NABOKOV, PERVERSELY

NABOKOV, PERVERSELY

ERIC NAIMAN

CORNELL UNIVERSITY PRESS
Ithaca and London

First published 2010 by Cornell University Press

Printed in the United States of America

Library of Congress Cataloging-in-Publication Data

Naiman, Eric, 1958–
   Nabokov, perversely / Eric Naiman.
      p. cm.
   Includes bibliographical references and index.
   ISBN 978-0-8014-4820-1 (cloth : alk. paper)
   1. Nabokov, Vladimir Vladimirovich, 1899-1977—
Criticism and interpretation.   2. Paraphilias in literature.
3. Sex in literature.   I. Title.
   PS3527.A15Z838   2010
   813'.54—dc22   2009049077

Cloth printing   10 9 8 7 6 5 4 3 2 1

for Thera

❧ CONTENTS

NABOKOV, PERVERSELY

Introduction

In 1926 Vladimir Nabokov wrote a short story called "*Skazka*" (A Fairy Tale). Published in *Rul'*, the Berlin émigré newspaper founded by his father, it opens with the protagonist riding in a tram. Every day, on his way to and from work, Erwin looks through the window and chooses girls for his harem. The harem is strictly imaginary; "only once in his life" has Erwin tried to pick up a woman, and that attempt ended badly: "You ought to be ashamed of yourself. Leave me alone" (*Stories,* 161). On this evening, however, Erwin meets a tall middle-aged lady who introduces herself as the Devil. She promises that on the morrow he can have all the women he fancies—they will be waiting for him at midnight. The only condition is that by that hour the number he has selected must be odd, not even. How will Erwin know that his choices have been duly noted? "In order that you may be sure that the deal stands, I shall have a sign given you every time—a smile, not necessarily addressed to you, a chance word in the crowd" (164).

The next day Erwin begins assembling the cast for the night to come, and each stirring of his desire is accompanied by a narrative non-sequitur that serves to confirm the Devil's recognition of his lust. "Yes, of course," a girl says to her friend—an acknowledgment that Erwin will have them both. After seeing another beauty, Erwin spots an advertisement with the word "Yes." In a café a man barks "All right, all right!" into a telephone when Erwin has made his next choice.

Eventually, Erwin collects eleven beauties. On his way to the address appointed by the Devil for the anticipated orgy, Erwin sees a child of fourteen walking with an older man, and he adds her to the group. Knowing he needs one more now that he has twelve, he begins following another, with whom he just cannot catch up. Finally, as midnight approaches, he draws near, ready to make her his thirteenth—but she turns out to be the same girl he selected first for his harem early in the day. "You ought to be ashamed of yourself," she tells him, "Leave me alone" (171).

When he translated this story into English years later, Nabokov gave it a provocatively inappropriate title: "A Nursery Tale." Eventually, it was included in a 1976 collection, *Details of a Sunset,* and Nabokov attached a coy, somewhat self-disparaging note:

> A rather artificial affair, composed a little hastily, with more concern for the tricky plot than for imagery and good taste, it required some revamping here and there in the English version. Young Erwin's harem, however, has remained intact. I had not reread my *"Skazka"* since 1930 and, when working now at its translation, was eerily startled to meet a somewhat decrepit but unmistakable Humbert escorting his nymphet in the story I wrote almost half a century ago. (quoted in *Stories,* 648)

Appearing in English so many years after its initial publication, the tale has struck at least one reader (Roy Johnson) as significant, not because it contains the initial appearance of Humbert but because it uses a technique that would become a hallmark of Nabokov's mature fiction: "Here we see Nabokov practicing those nudges and winks across the narrative to the reader which he was to bring to such a much more subtle stage of development in later stories" ("A Nursery Tale"). The hints that Nabokov would later convey covertly to the reader are here directed overtly to a character who serves as a model for Nabokov's later audience. As we shall see, the "good reader" of Nabokov must be alert to the hidden meanings suggested by all sorts of seemingly chance or inconsequential details in the text; he must work to distort the normal meaning of language, the expected functions of narrative, to arrive at an adequate understanding of Nabokov's prose. Admirers of Nabokov's fiction, trained to read him "well," in this fashion, ought to be somewhat disturbed to see their own first, ancestral representation in the figure of Erwin, a man whose "reading" of the world around him is driven by lust and is part of a deal with the Devil—and a losing deal at that.

Erwin's story belongs to a larger, fundamental narrative on which Nabokov drew throughout his career: the plight of a man both stimulated and undone by his interest in what he sees or reads. Looking through the tram window,

Erwin can watch with impunity the objects of his desire. He may not be able to have them, but at least he is protected from the dangers of excessive proximity. His situation is similar to that of a reader of erotic literature, who has only words (or pictures) and his own body to play with, but who risks no rejection and little shame so long as he remains in isolation. In "*Skazka*" the Devil tempts the sexual solipsist by taking away the barrier separating reader from text, and ultimately Erwin is rebuffed and shamed by the story into which he has moved. In the end, he is reminded of his inferior, second-rate status, his inability to have the girls he sees. Untouched by Erwin, the harem remains "intact."

Before his encounter with the Devil, at least one singular event had happened to Erwin: "only once in his life" he had been told, "You ought to be ashamed of yourself. Leave me alone." Now, not even that event is unique; the second shaming of Erwin is the ultimate put-down. "'A pity,'" said Erwin. 'A pity,'" the Devil echoes as the story closes (172). Erwin's shameful rejection has become part of a pattern, and this repetition, as we shall see when we turn to *The Defense* later in this study, is the mark of his having become a participant in a work of literature, a defining feature of which is lexical, semantic, or thematic echoing. Earlier, when he had assembled only half of his women, Erwin reflected that he might have been incautious in his initial selection: "Number one, the Maiden in White, she's the most artless of the lot. I may have been a little hasty" (168). This haste is repeated, in a more literal fashion, when Erwin races to catch up with the thirteenth girl, who proves to have been his first choice, too. The sentences become longer, as the periods stretch to capture Erwin's excitement:

> What enticed him? Not her gait, not her shape, but something else, bewitching and overwhelming, as if a tense shimmer surrounded her: mere fantasy, maybe, the flutter, the rapture of fantasy, or maybe it was that which changes a man's entire life with one divine stroke—Erwin knew nothing, he just sped after her over asphalt and stone, which seemed also dematerialized in the iridescent night. (171)

This passage recapitulates the opening sentence of the story—"Fantasy, the flutter, the rapture of fantasy!" (161)—and thus hints at the other repetitions soon to come. The word "life," as we shall see, often has a genital connotation in Nabokov's work, and the divine stroke mentioned here may be a hint at the sexual release anticipated by the hero. That release comes, after a fashion, when Erwin glimpses the girl's face:

> Once again Erwin came near. One more step, and he would be abreast of her. She stopped abruptly at an iron wicket and fished out her keys

from her handbag. Erwin's momentum almost made him bump into her. She turned her face toward him, and by the light a streetlamp cast through emerald leaves, he recognized the girl who had been playing that morning with a woolly black pup on a graveled path, and immediately remembered, immediately understood all her charm, tender warmth, priceless radiance.

He stood staring at her with a wretched smile.

"You ought to be ashamed of yourself," she said quietly. "Leave me alone." (171)

Far from being the most "artless," the first girl has turned out to be the marker of art. This is a different conclusion from the one desired by Erwin—and, perhaps, by the reader—but it arrives as the divine stroke of release from narrative tension and provides an aesthetic substitute for (or improvement on) sexual release. This "immediate understanding" of the girl's "charm, tender warmth, priceless radiance" exhausts Erwin, who can only respond "limply" to the Devil when she arrives in her chauffeured car, "bored to death" (172). The closure of the story has discharged the work's libidinal energy. Erwin's desire for multiple sexual partners has led only to the repetition of images and words: "the vernal lindens" with "the little black hearts of their shadows," mentioned before the moment of disappointing recognition, should have been seen by Erwin as hints that this girl was the one he had earlier glimpsed in a setting of "lustrous" linden leaves and their "ace-of-spades shadows" (171, 165). The defeat of Erwin's fantasies by a work of polished narrative would seem to signify—as Erwin submissively limps home—the boundary between pornography and art.

Details of a Sunset was not the first place "A Nursery Tale" appeared. The English version of the story was published earlier, in *Playboy*, in the January 1974 issue celebrating the magazine's twentieth anniversary. That occasion justified the inclusion of retrospective galleries of past playmates, and so there was an exceptionally large number of women between the covers. In fact, the first two pages of Nabokov's story were followed by thirty-three nude women on eight pages (102–11), and those who wanted to read the story more or less without stopping had to turn throughout the entire magazine to find the continuations. Even if few readers of *Playboy* counted the playmates to see if their quantity was even or odd, the association of Nabokov's readers with Erwin is striking, fully substantiating Jürgen Bodenstein's claim that Nabokov frequently "plays ironically with the reader's involvement in the fictional events, thwarting his expectations, mocking his inattention, and confronting him with unexpected developments; often he even puts the reader in the same situation of insecurity and doubt as the fictional characters" (1:294). With the passage of time and in its new context, "A Nursery Tale" was a more wickedly metafictive story. The English title of the story played a role in this transformation; as he assumes a pseudo-moralistic stance, Nabokov does to the genre of the nursery tale what Erwin would have liked to have done to the youngest girl in his harem.

One of the goals of *Playboy* was to include enough high-grade writing to enable its readers not to be ashamed of themselves, even as their magazine bound together the pleasures of reading and lust. Nabokov's story restates the sanction many of *Playboy*'s readers hoped to dodge: "You ought to be ashamed of yourself!" At the same time, by retrospectively providing a portrait of Nabokov's good reader as a lascivious young man, the story implicitly problematizes the notion of what it means to be a *good* reader in the first place.

And what was the good reader of *Playboy* supposed to conclude? For publication in *Playboy* Nabokov added several piquant details as part of the story's "revamping": the "red tufts" of a beauty's armpits, the promise of "cushions and rugs," the information that the two girlfriends whom Erwin decides to add to his harem are "sisters, or even twins" (166) (just like Mary and Madeleine Collinson, originally Playmates of the Month in October 1970, who now made a second appearance in the photographic pages following the opening of the story [110]). The final sentence assumed a particularly crude, and perhaps cruel, luster, punishing and tantalizing the reader by suggesting the ruins of an erection: "He walked with a heavy step, his legs ached, he was oppressed by the thought that tomorrow was Monday and it would be hard to get up" (172).[1] But most striking is the change introduced by the new context to the story's moral. Erwin is undone in part because he isn't a good enough reader; he fails to look closely enough at his specimens to make sure that each one is different. Are *Playboy*'s readers to look *more* closely at the pictures?

"A Nursery Tale" provides a particularly striking example of the dilemma besetting Nabokov's readers. Nabokov wants his readers to read closely, but reading too closely carries the risk of ridicule or sanction. His novels open up new worlds, but they carry with them the potential for shame and anxiety. Maurice Couturier describes Nabokov's reader as "always frustrated" (*Nabokov, ou la tyrannie,* 367); and "A Nursery Tale" poses the question whether that

---

1. In the English version the Devil's name (Monde) can be heard in the day (Monday) mentioned in the final line, allowing it to function as a demonic signature that effectively replaces the prospect of sexual satisfaction with the completion of a work of art.

frustration is a badge of honor, disgrace, or, paradoxically, both. Many readers of Nabokov's work may empathize with John Shade, the poet and apparent coauthor of *Pale Fire,* when he describes his first poetic epiphany. The experience brought the young man an all-encompassing vision, a powerful simultaneity of perception conducive to poetic creativity, but it inflicted on him a permanent, aesthetically induced trauma:

> But like some little lad forced by a wench
> With his pure tongue her abject thirst to quench,
> I was corrupted, terrified, allured,
> And though old doctor Colt pronounced me cured
> Of what, he said, were mainly growing pains
> The wonder lingers and the shame remains. (38)

As the following pages attempt to demonstrate, Shade's condition is emblematic of Nabokov's reader, who—if he reads well—is simultaneously corrupted and empowered, proud and ashamed of his insights into texts wonderfully complex and disconcertingly perverse.

Nabokov's opening lecture in his semester-long course at Cornell, "Masters of European Fiction," has been posthumously but appropriately entitled "Good Readers and Good Writers." Edited by Fredson Bowers, it now stands as the author's introduction to his *Lectures on Literature.* The lecture is the closest Nabokov ever came to writing a manifesto, and it begins with a sensuously inflected definition of the reader the author is looking for and the student he intends to reward:

> "How to be a Good Reader" or "Kindness to Authors"—something of that sort might serve to produce a subtitle for these various discussions of various authors, for my plan is to deal lovingly, in loving and lingering detail, with several European masterpieces. A hundred years ago, Flaubert in a letter to his mistress made the following remark: *Comme l'on serait savant si l'on connaissait bien seulement cinq à six livres:* "What a scholar one might be if one knew well only some half a dozen books." (1)

The pedagogic invocation of proper method is immediately supported by a quotation from Flaubert's intimate correspondence. The sentiment voiced by a great writer to the object of his affection is further eroticized by being quoted in French. Nabokov highlights the sensuality of proper reading throughout the lecture. "In reading, one should notice and fondle details" (1).

"Can anybody be so naïve as to think he or she can learn anything about the past from those buxom best-sellers that are hawked around by book clubs under the heading of historical novels?" (1). The art of literature is the "go-between" linking reality and invention, a term that has not lost all of its association with romance or with the pander. The apotheosis of good reading is presented as a fusion of author and audience: "Up a trackless slope climbs the master artist, and at the top, on a windy ridge, whom do you think he meets? The panting and happy reader, and there they spontaneously embrace and are linked forever if the book lasts forever" (2).

The pedagogic prose is so charmingly seductive that few of Nabokov's readers think to question the desirability of the image. What if we shy away from the author's sweaty embrace? Why can't we climb proximate but not identical peaks? The reader needn't thumb his nose at the author, but maybe a wave would be enough. Moreover, what kind of a term is "good reader"? Is it necessarily the same as a "close reader"? Isn't "good reader" a term most often applied to seven-year-olds? Is Nabokov simultaneously demanding both an interpretive exploit (reading as mountain climbing) and infantilization?

In his famous article in *Encounter* canonizing *Lolita,* Lionel Trilling acclaims Nabokov's success in restoring to prominence the novel of passionate love. Love, according to Trilling, has become the property of common sense, companionship, and health. Passionate, obsessive love is no longer believable, and to restore its former status, Nabokov has had to resort to the depiction of pedophilia: "our doubts are allayed if the obsession can be accounted for by the known fact of a sexual peculiarity, an avowed aberration." "Pathology," Trilling concludes, "naturalizes the strange particularity of the lover's preference" (18). *Lolita,* however, would not have disturbed so many readers had they been able to hide Humbert's appeal behind a diagnosis. With his rich language and seductive style, Humbert seeks, rather, to naturalize the pathology of pedophilia. A similar formulation might be applied to the process of reading Nabokov—as one becomes a good reader, one learns to perceive as natural and correct pathological forms of reading. Particularly in the first section of this book, I explore the way in which Nabokov pathologizes not only characters' sexual predilections but reading itself, pathologizes it in such a way that the reader may fear that the better he reads, the more perverse his reading practices become. Viktor Shklovsky, the Russian formalist critic, coined the term *ostranenie* ("defamiliarization" or "making strange") to describe what he viewed as the essence of art: the ability to make the habitual odd, to resist the automatization of things and ideas that result in our taking them for granted. Although Shklovsky wasn't as clear about this point as he might have been, he seems to have believed that art could produce a clearer appreciation of the real world, returning to us the stoniness of stone, as well as all the other things we've become used to: "clothes, furniture, one's wife, and the fear of war" (12).

Nabokov seeks a similar impact on the process of interpretation: he defamiliarizes reading and the manner in which the reader understands what he reads. Moreover, at least in Nabokov's mature work, this defamiliarization of reading often takes a transgressive, sexual turn, so that the mind awakened to hidden possibilities of understanding is figured in the text as sexually, and often inappropriately, aroused. The narrator of "The Vane Sisters" (written in 1951) derides Cynthia, a "perverse amateur of misshapen or illicitly connected words," for her willingness to assist an insane librarian in his search for "miraculous misprints such as the substitution of *l* for the second *h* in the world 'hither'" (*Stories,* 626), but Cynthia, with her "odds and ids" (629), proves to be the coauthor of the story, and the very paragraph that speaks of her penchant for twisted interpretation concludes by giving the key to the entire work: "I wish I could recollect that novel or short story (by some contemporary writer, I believe) in which, unknown to its author, the first letters of the words in its last paragraph formed, as deciphered by Cynthia, a message from his dead mother" (626). ("The Vane Sisters" ends: "I could isolate, consciously, little. Everything seemed blurred, yellow-clouded, yielding nothing tangible. Her inept acrostics, maudlin evasions, theopathies—every recollection formed ripples of mysterious meaning. Everything seemed yellowly blurred, illusive, lost" [631]). Nabokov's fiction offers a course of instruction in illicit connections, a series of lessons for the hermeneutic *Bildung* of a "perverse amateur." While depicting, aestheticizing, and—sometimes more explicitly than others—condemning such connections in the form of characters' sexual practices, Nabokov encourages and even trains his readers to make illicit, seemingly unwarranted, and often libidinally charged interpretive associations as an essential step in the understanding of his texts.

The crazed librarian combing tomes for Hitler's appearance in the form of a misprint is turning an ethical, political monstrosity (Hitler) into a textual blemish. In one significant respect, his "literary" practice follows Nabokov's. Russian writers tend to ask big questions:

What Is the Meaning of Life?
What Is the Essence of Humanity?
Isn't Property Weird?
Why Do People Reproduce?
Who is to Blame?
How Much Land Does a Man Need?

Implicit in these queries is the demand that the reader reflect on the value of her own life. Is she living in a manner commensurate with her life's worth? Does she measure up, morally, to her purpose on this earth?

The questions that haunt readers of Nabokov are not those that challenge the readers of Dostoevsky, Chekhov, and Tolstoy. But Nabokov's readers are haunted all the same, dogged by a variation of the self-reflexive inquiry that "rewards" readers of the great late nineteenth-century Russian authors. Nabokov's literature has a penchant for turning moral questions about life into procedural ones about reading. The intensity of his reader's engagement with his work has much in common with the tortured urgency of the conversations and internal debates that are so compelling in the heroes of Dostoevsky, Tolstoy, and, in some cases, Chekhov, but that engagement does not revolve around whether the reader is a good person or whether life is worth living but concerns whether he is a good reader and, implicitly, whether Nabokov is worth reading. These questions about reading, which take the place of the old moral ones about living, do not obliterate their predecessors; indeed, the Russian literary heritage both inspires and shadows his work, so that scholars of Nabokov continue to worry not only about whether they are good enough readers but also about whether being a good reader is enough.[2]

The word "perverse" has been applied frequently to Nabokov and his work. Not surprisingly, its use has most frequently had negative overtones. "The best parts [of your Gogol book] are brilliant," Edmund Wilson wrote to Nabokov in 1944, but "it does seem to me [...] that in some connections you've gone out of your way to be rather silly and perverse about the subject" (156). This detractive use of the word within a context that also admits to talent suggests a writer who lets his willfulness get in the way of his artistry. One early internal reviewer of *Lolita* noted: "That the passion should be such a sordid one is the mark of the author's perversity—and he is a remarkably perverse man—but it doesn't deprive the novel of the merits that it does have" (Stacy Schiff, 205). In these uses of the term, "perversity" is a kind of

---

2. Zinaida Shakhovskaia, a translator and critic, who was Nabokov's relative and, later, his detractor, tells a characteristic story: at one point in the 1930s Nabokov met a Soviet writer entrusted with the task of convincing him to return to Russia. As they sat in a Parisian café, Nabokov drew his interlocutor's attention to another patron avidly reading a newspaper. When the Soviet visitor asked about the paper's political orientation, Nabokov replied: "That's why I cannot return! What matters to me is *how* people read, what matters to you is *what* they are reading" (30).

excess, something not inherent in the writer's talent, and something which, presumably, the author might cure. This notion of the possibility of sifting the genuine Nabokov from the chaff has appealed to several critics, most recently Michael Wood, who tries ideally to separate Nabokovian "style" (which he prizes) from "signature" (which he finds somewhat tiresome) (21–27). But going back at least to John Hollander's 1956 essay on *Lolita* in *Partisan Review,* the term has also been used positively—"There is no clinical, sociological, or mythic seriousness about 'Lolita,' but it flames with a tremendous perversity of an unexpected kind" (Page, 82)—as the very feature that makes Nabokov worth reading. In 1966 Page Stegner took exception ("a flabby label") to Conrad Brenner's characterization of Nabokov's work as "the art of the perverse," even though Stegner used practically the same term himself to speak of *Lolita*'s transformative power. According to Stegner, Nabokov's technique of making "an art out of a perversion" is best seen as part of a redemptive procedure in which "Humbert's eye confronts vulgarity (his own and his world's) and converts it through imagination and subsequently language into a thing of beauty" (44, 114).

As Sarah Herbold notes, "good readers have recognized from the beginning that *Lolita* is a perverse book, if by 'perverse' we mean a book that induces readers to express symbolically and vicariously impulses they normally censor and suppress" ("'I have camouflaged everything,'" 79). That word itself, however, has remained a negative term in Nabokov studies, and it has been regularly resisted by Nabokov scholars, particularly when they are concerned—as they frequently are—with defending Nabokov outside of a strictly aesthetic framework. Recently, a use of "perverse" was flagged on the electronic Listserv NABOKV-L by a subscriber who relayed to the editors a book review of a biography of Edmund Wilson that referred to "Nabokov's altogether perverse edition of Pushkin's *Eugene Onegin.*" Stephen Blackwell, one of the Listserv's editors, expressed his sense of collective gratitude for the poster's vigilance:

> Our thanks to Victor Fet for calling Mr. Dickstein to task for his characterization of VN's translation and commentary. It would appear that either Mr. Dickstein has not looked at the translation and commentary (why would he?) and accepted Wilson's characterization [...] or else for his own reasons he shares Wilson's views. For those on the list who do not know Russian, it is worth noting that there will hardly be found a single Russian scholar who considers the translation a "perverse" or even frivolous exercise (unless one uses the word "perverse" in a very special rhetorical, theoretical sense, and even then—only one or two). The translation may, as all things must, be open to criticism,

but "perverse" it surely is not. I am constantly amazed by the refusal of otherwise reasonable people to accept VN's stated intention for the translation: as a "pony" and a "crib" for those attempting to read the work in the original before complete mastery of Russian. ("Edmund Wilson's Human Interest," online posting)

Dmitri Nabokov, the writer's son, seconded these sentiments: "My thanks, too, to Victor Fet for calling Mr. Dickstein to task and to the Editors for calling attention to Mr. Dickstein's assessment of my father's *Onegin*. Everyone, of course, has a right to his opinion, and I am certainly not a censor. But 'perverse' seemed such a bizarre epithet that I was sure, at first, that Mr. Dickstein's tongue was in his cheek" ("Edmund Wilson's Human Interest," online posting).

Both the word's repeated application to Nabokov and its continued propensity to provoke resistance among Nabokov's most well-intentioned readers demand that it be given a closer, more fixed look in connection with Nabokov's writing. The pages that follow do not attempt to apply a rigorous or even an inflected psychoanalytic analysis to Nabokov's texts, but we would do well to bear in mind the Freudian definition of perversion:

> Sexual activities which either (a) extend, in an anatomical sense, beyond the regions of the body that are designed for sexual union, or (b) linger over the intermediate relations to the sexual object which should normally be traversed rapidly on the path toward the final sexual aim. (62)

In many respects, the consumption and enjoyment of all art would seem perverse on these terms, particularly if an artist defines his activity precisely by its *uselessness* or if the artist's audience is bent on an experience founded as much in pleasurable lingering as in edification, self-improvement or social amelioration. One of the principal goals of the ensuing pages will be to explore the significance and consequences of Nabokov's insistence on bringing this issue of art's essential perversity to the fore.

This book is divided into three sections. The first offers a close reading of the interplay of sexuality and interpretation in the three novels that Nabokov wrote during the decade following his arrival in the United States, the period that witnessed his re-creation of himself as an American writer. The three books show us an author appropriating and taking license with the rich possibilities offered by the English language and American culture. As Sergei Davydov, among others, has shown, Pushkin was a crucial touchstone for Nabokov in his Russian-language work ("Nabokov and Pushkin," 482–96), and in this first American decade Nabokov marks his mastery of his new medium by displaying his command of Shakespeare, the writer whose authoritative status in English most approximates Pushkin's. Nabokov's novels had long been preoccupied with sexual themes and with questions of interpretation, and now Shakespeare's language served as a vehicle for the demonstration of his talents in English. Beginning with a reading of *Lolita* as a work of Shakespeare scholarship, I continue with an analysis of the use and sexual abuse of Shakespeare in the imaginary dictatorship of *Bend Sinister,* and then I proceed with an interpretation of *Pnin* as an exploration, inflected through *Hamlet,* of the painful necessity of perversion as a component of art. The first section concludes with a consideration of the homoerotics of interpretation in and of Nabokov's novels. The ordering of these chapters is not strictly chronological; rather, the structure of this first section is dictated by the conviction that a reading of *Lolita* is where an English-language book on Nabokov ought (im)properly to start.

The second part of the book looks closely at recuperative readings of Nabokov's fiction, most notably those by Azar Nafisi, Elizabeth Patnoe, and Stephen Blackwell. Here I examine the effort and rhetoric of scholarly and publicistic attempts to set Nabokov straight, to defuse the disturbing sexual and interpretive issues in his prose by placing them in a reassuring framework. The final third of the book presents a series of temporally preposterous interpretations that examine Nabokov's earlier work—and in several cases its subsequent revision—for clues to the origins of his hermeneutic perversity and with an eye toward its evolution in the late and, perhaps, overripe phase of his career. This section looks at Nabokov's work before and after he had discovered the sexual coding that would define his most famous English-language work. His insistence on perverse reading, however, and his focus on author-character and author-reader relations, was already present in his early novels such as *The Defense,* which I analyze in detail. Sexual topics and sexual perversions later became exemplary of Nabokov's core preoccupations; we can trace the process through which sexual coding became a dominant, even detrimental feature of Nabokov's art by examining its role in the revision of *King, Queen, Knave* and in Nabokov's longest novel, *Ada.* The book closes with a reading of Dostoevsky's "The Double" that heuristically inquires what happens when the interpretive practices developed in close reading of Nabokov are applied to other writers.

Throughout the book, I've had to contend with a basic feature of Nabokov's fiction, its tendency to repeat itself, usually in interesting variations. Nabokov returns to the same metafictive questions, exploring them from different angles and in different keys. In 1966 *The Paris Review* asked Nabokov if he agreed with Princeton professor Clarence Brown's claim that Nabokov was "extremely repetitious," albeit in "wildly different ways." Nabokov replied that he hadn't read Brown's essay but that the observation had some validity: "Derivative writers seem versatile because they imitate many others, past and present. Artistic originality has only its own self to copy" (*Strong Opinions,* 95). This characteristic poses a structural challenge to the Nabokov scholar. He can tackle Nabokov's entire oeuvre issue by issue, but the result will be a pastiche of quotations from various works that will have limited interest for the reader who has just finished a particular novel and wants to know how the scholar interprets it. Such a reader, if he reads the scholar's book at all, will be left chasing down references through the index. A novel-by-novel analysis, however, risks falling into repetition, continually spotting the same paradigm. This study adopts a hybrid approach, although wherever possible, I have tried to focus my attentions on a single text, using it to investigate phenomena that have relevance elsewhere in Nabokov's work. Although repetition is to a large degree my subject, I have tried not to make it my style. The goal has been to develop the theme of the necessity of readerly perversion but to use different texts by Nabokov to highlight distinct permutations and ramifications of this theme. Each chapter is intended to be separable, an answer of sorts to the reader who turns to scholarship with questions raised by a recent encounter with a specific work.

A central theme of this book is Nabokov's relationship with his readers. Obviously, Nabokov has different sorts of readers, and his encounter with a generalized reader must be something of an ideal myth. In this book I am chiefly concerned with those who to some extent define themselves *as* Nabokov readers. For the most part, these are scholars who write about Nabokov and who see their professional identity as bound up with his legacy. I will also make frequent reference to NABOKV-L, an electronic Listserv founded by D. Barton Johnson, a professor at the University of California, Santa Barbara, in 1993. Described as "an electronic discussion and information sharing group for those with a scholarly interest in the life and writings of Vladimir Nabokov" (NABOKV-L), its membership has grown to over seven hundred subscribers in more than twenty countries, the large majority of them from the United States (Johnson, "NABOKV-L Subscription Info" and "Boyd Proposal," online postings). Subscribing to the list is an act of conscious affiliation and identification. It can also be seen as an act of readerly bonding; those who post seek responses—not the least important of which is approval from members of a scholarly community. (Even on a formal level, all postings must be "approved" by the list's editors.) Postings are a form of publication, but since they undergo less revision than other public scholarly writings, they tend to be raw and thus symptomatic, a scholar's equivalent to patients' initial recitations of dreams. This makes them especially useful as gauges of readerly anxieties and desires.

Resistance to my book may well be based on the assertion that interpretive and sexual practices should be kept apart, that in my readings of Nabokov's work I slip too easily into sexual metaphors when discussing approaches to a text. I do not deny the subjectivity of my readings; in fact, as I argue, understanding Nabokov's poetics depends on taking stock of one's own anxieties and pleasures. I am aware, however, that *Nabokov, Perversely* will succeed only if I can convince its readers that my sexually oriented reading of Nabokov is not born primarily of my own quirkiness. Nabokov's readers and scholars seem to shift easily, albeit sometimes unconsciously, into metaphorical, sexually resonant discourse. Charles Lock derives the following truth from his wonderful reading of *Transparent Things:* "Paying attention to and in Nabokov often entails abnormal reading practices: the reader must focus on the characters, letters, and sounds instead of on the ideas that ought to be excited in her by them. Who could read straight through, in the way of prose, any sentence written by Nabokov after learning the 'solution' of 'The Vane Sisters'?" (115). Far from seeing this sort of abnormal reading, or this sort of language about deviant interpretation, as forced, we should see it as a brilliant effect of Nabokov's prose. As Nabokov wrote to Katherine White, after she and the *New Yorker* had rejected "The Vane Sisters" and thus "completely failed me as readers":

> You may argue that reading downwards, or upwards, or diagonally is not what an editor can be expected to do; but by means of various allusions to trick-reading I have arranged matters so that the reader almost automatically slips into this discovery. [...] When some day you re-read it, I want you to notice—I hope with regret—how everything in the tale leads to one recurving end, or rather forms a delicate circle, a system of mute responses, not realized by the Frenchman but directed by some unknown spirit at readers through the prism of his priggish praises. (*Selected Letters,* 116–17)

One sentence in the same letter seems especially poignant: "I am really very disappointed that you, such a subtle and loving reader, should not have seen the inner scheme of my story" (117). *Nabokov, Perversely* is all about loving Nabokov as he wanted to be loved. It is also about why it is difficult to do so.

❧ PART ONE

Sexual Orientation

✎ CHAPTER 1

A Filthy Look at Shakespeare's *Lolita*

"Not a single obscene term is to be found in the whole work" (4)—so states the fictitious Dr. John Ray, Jr., and until recently I had not thought that many readers would agree. *Lolita* has always struck me as a *stylistically* lewd book, an opinion I had not regarded as an original point of view. I was, therefore, surprised by an exchange in which I participated several years ago on NABOKV-L. The discussion began with a relayed query concerning "Chestnut Lodge," a motel in which Humbert Humbert discerns a clue left by his nemesis Clare Quilty. The author of the query asked whether this might be a reference to the insane asylum of the same name in Baltimore (Drescher and Edmunds). After the list's editor responded that he had once tried unsuccessfully to track down a motel by this name in old AAA tourbooks (Johnson, "Drescher Query"), I suggested that the first word in this hotel's name should be read as an anagram, beginning with the definite article and concluding with the possessive form of a word best not transported electronically across state lines.

Nothing I had ever written in my scholarly career had produced a response anything like that generated by this brief suggestion. Most of the comments displayed a mixture of astonishment and outrage: "we shouldn't underrate [Nabokov] by ascribing to him the kind of fun and pun that immature schoolboys enjoy in lavatories and suchlike places" (Kartsev); "I also had problems with the indecency unearthed: it's just not like the writer we all think we know. Eryx [referring to the site of a cult to Aphrodite], Kitzler [to the German word for clitoris], absolutely—but vocabulary on this level?" (Wendel). There were also several pointed ad hominem replies, observing that "there are cases when an interpretation tells us more of the critic's predilections and idiosyncrasies than the author's" (Kartsev; See also Dolinin, "Nabokov's Chestnut Lodge").

This outrage surprised me; *Lolita* at least masquerades as a story about sexual relations with a child and is littered with what might be called schoolboy humor, most notably in the list of faculty teaching at Beardsley College and the Beardsley School for Girls: Miss Redcock; Dr. Pierce; Miss Pratt, whose surname faces back and front and who insists that Lolita is "shuttling between the anal and genital zones of development" (194);[1] Miss Lester and Miss Fabian, whose names are to be cut and spliced; Miss Horn and Miss Cole, the first letters of whose names we are told Lolita likes to transpose; and Gaston Godin, the French "invert" whose name seems to derive from a slang term for an artificial phallus (*gode*) and who answers Humbert's need for "a label, a background, and a simulacrum" to protect him from suspicion about his interest in nymphets (175). The ribald nature of most of these names is fairly obvious; others require just a minimal familiarity with century-old English or current French slang. And Nabokov is, after all, the author of *Ada,* a novel that practically wears its salaciousness on its sleeve.

Yet ever since Lionel Trilling declared *Lolita* the great American love story, there has been a certain reluctance to tackle in any systematic fashion the bawdy linguistic games played in the novel or to discuss their purpose in the context of the novel's larger meaning. In part, this hesitancy may be due to the uneasiness still experienced by readers about the sexual nature of the novel's central plot—the theme of sexual abuse has provoked outrage from both the Left and the Right (Kauffman, Patnoe, and Podhoretz, inter alia). The necessity of responding to the implied charge of indecency has effectively traumatized many readings of the text, and even the efforts of a staunch defender such as Nabokov's biographer Brian Boyd are colored by the perceived necessity of showing that the novel serves as a condemnation of child abuse (*The American Years,* 228–54). Quite early on, Carl Proffer suggested that much of the erotic action in the novel was occurring on the level of wordplay generally missed by what he called the "outraged Congressmen and nervous mamas" (*Keys to Lolita,* 99), but since then the impression has generally been cultivated in Nabokov-scholarship that the lexical sex occurs at a fairly superficial level.

---

1. In addition to its older meaning—"buttocks"—prat(t) refers in England to the vagina, a usage that dates back at least to the 1930s. See Dalzell and Victor (2:1539); and Green (1130).

Alfred Appel, who claims that Nabokov may have had the last laugh on outraged critics by giving his novel a "racy" "substratum," soft-pedals this claim
with a calming adverb when he writes that "the erotica which seemed to be
there and turned out not to be was in fact present all along, most modestly"
(*The Annotated Lolita,* 441). In the pages that follow I intend to investigate
most immodestly the poetics and significance of this substratum; in particular
I will inquire into the extent to which Nabokov's technique of sexual reference is indebted to the tradition of Shakespearean bawdy and to writing
about it. In the process, I hope both to revise current understanding of the
poetics of Nabokov's novel and to place *Lolita* within the discourse of postwar
Shakespeare studies as a work of applied scholarship.

Before embarking on a consideration of Shakespearean bawdy in *Lolita,*
a short preface on technique is in order. In *Ada* there is a scene in which
the principal character's variety act is described at length:

> The stage would be empty when the curtain went up, then after five
> heartbeats of theatrical suspense something swept out of the wings,
> enormous and black, to the accompaniment of dervish drums. The
> shock of his powerful and precipitous entry affected so deeply the
> children in the audience that for a long time later, in the dark of sob-
> bing insomnias, in the glare of violent nightmares, nervous little boys
> and girls relived, with private accretions, something similar to the "pri-
> mordial qualm," a shapeless nastiness, the swoosh of nameless wings,
> the unendurable dilation of fever which came in a cavern draft from
> the uncanny stage. Into the harsh light of its gaudily carpeted space a
> masked giant, fully eight feet tall, erupted, running strongly in the kind
> of soft boots worn by Cossack dancers. [...] The unpleasant colossus
> kept strutting up and down the stage for a while, then the strut changed
> to the restless walk of a caged madman, then he whirled, and to a clash
> of cymbals in the orchestra and a cry of terror (perhaps faked) in the
> gallery, Mascodagama turned over in the air and stood on his head.
>
> In this weird position, with his cap acting as a pseudopodal pad, he
> jumped up and down, pogo-stick fashion—and suddenly came apart.
> Van's face, shining with sweat, grinned between the legs of the boots
> that still shod his rigidly raised arms. Simultaneously his real feet kicked
> off and away the false head with its crumpled cap and bearded mask.
> The magical reversal "made the house gasp." Frantic ("deafening,"
> "delirious," "a veritable tempest of") applause followed the gasp. He
> bounded offstage—and next moment was back, now sheathed in black
> tights, dancing a jig on his hands.

We devote so much space to the description of his act not only because variety artists of the "eccentric" race are apt to be forgotten especially soon, but also because one wishes to analyze its thrill. [. . . T]he rapture young Mascodagama derived from overcoming gravity was akin to that of artistic revelation in the sense utterly and naturally unknown to the innocents of critical appraisal, the social-scene commentators, the moralists, the idea-mongers and so forth. Van on the stage was performing organically what his figures of speech were to perform later in life—acrobatic wonders that had never been expected from them and which frightened children. (183–85)

Like so many other moments in Nabokov's oeuvre this is a metapoetic moment, indeed, it is perhaps *the* metapoetic moment in that it provides a model for what explication of a Nabokovian text ought to do: make a passage stand on its head to the amusement and delight of a critic's audience. This sort of revelation is not deconstructive—it is not reading against the grain but reading with a hidden one—and it is obviously in thrall to the old-fashioned notion of authorial intentionality on which Nabokov's aesthetics so stubbornly insist. The explication of a Nabokovian text entails providing readers with a different, but still authorial, "angle of vision" (*Stories,* 619); it involves doing what Nabokov asks his assistant to do in his poem "An Evening of Russian Poetry":

"My little helper at the magic lantern,
insert that slide and let the colored beam
project my name or any such-like phantom
in Slavic characters upon the screen.
The other way, the other way. I thank you.
(*Poems and Problems,* 158)

The command to turn a text "the other way" is an invitation to hermeneutic perversion, a notion that will serve as a pedal point for the chapters to come. A central metaphor for the relation between author and reader occurs during Humbert's first erotic contact with Lolita, when he licks a speck out of her eye:

Held her roughly by the shoulders, then tenderly by the temples, and turned her about. "It's right there," she said. "I can feel it." "Swiss peasant would use the top of her tongue." "Lick it out?" "Yeth. Shly try?" "Sure," she said. Gently I pressed my quivering sting along her rolling salty eyeball. "Goody-goody," she said nictating. "It *is* gone." "Now the other?"

"You dope," she began, "there is noth-" but here she noticed the pucker of my approaching lips. "Okay," she said cooperatively, and bending toward her warm upturned russet face somber Humbert pressed his mouth to her fluttering eyelid. She laughed, and brushed past me out of the room. My heart seemed everywhere at once. Never in my life—not even when fondling my child-love in France—never—. (43–44)

There is much to notice here, including the erotic charge of the excessive, useless act of licking the second eyeball: desire surfaces in a gesture which is superfluous and thus aesthetic. The verb "nictate" is placed on special erotic display, serving as a kind of verbal fetish apt to set the minds of readers who do not know it spinning from one part of the body to another. Most important for our purposes, though, is this scene's status as a representation of author-reader interaction. From his tongue to our eye—a reader just has to know how to dilate.

But what if we are dilating incorrectly? The notion of authorized perversion is a complex and paradoxical one. Is there a central difference between "*the* other way" and "*an* other way"? How can perversion ever be authorized? Once it is authorized doesn't it cease to be perverse? And when does close reading become *un*authorized perversion? While Nabokov was alive, this was a particularly fraught issue, as the close reader William Woodin Rowe, a professor at George Washington University, discovered when he wrote in detail about sexual symbols in Nabokov's work and Nabokov replied with a savage rejoinder in the *New York Review of Books*.

I must protest vehemently against a number of indecent absurdities. [...] If every "come" and "part" on the pages of my books is supposedly used by me to represent "climax" and "genitals," one can well imagine the naughty treasures Mr. Rowe might find in any French novel where the prefix "*con*" occurs so frequently as to make every chapter a veritable compote of female organs. I do not think, however, that his French is sufficient for such feasts. (*Strong Opinions,* 305–6)

Ever since that attack, Rowe has served as a tempting whipping boy for Nabokovians eager to tar a reading as an *over*-reading. Yet Rowe ought not to be dismissed so quickly. His mistake was more one of method than of madness: his skills as a scholarly prosecutor fell far short of his gifts as a close-reading detective. First, he offended Nabokov by claiming that Nabokov was using sexual *symbols,* a word that the author of *Lolita* found disagreeable because it implied the use of a tawdry, all too handy code developed outside literature and imposed on art from without. Moreover,

Rowe failed—did not even try, really—to provide an explanation for *why* Nabokov used sexual imagery.

Let us see what happens when we move the focus from sexual symbols to sexual *language,* to the literary and scholarly use of such language, and to a kind of sexual traffic that takes place between languages in translinguistic puns. In the process of so doing, I want to take up Nabokov's challenge regarding the use of the French *con,* but I suggest that we read his remarks as we might if we had found them in one of his novels—less as an injunction about how not to read French texts than as a hint about how to read his own.

Nabokov ranked Shakespeare as one of the world's greatest poets; he refers to Shakespeare's works with great reverence in his interviews. (*Strong Opinions,* 63, 89–90, 146). *Bend Sinister,* the novel completed prior to *Lolita,* provides striking and obvious evidence of Nabokov's intimate familiarity with the language of *Hamlet* in particular. In *Lolita,* Shakespeare is named on several occasions: Humbert muses about what "a real healthy sweetheart" might have discussed with Lolita: an abstract idea, a painting, stippled Hopkins or shorn Baudelaire, God or Shakespeare, anything of a genuine kind" (284). Nabokov was eager to share Shakespeare's divinity; he proudly noted that the two of them were born on the same day—April 23, although Nabokov's birthday was actually April 22 (Boyd, *The Russian Years,* 37). (Because gods are presumably immortal, Nabokov rarely mentioned that this purportedly shared birthday was also the day of Shakespeare's death). Nabokov admired Shakespeare's use of language far more than his development of characters or his feel for plot: "The verbal poetical texture of Shakespeare is the greatest the world has known, and is immensely superior to the structure of his plays as plays" (*Strong Opinions,* 89–90). Acknowledging Nabokov's debt to Shakespeare should entail reading the former's work with the care that we normally devote to the latter. What happens if we read *Lolita* as though it were as intricate as a Shakespearean sonnet?

Shakespeare's divine status once made the issue of his use of bawdy fraught with controversy. Although Gordon Williams is probably right in his claim that there was never "a time of innocence in the reading of Shakespeare, when [...] old gifted amateurs missed what the modern specialist takes for granted," Williams himself observes that from the middle of the nineteenth century to the middle of the twentieth Shakespeare studies were characterized by a certain reticence that included sanitized popular editions for young readers (9). When reading the editions of Shakespeare published during this time, one may be struck by either the amazing naïveté or the astonishing hermeneutic genius of complicated readings intended to demonstrate that

a certain passage is quite innocent. In fact, at least one Shakespearean commentator suggested that all the bawdy parts in Shakespeare's plays were actors'
interpolations (Cowden Clark, 52).[2]

A significant development in the public discussion of ribald moments in
Shakespeare's drama occurred in 1947, when Eric Partridge's *Shakespeare's
Bawdy* started what has become something of an industry within Shakespeare
studies—from Herbert A. Ellis to E. A. M. Colman to Gordon Williams to
James Henke to Frankie Rubinstein. Partridge's book consisted of an intro-
ductory essay followed by a glossary of words used by Shakespeare to bawdy
effect. Partridge was particularly interested in Shakespeare's preoccupation
with "the geography and topography of the female sexual features" (7). He
also provided a thesaurus for what he called "puden-synonymy": his list
includes *another thing, belly, bird's nest, blackness, bosom, box unseen, breach, case,
circle, city, constable, corner, coun, country, crack, dearest bodily part, den, dial, et cet-
era, eye, flower, forfended place, gate, hole, Holland, lap, low countries, mark, medlar,
naked seeing self, nest of spicery, Netherlands, O, peculiar river, plum, pond, ring,
rose, rudder, ruff, tail, tale, thing, treasure, venus' glove, vice, way, what, withered pear,
wound* (21–22). In many respects this catalogue is reminiscent of something
we might find in a vulgarized Freudian dreambook, but we should not be
so quick to assume that Partridge is projecting Freudian claims onto Shakespeare. Equally plausible is the possibility that Freud was projecting onto the
unconscious a symbolism and—just as important—a register of language that
was a conscious dramatic and poetic device in earlier times; Freudian reading
would probably not have prospered or even occurred had Freud lived in an
age when readings of Shakespeare were not so repressed. Partridge's moral-
istic eloquence, his reference to the female genitalia as Shakespeare's "one
unfailing lodestar" (21), and his defense of Shakespeare's sexual preoccupation
as "not uncommon among fervent, poetic intellectual men, whose superior
natures cause the pudend to become for them a mystic as well as a physical
goal, something esoteric as well as material, both a haven for the wary mind
and a harbour for their questing sexuality" (21) as well as his recommenda-
tion of Kenneth Walker's *The Physiology of Sex*—an "excellent [. . .] little book
[that] should be possessed by all laymen and many doctors and every priest
or clergyman" (13)—place him in the same discursive mode as John Ray, Jr.,

---

2. Do we hear just an echo of the Shakespeare scholar Charles Cowden Clark in "Clarence
Choate Clark, Esq.," Humbert's attorney who is responsible for cleaning up his dead client's manuscript? As Brian Boyd has shown, Nabokov drew upon Cowden Clark's commentary to *Hamlet*, via
the Furness *Variorum Edition*, when working on *Bend Sinister* ("Notes," 685). George Ferger views the
lawyer's name as a mask for "Clare Q" (137), but the two readings are not mutually exclusive.

the fictitious psychologist and author of the introduction to *Lolita*. This over-lap suggests a possible analogy between lexicography and psychoanalysis. In a 1969 interview, responding to a question about the neighbors he would like to have in heaven, Nabokov responded: "It would be fun to hear Shakespeare roar with ribald laughter on being told what Freud (roasting in the other place) made of his plays" (*Strong Opinions*, 126–27).

The coincidence of the publication date (1947) of Partridge's book with the beginning of Nabokov's English-language work on the novel that was to become *Lolita* is intriguing; *Lolita* was finished in late 1953, by which time *Shakespeare's Bawdy*, originally published in a small British edition, had begun achieving greater prominence. And Nabokov did keep his eye on Shakespeare scholarship. One of his first published reviews in the United States was of Frayne Williams's *Mr. Shakespeare of the Globe*. *Bend Sinister* (1947) includes a chapter where the philosopher-hero Krug and his transla-tor friend Ember discuss absurd interpretations of *Hamlet*. A sense of the resources offered to a novelist by Shakespeare's rich bawdy wordplay, how-ever, is largely absent in *Bend Sinister* and would await exploitation in *Lolita*. It is tempting to speculate that an acquaintance with Partridge's book made the difference. Yet Nabokov may not have needed Partridge for access to Shakespearean bawdy language; he was a sufficiently good, suspicious, and prurient reader to catch some of these on his own as he continued to draw on Shakespeare and Shakespeare scholarship in his writing. Partridge's book, after all, probably represented less of a scholarly discovery than a codification and dissemination of what many astute readers of Shakespeare knew but did not write. As such, Partridge "was not so much a pioneer as a watershed" (Williams, 10).

Let us recall some of the most obvious and well-known examples from Shakespeare. Most who have seen the play will remember the English les-son from *Henry the Fifth* (3.4.1–55), which is followed by further play on *con* in Harry's subsequent banter with Burgundy (5.2.260–90).[3] Mercutio's

---

3. King Harry: "Our tongue is rough, coz, and my condition is not smooth, so that having nei-ther the voice nor the heart of flattery about me I cannot so conjure up the spirit of love in her that he will appear in his true likeness."

Burgundy: "Pardon the frankness of my mirth, if I answer you for that. If you would conjure in her, you must make a circle; if conjure up love in her in his true likeness, he must appear naked and blind. Can you blame her then, being a maid yet rosed over with the virgin crimson of modesty, if she deny the appearance of a naked blind boy in her naked seeing self? It were, my lord, a hard condition for a maid to consign to."

Unless otherwise specified, all citations of Shakespeare, with the exception of the sonnets, refer to *The Norton Shakespeare*. For the sonnets, I have used Stephen Booth's edition.

bawdy language in *Romeo and Juliet*—"Twould anger him to raise a spirit in his mistress' circle / Of some strange nature, letting it there stand / Till she had laid it and conjured it down. / That were some spite. My invocation / Is fair and honest. In his mistress' name, / I conjure only but to raise him up" (2.1.23–29)—closely precedes one of the best-known lines in Shakespeare's corpus ("But soft, what light through yonder window breaks?" [2.1.44]). The sharp transition between these types of lovers' discourse has been rendered less jarring by editors who interpolate a scene break where none is warranted. (As a result, audiences may not catch the bawdy gibe in Romeo's retort bridging these two "scenes": "He jests at scars that never felt a wound" [2.1.43]). *Twelfth Night* is replete with bawdy, perhaps most unabashedly in the envelope scene: "By my life, this is my lady's / hand. These be her very C's, her U's, *and* her T's; and thus / makes she her great P's. It is in contempt of question her hand" (2.5.77–80; emphasis added). The *Merry Wives of Windsor* offers an outrageous grammar catechism, which includes the "focative" and "Jenny's case" (4.1.42–55). Finally, we might recall the famous exchange on "country matters" in *Hamlet:*

> [HAMLET]: Lady, shall I lie in your lap?
> [OPHELIA]: No, my lord.
> [HAMLET]: I mean my head upon your lap?
> [OPHELIA]: Ay, my lord.
> [HAMLET]: Do you think I meant country matters?
> [OPHELIA]: I think nothing, my lord.
> [HAMLET]: That's a fair thought to lie between maids' legs.
> [OPHELIA]: What is, my lord?
> [HAMLET]: No thing.
> [OPHELIA]: You are merry, my lord. (3.2.101–10)

Because of its relation to "o," a standard Shakespearean vaginal term, the word "nothing" was especially apt to produce bawdy punning—as, for example, in Sonnet 136: "Though in thy store's account I one must be, / For nothing hold me, so it please thee hold / That nothing me, a something sweet to thee" (lines 10–12).[4] (Thomas Pyles made one of the first post-Partridge contributions to the study of Shakespearean bawdy with the publication of a short article entitled "Ophelia's Nothing" in *Modern Language Notes* in 1949). At times the meaning of sexual language in Shakespeare is explicit and logical, as in Partridge's first extensive quotation, from *Venus and Adonis*

---

4. See Booth's commentary on these lines (471–72).

(229–40).[5] At other times passages are founded on what one commentator has called "pudendal suggestiveness" (Colman, 17), and we are left with a sense of verbal conjuration that stuffs a dazzling array of possibly double-edged words into a minimal number of lines.

The genital punning in Shakespeare is particularly apt to utilize English words beginning with the prefix *con.* Partridge and his successors have had a field day here; Partridge singles out *confessor* and *constable,* quoting a prominent slang lexicographer's comment that he knew one lady who would never use the latter word because "it had such an ill sound" (85). In Shakespeare, plays on *con* are particularly liable to surface in—but are not restricted to—scenes where French is at issue. In *Lolita*—and *Ada,* for that matter—French is at issue much of the time, and this language is explicitly eroticized by Nabokov when Humbert asks, "I wonder what my academic publishers would say if I were to quote in my textbook Ronsard's '*la vermeillette fente*' or Remy Belleau's '*un petit mont feutré de mousse délicate, tracé sur le milieu d'un fillet escarlatte*'" (47).[6] (Is the misspelling of *filet* (thread)—which would be a rare error for Nabokov—a baring of the novel's device, the reduction of a girl (*fille*) to her genitals?)[7] If we look at Ronsard's poem, we find that the original plays quite overtly with the expected pun:

> *Je te salue ô vermeillette fante,*
> *Qui vivement entre ces flancs reluis:*
> *Je te salue ô bienheuré pertuis,*
> *Qui rens ma vie heureusement contante.* (2:775–76)[8]

The final line is a double double entendre, because the French word for sexual member (*vit*) is a homonym for the word for life (*vie*). This play is frequent in French poetry of the period, and we will see Nabokov using it as well. Less obvious than these florid quotations is Nabokov's hint in the preceding paragraph, the end of Humbert's journal entry for the preceding day: Charlotte has just expressed her hope that Humbert will stay and help Lolita "with her home work—you seem to know everything, geography, mathematics, French."

---

5. "I'll be a park, and thou shalt be my deer./ Feed where thou wilt, on mountain or in dale; / Graze on my lips, and if those hills be dry, / Stray lower, where the pleasant fountains lie. / Within this limit is relief enough, / Sweet bottom grass, and high delightful plain, / Round rising hillocks, brakes obscure and rough, / To shelter thee from tempest and from rain. / Then be my deer, since I am such a park; / No dog shall rouse thee, though a thousand bark."

6. "[A] small hill padded with delicate moss and traced down the middle with a scarlet thread."

7. I thank Stephen Booth for pointing this "mistake" out to me.

8. "I salute you, oh scarlet slit / That shines vividly between these flanks / I salute you, oh happy pit / That makes my life happily content."

"That means," said Haze quickly, "you'll *be* here!" I wanted to shout that I would stay on eternally if only I could hope to caress now and then my incipient pupil. But I was wary of Haze. So I just grunted and stretched my limbs nonconcomitantly (*le mot juste*) and presently went up to my room. (46–47)

The prefix *con* is also quite marked in this way in *Ada,* where Van refers to a predatory woman as a condor and then adds that this is "the best Franco-English pun" he has ever heard (481); it also is part of a rant in the same novel directed at French Communists and André Malraux's *La condition humaine,* a title Nabokov effectively changes into an obscene speech act (con-dit): nothing but organ talk (377). A similar moment occurs in *The Real Life of Sebastian Knight,* where Nabokov dispatches at once two detested colleagues. A famous author who sounds much like D. H. Lawrence rebukes Sebastian "for being 'Conradish'" and suggests "leaving out the 'con' and cultivating the 'radish' in future works" (40). Here Nabokov has turned the name of his fellow Slav into a combination of verbal stand-ins for male and female genitalia (*con*-radish). He has also managed to deride Lawrence's worship of the phallus by suggesting—with the verb *cul*-tivate—where Lawrence might be better off placing that organ. Writing to Edmund Wilson to thank him for a copy of David W. Mauer's book about tricksters, Nabokov remarks: "For one instant, I had the wild hope that *The Big Con* was French" (273).

Humbert and the principal figures in *Ada* are all Francophones, and it is particularly relevant that Humbert has worked on an "Histoire abrégée de la poésie anglaise" and is hoping to complete in Ramsdale a "manual of French literature for English-speaking students (with comparisons drawn from English writers)" (16). Humbert threatens to take Lolita to a secluded farmhouse and make her study French and Latin "under" him (149). In *Lolita* French is sexualized throughout: "*Soyons logiques,* crowed the cocky Gallic part of my brain" (238), a phrase that establishes an equivalency between the Gallic rooster—*coq Gaulois*—and the bawdy speech indebted to Gallic parts. Yet even where French is less or even not explicitly at issue, the play on *con* continues. Here is Humbert invoking nymphets for the first time:

You have to be an artist and a madman, a creature of infinite melancholy, with a bubble of hot poison in your loins and a super-voluptuous flame permanently aglow in your subtle spine [...] in order to discern at once, by ineffable signs [...] the little deadly demon among the *whole*some children; she stands unrecognized by them and un*con*scious herself of her fantastic power.

Furthermore, since the idea of time plays such a magic *part* in the matter, the student should not be surprised to learn that there must be a *gap* of several years, never less than ten I should say, generally thirty or forty, and as many as ninety in a few known *cases,* between maiden and man to enable the latter to *come* under a nymphet's spell. It is a question of focal adjustment, of a certain distance that the *inner eye* thrills to surmount, and a certain *con*trast that the mind perceives with a gasp of perverse delight. (17, emphasis added)

This focal adjustment relates as much to our reading of the passage as it does to Humbert's study of nymphets.

Humbert seeks to find in his first wife, Valechka, a cure for his sexual obsession. He hopes that "all the conventions of marriage, the prophylactic routine of its bedroom activities and, who knows, the eventual flowering of certain moral values, of certain spiritual substitutes, might help me, if not to purge myself of my degrading and dangerous desires, at least to keep them under pacific control" (24). Humbert also maintains that "there is no other bliss on earth comparable to that of fondling a nymphet. It is *hors concours*" (166). Rita is adopted by Humbert as "a constant companion"; "she would have given herself to any pathetic creature or fallacy" (258). Lolita is served "an elaborate ice-cream concoction topped with synthetic syrup. It was erected and brought her by a pimply brute of a boy in a greasy bow-tie who eyed my fragile child in her thin cotton frock with carnal deliberation" (115). The prefix we have been highlighting is particularly marked when Humbert has his second meeting with Miss Pratt:

"Let me ask a blunt question, Mr. Haze. You are an old-fashioned Continental father, aren't you?"
"Why, no, "I said, "conservative, perhaps, but not what you would call old-fashioned." (193)

Humbert's reflections about his orgasm on the davenport drew Rowe's attention, but a focus on the Shakespearean language in this passage would have made Rowe's assertions of its indecency far more compelling:

I felt proud of myself. I had stolen the honey of a spasm without impairing the morals of a minor. Absolutely no harm done. The *con*jurer had poured milk, molasses, foaming champagne into a young lady's new white *purse;* and lo, the *purse* was intact. Thus had I delicately *con*structed my ignoble, ardent, sinful dream; and still Lolita was safe—and I was safe. What I had madly possessed was not she, but my own creation, another, fanciful Lolita—perhaps, more real than Lolita;

over*lap*ping, en*cas*ing her; floating between me and her, and having no *will,* no *consciousness*—indeed, no *life* of her own. The child knew *nothing.* I had done *nothing* to her. And *nothing* prevented me from repeating a performance that affected her as little as if she were a photographic image rippling upon a screen and I a humble hunchback abusing myself in the dark. (62, emphasis added)[9]

Here Nabokov's beloved, oft-used word—conjurer—takes on additional, freighted meaning. In this passage conjuration becomes a kind of tacit swearing (*jurer*) with *con.* The incantation draws on a series of bawdy synonyms, an erotic thesaurus concluding with the word—"nothing"—that has sent Humbert over the edge on the davenport.[10]

Humbert recalls lying next to Lolita at the Enchanted Hunters:

If I dwell at some length on the tremors and gropings of that distant night, it is because I insist upon proving that I am not, and never was, and never could have been, a brutal scoundrel. The gentle and dreamy regions through which I crept were the patrimonies of poets—*not* crime's prowling ground. Had I reached my goal, my ecstasy would have been all softness, a case of internal combustion of which she would hardly have felt the heat, even if she were wide awake. But I still hoped she might gradually be engulfed in a completeness of stupor that would allow me to taste more than a glimmer of her. And so, in between tentative approximations, with a confusion of perception metamorphosing her into eyespots of moonlight or a fluffy flowering bush, I would dream I regained consciousness, dream I lay in wait. (131–32)

The equation of "eyespots of moonlight" with "a fluffy flowering bush" in "gentle regions" is worth pausing over.[11] Many years ago, Diana Butler

---

9. The British pronunciation of "purse" is close to "puss"; in 1949 Thomas Pyles suggested that this phonetic similarity might have an etymological basis in the development of the genital meaning of "pussy" ("Innocuous Linguistic Indecorum," 2). In this passage, purse may be read as a noun in apposition to "lo" (i.e., Lo).

10. "[A]nd because of her very perfunctory underthings, there seemed to be nothing to prevent my muscular thumb from reaching the hot hollow of her groin—just as you might tickle and caress a giggling child—just that—and: 'Oh it's nothing at all,' she cried with a sudden shrill note in her voice, and she wiggled, and squirmed, and threw her head back, and her teeth rested on her glistening underlip as she half-turned away, and my moaning mouth, gentlemen of the jury, almost reached her bare neck, while I crushed out against her left buttock the last throb of the longest ecstasy man or monster had ever known" (61). That this signal for pleasure comes from both Humbert and Lolita supports Sarah Herbold's contention that Nabokov (or, just as likely, Humbert) implies that Lolita is experiencing pleasure here too ("'I have camouflaged everything,'" 79–84).

11. The gentle/genital pun surfaces several times in Shakespeare, including the entendre-rich Sonnet 20 and *Henry IV, Part 1:* "She bids you on the wanton rushes lay you down / And rest your

made the claim that Lolita shares many of her characteristics with butterflies and might even be understood as a butterfly in girl's clothing. As she and others have pointed out, *nymph* is another term for the *pupa* in the butterfly's cycle of development, and one of Nabokov's discoveries—"Nabokov's Wood Nymph"—belonged to the family of *Nymphalidae* (Appel, 339). Butler's notion would find support in Alexander Etkind's more recent suggestion that the Russian word for butterfly—*babochka*, or little woman—might be translated literally as nymphet (359). But Butler may have taken a secondary metaphor for the primary one; the term *nymphet* owes its genesis as much to anatomy as to lepidoptery. The labia minora have traditionally been referred to as "nymphae" (*Webster's New International* [the second edition, Nabokov's dictionary], 1676) or "nymphes," (*OED*, 10:19), and the butterfly is still a popular metaphor for sex educators and body piercers ("Go Ask Alice," Bertrang, and, Oh, 18, inter alia). The association between butterflies and genitalia had particular significance for Nabokov, who used genitalia as a key to innovations in scientific classification. "I have dissected and drawn the genitalia of 360 specimens and unraveled taxonomic adventures that read like a novel," he writes to Edmund Wilson, "This has been a wonderful bit of training in the use of our (if I may say so) wise, precise, plastic, beautiful English language" (126). In a passage abounding in double entendre, Humbert calls attention to "the *twofold nature* of this nymphet—of every nymphet, perhaps."[12] Although he insists on Lolita's individuality, he is also transforming her into nothing but vulva, a feminine and genitalized version of the

---

gentle head upon her lap" (3.1.210) (see Rubinstein, 330). (Booth does not discuss this pun in Sonnet 20 but sees several other possible instances of bawdy wordplay there [164]). The pun may also be at work at the conclusion of *Lolita's* Part 1, undermining or, perhaps, even accentuating the pathos of that scene: "At the hotel we had separate rooms, but in the middle of the night she came sobbing into mine, and we made it up very gently. You see, she had absolutely nowhere else to go" (142). See also the passage in *Ada* describing Van's initial sexual experiences: "Things went better six minutes later, after Cheshire and Zographos were through; but only at the next mating party did Van really begin to enjoy her gentleness, her soft sweet grip and hearty joggle" (33). Nabokov was still putting this pun to work in his final manuscript: "Only some very expensive, super-oriental doctor with long gentle fingers could have analyzed her nightly dreams of erotic torture in so called 'labs', major and minor laboratories with red curtains" (*The Original of Laura,* 55).

12. For a genital definition of "nature," see Partridge, 130 (citing "the obsolete French literalism, *la nature*", as well as *OED,*10:248. *Lolita* plays with this connotation several times. Pratt tells Humbert that "everybody wonders why you are so firmly opposed to all the natural recreations of a normal child." "Do you mean sex play?" Humbert responds. When told that "dramatics, dances and other natural activities are not technically sex play," Humbert allows Lolita to participate in the play: "She can take part in that play. Provided male parts are taken by female parts." "I am always fascinated," Pratt responds, "by the admirable way foreigners—or at least naturalized Americans—use our rich language" (196–97). In his own defense, Humbert protests "I have but followed nature. I am nature's faithful hound" (135).

device of anatomical magnification immortalized in the Russian tradition by Nikolai Gogol's "The Nose":

> And neither is she the fragile child of a feminine novel. What drives me insane is the twofold nature of this nymphet—of every nymphet, perhaps; this mixture in my Lolita of tender dreamy childishness and a kind of eerie vulgarity, stemming from the snub-nosed cuteness of ads and magazine pictures, from the blurry pinkness of adolescent maid-servants in the Old Country (smelling of crushed daisies and sweat); and from very young harlots disguised as children in provincial broth-els; and then again, all this gets mixed up with the exquisite stainless tenderness seeping through the musk and the mud, through the dirt and the death, oh God, oh God. And what is most singular is that she, *this* Lolita, *my* Lolita, has individualized the writer's ancient lust, so that above and over everything there is—Lolita. (44–45)

Alexander Dolinin observes that by "neglecting details and thinking in generic terms (nymphet/non-nymphet), Humbert Humbert commits what is according to Nabokov the deadliest epistemological sin, the sin of general-ization, which renders the world and its mysteries impenetrable" ("Nabokov's Time Doubling," 24). One might go further: genitalization—the reduction of a human individual to his or her genitalia—is one of the most egregious forms of generalization.

At the start of *Lolita*'s second half, the phrase *"nous connûmes"* is applied to the various motels in which Lolita and Humbert stop. In the first of these Nabokov employs a bit of misdirection that has driven commentators to the wrong sorts of source books: "We came to know—*nous connûmes,* to use a Flaubertian intonation—the stone cottages under enormous Chateaubrian-desque trees" (145). Here French is playing a double role in a pun on *chatte* (pussy) that Nabokov uses elsewhere in *Lolita:* perhaps when he refers to Mrs. Chatfield, and certainly when Humbert encounters at Quilty's "two or three women [who] were chatting and chinking ice" (305). The synonyms proliferate. Humbert tries to drug Lolita: "the whole pill-spiel [. . .] had had for object a fastness of sleep that a whole regiment would not have dis-turbed" (128); later, Humbert describes how he got "the whole story" (137) of Lolita's loss of her virginity at summer camp. (When reading a column for teens in *The Beardsley Star* recommending that fathers allow their daughters

---

The association between butterflies and genitalia surfaces again with reference to this word when Humbert picks Lolita up at Camp Q: "photographs of girl-children; some gaudy moth or but-terfly, still alive, pinned to the wall ('nature study')" (110).

to have "wholesome fun" with boys, Humbert exclaims: "Wholesome fun? Good Lord!" [185]).[13] Humbert, we should remember, is "only a very conscientious recorder" (72), but now that "only" looks like something other than a declaration of modesty. Indeed, like Shakespeare in Sonnet 151 ("Love is too young to know what conscience is"), Nabokov may be providing "conscience" with a new etymology, according to which a conscientious recorder is a writer who knows cunt.[14] This definition turns the moral notion of conscience inside out.

The traditional French erotic play on the dual meaning of *vit* is incorporated by Nabokov at several points. "What adults did for purposes of procreation was no business of hers. My life was handled by little Lo in an energetic, matter-of-fact manner as if it were an insensate gadget unconnected with me. While eager to impress me with the world of tough kids, she was not quite prepared for certain discrepancies between a kid's life and mine" (133–34).[15] Valeria tells Humbert that there is "another man in my life," a phrase glossed by Humbert as "a translation from her French" and "ugly words for a husband to hear" (27). Charlotte wants Humbert as "a lifelong mate" who will "link up your life with mine forever" (68). Lolita has not only developed "a wholesome personality" at summer camp but has learned the Girl Scout's motto: "I fill my life with worthwhile deeds such as—well, never mind what. My duty is—to be useful. . . . I am a friend to male animals. [. . .] I am thrifty and I am absolutely filthy in thought, word and deed" (114). This meaning of life is prominent as well in Humbert's famous opening words: "Lolita, light of my life, fire of my loins" (9), which may also rely on the Elizabethan homonym of lines/loins (Booth, 579; Kökeritz, 216–17). Humbert imagines Lolita comparing him to Quilty: "*He* broke my heart. *You* merely broke my life" (279). An understanding of Nabokov's use of "life" changes the tonality of this remark, making it more consistent with Humbert's anatomical preoccupation and undermining the notion of a reformed narrator.[16]

---

13. In his response to Nabokov's review of his book, Rowe highlighted this pun as one of several in which *Lolita* places the word "fun" in highly sexualized surroundings ("Twenty-Seven Footnotes," 79).

14. See Booth's comment on the sonnet: "Here Shakespeare seems to derive a reading of *conscience* that is roughly paraphrasable as 'cunt knowledge'" (526).

15. Patnoe is one of the few readers to identify "life" in this passage with "penis" (124–25), but she neither notes the Shakespearean origin of this quibble nor sees its function elsewhere in the text. See also Couturier, *Nabokov, ou la cruauté,* 224. Rowe points out the relevance of this meaning of life to the opening lines of Humbert's confession ("Twenty-Seven Footnotes," 78).

16. In his afterword to the novel Nabokov coyly bemoans that his favorite scenes in the novel will remain unnoticed "or never even reached, by those who begin reading the book under the impression that it is something on the lines of *Memoirs of a Woman of Pleasure* or *Les Amours de Milord Grosvit*" (316). The second title may have been invented by Nabokov, but Grosvit is the hero of

As in Shakespeare the use of bawdy in *Lolita* is occasionally far from physiologically coherent and resembles something of a rant: "I pushed, instead of pulling, pulled, pushed, pulled, and entered. Look out! Some ten paces away Lolita, through the glass of a telephone booth (membranous god still with us), cupping the tube, confidentially hunched over it, slit her eyes at me, turned away with her treasure, hurriedly hung up, and walked out with a flourish" (206–7). Here, as in the description of Humbert's collection of his mail, Nabokov seems to be engaging in a bawdy exercise: how many pudendal synonyms can he place in a single sentence? "My letterbox in the entrance hall belonged to the type that allows one to glimpse something of its contents through a glassed slit" (263). Readers may well sympathize with Lolita when, just before she escapes, she tells Humbert: "do you mind very much cutting out the French! It annoys everybody" (243). As Humbert says in a line that should be read as a double pun: "My tale is sufficiently incondite already" (70).

Corporeal images are especially marked in descriptions of Humbert's and Lolita's voyages. The entire nation is transformed into a coyly obscene poem to the female genitalia of the sort that flourished in sixteenth-century France: a *blason du con:* "Our route began with a series of wiggles and whorls in New England, then meandered south, up and down, east and west; dipped deep into *ce qu'on appelle* Dixieland, [. . .]and finally returned to the fold of the East, petering out in the college town of Beardsley" (154).[17] The theme of travel seems especially apt to bring sexualized uses of *country* into the text: Nabokov frequently plays on the sexual dimension of that word's first syllable. Humbert looks for "a nice country road where to park in peace" (140). He discusses with the Farlows how Lolita is to be recalled from her camp excursion:

> John said it was perfectly simple—he would get the Climax police to find the hikers. It would not take them an hour. In fact, he knew the country and—
> "Look, he continued, "why don't I drive there right now and you may sleep with Jean—(he did not really add that but Jean supported his offer so passionately that it might be implied).
> I broke down. I pleaded with John to let things remain the way they were. (100)

Yvonne, a novel published in 1898 in Paris and London and reprinted by Grove Press—with authorship attributed to Mary Suckit—in 1970.

17. For a discussion of the anatomical blasons in their historical context, see Pike, 223–42; and Sawday, 188–212. Sawday notes the propensity of erotic poems in the seventeenth century to compare the exploration of a woman's body to the conquest of America, as in Donne's Elegie XIX: "License my roaving hands, and let them go, / Before, behind, between, above, below. / O my America! My new-foun-land, / My kingdome, safeliest when with one man man'd (27).

Farlow agrees, concluding—in a pun noted by Bodenstein (312–13)—"whatever you feel is right" (101).

Humbert tells Valechka that she will like America, "the country of rosy children and great trees, where life would be such an improvement on dull dingy Paris" (27); he casts around for "some place in the New England countryside, [...] where I could spend a studious summer subsisting on a compact boxful of notes" (35).[18] At one point Nabokov calls attention to the quintessential nature of his characters' journey in a passage that effectively genitalizes not only Lolita but the entire landscape of the New World:

> We had been everywhere. We had really seen nothing. And I catch myself thinking today that our long journey had only defiled with a sinuous trail of slime the lovely, trustful, dreamy, enormous country that by then, in retrospect, was no more to us than a collection of dog-eared maps, ruined tour books, old tires, and her sobs in the night—every night, every night—the moment I feigned sleep. (175–76)

This passage is often cited by moral or sentimental readings of the novel, but the bawdy undercurrent gives those sentiments a distinctly bitter edge. Lolita's tears never manage to transcend the preoccupation that Humbert refers to as his "private aesthetics," his propensity for imparting a genital sheen to his beloved's portrait:

> Lo [...] had been crying after a routine row with her mother and, as had happened on former occasions, had not wished me to see her swollen eyes: she had one of those tender complexions that after a good cry get all blurred and inflamed, and morbidly alluring. I regretted keenly her mistake about my private aesthetics, for I simply love that tinge of Botticellian pink, that raw rose about the lips, those wet, matted eyelashes; and, naturally, her bashful whim deprived me of many opportunities of specious consolation. (64)

Of course, not every appearance of the words *country, tail, case* or the prefix *con* has a sexual tinge; writing a novel in English without this prefix would be a feat. But there are times when Nabokov employs this lexical register quite heavily—perhaps most notably when describing the hotel in which Lolita

---

18. There may be a pun here on note and naught (vulva). See Booth's comment on "naught" (164, 521). The precise wording of Nabokov's response to Rowe should also be kept in mind: "If every 'come' and 'part' on the pages of my books is supposedly used by me to represent 'climax' and 'genitals,' one can well imagine the naughty treasures Mr. Rowe might find [...] (*Strong Opinions,* 306).

and Humbert begin their "concourse." This hotel is called "The Enchanted Hunters," and this is also the name of a faux-Elizabethan play written by Clare Quilty, the first mention of which is prefaced by a reference to Elizabethan poetry. Humbert is slightly perplexed by this doubling of names:

> Nothing prevented one, of course, from supposing that in quest of an attractive name the founder of the hotel had been immediately and solely influenced by the chance fantasy of the second-rate muralist he had hired, and that subsequently the hotel's name had suggested the play's title. But in my credulous, simple, benevolent mind I happened to twist it the other way round, and without giving the whole matter much thought really, supposed that mural, name and title had all been derived from a common source, from some local tradition, which I, an alien unversed in New England lore, would not be supposed to know. In consequence I was under the impression [. . .] that the accursed playlet belonged to the type of whimsy for juvenile consumption, arranged and rearranged many times. (200–201)

The name of the hotel first surfaces soon after Humbert's marriage to Charlotte. The bride has entered the room to find her husband "turning volume C of the *Girls' Encyclopedia* around to examine a picture printed 'bottom-edge' as printers say." Humbert speaks to her absent-mindedly as he thumbs through the pages "(Campus, Canada, Candid Camera, Candy)":

> Presently (at Canoeing or Canvasback) she strolled up to my chair and sank down, tweedily, weightily, on its arm, inundating me with the perfume my first wife had used. "Would his lordship like to spend the fall *here*?" she asked, pointing with her little finger at an autumn view in a conservative Eastern State. "Why?" (very distinctly and slowly). She shrugged. (Probably Harold used to take a vacation at that time. Open season. Conditional reflex on her part).
> "I think I know where that is," she said, still pointing. "There is a hotel I remember, Enchanted Hunters, quaint, isn't it? And the food is a dream." (92–93)

As far as I know, Alexander Dolinin is the only one to have pointed out that—to judge from the encyclopedia volume—this state has to be Connecticut ("Kommentarii," 375), but he stops short of the insight that this state has been selected because it uniquely manages to contain both the English (cut, cunt) and French words (*con*) for the same thing. The insertion of "quaint," set off by commas, might even be read as an apposition for the hotel, since *quaint* was itself a euphemistic genital term (*Webster's New International,* 2031;

OED, 12:968; Booth, 163).[19] The scene functions as a lexicographic variation on the device of the verbal striptease identified by Jenefer Shute as central to Nabokov's practice of erotic listing (540). When Humbert and Lolita approach the Enchanted Hunters, there is, appropriately, an orgy of body-language, and I suspect that in Humbert's inability to secure proper directions we should see a hint that he is somehow mispronouncing the name of the hotel, that in the Enchanted Hunters a letter is being switched, as one is, for instance, when his name cabled to the hotel becomes Humberg (or Humbug) instead of Humbert:

> Dusk was beginning to saturate pretty little Briceland [...], when we drove through the weakly lighted streets in search of the Enchanted Hunters. The air, despite a steady drizzle beading it, was warm and green, and a queue of people, mainly children and old men, had already formed before the box office of a movie house, dripping with jewel-fires. [...]
>
> If we did not get to the hotel soon, immediately, miraculously, in the very next block, I felt I would lose all control over the Haze jalopy with its ineffectual wipers and whimsical brakes; but the passers-by I applied to for directions were either strangers themselves or asked with a frown "Enchanted what?" as if I were a madman; or else they went into such complicated explanations, with geometrical gestures, geographical generalities and strictly local clues (... then bear south after you hit the courthouse ...) that I could not help losing my way in the maze of their well-meaning gibberish. [...] [T]o grind and grope thorough the avenues of Briceland was perhaps the most exasperating ordeal I had yet faced. In later months I could laugh at my inexperience when recalling the obstinate boyish way in which I had concentrated upon that particular inn with its fancy name; for all along our route countless motor courts proclaimed their vacancy in neon lights, ready to accommodate salesmen, escaped convicts, impotents, family groups, as well as the most corrupt and vigorous couples. [...]
>
> The miracle I hankered for did happen after all. A man and a girl, more or less conjoined in a dark car under dripping trees, told us we were in the heart of The Park, but had only to turn left at the next traffic light and there we would be. We did not see any next traffic light—in fact, The Park was as black as the sins it concealed—but soon

---

19. See also Andrew Marvell's "To His Coy Mistress": "then worms shall try / That long-preserved virginity: And your quaint honour turn to dust, / And into ashes all my lust. / The grave's a fine and private place, / but none, I think, do there embrace" (51). The poem's subject, as well as the poet's imagining himself "by the tide of Humber," make it particularly relevant to *Lolita.*

after falling under the smooth spell of a nicely graded curve, the travelers became aware of a diamond glow through the mist, then a gleam of lakewater appeared—and there it was, marvelously and inexorably, under spectral trees, at the top of a graveled drive—the pale palace of The Enchanted Hunters.

A row of parked cars, like pigs at a trough, seemed at first sight to forbid access; but then, by magic, a formidable convertible, resplendent, rubious in the lighted rain, came into motion—was energetically backed out by a broad-shouldered driver—and we gratefully slipped into the gap it had left. (115–17)

This passage provides ample reference to the common source for which Humbert has been searching. But the suggestive language here is not all connotative of female genitalia: we have the backside of the car, the queue of children and old men, and just a page earlier, when Humbert has been driving too fast, Lolita has yelled at him for forgetting that "the speed in this bum state is fifty" (113). This passage offers—right down to Quilty's convertible, which puns on the green (young) fruit that Humbert loves, the green sickness of desire and venery that afflicts Juliet and so many of Shakespeare's lovers—a veritable orgy of bawdy language frequently employed in Elizabethan drama. When the hotel is then turned by Quilty into a play, this transposition merely brings out what was latent in the hotel's description from the very first.

Finally, we are ready to return to the outrageous suggestion with which we began this journey cross-country. The anagram that so ruffled the feathers of Nabokovians occurs in the midst of a long passage describing Humbert's hunt for traces of Quilty in hotel registers.

I noticed that whenever he felt his enigmas were becoming too recondite, even for such a solver as I, he would lure me back with an easy one. [...] An ordinary encyclopedia informed me who the peculiar looking "Phineas Quimby, Lebanon, NH" was; and any good Freudian, with a German name and some interest in religious prostitution, should recognize at a glance the implication of "Dr. Kitzler, Eryx, Miss." [...] But the most penetrating bodkin was the anagramtailed entry in the register of Chestnut Lodge "Ted Hunter, Cane, NH."

The garbled license numbers left by all these Persons [...] only told me that motel keepers omit to check if guests' cars are accurately listed. References—incompletely or incorrectly indicated—to the cars the fiend had hired for short laps between Wace and Elphinstone were of course useless; the license of the initial Aztec was a shimmer of shifting numerals, some transposed, others altered or omitted, but somehow forming interrelated combinations (such as "WS 1564" and "SH 1616," and Q32888" or "CU 88322") which however were so cunningly contrived as to never reveal a common denominator. (250–51)

The sentence ending the first paragraph quoted is a tour de force. The word "bodkin"—meaning a dagger—should provoke a hermeneutic toggle into Shakespearean discourse; it is used twice in *Hamlet,* and one of these occurrences is in the most famous soliloquy in the English language (3.1.78). Once we are in a Shakespearean mode, the word "lodge" has a markedly venereal look. In Shakespeare's plays it may refer as a noun to venery in both senses of that word and to the pudendum or, as a verb, to sexual intercourse.[20] Alfred Appel and other Nabokov commentators see no more than the surface anagram here—*Ted Hunter, Cane, NH* is obviously *The Enchanted Hunters*—but they have not been reading in the right register. If we read the phrase "anagramtailed entry" as itself a pun, an anagramtailed entry in the register of Chestnut Lodge the name of the lodge itself might lead us to look for that entry in the immediate lexical vicinity, and functions quite nicely in that respect as an anagram for a more vulgar term for "tail."

Shakespearean bawdy emerges openly in the second paragraph just quoted, its relevance proclaimed by those "*license* numbers," a term that is itself a pun. Appel points out that WS 1564 and Sh 1616 refer to the years of Shakespeare's birth and death. He notes that the letters on the other two plates refer to Quilty, and he opines that the numbers are significant because they add up to fifty-two, which is, he says, the number of weeks Humbert and Lolita are on the road, the number of lines in the poem addressed to her, the number of cards in a deck, and the year—1952—in which all the characters die (428). Perhaps. It might also be pertinent that Shakespeare lived fifty-two years. But the essential thing to note is that the text establishes an equivalence between Quilty and Shakespeare. Quilty is, in effect, a Shakespeare run amok, a Shakespeare who exists *only* at the level of bawdy. (He might even be the "Wild Bill Something" whose rodeo Humbert and Lolita visit in Kansas [156]). When Humbert tracks Quilty down at last, the latter makes a pun that is so bad that, Appel asserts, he does indeed deserve to die for it: "I promise you […] you will be happy here, with a magnificent cellar, and all the

---

20. See the uses of "lodge" cited by Henke (158–59) and Rubinstein (150), who also suggests that there is sexual innuendo at the end of the Ghost's injunction to Hamlet: "Leave her to heaven / And to those thorns that in her bosom lodge, / To prick and sting her" (1.5.86–88). Humbert is "perfectly aware that if by any wild chance I became [Charlotte's] lodger, she would methodically proceed to do in regard to me what taking a lodger probably meant to her all along"; a few paragraphs later he is already Charlotte's "lodger-lover" (37–38).

royalties from my next play—I have not much at the bank right now but I propose to borrow—you know, as the Bard said, with that cold in his head, to borrow and to borrow and to borrow" (301). "To borrow" and "tomorrow" is not the only cold-induced pun here. There is a tape of Nabokov reading this passage, and he pronounces "bard" in the English way—without an "r" (*Lolita, Poems*). "Bard" when pronounced in London is closer to "bawd" than it would be in American English. Humbert has had to miss a rendezvous with the prostitute Monique when he catches "a cold" from her (23). A bard with a cold, Quilty suffers from a verbal venereal disease.

Does Quilty have a Shakespearean prototype? Indeed, he does. The King Edward VII Professor of English Literature at Cambridge while Nabokov was a student there was the noted lecturer, prolific scholar, and poet Arthur Quiller-Couch. Between 1921 and 1931 Quiller-Couch was the coeditor of *The New Cambridge Edition of the Works of Shakespeare,* serving in that position until the edition had published all of Shakespeare's comedies. He was also the editor of a wide range of material that would indicate the extent of his Quilty-esque erudition: *The Oxford Book of English Verse, Select English Classics, The Oxford Book of Victorian Verse, The Oxford Book of Ballads, The Oxford Book of English Prose.* He wrote several collections of fairy tales, a children's book about the bard's life entitled *Shakespeare's Christmas,* and many volumes of critical essays, including some on Shakespeare collected in a volume entitled *Shakespeare's Workmanship;* he also was the author of over twenty novels and several books of poems, including parodies that were published in his collection of verse entitled *Green Bays.*[21] For our purposes, though, the most significant feature of his huge output may be the name under which he published his poems and fiction and by which he was known to his friends: "Q." After Quiller-Couch's death in 1944, F. Brittain, Fellow of Jesus College, subtitled his encomium "A Biographical Study of Q."[22] J. M. Dent and Sons published *A Q Anthology* in 1948, and Quiller-Couch's successor as the King Edward VII Professor entitled his inaugural lecture "The Q Tradition."

Quiller-Couch was in no sense a bawdy writer; in fact, his editions of Shakespeare's comedies are occasionally risible in their efforts to avoid bawdiness.[23] The name Quilty is assuredly overdetermined—Nabokov plays with

---

21. A partial list of Quiller-Couch's publications is provided by F. Brittain (*Q Anthology,* xii–xiv).

22. Given Quilty's "many plays for children," it is worthy of note that in 1923, while Nabokov was at Cambridge, Quiller-Couch was at work coediting *The Children's Bible* and *The Little Children's Bible* (Brittain, *Arthur Quiller-Couch* 114–15).

23. In their introduction to *Twelfth Night,* Quiller-Couch and his coeditor assert that the play has absolutely no ribald moments, and their puzzlement at the meaning of 2.5.77–80 ("These be

it endlessly, and he needed a name beginning with a rarely used letter to mark that figure's presence—yet Quilty's name—and his nickname, Cue—probably has its origin in this figure of erudition so closely associated with Shakespeare. Nabokov was not loathe to use other aspects of his college days in a similar manner. In *Ada*'s world of Anti-Terra, Cambridge is transformed into "Chose University."

Quilty is probably a composite, combining two wide-ranging giants of successive generations: Quiller-Couch and Nabokov's friend Edmund Wilson. Although Wilson and Nabokov would fall out irretrievably only after Wilson's condemnation of Nabokov's *Onegin* translation in the 1960s, their relations were competitive from the first and full of sexual banter. Wilson supplied Nabokov with erotic literature and later playfully credited these gifts with having inspired *Lolita* (*The Nabokov-Wilson Letters,* 368). It is more likely, though, that Nabokov was inspired by the scandal that ensued after the banning in 1946 of Wilson's *Memoirs of Hecate County.* Wilson's book was prosecuted chiefly on account of a single passage, an extended and explicit description of the female genitalia prior to and during intercourse (*Memoirs,* 250–51; Updike, 449–59). The passage is founded on a poetics best described as clinical, with a few lexical sprinklings from Victorian erotica:

> She seemed perfectly developed and proportioned, with no blight from her spinal disease: she was quite straight and had the right kind of roundness. I found that I was expressing admiration of her points as if she were some kind of museum piece, and that she seemed to enjoy being posed in the setting of the fresh rose sheath, as if some frank and unashamed self-complacency coexisted with her morbid self-doubt. [...] But what struck and astonished me most was that not only were her thighs perfect columns but that all that lay between them was impressively beautiful, too, with an ideal aesthetic value that I had never found there before. The mount was of a classical femininity: round and smooth and plump; the fleece, if not quite golden, was blond and curly and soft; and the portals were a deep tender rose, like the petals of some fleshly flower." (250–51)

On reading the novel, Nabokov claimed to have derived "no kick from the hero's love-making. I should have as soon tried to open a sardine can with my penis" (*The Nabokov-Wilson Letters,* 188). But the passage at issue

---

her very C's, her U's, and her T's") seems comically naïve today. They suggest that the T must be an error, that originally it was an e, thus turning the word into CUE, a reference to minding one's ps and qs (1383–89).

nevertheless stayed with him. Writing to Wilson in 1953 from Portal, Arizona, a town that he identified in "On a Book Entitled Lolita" as one of the four places the novel was written (312), he admitted: "The word 'portal' is rather dreadfully associated in my mind (which has always contained more associations than thoughts) with a certain euphemism in your *Hecate*" (*The Nabokov-Wilson Letters,* 311). It may well be that just as Humbert and Quilty compete for Lolita, so Nabokov saw *Lolita* as competing with, and surpassing, Wilson's *Memoirs. Lolita* is not only more seductive as a text, but with its covert genital proliferation it also gets away with putting everywhere what Wilson was punished for putting in a single passage. (Lolita tells Humbert that "this world is just one gag after another, if somebody wrote up her life nobody would ever believe it" (273). In *Lolita* Nabokov *has* written up his heroine's 'life,' and few people seem to have noticed). Treating the same subject as Wilson, Nabokov effectively appropriates the "ideal aesthetic value" from the object and applies it to his text itself, so that not genitalia but writing "about" them attains the status of art.[24]

Does all the bawdiness in *Lolita* have its source in Quilty? Not exactly, because—ignoring for a moment the question of whether Quilty is simply Humbert's double—most of the passages we have examined are at least superficially Humbert's. And even in John Ray's introduction we encounter bawdy wordplay. Ray asserts: "not a single obscene term is to be found in the whole work; indeed, the robust philistine who is conditioned by modern conventions into accepting without qualms a lavish array of four-letter words in a banal novel, will be quite shocked by their absence here" (4). He goes on to provide a few phrases which—in generic terms—turn the entire text into a bawdy item. *Lolita* is "a tragic tale," "a case history," "a memoir permitted to come under my reading lamp" (4–5).[25] Most telling is the subtitle he provides: "the confessions of a white widowed male"—and in that con-fession we may

---

24. Wilson himself seems to have suspected that Nabokov's writing was more effectively seductive than his own. In 1946 he recorded in detail his sexual relations with the woman who would soon become his next wife: "E[lena] at Wellfleet, July—second time when she was dry: thrusting it down into her with deliberate strong strokes that finally set the spring flowing. She would groan—said it hurt at first but later on was wonderful. Marvelous afternoon in room above my study: tuna sandwiches and white wine. I made her laugh a lot the time before with Russian stories from V. Nabokov: she would say: more stories! (When I had read her the German sex book, she had said at last: enough theory!)" (Wilson, *The Forties,* 173). Not only does writing about sex lead Wilson here immediately to mention Nabokov, but through a compositional parallel Nabokov's stories in the second paragraph do the work eventually accomplished by good sex in the first.

25. D. Barton Johnson discusses quibbles on "case" and several other genital puns in *Ada* (*Worlds in Regression,* 56–58). George Ferger has argued that Ray's prose style is sufficiently similar to the rest of the novel to warrant the conclusion that he is a coauthor of the entire text. Ferger may have a point, although his methodology—finding elsewhere in the text individual words used by Ray

hear shuttling between the genital and anal zones of development: from *le con* to *les fesses*. If America is not a real country, if Humbert and Lolita have seen nothing, if the entire novel is a case, a tail, a confession, then what indeed is the whole book about? Seen in this light, the novel begins to become not a journey around America, and not even a trip around the body, but travel around language about the body. Nabokov insisted that *Lolita* was the story of his love affair with the English language, and we certainly do see his appreciation of the Shakespearean bottom edge. Like Shakespeare, Nabokov can play high or low, sending us either to the *OED* or to Partridge and his many successors. He certainly understood that the inclusion of a bawdy, bodily register can imbue high literature with a vital, regenerative, even juvenile force appropriate to the meeting of the Old and New Worlds.

And a love affair, after all, does have its physical, crude dimension. Yet we can also see this novel as a tragedy about both the riches *and* the limitations of language. Humbert's dream is to incarnate the spell of Annabel Lee in another; the novel depicts a failed incarnation, and it both begins and ends with the death of Lolita and her stillborn daughter on Christmas Day. That, I think, explains the name of the fictitious introducer—John Ray, Jr.—whose name, resonant with the Johannine preamble's emphasis on light, should make us consider the novel a poor, even failing second attempt to provide a gospel of incarnation, of the word becoming flesh. All the Shakespearean verbal play with the body's lower stratum should remind us that there is no flesh here. The poem by Remy Belleau cited by Humbert is entitled *"Impuissance."* As Humbert says himself, he has "only words to play with."

In this sense, one could say that Lolita is all about "oral sex," but only if Nabokov is redefining the concept. The novel begins with an oral how-to—"the tip of the tongue taking a trip of three steps down the palate to tap, at three, on the teeth. Lo. Lee. Ta" (9)—that recalls pronunciation exercises (Nabokov at Wellesley: "Please take out your mirrors, girls, and see what happens inside your mouths" [The Nabokov-Wilson Letters, 105]) and serves as an initial appeal for the reader's oral complicity. (Reading ordinarily requires the movement of our eyes, the start of *Lolita* makes a claim on our tongues as well.) Humbert uses "fancy" as part of a euphemism to refer to fellatio— "Knowing the magic and might of her own soft mouth, she managed— during one schoolyear!—to raise the bonus price of a fancy embrace to three, and even four bucks!" (184)—but he also uses that word to characterize his entire style of writing: "You can always count on a murderer for a fancy prose

---

(i.e., "ghost") and capacious anagrams for Ray's name ("born in Ocean City," "you bear south")— often leads to highly tenuous results.

style" (9). The number of chapters in Lolita (69) is also probably significant in this regard, Nabokov's denial to the contrary notwithstanding (Mason, 75), as is Humbert's erotic obsession with lips, which builds to a climax in the davenport scene:

> Lola the bobby-soxer, devouring her immemorial fruit, singing through its juice, losing her slipper, rubbing the heel of her slipperless foot in its sloppy anklet, against the pile of old magazines heaped on my left on the sofa—and every movement she made, every shuffle and ripple, helped me to conceal and to improve the secret system of tactile correspondence between beast and beauty—between my gagged, bursting beast and the beauty of her dimpled body in its innocent cotton frock. (59)

This labial incitement reaches its apex several sentences later, when Lolita is "safely solipsized." (60). However, this succinct expression for Humbert's appropriation of Lolita reveals the limits of his possession, built as it is on the idea that sexual satisfaction can be predicated on talk about parts of the body that produce language. The oral sex in *Lolita* is sex that never moves beyond talk. Beardsley headmistress Pratt, generally so clueless about Lolita's relationship with Humbert, grasps the narrative's fundamental contradiction:

> You say that all you expect a child to obtain from school is a sound education. But what do we mean by education? In the old days it was in the main a verbal phenomenon; I mean, you could have a child learn by heart a good encyclopedia and he or she would know as much as or more than a school could offer. Dr. Hummer, do you realize that for the modern pre-adolescent child, medieval dates are of less vital value than weekend ones [twinkle]?—to repeat a pun that I heard the Beardsley college psychoanalyst permit herself the other day. We live not only in a world of thoughts, but also in a world of things. Words without experience are meaningless. What on earth can Dorothy Hummerson care for Greece and the Orient with their harems and slaves?" (178, brackets in original)

Significantly, if still ludicrously, this insistence on the value of experience rather than language is paired with a rejection of Humbert's bawdy poetics in favor of bodily communication: "with due respect to Shakespeare and others, we want our girls to communicate freely with the live world around them rather than plunge into musty old books. We are still groping perhaps, but we grope intelligently, like a gynecologist feeling a tumor" (177).[26]

---

26. The adverb "intelligently," while returning the reader to the gentle/genital pun discussed above (note 11), also serves to describe the bawdy poetics of *Lolita* in general as well as the manner in

In the tradition of Russian Symbolism from which Nabokov sprung, words ought to be more than enough, since they are magic and meant to have an impact on the world.[27] In Andrei Bely's celebration of verbal majesty "language is the most powerful instrument of creation," the creative word is automatically "incarnate," and "in the creation of words, in the naming of unknown phenomena, we subdue and enchant these phenomena with sounds" ("The Magic of Words," 123, 127). An application of Bely's manifesto to language about sex would suggest that bawdy language is a way of obtaining mastery over the body's essential drives, but we can also see bawdy talk as a self-perpetuating verbal prison that traps the speaker in lexical solipsism that never reaches the physical object of desire. *Lolita* is an incantation, but its conjuring never moves from word to flesh; the brilliance and tragedy of language is that it is only language and therefore useless. Its glory arises from its inability to transcend the distinction between word and matter just as—for Nabokov—the value of life arises through its limitation in time. However, there is another, metafictive form of incarnation occurring here. In *The Real Life of Sebastian Knight,* Sebastian's novel *The Prismatic Bezel* "can be thoroughly enjoyed once it is understood that the heroes of the book are what can be loosely called 'methods of composition'" (93). If *Lolita* is a sick book, it is so because in it the hermeneutics of perversion, which have lain at the core of Nabokov's work since the late 1920s, are finally configured: a constructive poetic principle is here incarnated in a character (Humbert) and his double (Quilty). The result, though, is hardly the hideous universe and the "monstrously distorted" language of *Bend Sinister,* a novel in which wordplay, Nabokov's preface tells us, is a "verbal plague, a contagious sickness in the world of words" (xv). In *Lolita,* the pervert may be apparent, but the principle of poetic contortion remains masked, accessible only to a reader who is complicitly perverse.

Here is where a fundamental tension in Nabokov scholarship plays a central role. The thrill of reading Nabokov well results from the interplay of two possibilities: the triumphant bringing to light of hidden, undiscovered meaning, and the risk of appearing ridiculous, of misguidedly "abusing [one]self in the dark" (62). The reader who seeks to understand *Lolita* fully by reading the novel with a leer runs the risk of becoming Quilty's double: a person who always thinks of *that.* A willingness to be complicitly perverse

---

which this libidinally charged, verbally playful novel ought to be read, even if the image of "groping" a text is far less elegant than "fondling details."

27. On Nabokov's relationship to major writers in the Russian Symbolist movement, see Alexandrov ("Nabokov and Bely") and Bethea.

exposes the reader to the danger of being required to provide the body—and the genitals—that Humbert and Quilty lack. This possibility of physiological possession haunts the reading of *Lolita* and accounts for the insistent rejection of the discoveries of sexually oriented readers.

Ironically, in engaging with the novel, the embodied reader of Lolita inevitably slips into a form of fetishism, replacing a desired body with a desired text. Reading *Lolita* closely becomes akin to Humbert's attempt to find traces of Quilty on Lolita—and thus to substantiate his feeling of being deceived:

> I pushed her softness back into the room and went in after her. I ripped her shirt off. I unzipped the rest of her. I tore off her sandals. Wildly, I pursued the shadow of her infidelity; but the scent I traveled upon was so slight as to be practically undistinguishable from a madman's fancy. (215)

As Maurice Couturier has pointed out, the difference between an initial reading of Lolita and a repeated one is the transition from "a reading both poetic, by identification with Humbert the narrator, and erotic, by identification with Humbert the character," to "a reading of investigation" that takes Humbert's and Nabokov's language as its object (*Nabokov, ou la tyrannie*, 177). The difficulty for the close reader lies in knowing when to stop, when to forgo the ripping apart of the text for the pleasure of fondling its details in an appreciation of its surface. Ideally, in an impossibly perfect reading, the savoring of the text would be indistinguishable from the pursuit of its shadows, a process best halted while there is still something—and not just nothing—left.

We will return to this question of the reader's sexual focus. Now let us move backward and take a look at the novel Nabokov wrote just before *Lolita,* a book no less sexually oriented, but oriented differently.

✍ Chapter 2

Art as Afterglow (*Bend Sinister*)

Received wisdom has it that *Bend Sinister,* completed a year after the defeat of the Nazis and in the face of Soviet expansion in Eastern Europe, is about the saving power of art and the importance of individual freedom. Such a reading is fundamentally rooted in the liberal, humanist tradition, and if *Bend Sinister* is generally considered one of Nabokov's least successful novels (Boyd, *American Years,* 105; Clancy, 92–100), it may be because it seems to choose such an easy target.[1] Who, after all, could argue with the notion that totalitarianism is a bad thing?

Even though Nabokov, in his subsequently written commentary placed at the start of later editions of the novel, emphasized that "*Bend Sinister* is not really about life and death in a grotesque police state" (xiii), few readers have believed him. To cite two very different commentators, Azar Nafisi treats the novel as one of several parables by Nabokov about the salvational power

---

1. Michael Wood, who appreciates *Bend Sinister* as a compassionate work by a "theorist of pain," dismisses its merit as a political novel: "The politics are surely trivial, not because the questions they address don't matter or because Nabokov is a mere aesthete, but because his overtly political formulations are always too broad and easy, have none of the interest and intricacy of a fully imagined political world" (59). Edmund Wilson was similarly disparaging: "You aren't good at this kind of subject, which involves questions of politics and social change, because you are totally uninterested in these matters and have never taken the trouble to understand them. [...] Now don't tell me that the real artist has nothing to do with the issues of politics. An artist may not take politics seriously, but, if he deals with these matters at all, he ought to know what it is all about" (Nabokov-Wilson, 210).

of literature for those living under dictatorship: "It is this world [of fiction] that prevents his heroes and heroines from utter despair, that becomes their refuge in a life that is consistently brutal" (32–33). Samuel Schuman, in an article on *Hamlet* in *Bend Sinister,* argues that "both works proclaim that art, including the art which they themselves manifest, stands in opposition to subhuman despots and rotten states. Indeed, it may be that the magic creative and recreative power of words, freshly imagined and imaginatively used, is the best and only defense available to Hamlet, to Krug, to their creators, and to us" (211).

It seems a shame to challenge this view of *Bend Sinister,* since its affirmation of the benevolent power of art is one that most of its readers would probably like to embrace. Here, though, I'm going to urge a contrary position, one that is almost Tolstoyan. Art, *Bend Sinister* argues, can be good or bad, but it is not democratic, nor is it related, except perhaps inversely, to salvation. On the contrary: this is the work by Nabokov that most conclusively establishes an affinity between totalitarianism and art.

At several points in his career, Nabokov equated authorship with dictatorial control. Fyodor says in *The Gift* that he wants to "reach a final dictatorship over words, because in my *Chernyshevski* they are still trying to vote" (364). In an interview with Alfred Appel, Nabokov dismissed the notion that a character might "dictate" the course of action to his author: "I have never experienced this. [...] Writers who have had it must be very minor or insane. No, the design of my novel is fixed in my imagination and every character follows the course I imagine for him. I am the perfect dictator in that private world insofar as I alone am responsible for its stability and truth" (*Strong Opinions,* 69). *Bend Sinister* takes these dicta literally. The phrase "an imaginary dictatorship" might refer not only to the novel's setting but to any strong work of art.[2]

Let's begin with the heart of the book, the longest chapter and the one that occupies its center, at least quantitatively. This is the scene where Adam Krug, the philosopher-hero, and his friend Ember discuss bad adaptations of *Hamlet.* Ember, a translator of Shakespeare, is in bed with a cold and incensed by the production of *Hamlet* currently being staged at the State Theatre. That version of the play has been heavily influenced, as Brian Boyd ("Notes," 684–91) has pointed out, by German scholars quoted in the New Variorum edition, a work first published in 1877 and dedicated "To The German

---

2. In his analysis of *Bend Sinister* Maurice Couturier observes: "To write a novel for [Nabokov] is most of all to exercise his power over a universe that he has invented entirely and for the existence of which he owes nothing to anyone else" (*Nabokov, ou la cruauté,* 148–49).

Shakespeare Society of Weimar, Representative of a People Whose Recent History Has Proved Once For All That 'Germany is *NOT* Hamlet'" (1:1), words that took on an ominous connotation in Nabokov's early American years, when Germany had again proved itself far from indecisive. The State Theatre's *Hamlet* makes Fortinbras the hero: "With God's sanction, this fine Nordic youth assumes the control of miserable Denmark which had been so criminally misruled by degenerate king Hamlet and Judeo-Latin Claudius" (*Bend Sinister,* 108). Krug replies with his own memories of bad adaptations of Shakespeare, and the ensuing discussion attests to Nabokov's thorough knowledge of both *Hamlet* and Shakespeare scholarship.

Stylistically, the scene seems to owe much to Stephen's discourse in the National Library in *Ulysses.* In his lectures at Cornell, Nabokov spoke disparagingly about that chapter:

> *Action:* Stephen discoursing on Shakespeare argues (1) that the Ghost in *Hamlet* is really Shakespeare himself, (2) that Hamlet is to be identified with Hamnet, Shakespeare's little son; and (3) that Richard Shakespeare, William's brother, had an intrigue with Anne, Shakespeare's wife, thus accounting for the bitterness of the play. When he is asked if he believes his own thesis Stephen promptly answers: no. Everything is fouled up in this book. The discussion in this chapter is one of those things that is more amusing for a writer to write than for a reader to read, and so its details need not be examined. (*Lectures on Literature,* 326)

For someone who lectured on the importance of "fondling details" (*Lectures on Literature,* 1), this is a surprising statement, but the point seems to be that Nabokov disliked the Shakespeare scene in *Ulysses* because he did not find in it a sufficient connection to the work as a whole. In writing his own Shakespeare scene he sought to outdo Joyce by revising that chapter so as to make it central to the thematics of his own novel.

On a first reading, it might appear that the centrality of this chapter has much to do with the poetics and politics of resistance. Ember's apartment and the topic of the chapter appear to provide a welcome respite from the oppressive dictatorship outside, the realm of Paduk, the leader of The Party of the Average Man and the son of the inventor of the padograph, "a typewriter made to reproduce with repellent perfection" an individual's handwriting (69). Initially Shakespeare seems important because he stands above Paduk's tawdry world, an original genius rather than a mere replicator. The security of Ember's abode turns out to be illusory, however, and at the end of the chapter he is taken away under arrest. But Shakespeare's majestic aloofness is also illusory; it proves to be implicated in the novel's dynamics of repression.

In responding to Ember's critique of a bad German-inspired production, Krug provides one of his own. He recalls a train journey through America, where in the "toilet lounge" he met a man who wanted to make a movie of *Hamlet*. This "hawkfaced shabby man, whose academic career had been suddenly brought to a close by an awkwardly timed love affair," evidently harbored resentment against the underage girl who had got him into trouble: "He added that he had thought she was eighteen at least, judging by her bust, but, in fact, she was hardly fifteen, the little bitch." The American then launched into a discussion of how he would film the death of Ophelia, at whom he intended to redirect his sexual rage (112–13).

Filtering this potential cinematic version of *Hamlet* through his own words, Krug imagines showing Ophelia "trying to reach, trying to wreathe a phallacious sliver," followed by shots of Ophelia lying on her back and then of a "liberal shepherd on marshy ground where *orchis mascula* grows: period rags, sum-margined beard, five sheep and one cute lamb" (113–14). In this context the phrase "period rags" looks like a double entendre. There is a history of casting scholarly aspersions at Ophelia's chastity, from Ludwig Tieck's suggestion, reproduced in the New Variorum edition, that Shakespeare "has meant to intimate [...] that the poor girl, in the ardor of her passion for the fair prince, has yielded all to him" (2:286), to Rebecca West's pronouncement that "Ophelia was a disreputable young woman: not scandalously so, but still disreputable" (19). Early and mid-twentieth-century critics were particularly shocked by the language Hamlet uses and Ophelia tolerates. John Dover Wilson noted that Hamlet treats Ophelia "like a prostitute" (103), Arthur Quiller-Couch (a.k.a. "Q") admitted: "I could never quite understand (or forgive) that Ophelia, being Ophelia, should so readily lend herself in Act III, Scene 1, to entrap Hamlet to confession, with the king and her father for eavesdroppers; as far less could I forgive Hamlet, a gentleman, for speaking to her (in the play-scene, for example) so vilely as he does. My instinct all through prompts me to say, 'Yes, yes, you are driven. But for God's sake, need you speak to this child as to a strumpet? O man, leave *her*, at least, alone!'" (*Shakespeare's Workmanship,* 163). Quiller-Couch explained the grossness of Hamlet's banter by Ophelia's having been a courtesan in an earlier text used by Shakespeare as a source: "[Shakespeare], in his great wisdom, preferred to replace this experienced lady by the innocent Ophelia [...] but, I hold that, being an indolent man, he failed to remove or to recast some sentences which, cruel enough even when spoken to a woman of easy virtue, are intolerable when cast at Ophelia" (164). Nabokov's heroes take this dynamic very far indeed, turning Shakespeare's tragedy into the stuff of a dirty joke. After listening to Krug, Ember "enters into the spirit of the game" (114)—the word *spirit* was used by Shakespeare and other Elizabethan poets to refer not just to genius or inspiration but also to an erection, semen, or sexual excitement (*Romeo and Juliet,* 2.1.24; Ellis 95–97)—and offers a reading of Ophelia and "her sleazy lap" as "Amleth's wet dream":

> She was one of those thin-blooded pale-eyed lovely slim slimy ophidian maidens that are both hotly hysterical and hopelessly frigid. Quietly, with a kind of devilish daintiness she minced her dangerous course the way her father's ambition pointed. Even mad, she went on teasing her secret with the dead man's finger. Which kept pointing at me. Oh, of course I loved her like forty thousand brothers. (114–15)

Krug responds with his own, German-inflected reading of Hamlet's name. "Take 'Telemachos,' he says, which means 'fighting from afar'—which again was Hamlet's idea of warfare. Prune it, remove the unnecessary letters, all of them secondary additions, and you get the ancient 'Telmah.' Now read it backwards. Thus does a fanciful pen elope with a lewd idea and Hamlet in reverse gear becomes the son of Ulysses slaying his mother's lovers. *Worte, worte, worte.* Warts, warts, warts. My favourite commentator is Tschischwitz, a madhouse of consonants—or a *soupir de petit chien*" (115). This gloss on Hamlet's name is just a brief diversion, for Ember, Nabokov tells us, "has not quite finished with the girl" (115). Krug's friend dwells for another paragraph on the details of Ophelia's body, including her morning breath and "the ghost of a blond fluff (most delicately bristly to the eye) at the corners of her mouth, remind[ing] him [...] of a certain anaemic Esthonian housemaid, whose pathetically parted poor little breasts palely dangled in her blouse when she went low, very low, to pull on for him his striped socks" (116).

In his comment on this scene Samuel Schuman agrees with G. M. Hyde that "there is an important and revealing contrast between the 'civilized literary consciousness represented by these two men [and] the vulgar materialistic assaults on Shakespeare' they discuss" (208–9). I don't think this is the case; in fact, I would argue that this is an example of how the novel has suffered from simplification arising out of the scholarly desire to find in it an uplifting message. Krug and Ember derive great sport from this vulgarization of *Hamlet.* Beginning with others' crude treatments of Shakespeare, they imagine cruder ones, their fanciful minds directing the pens eloping with lewd ideas. We should remember that Ember "has a bad cold" (105), and keeping in mind the code language of an earlier time we can view this chapter as a preview of Quilty's venerialization of Shakespeare.

Midway through the scene, when Ember has stopped joking and is reading his translation of *Hamlet* to Krug, the narrator pauses to introduce what
he calls his "favorite scene":

> As he sits listening to Ember's translation, Krug cannot help marvel-
> ling at the strangeness of the day. He imagines himself at some point
> in the future recalling this particular moment. He, Krug, was sitting
> beside Ember's bed. Ember, with knees raised under the counterpane,
> was reading bits of blank verse from scraps of paper. Krug had recently
> lost his wife. A new political order had stunned the city. Two people
> he was fond of had been spirited away and perhaps executed. But
> the room was warm and quiet and Ember was deep in *Hamlet*. And
> Krug marvelled at the strangeness of the day. He listened to the rich-
> toned voice (Ember's father had been a Persian merchant) and tried
> to simplify the terms of his reaction. Nature had once produced an
> Englishman whose domed head had been a hive of words. [...] Three
> centuries later, another man, in another country, was trying to ren-
> der these rhythms and metaphors in a different tongue. This process
> entailed a prodigious amount of labour, for the necessity of which no
> real reason could be given. [...] From a practical point of view, such
> a waste of time and material (those headaches, those midnight tri-
> umphs that turn out to be disasters in the sober light of the morning!)
> was almost criminally absurd, since the greatest masterpiece of imita-
> tion presupposed a voluntary limitation of thought, in submission to
> another man's genius. Could this suicidal limitation and submission be
> compensated by the miracle of adaptive tactics, by the thousand devices
> of shadography, by the keen pleasure that the weaver of words and their
> witness experienced at every new wile in the warp, or was it, taken all
> in all, but an exaggerated and spiritualized replica of Paduk's writing
> machine? (119–20)

As we will later see in more detail, the word "strange" is often coded in
Nabokov's fiction as a marker of art, and this scene is as aesthetically bur-
nished as any in *Bend Sinister*, but it also has its homoerotic glow. The reader
of *Lolita* should be familiar with the sensuous oriental touch of Ember's
ancestry—"sleep is a rose, as the Persians say" (*Lolita*, 127)—and the warmth
of the scene by Ember's bedside, with the translator "deep in Hamlet," may
owe something to those male mellow moments Nabokov so appreciated in
The Strange Case of Dr. Jekyll and Mr. Hyde (*Lectures on Literature*, 179–204).
The scene has been prefaced by an odd feint at physical contact between the

men. Olga's "monstrous absence"—Krug's wife has just passed away—causes the two men "dreadful embarrassment":

> This was, this is, their first meeting since she died. Krug will not speak of her, will not even inquire about her ashes; and Ember, who feels the shame of death too, does not know what to say. Had he been able to move about freely, he might have embraced his fat friend in silence (a miserable defeat in the case of philosophers and poets accustomed to believe that words are superior to deeds), but this is not feasible when one of the two lies in bed. Krug, semi-intentionally, keeps out of reach. (106)

In one respect, the fun Krug and Ember have at Ophelia's expense is reminiscent of Krug's rapport with his wife. Right after her death, Krug fondly recalls how the couple had delighted in mockery. "He remembered other imbeciles he and she had studied, a study conducted with a kind of gloating enthusiastic disgust" (11). This sentence occurs at the start of one of the most tender paragraphs in the book, and it is remarkable how quickly "murderers," "Flaubertian farceurs," "fraternities, mystic orders," "people who are amused by trained animals," and "the members of reading clubs" give way to unbearable grief at the recollection of lost love. The scene with Ember provides a reprise of this earlier mode of intimacy. At least overtly, Krug is resolutely heterosexual; Ember, who considers "going out to mail his letter as bachelors are wont to do around eleven o'clock at night" (32), Ember we can't be so sure about.[3] Their treatment of Ophelia, however, has been an act of homosocial intimacy, a moment of mutual excitement. The scene will end, as will Krug's later sexual tantalization by the nubile nanny Mariette, with an arrest, here executed by a sexually excited thug who wants to enlist his girlfriend to put Ember's bed to the use that it has hinted at through the entire scene: "these mirrors and rugs suggest certain tremendous Oriental sensations which I cannot resist" (127).

Just before the arrest, as Ember is discussing his translation's fine points, Krug notices something strange by looking out the window:

> "Some of his puns—" said Krug. "Hullo, that's queer." He had become aware of the yard. [...] "Never in my life, said Krug, have I seen *two* organ grinders in the same back yard at the same time. [...] I wonder what has happened? They look most uncomfortable, and they do not, or cannot play."

---

3. In *Ada* Van asks Johnny Rafin, the homosexual second of a man Van has challenged to a duel, where he can find a brothel: "With increasing disdain Johnny answered he was a confirmed bachelor" (306).

"Perhaps, one of them butted into the other's beat," suggested Ember, sorting out a fresh set of papers. "Perhaps," said Krug. [...]

Well, Adam, sit down and listen. Or am I boring you?" "Oh non-sense," said Krug, going back to his chair. "I was only trying to think what exactly was wrong. The children seem also perplexed by their silence. There is something familiar about the whole thing, something I cannot quite disentangle—a certain line of thought." (121)

That "line of thought" is the tangle of the novel itself, entwined with multiple references to homosexuality. The dictator, Paduk, has been molested by the school janitor as a child, and he seems to have been in love with Krug since their school days. Krug still remembers as "loathsome" the soft wet kiss left by "the Toad" on the back of his hand (88). The narrator, at one point appears bewildered by Paduk, whose failings "would have been readily excused had be been a likable fellow, a good pal, a co-operative vulgarian or a pleasantly queer boy with most matter-of-fact muscles (Krug's case)" (68). When Krug screams at one of Paduk's toadies at the university to shut up, the narrator mentions a "queer streak of vulgarity and even cruelty" that runs through the philosopher (59). Much of the novel is spent trying to make the reader forget about Krug's pleasant queerness and cooperative vulgarity, as in the passage where the text draws on Paduk's manifesto to recruit the reader into an ideologically inflected homosexual panic:

From now on [...] the way to total joy lies open. You will attain it, brothers, by dint of ardent intercourse with one another, by being like happy boys in a whispering dormitory, by adjusting ideas and emo-tions to those of a harmonious majority; you will attain it, citizens, by weeding out all such arrogant notions as the community does not and should not share; you will attain it, adolescents, by letting your person dissolve in the virile oneness of the State; then, and only then, will the goal be reached. Your groping individualities will become interchange-able and, instead of crouching in the prison cell of an illegal-ego, the naked soul will be in contact with that of every other man in this land; nay, more: each of you will be able to make his abode in the elastic inner self of any other citizen, and to flutter from one to another, until you know not whether you are Peter or John, so closely locked will you be in the embrace of the State. (97)

"We are for the virile harmony between lover and beloved" one of Paduk's leaflets states (168), and in keeping with the theme of homosexual disgust associated with Paduk, *Bend Sinister* insists on the physiological location of this virility in the anus. Paduk has "gnawed his way into the bowels of [the] country" (45), his very name hints not only at a Shakespearean toad—via *Macbeth* (1.1.9)—but also at something that has fallen or been excreted. (The Russian root *pad/past'* means to fall). This theme of anality is not limited to scenes that speak directly of Paduk—it runs through the entire text, even in moments of unmistakably Nabokovian aestheticization, such as where two grizzled riders are "inspecting the anal ruby" (15) of one of their bicycles. Sometimes the theme surfaces in playful passages, as in the one describing Schimpffer, a former classmate of Krug's with a speaking name who has "a big factory of sport articles in Ast-Lagoda" and "had been a brave b*anal* red-haired boy, but now had a pale puffy face with freckles showing through his sp*arse* hair" (237, emphasis added). These are examples of what Jürgen Bodenstein, employing a term coined by W. K. Wimsatt, calls Nabokov's "momentary morphemes" (1:132–33), one of the most prominent of which, uttered by the sexually conflicted Hermann in *Despair,* hints at a link between wordplay and perverse sexual attraction: "What is this jest in majesty? This ass in passion?" (46). (See also Van's remark in *Ada*: "Art, my *foute*. This is the hearse of *ars,* a toilet roll of the Carte du Tendre!" [406].) *Bend Sinister* begins under the sign of posteriority, with a variant of the anal ruby: "An oblong puddle inset in the co*arse as*phalt; like a fancy footprint filled to the brim with quicksilver; like a spatulate hole through which you can see the nether sky. Surrounded, I note, by a diffuse tentacled black dampness where some dull dun dead leaves have stuck" (1, emphasis added).[4] Even escape from Paduk's captivity operates as both excretion and retention, a demonstration of the

---

4. The word "fancy" occasionally has erotic connotations in Nabokov's novels, signaling something that departs from normal sexual—or by implication—writerly style. Hitchhikers "vigorously, almost priapically" thrust out "tense thumbs to tempt lone women or sadsack salesmen with fancy cravings" (*Lolita,* 159). Gaston Godin knows by name all the small boys in his neighborhood and has them "clean his sidewalk and burn leaves in his back yard [...] and even perform simple chores about the house, and he would feed them fancy chocolates, with *real* liqueurs inside—in the privacy of an orientally furnished den in his basement" (181). A boy in *Ada* is called "Fancytart" (146), and Van feels sorry "for all the trouble that underpaid, tired, bare-armed, brunette-pale shopgirls had no doubt taken in trying to tempt dour homosexuals with his stuff ('Here's a rather fancy novel about a girl called Terra')" (343). The appearance of "fancy" in the first paragraph of *Bend Sinister* initially appears innocent. It next surfaces, however, in a context that is anatomically specific, when Krug and his colleagues look out into the empty streets as they are being driven to the university: "the only live creature encountered was a young man going home from an ill-timed and apparently badly truncated fancy ball: he was dressed up as a Russian mujik—embroidered shirt spreading freely from under a tasselled sash, *culotte bouffante,* soft crimson boots, and wrist watch. '*On va lui torcher la derrière, à ce gaillard-là,*' remarked Professor Beuret grimly" (36). (*Torcher la derrière* means "to wipe someone's bottom," but here it also encompasses another meaning of "*torcher*"—"to beat"—and certainly serves to render more salient the *cul* in *culotte*). On rereading, the "fancy" in the opening paragraphs becomes an early instance of the novel's homosexual and posterior thematics.

principles of anal eroticism. Jailed, Krug listens to "the heartbeats of younger men noiselessly digging an underground passage to freedom and recapture, the pattering sound made by the excrementa of bats" (233). The landscape in Krug's dream about his childhood seems to have been decorated with the jewels of the bicycle riders encountered earlier: "Now he found himself running (by night, ugly? Yah, by night, folks) down something that looked like a railway track through a long damp tunnel (the dream stage management having used the first set available for rendering 'tunnel,' without bothering to remove either the rails or the ruby lamps that glowed at intervals along the rocky black sweating walls)" (66). In the Maximov bathroom—where Sholokhov is kept next to the toilet paper—Krug sees floating at the bottom of the toilet bowl "a safety razor blade envelope with S. Freud's face and signature" (85)—an indication not only of Nabokov's general opinion of Freud but also of the particular Freudian paradigm here in play.[5] In the bathroom not only the officially acclaimed hero of Soviet literature but also the Russian Formalist Viktor Shklovsky's influential definition of art as "making strange" (i.e., overcoming habit) is taken to the toilet: "If I stay for a week," Krug thinks as he sits there, "this alien wood will be gradually tamed and purified by repeated contacts with my wary flesh" (85–86). The abbreviation by which the novel is usually indicated in scholarly works is highly revealing, particularly since Nabokov himself used that abbreviation when he revealed the new title to Wilson: "My novel, the final title of which is Bend Sinister, has gone to the printers. The second copy of the MS is more or less dismembered (parts will be published in magazines, I think), so I still cannot show you B.S." (Nabokov and Wilson, 201).

The most surprising deployment of this anal and homosexual theme is its connection to Krug. As Anne Dwyer has pointed out, readers of Bend Sinister often forget or dismiss the many references to Krug's cruel schoolyard behavior (1–2). Krug and his buddies tormented Paduk as a child:

> If you opened that door you found a few [zaftpupen] "softies" mooning on the broad window seats behind the clothes racks, and Paduk would be there, too, eating something sweet and sticky given him by the janitor, a bemedaled veteran with a venerable beard and lewd eyes. When the bell rang, Paduk would wait for the bustle of flushed begrimed class bound boys to subside, whereupon he would quietly make his way up

---

5. Technically, it is impossible for anything to "float" "at the bottom" of a toilet bowl, but Nabokov's description of Freud's location reinforces even further the association of the psychiatrist—and the value of his work—with anality and excretion.

the stairs, his agglutinate palm caressing the banisters. Krug, whom the putting away of the ball had detained (there was a big box for play-things and fake jewellery under the stairs), overtook him and pinched his plump buttocks in passing. (67)

It is odd how scholars have read the relationship between Paduk and Krug as *unrequited* homosexual desire. Here is L. L. Lee's summary of their relationship:

Krug and Paduk had been schoolmates as children; the new State wants Krug's endorsement for propaganda reasons, although there is an over-tone of homosexuality in Paduk's desire for Krug. It would not be an over-reading to interpret Paduk's implied homosexuality as a personal and political commentary: the dictator, the seeker for power (an essen-tially sterile personality), lusts after the life of the mind at the same moment that he needs to degrade it. (96)

However, if Krug represents "the life of the mind," that life itself is char-acterized in this novel by homosexual ideation and the desire to subject oth-ers to degradation. Paduk is described as "a veritable hero in the domain of meanness, since every time he indulged in it he must have known that he was heading again towards that hell of physical pain which his revengeful class-mates put him through every time" (68). It is not clear that he deserved this treatment: "Curiously enough, we cannot recall any single definite example of his meanness, albeit vividly remembering what Paduk had to suffer in retaliation of his recondite crimes" (68). Is this because meanness is inherently unmemorable, or because Paduk was treated unfairly? Krug recalls: "What I and the Toad hoard *en fait de souvenirs d'enfance* is the habit I had of sitting upon his face. [...] I was something of a bully, I am afraid, and I used to trip him up and sit upon his face—a kind of rest cure. [...] I sat upon his face every blessed day for about five school years—which makes, I suppose, about a thousand sittings" (50–51). Retrospectively, Krug's abuse of the young Paduk seems a pattern of *proactive* dissent; in this respect *Bend Sinister* does for bully-ing what *Lolita* does for pedophilia. At least on the surface, the novels work to naturalize these practices, and the reader must actively resist the narrator's logic to reassert his initial moral position that bullying or pedophilia is evil.

At points where Krug is aroused by Mariette, and where the text seems to wonder why he does not act, the excessive virility of Nabokov's Hamlet is stressed, in a manner that perhaps suggests protesting too much:

It is not quite clear why he indulged in all this ascetic self-restraint business when he might have ridden himself so deliciously of his quite natural tension and discomfort with the assistance of that keen

puella. [...] Perhaps he was held back by certain subtle supermatrimo-
nial scruples or by the dismal sadness of the whole thing. Unfortunately
his urge to write had suddenly petered out and he did not know what
to do with himself. He was not sleepy having slept after dinner. The
brandy only added to the nuisance. He was a big heavy man of the
hairy sort with a somewhat Beethovenlike face. He had lost his wife in
November. He had taught philosophy. He was exceedingly virile. His
name was Adam Krug. (195)

Mariette's temptations, while often (very) explicitly depicted as female, are
of uncertain and multiple anatomical origins. Although, as we will see, there
are several prurient references to her genitals, her charms are markedly posterior. When he first sees her in the bathroom, Krug is struck by the sight of her
from behind, and later the image of her "adolescent buttocks" (163) inter-
rupts his thoughts. At one point, in a coming attraction of *Lolita*'s davenport
scene, he fantasizes about her sitting on his lap. Ultimately he is prepared to
accept her "banal invitation" to engage in sex. The most curious description
of her body occurs when Krug has a look in on her habitat:

For no special reason (or was he looking for something? No) he had
been led to peep into her room in passing while she was out with
David. It smelt strongly of her hair and of *Sanglot* (a cheap musky per-
fume); flimsy soiled odds and ends lay on the floor and the bed-table
was occupied by a brownish-pink rose in a glass and a large X-ray
picture of her lungs and vertebrae. (158–59)

This "brownish-pink rose in a glass" hints at some sort of erotic charge:
just a couple paragraphs later Krug averts his eyes "from the brownish-pink
shadows" revealed by this "queer child" as she lies scantily dressed "athwart"
David's bed (159).

Even in his scholarship and professional activity, Krug is linked in various
ways with posteriority. Under the recent shock of learning of Krug's wife's
death, Ember notes: "At first I was struck by the unpardonable thought that
he was delivering himself of a monstrous joke like the time he read backwards
from end to beginning that lecture on space to find out whether his students
would react in any manner" (28). The backwards action recalls not only
the inverse path of Dante's sodomites (265) but also Krug's being forced to
retrace his steps over the bridge in the book's second chapter, an action preceded by his remark to the sentry holding his pass upside down: "Inversion
does not trouble me" (9). (We should recall, too, the description of Krug's
playful treatment of Shakespeare's play: "Thus does a fanciful pen elope with
a lewd idea and Hamlet in reverse gear becomes the son of Ulysses slaying his

mother's lovers" [115]). Ember's recollection continues to touch on Krug's most important work, in a passage into which Nabokov, as he reveals in his introduction, has introduced a "lavatorial injunction" (xvii):

> An obscure scholar, a translator of Shakespeare in whose green, damp country he had spent his studious youth—he innocently shambled into the limelight when a publisher asked him to apply the reverse process to the *Komparatiwn Stuhdar en Sophistat tuen Pekrekh* or, as the title of the American edition had it, a little more snappily, *The Philosophy of Sin* (banned in four states and a best seller in the rest). What a strange trick of chance—this masterpiece of esoteric thought endearing itself at once to the middle-class reader and competing for first honours during one season with that robust satire *Straight Flush,* and then, next year, with Elisabeth Ducharme's romance of Dixieland, *When the Train Passes,* and for twenty-nine days (leap year) with the book club selection *Through Towns and Villages.* (29)

Here "the reverse process" leads quickly to the themes of trashy literature and excretion. Are these echoes of the anal, excremental, and homosexual themes simply parodies; does Krug mirror them in opposition, in ways that emphasize their *dis*similarity? I think not: Krug here seems too bound up in these thematics, through his abuse of Paduk too implicated in their genesis. Even Krug's affection for his son connects to the novel's anatomical thematics. Nabokov's introduction specifies that "the main theme of *Bend Sinister* [...] is the beating of Krug's loving heart" (xiv), but cardiac imagery also surrounds Paduk: his organ's thumps are followed closely in his cardiarium. For every positive reference to the heart as a measure of genuine emotion (i.e., "the thumping of his heart was suddenly interrupted by his little son's special bedroom voice" [25]), there is a reference to fraudulent sentiment ("a heart-to-heart talk with a fellow prisoner who really is one of our agents" [212]). In *Bend Sinister* hearts are rent, broken, made of stone, diseased, weak, and, following *Hamlet,* the origin of sickness ("Imagine the morale of an army where a soldier [...] says he is sick at heart" [108]). Even when the heart is used in a positive idiomatic construction, the context often undermines it as a positive marker: "Several times clerks crossed the room at a breathless run and once a telephone operator (a Miss Lovedale) who had been disgracefully manhandled, was carried to the prison hospital on a stretcher by two kind-hearted stone-faced colleagues" (217).

In a comic but extremely important image the wife of the history teacher tries to seduce Paduk "with an eager jiggle of her rump (which in those days of tight waists looked like an inverted heart)" (71). Another scene from Krug and Paduk's school days amplifies the dynamic further: "Soccer was played in the windy pale interval between two series of lessons. The yawn of the tunnel and the door of the school, at the opposite ends of the yard, became football goals much in the same fashion as the commonplace organ of one species of animal is dramatically modified by a new function in another" (65). For all its overt pretensions to keep them apart, *Bend Sinister* ultimately ends up equating the heart and the ass. The novel's first sentence—with its "coarse asphalt" and "nether sky"—already captures the transformation of one (*cor*) into the other (arse). The relation between Krug and David is as saccharine as it is privileged, and we should see it as part of a discourse of impoverished sentimentality.

Chapter 6, which concludes with David's question about his dead mother—"Will my mummy be back when we come [home]?" (104)—also contains in Krug's conversation with Maximov the most extensive description of Paduk's affection:

"I dreamed of him," said Krug. "Apparently this is the only way that my old schoolmate can hope to *asso*ciate with me nowadays."

"I understand you were not particularly fond of each other at school?"

"Well, that needs *anal*yzing. I certainly loathed him, but the question is—was it mutual? I remember one queer incident. The lights went out suddenly—short circuit or something."

"Does happen sometimes. Try that jam. Your son thought highly of it."

"I was in the classroom reading," continued Krug. "Goodness knows why it was in the evening. The Toad had slipped in and was fumbling in his desk—he kept candy there. It was then that the light went out. I leaned back, waiting in perfect darkness. Suddenly I felt something wet and soft on the back of my hand. The Kiss of the Toad. He managed to bolt before I could catch him."

"Pretty sentimental, I should say," remarked Maximov.

"And loathsome," added Krug.

He buttered a bun and proceeded to recount the details of the meeting at the President's house. (87–88, emphasis added)

The passage has several moments connoting disgust at anal affection: "associate," "analyzing," perhaps "classroom" and "bun".[6] The reference

---

6. See also the play with assonance in Ember's remark immediately following Krug's attempt to catch the line of thought provoked by the two male organ grinders: "The chief difficulty that assails the translator of the following passage" (121–22).

to David and his confectionary pleasure in the jam serves to tie these two relations closer together and emphasizes that Krug's disgust at Paduk and his sweet love for David are part of the same flawed emotional phenomenon of suspect sentimentality.

Brian Boyd, who admits to liking *Bend Sinister* less than Nabokov's other mature works, is representative of many who have written about it:

> The plot has its poignancy, but it remains too meager in proportion to the self-consciousness and scholarly obscurity that surround it. Krug's intense concentration of feeling on his wife and son may strike us as less wholly endearing and more cloying and unhealthily exclusive than Nabokov appears to have intended. And the boyhood relationship between Paduk and Krug seems both gratuitous and unconvincing. The schoolboy Krug who could sit on Paduk's face not just once but a thousand times is not merely a bully and a boor but a bore with no conceivable relationship to the Krug of later years. (*American Years,* 105–6)

In this respect, Boyd strikes the same note as Quiller-Couch, who seeks to discount Hamlet's treatment of Ophelia as an authorial mistake.

Boyd is puzzled by Krug's reluctance to flee into exile—"Still dazed by grief for his wife, he feels he can no longer write or think—and indeed only his mental disarray can explain his failure to perceive his real vulnerability" (*American Years* 93). Boyd's dissatisfaction arises, I think, from a fundamental and generally shared failure to understand the logic of the plot: "Even before Krug declares himself ready to cooperate, alas, a series of bureaucratic bungles leads to David's murder" (*American Years,* 93). In fact, David's murder is a completely logical, indeed inevitable development. It is prepared not only by the mention of the other Dr. Krug (the father of the boy who "should" have been murdered) at the start of the novel, but also by Adam Krug's conduct throughout.

Let's look more closely at the scene of David's death, a scene so repellant that close looking has been avoided by many critics.[7] David is killed at a psychiatric center for juvenile delinquents: "The theory [...] was that if once a week the really difficult patients could enjoy the possibility of venting in full their repressed yearnings (the exaggerated urge to hurt, destroy, etc.) upon

---

7. Wood is an exception, though he appreciates the sentimental pathos of the scene rather than its metafictive dimension and its clever reinscription of a Dostoevskian trope—the recounting of stories about child abuse—in an updated psychoanalytic setting that urges a reappraisal (as kitsch) of Ivan Karamazov's rebellious protest against divinely countenanced cruelty.

some little human creature of no value to the community, then, by degrees, the evil in them would be allowed to escape, would be, so to say, 'effundated,' and eventually they would become good citizens" (218). Apparently, David has been sent there by mistake, but he is to be restored to Krug when Krug agrees to capitulate to the will of the dictatorial state.

On his arrival at the Institute for Abnormal Children, Adam Krug is treated like royalty—everyone caters and bows to him—and taken to a hall where a movie is projected. The film is silent and of low quality. It shows the delinquents waiting in a garden and being searched for concealed weapons, then we see David going into the garden. The action is intercut with titles like "Frau Doktor von Wytwyl, Leader of the Experiment (No Whistling Please): "Watch Those Curves" (about her body), "Bad Luck, Fatso" (an entire arsenal of torture tools are found up one boy's sleeve) "What a Treat For a Little Person to be Out Walking in the Middle of the Night" (as David walks out onto the lawn), and "Uh-Uh. Who's That." At this point the lights go on and the film is given o'er (223–24).

The presentation of David's death is a replay of *Hamlet*'s play within a play, staged not for Claudius but for Krug, who reacts to it much as does Hamlet's uncle. In both cases, though, the show is no arbitrary representation but is meant as a punishment, in this instance for Krug's aesthetic sins. Having taken part in the mockery of Ophelia, Krug suddenly finds himself (or David) in her place, forced to act virtually in her stead.[8] The genre of the movie is particularly appropriate. What kind of film has Krug watched? The poor quality and crude, joking titles are indicative enough, but the genre is virtually named at the end of the chapter, when Krug recalls how a deer had once jumped into the blaze of his headlights. Ember has mentioned this episode much earlier; and the doe, over which Krug's wife Olga had grieved, now becomes an emblem for David, as well as recalling Hamlet's words right

8. There is precedent in Nabokov's fiction for this sort of punishment. *The Gift* offers several instances of writers hoisted—with the help of the author—by their own poetic petard. Chernyshevski "did not understand the rhythm of Russian prose; it is only natural, therefore, that the very method he applied to prove his theory had its revenge on him" (242). Indeed, all of the fourth chapter of *The Gift* can be seen as a retributive punishment by poetry of someone who "castigated" (*kaznil*) art (238). Even Fyodor, the positive hero and good writer is not immune. His fellow poet Koncheyev points out that "you sometimes bring up parody to such a degree of naturalness that it actually becomes a genuine serious thought, but on *this* level it suddenly falters, lapsing into a mannerism that is yours and not a parody of a mannerism, although it is precisely the kind of thing you are ridiculing—as if somebody parodying an actor's slovenly reading of Shakespeare had been carried away, had started to thunder in earnest, but had accidentally garbled a line" (339). *Laughter in the Dark* offers a similar moment of cinematic punishment. As she watches her own miserable acting on the screen, Margot "felt like a soul in Hell to whom the demons are displaying the unsuspected lining of its earthly transgressions" (189).

after the abrupt end of the Mousetrap: "Why, let the stricken deer go weep, The hart ungalled play" (3:2:49–50). It also stands, however, for a kind of ultimate vulgarization of Shakespeare, the transposition of *Hamlet* into a *stag* film, a proper destination for a play that began in the "men's lounge."[9] Here, though, it is not ejaculation but "effundation" that replaces catharsis or at least combines the medical (purgative) and aesthetic meanings of that term.

David's death or, rather, the torture of Krug by David's death is thus a literal instance of poetic justice. (Even the awful, kitschy little dog "prettily placed" at the foot of the dead boy's bed, which suddenly comes snarlingly to life [224], recalls the *"soupir de petit chien"* that Krug heard earlier in the name of Tschisichwitz, "my favorite commentator" and "a *madhouse* of consonants" [115, emphasis added]). Ember's entry "into the spirit of the game" of mocking Ophelia is horrifically replayed in the description of David's torturers: "It was interesting to observe how the 'gang' spirit gradually asserted itself. They had been rough lawless unorganized individuals, but now something was binding them, the community spirit (positive) was conquering the individual whims (negative)" (219). Krug has insisted on the presence of "one cute lamb" in his portrait of Ophelia's dead, verbally defiled body: "An important point this lamb, despite the brevity—one heartthrob—of the bucolic theme" (114). David's death scene, in which he takes the role of a lamb led to the slaughter, is equally bucolic, set in an "enclosure," "a beautiful expanse of turf, and the whole place, especially in summer, looked extremely attractive, reminding one of some of those open-air theatres that were so dear to the Greeks" (219). In his remarks in the preface to the novel Nabokov paves the way for this interpretation of the plot as punishment for past sins:

> Is there any judgment on my part carried out, any sentence pronounced, any satisfaction given to the moral sense? If imbeciles and brutes can punish other brutes and imbeciles, and if crime still retains an objective meaning in the meaningless world of Paduk (all of which is doubtful), we may affirm that crime *is* punished at the end of the book when the uniformed waxworks are really hurt, and the dummies are at last in quite dreadful pain, and pretty Mariette gently bleeds, staked and torn by the lust of forty soldiers. (xiv)

---

9. On the poetics of the stag film, and, in particular, the genre's penchant for crude humor, see Penley, 309–31; and Lehman, 3–16. The phrase "toilet lounge" is one of two terms used to describe the location of Krug's conversation with the would-be filmmaker, and the substitution of one expression for the other ("men's lounge," "toilet lounge") hints at both the homoerotic and excremental charge of the motif. David's ultimate fate is presaged by a lavatorial response when Krug pleads earlier for his safety: "'I cannot leave my child to be tortured. Let him come with me wherever you are taking me.' A toilet was flushed. The two sisters joined the men and looked on with bored amusement" (202).

Ember seals this interpretation himself, when he is facing death.

"I am ready to die.... But there is one thing that I refuse to endure any longer, *c'est la tragédie des cabinets,* it is killing me. As you know I have a most queasy stomach, and they lead me into an enseamed draught, an inferno of filth, once a day for a minute. *C'est atroce.* I prefer to be shot straightaway." (239)

The impetus for this tragedy of the toilets has been given by Krug himself, by the text he has helped create, and that word—"cabinets"—hints at the link here between the sites of artistic creativity and excretion.[10] There is nothing humane about this justice, and Krug's punishment must strike nearly all readers, as excessively cruel—indeed, atrocious. Yet there is no contradiction, art does not move along a "straightaway" but is necessarily inflected and bent. (Here the term "poetic justice" might be replaced by "poetical vengeance," a phrase used in *Pnin* to describe a narrator punished for his cruelty by being required to substitute for the original object of his vicious storytelling [189]).

Mariette's death is more explicitly presented as a fitting moment of retribution, and it may strike us as equally nasty. She has tempted Krug and, perhaps, the reader throughout the novel. Krug has threatened her with "a bestial explosion" if she succeeds in seducing him (197), and in the end the lust she provokes has been satisfied, though Krug has been protected from responsibility for it by others' serving as its agent. In at least one respect, Mariette is linked to the subject of Krug's scholarship (*The Philosophy of Sin*); her nickname ("Cin") provides the text an excuse for finding the "sin" in Cinderella. But Mariette has profaned more than a fairy tale:

"When I'm alone," she said, "I sit and do like this, like a cricket. Listen, please."
    "Listen to what?"
    "Don't you hear?"
    She sat with parted lips, slightly moving her tightly crossed thighs, producing a tiny sound, soft, labiate, with an alternate crepitation as if she were rubbing the palms of her hands which, however, lay idle.
    "Chirruping like a poor cricket," she said. (194)

---

10. Mariia Dmitrovskaia notes that Nabokov's biography provided a justification for the linkage of toilets with authorial creativity (47). In Germany and France he lived in such cramped quarters that he had to retreat to the bathroom to write. At one point his desk was a suitcase perched on a bidet.

"Cricket" was Pushkin's nickname in the literary society Arzamas, and this genitalization is equivalent to taking Ophelia, period rags and all, to the toilet. Pushkin and Shakespeare have extended hands to each other across most of Nabokov's career; their treatment is parallel here, both being sinned against by a character, who is subsequently punished.[11] In both cases, too, the work of a national genius is subject to a plot inversion. Nabokov's Hamlet loses his son at the end of the narrative, not his father (Bader, 116). This story's princess is not one of forty sisters without genitalia, as in Pushkin's ribald tale in verse, "Tsar Nikita and His Forty Daughters"; rather, she is raped by forty soldiers (or "brothers"), tortured through the body part that in "Tsar Nikita" she would have lacked. Although Nabokov himself was certainly not averse to parody, when characters in this novel parody great authors, their fates are similar to those of the benighted protagonists of Greek myths, punished for poaching on the realm of the gods. Here the creator of *Bend Sinister*—for all his professed sympathies for his protagonist, is careful to place himself on the side of the immortals.

Nabokov seems to enjoy the image of Mariette's punishment. His comment in the introduction—"pretty Mariette gently bleeds, staked and torn by the lust of forty soldiers" (xiv)—is an echo of the final chapter of the text: "Mariette sat with closed eyes, in a rigid faint, bleeding gently. [...] The Elders heard a drop of blood fall upon the floor. They heard forty satisfied soldiers in the neighbouring guardhouse compare carnal notes" (228–30). That "gentle" bleeding—a first use by Nabokov of the pun (gentle/genital) he would soon employ in *Lolita*—has earlier been raised as a theme by Paduk in his imagined conversation with Krug: "I beseech you to be careful. The walls are full of camouflaged holes, each one with a rifle which is trained upon you. Please do not gesticulate. They are jumpy today. It's the weather. This grey menstratum" (146). This phrase is the clearest indication of the extent to which the entire text is awash in waste. *Bend Sinister* is a world characterized by what Bakhtin called "the bodily lower stratum" (368–436), although here it is hardly celebrated as in Rabelais. Instead, the lower body evokes shame and disgust, as if the novelist's art has been reduced to a dirty joke. Not for nothing is the spokesman of the Council of Elders Schamm ("Scham" means "shame" or "genitalia" in German), an official whose name seems to have been transposed into French when he says "in very careful accents": "The programme must be carried out without all this *chatt*er and *conf*usion" (emphasis added, 239).

---

11. See Dolinin on the importance of these figures throughout Nabokov's career and on Quilty's profanation of both Pushkin and Shakespeare in *Lolita* ("Nabokov's Time Doubling," 24).

Bend Sinister may be Nabokov's most excremental text, but it does not contain his only references to the topic. Brian Boyd has discussed the significance of excrement in *Ada,* where he relates it to the reader's moral judgment of Van and explains its presence by nodding to Nabokov's interest in everything human:

> Disgust is a key human emotion, one of seven recognized cross-culturally as one of the seven basic human emotions (happiness, sadness, anger, fear, surprise, contempt, and disgust). Art aims to elicit response, and Nabokov, like other writers and artists, avails himself from time to time of disgust as one note in his emotional keyboard. (Boyd, "Scatology")

I think there is more to it than that, and that Nabokov is making a specific point about the nature of art. Literature is coded in *Bend Sinister* as waste. In addition to the description of Krug's *Philosophy of Sin,* we find the toilet surfacing in connection with reading material at the Maximovs: "A bottle of mineral oil, half full, and a grey cardboard cylinder which had been the kernel of a toilet paper roll, stood side by side on a shelf. The shelf also held two popular novels (*Flung Roses* and *All Quiet on the Don*)" (86). These texts will presumably be put to a use other than that intended by their authors. A more interesting example of the contiguity of the novel with waste occurs when Krug himself describes the process of artistic creation:

> I might start writing the unknown thing I want to write; unknown, except for a vague shoe-shaped outline, the infusorial quiver of which I feel in my restless bones, a feeling of *shchekotiki* (as we used to say in our childhood) half-tingle, half-tickle, when you are trying to remember something or understand something or find something, and probably your bladder is full, and your nerves are on edge, but the combination is on the whole not unpleasant (if not protracted) and produces a minor orgasm or *"petit éternuement intérieur"* when at last you find the picture-puzzle piece which exactly fits the gap. (157–58)

This description of artistic creativity may be indebted to Pushkin's notion of "poetic diarrhea," his reference to "shitting in hexameters," and his comment about the emergence of fairy tales from his gastro-intestinal tract (*Sobranie sochinenii,* 10:57, 60). Near the book's end, Krug hears "the pattering sound made by the excrementa of bats, the cautious crackling of a page which had been viciously crumpled and thrown into the wastebasket and was making a pitiful effort to uncrumple itself and live just a little longer" (233–34). This crumpled page is not only a sign that the novel is nearing its end; it is also further evidence of the novel's status as refuse. As Krug speculates in a cosmological key when considering first principles: "we give a good shake to the telescopoid kaleidoscope (for what is your cosmos but an instrument containing small bits of coloured glass which, by an arrangement of mirrors, appear in a variety of symmetrical forms when rotated—mark: when rotated) and throw the damned thing away" (172).[12]

One could see these references to waste as signs that *Bend Sinister* should be read as a broken text. How many damaged or poorly constructed objects does this novel contain? When he uses the term *"tragédie des cabinets"* Ember complains about the "enseamed draught" plaguing him there (239), and we can think of that as a comment on the book he is in, a metafictive equivalent of the "enseamed" sheets on Gertrude's bed (*Hamlet*, 3.4.82). Nabokov refused to publish or show his drafts to scholars, since doing so would be "like passing around samples of one's sputum" (*Strong Opinions*, 4). Is this a finished novel masquerading as a rough draft? Perhaps. The notion of waste, however, is universalized at several points where art is contemplated from the point of view of a useless expense of effort: "Just think of all the trash we used to be taught.... Think of the millions of unnecessary books accumulating in libraries. The books they print!" (19-20). Even in his loving exaltation of Shakespeare and Ember's translation of it, Krug admits, "From a practical point of view, such a waste of time and material [...] was almost criminally absurd" (120). In other words, waste is a fundamental characteristic of literature and serves as a marker for Nabokov's notion of art. We can understand Humbert's remark that, along with telephones, "I felt instinctively that toilets [...] happened to be, for reasons unfathomable, the points where my destiny was liable to catch" (*Lolita*, 211).

The presence of toilets in Nabokov's work was first noted in a letter by the émigré scholar and critic Gleb Struve: "Toilets in Sirin [Nabokov]. Have you never noticed that there is almost no novel or story by him (and sometimes this is true of his poetry) in which a toilet or an act carried out in one does not figure?" (Mel'nikov, 615). In Nabokov's English work, the theme becomes even more marked, so that one of the things he does when translating *King, Queen, Knave* is to place a chamber pot in each room. Struve's letter is quoted by Maria Dmitrovskaia in a wonderful article on *Mary*, in

---

12. See also the early scene of Olga painting, which presages the feeling of emptiness with which the reader of *Bend Sinister* is left at the close of the novel after Krug and his world have dissolved into the author's night: "But it all fades, it fades, she used to sit in a field, painting a sunset that would never stay, and a peasant child, very small and quiet and bashful in spite of its mousy persistence would stand at her elbow, and look at the easel, at the paints, at her wet aquarelle brush poised like the tongue of a snake—but the sunset had gone, leaving only a clutter of the purplish remnants of the day, piled up anyhow—ruins, junk" (3).

the course of which she also surveys the theme of toilets in Nabokov's other Russian texts and suggests that the equation of creativity with excretion may be related to the similarity in Russian between *pisat'* ("to write", stress on second syllable) and *pisat'* ("to piss", stress on the first), to the importance of privacy in both acts, and to the Freudian equation of excrement to riches (43–48). These may be important considerations, but the primary one is probably the shared *uselessness* of both writing and excrement: at several points in his writing Nabokov virtually defines art by its impracticality and lack of useful application. In his memoir, Nabokov recalls discovering "in nature the nonutilitarian delights that I sought in art" (*Speak, Memory,* 125). In *King, Queen, Knave* Dreyer attempts to give his nephew a lesson in salesmanship, but instead he "soared into the ravishing realm of inutile imagination, demonstrating not the ways ties should be sold in real life, but the way they might be sold if the salesman were both artist and clairvoyant" (70). In *Bend Sinister* Nabokov makes the idea of art as a fundamentally useless activity explicitly excremental.

The linkage of art to waste is in some respects traditional, but in most cases an insistence on transcendence validates the connection. This is true either in purely aesthetic terms—"If you only knew from what trash / poetry grows" (Akhmatova, 44)—or in Christian or socialist recuperative narratives, such as Rodolphe's trawling through the urban dregs for slum dwellers worthy of salvation in Sue's *The Mysteries of Paris.* There is also the particularly modernist gesture, epitomized by Duchamp's urinal, of presenting trash as art, a carnivalesque gesture that defies prevailing hierarchies of value while celebrating the power of the artist to make art of anything he pleases. In Nabokov's fiction the transformation of waste is occasionally an important element: *The Gift*'s hero experiences "a piercing pity [...] for all the trash of life which by means of a momentary alchemic distillation—the 'royal experiment'—is turned into something valuable and eternal" (164), a figure Alexander Dolinin traces back with the help of Omry Ronen to Shelley's comment that poetry's alchemy "turns to potable gold the poisonous waters that flow from death through life" ("Primechaniia," 689). This formulation, however, essentially undoes the exaltation of aesthetic nonutilitarianism by depicting art as transforming the useless into the useful, making of art a kind of fertilizer. Elsewhere in Nabokov's work, the relationship between art and trash seems entirely antithetical, but on closer inspection these two concepts are found to be bound together in a reinforcing rapport. Few critics who write about Nabokov can long refrain from quoting the credo in the afterword to *Lolita*: "a work of fiction exists only in so far as it affords me what I shall bluntly call aesthetic bliss; that is a sense of being somehow, somewhere, connected with other states of being where art (curiosity, tenderness, kindness, ecstasy) is the norm." Only a couple, however, follow this paragraph through to the end: "There are not many such books. All the rest is either topical trash or what some call the Literature of Ideas, which very often is topical trash coming in huge blocks of plaster that are carefully transmitted from age to age until someone comes along with a hammer and takes a good crack at Balzac, at Gorki, at Mann" (314–15).[13] Scholars probably cut the quotation short because the latter two sentences seem unworthy of the famous preceding maxim, but the proximity is important; in Nabokov's mind the connection between art and trash is extremely close. Another permutation of this paradigm can be felt in *The Gift,* where Fyodor is attacked for the excretory nature of his poetics:

> There is no detail too repulsive for him to disdain. He will probably reply that all these details are to be found in the "Diary" of the young Chernyshevski; but there they are in their place, in their proper environment, in the correct order and perspective, among many other thoughts and feelings which are much more valuable. But the author has fished out and put together precisely these, as if someone had tried to restore the image of a person by making an elaborate collection of his combings, fingernail pairings, and bodily excretions. (307)

Virtually all Nabokov's novels play with the same metafictive concerns, but they explore them in different ways—making now this and now that aspect of metafictive aesthetics dominant. *Bend Sinister* is Nabokov's most sustained effort rigorously—indeed, relentlessly—to think through this connection between art and trash, to take it to its ultimate ends. The consequences in this novel are horrific and much different in tone from another text written by Nabokov at about the same time. Two days after D-Day, during the period when he was working on *Bend Sinister,* Nabokov sent a long letter to Edmund Wilson in which he described at great length—literally ad nauseam—his symptoms during a bout of food poisoning. Although the touch is light, even in this friendly epistle the affairs of nations are figured in

---

13 Frank Kermode is a prominent exception, and he offers the entire quotation in support of Nabokov's pronouncement that *Bend Sinister* is not about politics: "It is a work of art or nothing" (234, see also 228–29). One of the most extreme examples of the purification of this passage is provided by Leland de la Durantaye, who cuts the passage off right after "Literature of Ideas" and then paraphrases the rest of the sentence in a footnote nearly fifty pages later, without mentioning that it is from the same, crucial paragraph (*Style Is Matter,* 77, 120).

digestive (and indigestive) terms, and even here Nabokov's writing seeks to turn bodily effusions into the object of art:

> On the day of the invasion certain "bacilli" mistook my innards for a beachhead. I had lunched on some Virginia ham in a little Wursthaus near Harvard Square and was happily examining the genitalia of a specimen from Havilah, Kern co., Calif. at the Museum when suddenly I felt a strange wave of nausea. [...] My stomach rose with an awful whoop. I managed somehow to reach the outside steps of the Museum, but before attaining the grassplot which was my pathetic goal, I threw up, or rather down, i.e. right on the steps, such sundry items as pieces of ham, some spinach, a little mashed potatoes, a squirt of beer—in all 80 cents worth of food. Excruciating cramps racked me and I had just the strength to reach the toilet where a flow of brown blood rushed out of me from the opposite part of my miserable body. Since I have in me a heroic strain, I forced myself to climb the stairs, lock my lab, and leave a note in Clark's office canceling the tennis game. Then, vomiting every three steps, I proceeded to stagger home, much to the amusement of passers-by, who thought I had been overcelebrating the invasion. [...] Incidentally I vomited *into* the telephone, which I think has never been done before. (Nabokov and Wilson, 146–47)

In this friendly letter Nabokov can make the connection between art and waste retrospectively comic—Rabelais would have approved[14]—and there is even a competitive edge as Nabokov aestheticizes the sort of activity that can be found described more prosaically in Chernyshevsky's diaries—of which the list of precisely priced items vomited up is probably an undigested reminder.

In the metafictive laboratory of *Bend Sinister,* Nabokov portrays the relation of art to waste in far more sinister hues. *Bend Sinister* is not about the salvational power of literature. On the contrary, it is about literature's power to waste. In his introduction Nabokov refers to his choice of title as an attempt to suggest "a wrong turn taken by life, a sinistral and sinister world" (xii). It would, I think, be more accurate to speak of a wrong turn taken by *art,* an attempt by Nabokov to think through the logic of some of his aesthetic principles. He certainly does this elsewhere in his oeuvre: as several critics have pointed out, *Lolita* is partly about what happens when a person lets his aesthetic impulses run away with him (Bell, 171; Dolinin, "Nabokov's Time

---

14. On the Rabelasian tradition—and Nabokov's debt to Cervantes in departing from it—see Couturier, *Nabokov, ou la tyrannie,* 253–58.

Doubling," 21; de la Durantaye, *Style Is Matter,* 51, 95, 187). Just as Krug is undone by his interpretive practices, so *Bend Sinister* shows us a world undone by art, two principal features of which are authorial control and uselessness, here taken to their extremes as totalitarianism and excrement.

Several passages in the novel provide the reader with nearly Joycean streams of consciousness. In addition to serving as an homage to the author of one of Nabokov's favorite novels, these moments of mental and creative drift allow Nabokov to smuggle into the text descriptions of the novel as a whole: metafictive set pieces of the sort he loved. One passage is particularly important:

> Speaking of Roman *venationes* (shows with wild beasts) of the same epoch, we note that the stage, on which ridiculously picturesque rocks (the later ornaments of "romantic" landscapes) and an indifferent forest were represented, was made to rise out of the crypts below the urine-soaked arena with Orpheus on it among real lions and bears with gilded claws; but this Orpheus was acted by a criminal and the scene ended with a bear killing him, while Titus or Nero, or Paduk, looked on with that complete pleasure which "art" shot through with "human interest" is said to produce. (155–56)

This passage connects to many other crucial moments in the text—the toilet-lounge version of Ophelia, the film of David's death, and the "practical point of view" that would characterize the Shakespearean "waste of time and material" as "almost criminally absurd" (120). The urine-soaked arena captures the aesthetic settings of Nabokov's novel, as does the identification of the criminal with art. The Latin word *"venationes,"* highlighted here as a lexical item on display, hides behind it the phonetic identification of the signature "VN," of the creator of "The Vane Sisters" and of *Ada's* hero Van, and recalls the child molester at the school, the janitor "with a venerable beard and lewd eyes" (67). In other works by Nabokov the author's function is equated with the work of a tailor, department store owner, dancing master, or inventor. Here he is a janitor with a dirty mind. The end of the quoted passage returns to the theme of pure and corrupt hearts and raises the question whether the novel's frequently treacly sentimentality, persistently linked to David, is not something of a "human interest" trap, the work of an Orpheus with aesthetically criminal inclinations.

In his introduction Nabokov portrays the end of *Bend Sinister* as a happy one:

> Krug, in a sudden moonburst of madness, understands that he is in good hands: nothing on earth really matters, there is nothing to fear,

and death is but a question of style, a mere literary device, a musical resolution. And as Olga's rosy soul, emblemized already in an earlier chapter (Nine), bombinates in the damp dark at the bright window of my room, comfortably Krug returns unto the bosom of his maker. (xviii–xix)

Krug's "comfort" arises from his discovery that he has been "living" in a totalitarian fiction. One wonders how affectionate his imminent reunion with his creator will be, because, as Alexander Etkind has argued, its selenian tenor—the sudden moonburst of madness—recalls the illumination that often signifies homosexuality in the Russian philosophical tradition first delineated and attacked by Vasily Rozanov in his 1911 book *People of the Lunar Light* (399–409). The author slides toward Krug, "along an inclined beam of pale light" (233), which can recall either Kinbote's "Pale Fire" or the janitor's collection of "'softies' mooning on the broad window seats behind the clothes racks." Moreover, while the conclusion obviously suggests a link to the metafictive escape at the end of *Invitation to a Beheading,* it might be equally close to the eternity of repetition suggested by the end of *The Defense,* where the hero's flight from the text leads him only to further versions of what he has already experienced.[15]

Waking in his prison cell and about to meet his maker, Krug is conscious of a half-remembered nightmare: "It would seem that some promise had been broken, some design thwarted, some opportunity missed—or so grossly exploited as to leave an afterglow of sin and shame" (233). The presence of so many German words in the novel, and Nabokov's reference to the "hybridization of tongues" in Padukgrad might lead us to question whether the "after" (German, "anus") in "afterglow" might be read in keeping with the more evident Teutonic meaning of "Schamm." *Bend Sinister* is a "gross exploitation" of the nature of art. It has nothing to do with the evil of eradicating art or driving art to society's margins; and if the novel is about the oppression of art, that term must mean a situation in which art is doing all the oppressing. In effect, the novel draws on the registers of politics

---

15. In the course of a comparison of Nabokov and Pasternak, Etkind presents a fascinating analysis of Nabokov as a bigger, more respectable, more competent Paduk: "The narrator does his work—that of tailing and reporting—incomparably better than the agents of the Average Man. The storyteller not only enters Krug's house—the agents can do this too,—but also listens to his thoughts and registers his slightest desires. . . . In fact, a dictator like Paduk can only dream about knowing as much about his subjects as an author like Nabokov knows about his heroes" (385). A similar suggestion is made by Maurice Couturier: "Pretending to forget that he has in fact been the sole torturer of Adam Krug from the start, [Nabokov] now claims to liberate him, if not to ensure his salvation" (*Nabokov, ou la cruauté,* 148).

and homophobia to produce a narrative of revulsion provoked by art's own charms. Artistic freedom and the ability of the author, unfettered, to work in perfect serenity turn out not to be not the antitheses of dictatorship but its necessary complements. Artistic virtuosity requires unlimited control, and this aesthetic absolute power leads to a world with distinctly totalitarian contours.[16] In some respects we have heard this story before, from Boris Groys, whose account of the Russian avant-garde's conceptual complicity in the worldview of Stalinism can be read as a historical morality tale (*The Total Art of Stalinism,* passim). What most distinguishes the world of *Bend Sinister* from real-world totalitarianism, however, is the overall sense of textual self-loathing, an artist's disgust at the total freedom that an artistic refusal to compromise necessitates. Nabokov's description of life in Padukgrad should be read as a nightmarish story about the fulfillment of an artist's desires. The driving force behind *Bend Sinister* might best be characterized as aesthetic panic. Essentially, Nabokov has inverted and transposed the stark warning of *The Brothers Karamazov* from theological to aesthetic terms: precisely because there *is* a God, everything is permitted.

In this context it is interesting to note that the suffering and death of children—the most horrible of the awful phenomena that serve Ivan Karamazov as the basis for his rejection of God—is a frequent theme in Nabokov's work. In addition to its status as the hallmark of divine injustice, the death of children is an easily grasped sign for the failure of hope for the future. A work of art, finished, fixed, has no future outside itself—it stands as a mark of resistance to the cruel onslaught of time, just as in its lasting value it defies the contextual social or political demands of a given time. The torture or elimination of children can serve as markers both of absolute authorial power (for which all is permitted) and of the imperviousness of art to the

---

16. *Bend Sinister* thus points to the potential for human tragedy implicit in the creation of art. In this respect it may be read in tandem with other works such as *Lolita* and *Ada*. According to de la Durantaye, *Lolita* demonstrates that "the artist cannot live in the world as he lives in the world of words—and that this is a lesson worthy of expressing in the world of words" (*Style Is Matter,* 95). Brian Boyd treats *Ada* as something of a morality tale, "a radical exploration of the moral consequences of human consciousness." According to Boyd, "[Nabokov] lets Van and Ada revel in the infinity of their emotion for each other, and then shows the absurdity of their acting as if the privilege of such feeling could exist without their being interconnected with other lives and without their being responsible for each of those interconnections. Subjecting his hero and heroine to rigorous scrutiny, he sets out an exhaustive criticism of the romantic egotism that in certain lights and at certain moments they can make seem so seductive. And he shows that even the greatest gifts of consciousness offer insufficient protection against the blindness of the ego" (*The American Years,* 554). Nabokov, however, is not primarily preaching compassion but expressing a tragic paradox about the nature of art. A more adequate and, in the long run, more disturbing reading of much of his fiction would require the replacement in Boyd's summation of "absurdity" with "beauty."

contingent demands of time and place, including the need to move from an imperfect present into another generation's future. In contradiction to the typical nineteenth-century realist novel, in which the next generation has an especially prominent place in the epilogue, of all Nabokov's novels I believe there is only one—*Look at the Harlequins!*—in which the hero's biological offspring survives to the end. This failure of children to thrive (or even to be produced) might be seen as a metafictive equivalent to the anti-procreative tendency identified by Rozanov as the central "sodomitic" strain in much Russian spiritual and social thought (97–147). In an interesting commentary on Nabokov's attitude toward "art for art's sake," de la Durantaye quotes Nabokov's half-hearted dismissal (or reluctant acceptance) of that doctrine:

> Although I do not care for the slogan "art for art's sake"—because unfortunately such promoters of it as, for instance, Oscar Wilde and various dainty poets, were in reality rank moralists and didacticists— there can be no question that what makes a work of fiction safe from larvae and rust is not its social importance but its art, only its art. (*Strong Opinions,* 33)

De la Durantaye concludes that Nabokov "thus adopts the conceptual outlines ["of art for art's sake"] and rejects its historical connotations" (33). An avatar of Wilde may appear early in *Bend Sinister,* in that young man returning from a "fancy ball" whose "derrière" is about to be the object of official attention.[17] Like Krug, this fellow is presented as a victim, but the sexual orientation of Paduk's state may be a further nod to the implication of "art for art's sake" in its mechanics of repression.

Were I a Freudian, I might suggest that *Bend Sinister* is the work of the anal stage in our émigré author's aesthetic development, something a boy even younger than David might write were he so lexically precocious as to have read all of Shakespeare and the entire dictionary. By the time of his next book, Nabokov will have developed a more psychoanalytically "mature," erotic passion for his new language, and although many of his aesthetic, metafictive concerns would remain the same, melancholic longing will have taken the place of disgust, enabling Nabokov to write an *enticingly* shocking, much more palatable work. As part of the process of his second linguistic maturation, Vladimir Nabokov would finally reach a wide audience as a great American writer, but only when he had rediscovered girls.

---

17. For a discussion of Wilde's caricatured association with fancy dress and effeminacy, see Shirland, 26–29.

CHAPTER 3

Perversion in *Pnin*

Perversion in *Pnin*? Even when we have begun to appreciate the narrative war being waged between Pnin and those who tell stories about him, the novel appears to lack the dark, salacious side of much of Nabokov's English work. *Pnin*'s virtual simultaneity to *Lolita*—it was written right after *Lolita* but published in the United States before it—reinforces this impression; it is as if the latter novel has unsexed the former, absorbing all the libidinal energy Nabokov was capable of producing at one time. Yet not only is *Pnin* frequently a lewd book, its *hidden* lewdness hints at a deeper poetic perversion that is central to nearly all of Nabokov's work. In *Lolita, Laughter in the Dark, Pale Fire,* and *Ada,* the figure of the pervert serves Nabokov as a representation within the text of the author's—and ideal reader's—basic hermeneutic stance; the text must be twisted to get at its essence. *Pnin* seems to stand out from Nabokov's English work because it lacks major characters whom 1950s readers of the *New Yorker* would classify as deviants. Yet the author's leer remains as a principal sign of his presence; and—far more important—in *Pnin* perversion, responding to the close reader's hermeneutic ministrations, bares its devices as nowhere else in Nabokov's fiction, so much so that this book might be read as a covert manifesto for the necessity of perverse reading.

One of the puzzling aspects of Nabokov scholarship is the reluctance of scholars to accept that having a dirty mind is a necessary, albeit insufficient, condition for appreciating Nabokov's work. To savor the fun and games in *Lolita,* you have to read bawdily, but an awareness of sexually suggestive language is essential to an adequate understanding of *Pnin* as well. *Pnin* seems to be Nabokov's warmest, most sentimental work, Nabokov's novel for readers who don't like Nabokov. As such it offers an apt challenge, a sort of limit case for a study of Nabokov's penchant for the perverse. If the reader can make perversion out here, can he make it out anywhere? In this and subsequent chapters I want to dwell on the implication of that question for the reader's subjectivity.

In *Pnin* lewdness lurks so snugly in innocence's bosom that the perverse interpreter is especially apt to expose himself as a hermeneutic lunatic, or, at the very least, to offer himself as an object for derision. A wonderful example of this dynamic is presented by an epistolary exchange that several years ago spilled over from the pages of *Nature Conservancy* into NABOKV-L. In 1999 that journal published a short note on Nabokov's lepidopteral interests. On the issue's last page a large photograph of a Karner Blue appeared above a large-print quotation from *Pnin:* "A score of small butterflies, all one of a kind, were settled on a damp patch of sand. . . . One of Pnin's shed rubbers disturbed them and, revealing the celestial hue of their upper surface, they fluttered around like blue snowflakes before settling again" ("Natural Selection," 42). This quotation provoked an irate letter to the editor in the following issue. Susan Cadwalader, from Villanova, Pennsylvania, wrote that she had been a member of the conservancy for over thirty years and had always given the magazine to her younger son to take to school. "I am appalled by your use of the *Pnin* quote. If it was to be some double-edged quote on both the beauty of nature and man's disregard by 'littering,' it fails miserably" (40). This information was relayed to NABOKV-L by lepidopterist Kurt Johnson, the coauthor of *Nabokov's Blues,* who reported that he had sent in his own letter defending Nabokov's ethics and added that since Nabokov was obviously referring to footwear rather than to prophylactics, the fuss raised by Ms. Cadwalader was "pretty funny and appears to strengthen the comments by all biographers of Nabokov that the sector of the public only identifying Nabokov with erotic subjects is apt to read that kind of thing into any mention of him, etc." But this episode was equally symptomatic of scholars who have invested heavily in Nabokov as a great artist or scientist and see attention to his lubricity as a threat to their professional capital.

Let's read that passage in *Pnin* closely:

"Look, how pretty," said observant Chateau.

A score of small butterflies, all of one kind, were settled on a damp patch of sand, their wings erect and closed, showing their pale undersides with dark dots and tiny orange-rimmed peacock spots along the hindwing margins; one of Pnin's shed rubbers disturbed some of them and, revealing the celestial hue of their upper surface, they fluttered around like blue snowflakes before settling again.

"Pity Vladimir Vladimirovich is not here," remarked Chateau. "He would have told us all about these enchanting insects."

"I have always had the impression that his entomology was merely a pose."

"On, no," said Chateau. "You will lose it some day," he added, pointing to the Greek Catholic cross on a golden chainlet that Pnin had removed from his neck and hung on a twig. Its glint perplexed a cruising dragonfly. "Perhaps I would not mind losing it," said Pnin. "As you well know, I wear it merely from sentimental reasons. And the sentiment is becoming burdensome." (128)

Rubbers, of course, do mean "boots," but their appearance in this passage is hardly innocuous. Pnin is wearing rubber overshoes as "a sensible precaution" (124). The word "rubbers" appears in a paragraph with a number of words that might accompany it also in quite a different sort of literature (*erect,* the *cock* in peacock). These butterflies are "all of one kind." The passage describing Pnin at swim suggests a transplantation of Pushkin's poem "Tsar Nikita" to American soil, birdies to small butterflies, female to male. In Pushkin's bawdy verse tale, a tsar's forty daughters are perfect in every way but one— each lacks her sex. A messenger is sent to an old woman who hands him forty pudenda in a box. But the curious young man opens the container, and the genitalia fly out like "little birdies" before settling, tails aflutter, on branches nearby. And if we recall that Nabokov's transliteration scheme uses *h* for *kh* (*Eugene Onegin,* I:xxiii), it may be that in the midst of this lexical flora and fauna, *"hue"* stands as an oblique form of the Russian word for "cock" and thus is hardly a bilingual innocent.[1]

Vladimir Vladimirovich "would have told us all about these enchanting insects." A natural suggestion, given Nabokov's interest in butterflies. But

---

1. Nabokov plays a similar game in *Ada,* where Van reprimands Lucette for saying "Pah!": "And please, do not use that expletive" (371). *Pakh,* or *pah* in Nabokov's transliteration, means "groin."

the next line—"I have always had the impression that his entomology was merely a pose"—may, in *this* instance, be true. To steal a phrase from *Transparent Things,* here lepidoptery is a *pose osée* (19). Or, perhaps, in this instance of extensive double entendre, Nabokov has managed to give covert literary expression to his scientific interest in butterfly genitalia.

What follows? "'Oh, no,' said Chateau. 'You will lose it some day,' he added, pointing to the Greek Catholic cross." The placement of the pronoun's referent after the statement about loss sounds humorous once one's lexical focus has been adjusted. Until we reach "pointing to the Greek Catholic cross" the statement is not sufficiently anchored to prevent misapplication. "Perhaps I would not mind losing it," said Pnin—continuing this line of thought. The Russian radical Nikolai Chernyshevsky and the great friend of his youth express a similar thought (about penises) in the published diaries that Nabokov had read two decades before when he prepared the Chernyshevsky section of *The Gift* (Chernyshevskii, Polnoe sobranie, 1:82). Both "erotic galoshes" and "a cross" have already been scornfully mentioned in *Pnin* as examples of symbols beloved to psychologists (92). Nabokov surreptitiously links these two words—not as Freudian symbols but, through Chernyshevsky, as eroticized literary facts.[2]

It is hardly a coincidence that these butterflies are noticed by a professor named Konstantin Chateau. Upon our introduction to Chateau, we are told that he derived his surname from his grandfather, a "Russianized Frenchman" (125). The first syllable of that surname is close to *chatte* (pussy), a French term for the female genitalia. And in a reprise of the bawdy combinational play we saw in *Bend Sinister* (Schamm's remark about "chatter and confusion"), the first syllable of Chateau's Christian name is close to another French word (*con*) with a related meaning. The first of these near-synonyms makes at least one cameo appearance elsewhere in the novel, when Victor is forced to take "the charming Bièvre Attitude Game (a blessing on rainy afternoons), in which little Sam or Ruby is asked to put a little mark in front of the things about which he or she feels sort of fearful, such as dying, falling, dreaming, cyclones, funerals, father, night, operation, bedroom, bathroom, converge, and so forth." (91) The Marquis de Bièvre was a famous punster, but the puns here are Nabokov's and involve English/French translation, for *bièvre* translates as "beaver," and converge, which draws attention to itself as a verb among nouns, is "a veritable compote" of French sex organs, a semantic

---

2. It may also be relevant that the theme of "Pushkin or a pair of boots" was a stock figure of derision used to parody the utilitarianism of Chernyshevsky and his colleagues at the journal *The Contemporary.* In the context of this scene Nabokov may be putting this literary fact to work as well.

if not a grammatical copula. ("Con" and "verge" are French words for the female and male sex organs).

When writing her doctoral dissertation in 1971, Jessie Lokrantz got in touch with Nabokov and asked him about the origin of Professor Chateau's last name. Sometimes, Lokrantz reported, a "name may be a personal or private allusion known only to the author or his immediate circle":

> One such private allusion is found in the name, Professor Chateau, in *Pnin*. According to the author's own admission, this name is a private allusion and a complicated bi-lingual play on words. Chateau, when broken into syllables, comes out *chat-eau,* or literally, cat water. There is also an earlier poem by Nabokov titled *To Prince S. M. Kachurin.* Kachurin, when repeated, leads one, in sound, to cat-urine, and the plays on the words are similar. To whom these two names allude, I do not know, but I feel sure they are one and the same person. (64)

This appears to be a wonderful example of an authorial prank at a scholar's expense. Lokrantz, whose published dissertation included an entire chapter on puns, may have been misled by the phrase "*private* allusion," which in this case Nabokov seems to have used as a meta-pun.[3]

Chateau's name, however, is not just a little joke, for it ties together two of the story's crucial motifs. The thematic prominence of water is the more obvious. This element is particularly marked in *Pnin,* often appearing in contexts that seem to have invented as excuses for yet another appearance of the motif. *Pnin* is the "water father" (55) and knows that "water in Turkish is *su*" (33); Liza's lover is the son of a man who owned "a floating casino" (56). The text is replete with all sorts of liquid figurative expressions: Pnin "took the plunge" (34), a "buoyantly thriving German Department" (9), everything is "swimming a little in the radiance of [Joan's] relief" (59). The genital theme is less evident, but it begins to sound in the second chapter and continues throughout—often, as in Chateau's name, with feline markings. At the start of that chapter, Mrs. Clements calls Mrs. Blorenge "a vulgar old cat!" (30). (That Mrs. Blorenge is the wife of the chair of the French Department is another hint at the novel's preoccupation with French genital slang.) Later she shows Pnin a cartoon:

> "So this is the mariner, and this is the pussy, and this is a rather wistful mermaid hanging around, and now look at the puffs right above the sailor and the pussy."

---

3. Lokrantz does not give Nabokov's exact words, so we cannot be absolutely sure that Nabokov actually used the words "private allusion"; Lokrantz may have been paraphrasing another expression. At the very least, though, she provides evidence that Nabokov had bilingual wordplay in mind when he named his character "Konstantin Chateau."

"Atomic bomb explosion," said Pnin sadly.

"No, not at all. It is something much funnier. You see, these round puffs are supposed to be the projections of their thoughts. And now at last we are getting to the amusing part. The sailor imagines the mermaid as having a pair of legs, and the cat imagines her as all fish." (60–61)

This is also the chapter in which Pnin enters Isabelle's room and inspects "Hoecker's 'Girl with a Cat' above the bed, and Hunt's 'The Belated Kid' above the bookshelf" (34). Gennady Barabtarlo strives mightily to identify these paintings, noting that although the two German artists named Hoecker never produced such a painting, "among a few American paintings bearing that title the most plausible seems to be the 'Girl with a Cat' by Paula Modersohn-*Becker* (1876–1907), while if, instead of changing one letter in the artist's name, one would tamper in like manner with the title, one would come up with the 'Girl with a *Hat*' (1908) by E. C. Tarbell, or, even more to the point, with the rather well-known 'Girl with the *Cap*' by none other than William Morris Hunt" (*Phantom of Fact,* 90). There was, in fact, a painting by Thomas Hoecker of a girl with a cat (Figure 1),[4] but I believe that Barabtarlo is, indeed, engaging in a phonetic exercise designed by the text, with the letter to be changed the first one in Hunt. Furthermore, there may well be a second painting in play, "*Jeune Fille au Chat*" (Girl with a Cat) (1938) by Balthus, a painter whom Nabokov admired (Figure 2).[5] Balthus's painting shows a young girl reclining on her chair, her legs apart, with her crotch near the center of the canvas. Next to her, at lower right, is a cat, iconically and verbally serving as a substitute for the place to which the girl's panties preclude the viewer's access. (The name "Chateau" is a phonetic near-anagram of the last two words of the title of Balthus's painting, the genitally suggestive *au chat*.). Nabokov follows this glimpse of the painting with more of Joan

---

4. I am grateful to Jonathan Rowen for pointing out to me that this 1887 painting by Paul Hoecker was reproduced in the 1889 Christmas edition of *The Illustrated London News* with the caption "Cat's Eyes." The same painting, alongside the title *Girl with Cat,* later appeared on the September 1935 cover of *The Instructor: The Classroom Magazine for Grade Teachers,* published in Dansville, New York (about ninety miles from Ithaca). That issue contained many miniature reproductions of the painting (presumably for distribution to schoolchildren), provided courtesy of The Art Extension Press, Inc., in New York.

5. *Strong Opinion,* 167. Further, unattested evidence for Nabokov's appreciation of Balthus is provided by Nicholas Fox Weber (400). A posting by Phillip Iannarelli on NABOKV-L brought Weber's biography of Balthus and *Jeune Fille au Chat* to my attention. "Nabokov and Balthus," 22 December 1999 (http://listserv.ucsb-edu/lsv-cgi-bin/wa?A2=ind9912&L=nabokv-l&F=&S=&P=4108). From 1937 to 1963 the painting was owned by the Pierre Matisse Gallery in New York, where Nabokov may have seen it (Ades, 6). After Nabokov's death, *Jeune Fille au Chat* graced the Penguin cover of *Lolita.*

THE INSTRUCTOR

THE CLASSROOM MAGAZINE FOR GRADE TEACHERS

SEPTEMBER 1935

30 Cents a Copy $2.50 a Year

GIRL WITH CAT
By Paul Hoecker
Courtesy, The Art Extension Press, Inc.,
New York

From INSTRUCTOR, September 1935. Reprinted by permission of Scholastic Inc. Paul Hoecker's *Girl with a Cat* was used in INSTRUCTOR through the courtesy of The Art Extension Press, Inc.

Balthus (Balthusz Klossowski de Rola), French, 1908–2001, Girl with Cat (*Jeune Fille au Chat*), 1937, oil on board, 87.6 x 77.5 cm, The Lindy and Edwin Bergman Collection, 1991.595, The Art Institute of Chicago. Photography © The Art Institute of Chicago. Copyright © 2010 Artists Rights Society (ARS), New York/ADAGP, Paris.

Clements's house tour, and in just a few paragraphs we reach the first mention of Professor Chateau:

> "And here is the bathroom—small, but all yours." "No *douche*?" inquired Pnin, looking up. "Maybe it is better so. My friend, Professor Chateau of Columbia, once broke his leg in two places." (34)

In his commentary, Barabtarlo observes: "In both Russian and French the meaning of the word is limited to shower bath" (*Phantom of Fact,* 91), thus providing a wonderfully symptomatic instance of the penchant for authoritative Nabokovians to go out of their way to close off libidinal readings of the master's prose. It seems oddly necessary to insist that the language of *Pnin* is English: in this context douche is a private allusion not out of place with the text's drift. We should once again recall Pushkin's "Tsar Nikita." It makes sense that someone named "Chateau" would attract those butterflies.

Pnin's theme of aquatic pussy is further developed when Nabokov takes up the drowning of Ophelia. This is territory he explored in *Bend Sinister,* but here the casting of aspersions on Ophelia flows through the entire novel and serves as the fundamental reference for the narrative's tendency to mistreat its human subjects. Gertrude's description of Ophelia's death is worth a close look:

> There is a willow grows aslant a brook
> That shows his hoar leaves in the glassy stream.
> Therewith fantastic garlands did she make
> Of crow-flowers, nettles, daisies, and long purples,
> That liberal shepherds give a grosser name,
> But our cold maids do dead men's fingers call them.
> There on the pendent boughs her crownet weeds
> Clamb'ring to hang, an envious sliver broke,
> When down the weedy trophies and herself
> Fell in the weeping brook. Her clothes spread wide,
> And mermaid-like a while they bore her up;
> Which time she chanted snatches of old tunes,
> As one incapable of her own distress,
> Or like a creature native and endued
> Unto that element. But long it could not be
> Till that her garments, heavy with their drink,
> Pulled the poor wretch from her melodious lay
> To muddy death. (4.7.137–54)

The grosser name for long purples—a variety of orchid which, like "crow-flowers," was traditionally associated in England with fertility—is identified by the editors of *The Norton Shakespeare* as "Priest's pintle" or "Fool's ballochs" (1739–40),[6] but Frankie Rubinstein goes further, asserting that the entire passage is an assault on Ophelia's chastity, with *clothes* being a pun on *close*—a reference to the female genitals—spread wide, and one might stress as well the *snatches* of old tunes, her melodious *lay* (251). As far as Shakespearean intention is concerned, this reading may be fantasy... but *Bend Sinister* strongly suggests that Nabokov had similar thoughts about how that passage might be perversely read.[7] Pnin is unconsciously reminded of Ophelia when he reads a passage about fertility rites from Kostromskoy's book on Russian myths, but he can't "catch it by its mermaid tail" until several paragraphs later:

> Of course! Ophelia's death! *Hamlet!* In good old Andrey Kroneberg's Russian translation, 1844—the joy of Pnin's youth, and of his father's and grandfather's young days! And here, as in the Kostromskoy passage, there is, we recollect, also a willow and also wreaths. But where to check properly? Alas, *"Gamlet" Vil'yama Shekspira* had not been acquired by Mr. Todd, was not represented in Waindell College Library, and whenever you were reduced to look up something in the English version, you never found this or that beautiful noble, sonorous line that you remembered all your life from Kroneberg's text in Vengerov's splendid edition. (79)

One will not find those beautiful, noble sonorous lines in the English version of Hamlet provided in *Pnin*. On the contrary, the persistent echoes of Ophelia's death highlight the elements of Gertrude's language most susceptible to lewd interpretation. "Where to check properly?" Proper investigation of intertextual echoes in *Pnin* entails checking *im*properly. Pnin's reading of Kostromskoy includes references to peasant maidens making "wreaths of buttercups and frog orchises" and "singing snatches of ancient love chants." In the next section of the chapter, Nabokov restages these lines in modern undress in a ludicrous context: Pnin sees a Soviet documentary in which "handsome, unkempt girls marched in an immemorial Spring Festival with

---

6. For a thorough inventory of the grosser names of the flowers that compose the "obscenity of [Ophelia's] funerary wreath," see Otten (297–402).

7. In a 1941 article cataloguing translators' sins, Nabokov criticized Russian versions of *Hamlet* which gave Ophelia "richer flowers than the poor weeds she found." He continued: "The Russian rendering of 'There with fantastic garlands did she come / Of crowflowers, nettles, daisies and long purples,' if translated back into English would run like this: 'There with most lovely garlands did she come / Of violets, carnations, roses, lilies.' The splendor of this floral display speaks for itself; incidentally it bowdlerized the Queen's digressions, granting her the gentility she so sadly lacked and dismissing the liberal shepherds" (*Lectures on Russian Literature,* 316–17).

banners *bearing snatches* of old Russian ballads such as *"Ruki proch ot Korei"* (81, first emphasis added). (The drowned Ophelia is literally "unkempt"— her hair uncombed.) This phrase literally bares two of the novel's principal devices—puns and what might be called surreptitious indecent exposure. Pnin bursts out laughing on being exposed to such trash, but the scene describing his physical reaction hints at a different sort of stimulus, a different reaction and an altogether different genre of writing: "'I must not, I must not, oh it is idiotical,' said Pnin to himself as he felt—unaccountably, ridiculously, humiliatingly—his tear glands discharge their hot, infantine, uncontrollable fluid" (81–82). The phonetics here (una*cco*untably, un*co*ntrollable) are suggestive, reinforcing the connotation offered by "snatches," and even the "idiotical" may hint in this direction through a French detour (idiot=*con*).[8]

Ophelia's death has several sexual echoes in *Pnin*—as if the narrative voice understood the scene's double entendre better than its tragedy. The *poshlost'* of modern transpositions of *Hamlet* (and the vulgarity of much modern life) is reflected not only in the Soviet newsreel but in communism's American counterpart—group therapy. Pnin is struck by "a curious verbal association" when reading Kostromskoy's book on Russian myths, and he is set musing in particular by a passing reference "to the old pagan games that were still practiced at the time, throughout the woodlands of the Upper Volga [...][d]uring a festive week in May" (77). Ostensibly, this association is brought to consciousness a few pages later—with the mention of the death of Ophelia—but as often happens with Nabokov, the proffered solution to a riddle is not the only right one. The words "woodlands" and "May" should provide a different verbal association for the reader. They ought to recall the description— earlier in the novel—of the practice of Bernard Maywood, Eric Wind's boss at a Planned Parenthood Center. Inspired by Maywood, "Eric evolved the ingenious idea (possibly not his own) of sidetracking some of the more plastic and stupid clients of the Center into a psychotherapeutic trap—a 'tension-releasing' circle on the lines of a quilting bee, where young married women in groups of eight relaxed in a comfortable room amid an atmosphere of cheerful first-name informality, with doctors at a table facing the group, and a secretary unobtrusively taking notes, and traumatic episodes floating out of everybody's childhood like corpses" (51). This idea is, indeed, not Eric's own but is—perversely—indebted to Shakespeare: a pale reflection of Ophelia's death. The verbal association that strikes Pnin while reading Kostromskoy

---

8. For an analogous moment in Pushkin (Lensky's "living tears" [*zhivye slezy*]), see Proskurin, who observes that "the Russian tradition of indecent poetry had by this time already adopted and widely used the image of crying as a metaphor for ejaculation" (156).

("woodlands," "May," "singing snatches," "wreaths ... unwinding," "maidens floated and chanted"—all part of a description of fertility rituals) refers not only to Shakespeare's play and its vulgar cinematic hypostasis but also to that earlier chapter of the text of *Pnin* itself where many of the same elements appeared in degraded form ("Maywood," "Eric and Liza Wind," "young, married women," "traumatic episodes floating like corpses"). The "singing snatches" and the mad Ophelia's sexually charged songs may find their travestied modern parallel in the modern wives' reports of the success of their sex education training: "after this or that lady had gone home and seen the light and come back to describe the newly discovered sensation to her still blocked but rapt sisters, a ringing note of revivalism pleasingly colored the proceedings ('Well, girls, when George last night—')" (51). The world of this novel may itself, Laurence Clements suggests, be "really a fluorescent corpse" (166), as if the entire work has become identified with Ophelia's flowing body. Ophelia's identification with water—"Too much of water hast thou, poor Ophelia" (5.1.157)—reinforces this association of Shakespeare's heroine with *Pnin*'s dominant element; Laertes' mournful words might well serve as a motto for the novel's poetics as a whole.

Following the scent of Ophelia's lewd treatment in *Hamlet,* we find several echoes in *Pnin* of the play's "country matters" scene, with its equation of the female genitalia and "nothing." Here, though, Nabokov effectively makes that pun through translation, thus linking it to Russian and English traditions. Pushkin drew on this pun in "Tsar Nikita," probably relying on French convention:[9]

> *Odnogo ne dostavalo*
> *Da chego zhe odnogo?*
> *Tak, bezdelki, nichego.*
> *Nichego il' ochen' malo,*
> *Vse ravno—ne dostavalo.* (2:1:248)

There was one thing missing. What was it? Oh, a trifle, nothing at all. Nothing at all or very little, all the same, it wasn't there.

Pushkin's pudendal word play is picked up in Liza's poetry:

> *Samotsvétov króme ochéy*
> *Net u menyá nikakíh,*
> *No est' róza eshchó nezhnéy*

---

9. The common source may have been French erotic poetry or Diderot's *Les bijoux indiscrets.* See Levinton and Okhotin, 29.

Rózovïh gúb moíh.
I yúnosha tíhiy skazál:
"Vashe sérdtse vsegó nezhnéy ..."
I yá opustíla glazá....

I have marked the stress accents, and transliterated the Russian with the usual understanding that *u* is pronounced like a short "oo," *i* like a short "ee," and *zh* like a French "j." Such incomplete rhymes as *skazal-glaza* were considered very elegant. Note also the erotic undercurrents and *cour d'amour* implications. A prose translation would go: "No jewels, save my eyes, do I own, but I have a rose which is even softer than my rosy lips. And a quiet youth said: 'There is nothing softer than your heart.' And I lowered my gaze...." (181)

The narrator's English "translation" has added an indecent double entendre with a Shakespearian/Pushkinian pedigree ("there is nothing softer than your heart") that supplements the vulgar aesthetic content of the original Russian, which would more literally translate as "Your heart is more tender than everything else." When this passage is lewdly illuminated, the phrase "*cour d'amour*" (court of love) becomes an anatomical reference as well as a stylistic and historical one.

Bawdy echoes of Ophelia serve as a central "erotic undercurrent" in *Pnin;* at several additional places it flows through the "limpid mermaid" (44) who was once Pnin's wife. If we recollect the "pussy"-mermaid connection in the cartoon discussed above, we begin to see that Liza, with those "feline little lines" fanning out from the eyes, is particularly implicated in the novel's submerged bawdy theme. "[T]here was hardly a flaw to her full-blown, animated, elemental, not particularly well-groomed beauty" (44). Barabtarlo notes that Liza's defects in grooming tie her to those "handsome unkempt" girls in the Soviet spring festival (*Phantom of Fact,* 97), and her sloppy appearance also leads to the bawdily drowned Ophelia, a direction reinforced by the word "elemental," echoing Gertrude's description of the drowning Ophelia ("a creature native and endued / Unto that element"). Nabokov has focused on this line before. In *The Gift* Fyodor finds the world of writing "as natural to him as snow to the white hare or water to Ophelia" (125); and, as Dolinin observes ("Primechaniia," 4:694), there is a further echo of the line in Zina's first appearance: "She always unexpectedly appeared out of the darkness, like a shadow leaving its kindred element" (177). The film of the Soviet girls with snatch-bearing banners has been preceded by a Chaplin movie, a seemingly strange combination until one recalls Chaplin's nickname: "The Little Tramp." (The regendering of Chaplin's affectionate moniker first occurs in reference to the ex-beau of Betty Bliss, "a handsome heel for a lover, who had jilted her for a little tramp" [42], and continues with an implicit critique of Liza's low morals: "one damp April day in 1940 there was a vigorous ring at his door and Liza tramped in, puffing and carrying before her like a chest of drawers a seven-month pregnancy" (46–47). Preparing to introduce Liza, the narrator employs a Pninism that reflects as much on his ex-wife as on him: "The cat, as Pnin would say, cannot be hid in a bag" (43). The triple association—linking Liza, Ophelia, and the flower of Soviet youth—is reinforced further in the narrator's description of Liza's and Pnin's first meeting: "at one of those literary soirees where young émigré poets, who had left Russia in their pale, unpampered pubescence, chanted nostalgic elegies dedicated to a country that could be little more to them than a sad stylized toy, a bauble found in the attic" (44–45).[10]

Liza's language can be suggestively crude. Pnin should provide money for Victor, she insists, because her ex-husband's salary is "more than enough for your needs, for your microscopic needs" (55). The text that follows picks up the sexual innuendo: "Her abdomen tightly girdled under the black skirt jumped up two or three times with mute, cozy, good-natured reminiscential irony—and Pnin blew his nose, shaking his head the while, in voluptuous, rapturous mirth" (55). As we have seen in *Lolita,* good-*nature*d may itself be a pudendal quibble, and Pnin's laughter implies his own good-natured appreciation of the joke. Most of the verbal-genital play surrounding Liza, however, is of a different nature and pains Pnin greatly. Of Pnin's sea voyage to America with Liza we learn: "It was a little disappointing that as soon as she came aboard she gave one glance at the swelling sea, said '*Nu, eto izvinite* (Nothing doing),' and promptly retired into the womb of the ship" (47–48). The Russian here literally means "well, excuse me." Once again we see that in Nabokov's novels the act of translation, through which here, for a second time, he adds "nothing," is rarely gratuitous. Pnin's disappointment (that word may itself be an apt pun) later reaches the level of despair: "'I haf nofing,' wailed Pnin between loud, damp sniffs, 'I haf nofing left, nofing, nofing!'" (61). And it is on this note that—to appropriate Barabtarlo's useful terminology (*Phantom of Fact,* 20)—the drawstrings of chapter 2 are closed.

Yet all this sex is as much figure as ground, for as every reader of Nabokov knows, "sex is but the ancilla of art" (*Lolita,* 259). The treatment of Ophelia amounts to a kind of slander, a perverse retelling of her story. The narrator

---

10. On Shakespeare's bawdy uses of "toy" and "bauble," see Partridge, 203.

of *Pnin*—and his source, Jack Cockerell—subject Pnin to a similar outrage, a different sort of indecent exposure.[11] Where *Lolita* seeks to safely solipsize its heroine as an eternally young sex object, *Pnin* attempts to infantilize its hero by reducing him to a comic character. Both are a form of character assassination and highlight the lethal aesthetic dimension of turning someone into the hero of a story: all characters imprisoned in fiction are less than human. "You can always count on a murderer for a fancy prose style" (9), Humbert says at the outset of *Lolita,* and the narrator of Pnin seeks to put this precept into practice: "If his Russian was Music, His English was Murder" (66)—that's a catchy zinger of a sentence that helps put Pnin in his anecdotal casket. Both stories begin with powerful attempts to coopt the reader. With *Lolita* it is the reader's tongue—"Lolita—the tip of the tongue taking a trip of three steps down the palate to tap....." In *Pnin* it is the reader's imagined pencil:

> [H]e began rather impressively with that great brown dome of his, tortoise-shell glasses (masking an infantile absence of eyebrows), apish upper lip, thick neck, and strong-man torso in a tightish tweed coat, but ended, somewhat disappointingly, in a pair of spindly legs (now flannelled and crossed) and frail-looking, almost feminine feet. (7)

Diminishing Pnin as cute and characterizing Ophelia as a loose woman are parallel practices. The narrator's implication in the malevolent shadowing of Pnin and in Ophelia's genital theme is made most apparent in the novel's seventh chapter, the one that exposes him in his turn as a character:

> One afternoon, as in concentrated ecstasy I was spreading, underside up, an exceptionally rare aberration of the Paphia Fritillary, in which the silver stripes ornamenting the lower surface of its hindwings had fused into an even expanse of metallic gloss, a footman came up with the information that the old lady requested my presence. (177)

The narrator's interrupted activity—he is about to meet Pnin for the first time as an adult—is a reflection of his method of writing about Pnin and, for all we know, of his writing in general: the name of the Paphia Fritillary hints at Paphos, the Cyprian site of a shrine to Aphrodite which has produced the adjective "paphian," defined by Nabokov's dictionary as "pertaining to

---

11. Placing *Pnin* within the tradition of the detective novel, Couturier notes that typically that genre begins with "an initial recognition of a reprehensible action, usually a murder": "This logic has already been perverted in the novels [*Despair* and *Lolita*] where it was the murderers themselves who did the investigating. It is even more so [in *Pnin* and *Transparent Things*]: the reprehensible act is the narration itself, the investigator is the reader, and the 'guilty party' is the author" (*Nabokov, ou la tyrannie,* 186).

illicit love" and "wantonness" (*Webster's New International,* 1768).[12] The narrator turns his world underside up, spreads it wide, imbuing his text with a genital hue.[13] In this respect, Joan's comment about the sailor and the pussy— "now comes the amusing part"—can be read metapoetically: this book's narrator seems to have a genital muse.[14] But Nabokov's novel does not content itself with the drawing of an analogy between Pnin and a Shakespearean prototype, nor does it seek simply to condemn the leering mistreatment of both characters. The role of perversion in *Pnin* is much more complex, for the novel insists on the fundamentality of perversion to art.

To get at the hard core of perversion in *Pnin,* we must leave the philological locker room and turn to the squirrel. No argument need be made for the centrality of this beast, which puts in several crucial appearances. Etymologically "squirrel," we are told by a postcard from Pnin to Victor, means "shadow tail," and an obvious pun (tail/tale) makes the beast an image for the novel as a whole with its shadow narrators and metafictive plot. Robert Alter and Gennady Barabtarlo have argued that the squirrel represents no more than the principle of pattern. "[D]oes the squirrel Theme have a special allegoric mission," Barabtarlo asks, "besides sharing in the general symbolism of all artistic expression? Not in Nabokov's novel" (*Phantom of Fact,* 23).[15] That favorite whipping boy of Nabokovians, W. W. Rowe, argues that the squirrel—in Russian *belka*—represents the ghost of Pnin's former beloved, Mira Belochkin, who haunts and inspires the entire work (62–66). To my mind the squirrel represents something else, the fundamental principle of poetic perversity so dear to Nabokov. One of its last appearances in the novel occurs when Pnin discusses Cinderella's shoes, which were "not made of glass but of Russian squirrel fur—*vair,* in French. It was, Pnin said, an obvious

---

12. Bodenstein calls attention to the added connotative value often inherent in Nabokov's use of lepidopteral terms: "In Nabokov's use of scientific words, the naturalist's precision is supplemented by the artist's appreciation of associative and etymological values in words" (1:47).

13. What the narrator does with butterflies, Nabokov does with words. Couturier quotes Nabokov's comment to Bernard Pivot: "If I like to take a word and turn it over to see whether its underside is shiny or dull or decorated with variegation missing on its top side, it is not because of idle curiosity. One always finds all sorts of curious things in studying the underside of a word (*en étudiant le dessous d'un mot*); one finds there the unexpected shadows of other words, or other ideas, the relations between them, hidden beauties which suddenly reveal something beyond the word" (Nabokov, ou la tyrannie, 374). The entire televised interview—an episode of *Apostrophes*—is available on YouTube (www.youtube.com/watch?v=XheZIhnRKQI).

14. In an analogous moment, at the start of *Pale Fire* Kinbote invokes the principle of play as the work's dominant mode: "There is a very loud amusement park right in front of my present lodgings" (13).

15. Alter treats the squirrel in similar terms: "the literary high fun of the squirrel is not that it serves as the half-hidden key to an elaborate code (for which, of course, Nabokov had a well-known fondness) but, on the contrary, because it sets our minds spiraling with swarming prospects of meaning and connection" (236).

case of the survival of the fittest among words, *verre* being more evocative than *vair*" (158). A game of homonymity is being played here, and it has repercussions for the entire text, in which these two French words—through their English translations—serve as principal poetic motifs. But as so often in Nabokov's work, the answer is not (or not only) the one ostensibly provided, for squirrel fur has a homonym other than glass—it is, quite simply, *vers,* verse, which stands here for the poetry of all art and is derived from *vertere*—the Latin word meaning "to turn."[16] The verb "pervert" is derived from the same root—it means to turn something excessively or to turn it the wrong way.

Images of bending and twisting are central to Nabokov's portrait of creativity throughout his oeuvre. This is as true in Nabokov's lexicon for bad, parodic art as it is for the real thing. The evil world of *Bend Sinister* has its companion in the world in which the narrator of *Pnin* continually tries to place his hero. "Important lecture!" cries Pnin when he finds himself on the wrong train: "It is a cata-stroph" (17)—Nabokov's hyphenation of this last word represents not only Pnin's pronunciation but the word's etymology— a "catastrophe" is literally a downward turn or an over-turning. In the *Lolita* screenplay, on the day after their first sexual intercourse, Humbert and Lolita squash a squirrel and take "the wrong turning" (114, 116); in the novel the progression is quicker: "poor Humbert Humbert... kept racking his brains for some quip, under the bright wing of which he might dare *turn* to his seatmate. It was she, however, who broke the silence: 'Oh, a squashed *squirrel,*'

---

16. Barabtarlo nearly reaches the same conclusion when he mentions one scholar's tracing of the etymology of *belka,* but he is characteristically reluctant to assume the responsibility of interpretation: "J. Endzelin thinks that the word is somehow connected with *ver*—to bend, having to do with the squirrel's crooked tail" (*Phantom of Fact,* 243).

"Vair" has at least two other homonyms other than *verre* and *vers: vert* (green) and *ver* (worm). Neither word seems particularly important in *Pnin,* although Nabokov does employ a related pun in *Look at the Harlequins!:* "I let my index finger stray at random over a map of northern France; the point of its nail stopped at the town of Petiver or Petit Ver, a small worm or verse, which sounded idyllic" (75). Green is one of the most frequently mentioned colors in *Pnin* (Barabtarlo: *Phantom of Fact,* 303), but only its penultimate appearance seems particularly meaningful: "a quiet lacy-winged little green insect" circles above Pnin when he fears that he has broken Victor's glass bowl. (Nicol sees this insect as evidence of the real author's presence in this scene, but he does not comment on the insect's particular color [208]). In his youth, Pnin earned his livelihood from two jobs, one in the rue Vert-Vert, and the other in the rue Gresset (44). As Barabtarlo notes, "Vert-Vert" is the parrot hero of the eponymous poem by Jean Baptiste Louis de Gresset (*Phantom of Fact,* 98). Nabokov's reference to Gresset's poem in his commentary to *Eugene Onegin* is suggestive of its implication in the homonym game of *Pnin:* "Incidentally, the variations in the spelling of the name of Gresset's parrot are amusing. My copy has the following title: *Les Oeuvres de Gresset, Enrichies de la Critique de Vairvert / Comédie en I acte* (Amsterdam, 1748). In the table of contents the title is *Vert-Vert.* In the half title (p. 9) and in the poem itself it is 'Ver-Vert,' and in the critique in comedy form appended to the volume, 'Vairvert'" (2: 119).

she said. 'What a shame.'"(140, emphasis added) In "Time and Ebb" we are told that the poet Richard Sinatra remained undiscovered throughout his lifetime, "an anonymous 'ranger' dreaming under a Telluride pine or reading his prodigious verse to the squirrels of San Isabel Forest, whereas everybody knew another Sinatra, a minor writer." A bit of doggerel in *Lolita* is perhaps the closest Nabokov comes to decoding the meaning of the squirrel:

> I recalled the rather charming nonsense verse I used to write her when she was a child: "nonsense," she used to say mockingly, "is correct."

> The Squirl and his Squirrel, the Rabs and their Rabbits
> Have certain obscure and peculiar habits.
> Male hummingbirds make the most exquisite rockets.
> The snake when he walks holds his hands in his pockets. (254–55)

Here "nonsense verse" is instantiated by a poem in which "Squirrel" is misspelled and becomes literally nonsensical. Yet although the use of the squirrel as a symbol of poetry may be found elsewhere in Nabokov, *Pnin* is the novel that most insistently presents images of turning—narrative version and perversion within the universe of the novel—and in the process turns this action into an iconic and lexical mantra for the struggle among characters and between character and author for control of the text.

There is a great deal of winding, turning, and twisting in *Pnin*. Victor is faced by an awful travesty of the squirrel: "a communal supply of athletic supporters—a *beastly gray* tangle, from which one had to *untwist* a strap for oneself to put on at the start of the sport period" (95, emphasis added). Pnin twists his head, checking the numbers of cross streets as he recites "a magnificent account of the rambling comparison in Homer and Gogol." The narrator recalls a fleeting glance of Pnin's childhood room: "Through the open door of the schoolroom I could see a map of Russia on the wall, books on a shelf, a stuffed squirrel, and a toy monoplane with linen wings and a rubber motor. I had a similar one but twice bigger, bought in Biarritz. After one had wound up the propeller for some time, the rubber would change its manner of twist and develop fascinating thick whorls which predicated the end of its tether" (177). The "writhing pattern" (158) of Victor's "perfectly divine bowl" might also be fit into this theme, capturing the poetic equivalence of twisting and writing.[17] (Here we should recall Nabokov's "An Evening of

---

17. The writhing/writing pun goes back at least to Lewis Carroll and his *Alice,* which Nabokov had translated some thirty years earlier. Compare Carroll's "Reeling and Writhing" (101) with Nabokov's "*chesat'i pitat'*" (transforming "reading and writing" into "scratching and feeding") (*Ania v strane chudes,* 85).

Russian Poetry," which Nabokov, anticipating Pnin, delivers as a fictitious guest lecture: "Not only rainbows—every line is bent, and skulls and seeds and all good worlds are round / like Russian verse, like our colossal vowels" [*Poems and Problems,* 158–59]).[18]

Pnin "felt very grateful to Herman Hagen for many a good turn," and I want to draw attention to the "ver" in "very," for it has not been pointed out, I think, that Nabokov uses "very" with astonishing frequency for such a good writer. Indeed, the syllable "ver"—admittedly unavoidable in English—eats away like a worm at the novel's "fluorescent corpse," establishing a network of connections far more numerous than the appearance of the squirrel. Yes, Nabokov loves alliteration and, yes, it would be a feat to write in English without this syllable, but its use in *Pnin* is so frequent—often in the context of images concerning poetic creativity—that the attentive reader should be on the lookout for an unexpected rustle in the leaves.

Let us begin by examining a few of these moments in which the syllable "ver" is explicitly tied to words formed on the winding root of "version," to the presence of the squirrel or to discussions of artists or artistic creativity. Waindell is characterized "by a huge, active, buoyantly thriving German Department which its Head, Dr. Hagen, smugly called (pronouncing every syllable very distinctly) 'a university within a university'" (9). When, toward the conclusion of chapter 5, the "pang of tenderness" experienced by Pnin after recollecting Mira Belochkin is compared to "the vibrating outline of verses you know you know but cannot recall," the reader should recollect a moment earlier in the chapter, where branches vibrate and a hunted but hidden squirrel can be glimpsed through an anagrammatic outline: "The dense upper boughs in that part of the otherwise sti*rl*ess forest started to move in a receding *seq*uence of shakes or jumps, with a swinging lilt from tree to tree, after which all was still again" (115, emphasis added). The squirrel is just as present to our ear in this sentence as it would be to a character's eye.

Our syllable continues on its sinuous course: "Germany, that nation of universities, as the President of Waindell College, renowned for his use of the *mot juste,* had so elegantly phrased it" (135). The French phrase here may

---

18. In a similar play, Nabokov introduces a turn to Marina Tsvetaeva's poem "To My Poems, Written so Early" (Moim stikham, napisannym tak rano), which he translated for Alfred Appel: *"Razbrossanym v pyli po magazinam / (Gde ikh nikto ne bral i ne beret!), / Moim stikham, kak dragotsennym vinam, / Nastanet svoi chered"* (I:36) (Amidst the dust of bookshops, wide dispersed / And never purchased there by anyone, / Yet similar to precious wines, my verse / Can wait: its turn shall come) (*Nabokov's Dark Cinema,* 315). The word translated as "turn" (*chered*) is associated with order and place; etymologically it has nothing in common with turning, an association added by Nabokov in his English translation.

hint at the Latin root of uni*ver*sity despite the German decoy—a universe or a university becomes a work turned to the purpose of a controlling poet. "Moreover, Liza wrote verse" and "every intonation, every image, every simile had been used before by other rhyming rabbits" (44–45). Liza, who "should be treated as a very sick woman," combines "lyrical outbursts with a very practical and very commonplace mind" (182). According to Pnin, Pushkin's poem "Whether I wander along noisy streets" describes "the morbid habit he always had—wherever he was, whatever he was doing—of dwelling on thoughts of death and of closely inspecting every passing day as he strove to find in its cryptogram a certain 'future' anniversary" (68); "I ran into Pnin several times during those years at various social and academic functions in New York; but the only vivid recollection I have is of our ride together on a west-side bus, on a very festive and very wet night in 1952, [. . .]the occasion of the hundredth anniversary of a great writer's death" (185–86). The opening of the Victor chapter reads like an incantation by the novel's central sound: "The King, his father, wearing a very white sports shirt open at the throat and a very black blazer, sat at a spacious desk whose highly polished surface twinned his upper half in reverse" (84). In all three instances the sound "ver" is repeated in a context which unites it with a word etymologically linked to the French root meaning "turn": university, verse, anniversary, anniversary, reverse.

At one point, Nabokov obliquely calls attention to the importance of this syllable: "Before leaving the library," Pnin "decided to look up the correct pronunciation of 'interested,' and discovered that Webster, or at least the battered 1930 edition lying on a table in the Browsing Room, did not place the stress accent on the third syllable, as he did" (78). Let us place the stress on another, adjacent word, on what pretends to be process rather than object. A disco*ver*y indeed! Here, as often in Nabokov, the interpretive key is provided but we have to realize that the text is ostensibly fitting it to the wrong lock. "It stood to reason that if the evil designer—the destroyer of minds, the friend of fe*ver*—had concealed the key of the pattern with such monstrous care, that key must be as precious as life itself and, when found, would regain for Timofey Pnin his e*ver*yday health, his e*ver*yday world; and this lucid—alas, too lucid—thought forced him to perse*ver*e in the struggle" (23, emphasis added). The key to the work is concealed many times in the passage we have just read—as with all other keys, this one is powerful only when it is turned. Let's look at one more subtle baring of the device. Pnin is teaching:

[F]e*ver*ishly, he would flip right and left through the volume, and minutes might pass before he found the right page—or satisfied himself that he had marked it correctly after all. Usually the passage of his choice would come from some old and naive comedy of merchant-class habitus rigged up by Ostrovski almost a century ago, or from an equally ancient but even more dated piece of trivial Leskovian jollity dependent on *ver*bal contortions. He deli*ver*ed these stale goods with the rotund gusto of the classical Alexandrinka (a theater in Petersburg), rather than with the crisp simplicity of the Moscow Artists; but since to appreciate whate*ver* fun those passage still retained one had to have not only a sound knowledge of the *ver*nacular but also a good deal of literary insight, and since his poor little class had neither, the performer would be alone in enjoying the associative subtleties of his text. The heaving we have already noted in another connection would become here a *ver*itable earthquake. (12, emphasis added)

Appreciation of this passage does indeed require "a *sound* knowledge of the *ver*nacular." This sound knowledge clues the reader in to the presence of the poet. "I made friends with a squirrel. We'll meet at the Siren Cafe," says Dreyer in a passage added in the English version of *King, Queen, Knave* (244), and we meet the poet at every moment when we encounter the telltale syllable of the artist's poetic beast. "And indeed progressive, idealistic Wind dreamed of a happy world consisting of Siamese centuplets, anatomically conjoined communities, whole nations built around a communicating liver" (52). Here li*ver* is a triple pun, standing not only for the bodily organ but for the poetic, living author.

The move in the passage just quoted—from Wind to liver, is indicative of another conjunction for motifs of aesthetic creativity in *Pnin*. From as far back as *The Defense,* Nabokov has been using images of breath (inspiration) and of rotation as markers of authorial presence.[19] Only in *Pnin,* however, does Nabokov bring these two themes together in a homographic pair that leaves almost as pervasive a trail as the poetic squirrel. This couple is wind (breath) and wind (turn).[20] A bad poet, Liza Wind represents a typical case of creative sinistrality and serves, along with the narrator and even a hairy-armed attendant (who misdirects Pnin at a gas station), as examples of substandard

---

19. See Davydov, *Teksty-Matreshki,* 80–83; Rowe, *Nabokov's Spectral Dimension, passim;* and Dolinin, who remarks that "in the iconic system of Nabokov" "wind is the attribute of the divine author, the pneuma of the creator" (*Istinnaia zhizn',* 89).

20. In Shakespeare's day the two words were homonyms, both pronounced more closely to the sound of the verb "wind" (twist) today (Kökeritz, 218). The phonetic and semantic ambiguity associated with Liza's surname finds its parallel in the two possible pronunciations of her first name, which would contain a short initial vowel in Russian but a long one in English.

creative directors. Additional words are used in _Pnin_ to describe air currents or twisting, but this pair is accorded special prominence, and Nabokov drops hints about their metafictive equivalence, bringing each into syntactic contiguity with synonyms for the other. Referring to Liza's predecessor, the narrator informs us that "Dr. Wind had a wife with a tortuous mind" (46). (Here the connection of the two meanings of "wind" is helped by a visual cue to the no-longer extant rhyme.) Wind is closely linked with the squirrel in _Pnin;_ both stand not—as Rowe thought—for the ghost of Mira Belochkin but for authorial, poetic power. Nabokov has drawn these images together before, most notably in _Laughter in the Dark,_ where the pair of words hints at the evil king (Rex) who rules as a false divinity over Albinus's world. Rex has thrown a stone at a squirrel.

> "Oh, kill it—they do a lot of damage to the trees," said Margot softly.
> "Who does damage to the trees?" asked a loud voice. It was Albinus. [...] "Lead me back to the house," he said, almost in tears. "There are too many sounds here. Trees, wind, squirrels and things I cannot name." (264–65)

Nabokov's use of trees, wind, and squirrels may serve as an example of the aesthetic process Victor's teacher, Lake, calls the "'naturalization' of man-made things" (97).

The pages that open chapter 5 of _Pnin_ are especially rich in the condensation of wind, winding, and squirrels. Pnin has recently learned to drive, an achievement that signals a certain degree of autonomy from his authors, although it has been won only after a series of tense encounters "with a harsh instructor who cramped his style" and "issued unnecessary directives" and with an examiner who refused to be convinced by Pnin's arguments about the ludicrous nature of some rules of the road. Pnin's car is turning aimlessly along forest roads as he desperately searches for his friend's summerhouse. Our hero has been misdirected by the gasoline attendant: "'[T]here is a better way to get there. [...] The trucks have messed up that road, and besides you won't like the way it winds. Now you just drive on. [...] Take the first left turn. It's a good gravel road.' He stepped briskly around the hood and lunged with his rag at the windshield from the other side. 'You turn north'" (114). Pnin follows the directions of this "chance busybody" and gets lost. The nadir of desperation is reached when the wind subsides and a squirrel is shot at in the trees. (Its would-be killer is a gameskeeper who is also a pathological bookbinder—a perfect counter-agent for Nabokov.) But the squirrel escapes and so does Pnin. "Everything happen[ed] at once," the sun comes out, an ant's "inept perseverance" at reaching the top of an observation tower is rewarded, and Pnin's "*vari*ous indecisions and gropings" finally lead him to a sign "directing" wayfarers to "The Pines" (112–15, emphasis added).

This scene is a forerunner of the novel's finale, in which Pnin wins his battle against the narrative that so seeks to misdirect him, to turn him wrong and so—narratively—to pervert him. In chapter 7 the narrator claims that his first recollection of Pnin "is connected with a speck of coal dust that entered my left eye" on a "gusty" morning in 1911. He is bothered by "the granule of smarting pain in the far north of my eyeball" (175). "Home remedies, such as the application of wads of cotton wool soaked in cool tea and the tri-k-nosu (rub noseward) device, only made matters worse" (175). The ocular locus of the narrator's pain repeats the hairy-armed attendant's misdirection—left and northward; in the "*tri-k-nosu* device" readers should hear the final sound of the parasite theme that has already been provided as a narrative figure of author-hero relations.[21] Now, however, Pnin is protected from "insidious drafts" and the narrator is the object of *his* author's gust.[22]

On the last day described in the novel, the narrator is eager to have a look at Pnin before his erstwhile "friend" escapes, and so he rises early and sets out for a walk. His route retraces the instructions of the gasoline attendant: "I turned left, northward, and walked a couple of blocks downhill," but suddenly he sees Pnin driving off in a sedan. "Then the little sedan boldly swung past the front truck and, free at last, spurted up the shining road, which one could make out narrowing to a thread of gold in the soft mist where hill after hill made beauty of distance, and where there was simply no saying what miracle might happen" (190–91). Here Pnin—like Krug and Cincinnatus before him—manages something of an escape from narrative—there is now *no saying* what might happen to him. (Are those two trucks the covers of the book?) A captive audience of the obsessive Pnin-mimicry of Cockerell, the narrator seems to have fallen victim to his own devices:

> By midnight the fun began to thin; the smile I was keeping afloat began to develop, I felt, symptoms of labial cramp. Finally the whole thing grew to be such a bore that I fell wondering if by some poetical

---

21. According to the narrator, Pnin regards his heart "with a queasy dread, a nervous repulsion, a sick hate, as if it were some strong slimy untouchable monster that one had to be parasitized with, alas" (20).

22. The narrator's last night in *Pnin* is in some respects similar to the last night of the child molester in *The Enchanter*. Both are about to be undone on the last page of the work that contains them, and in both cases their final evening is disturbed by trucks: "The thunder of trucks rocked the house every two minutes or so; I kept dozing off and sitting up with a gasp, and through the parody of a window shade some light from the street reached the mirror and dazzled me into thinking I was facing a firing squad" (*Pnin,* 190). Cf. *The Enchanter,* 71: "With the roar of cannon fire a truck ascended from the bottom of the night."

vengeance this Pnin business had not become with Cockerell the kind
of fatal obsession which substitutes its own victim for that of the initial
ridicule. (189)

Here part of the vengeance entails the employment of the book's genital
thematics at not only Cockerell's but also the narrator's own expense: *afloat,
labial cramp, the whole thing* become a bore. The novel's penultimate paragraph
describes Cockerell letting in his "cocker" (spaniel) and leading the narrator
"to a British breakfast of depressing kidney and fish." We have returned to
the cartoon of chapter 2: "the sailor imagines the mermaid as having a pair
of legs, and the cat imagines her as all fish." The cat has had its way, but now
it is the narrator who has nofing left.[23]

Of course, Pnin does not escape from the novel *Pnin;* Nabokov has created him and this is a game that the character can never win. Spurting free
of the book on his birthday, the "infantine-eyed" (179) Pnin forgets Liza's
mentor's "theory of birth being an act of suicide on the part of the infant"
(183).[24] But there are various degrees of defeat, and Pnin has succeeded in
escaping from one plot to another, from a merely perverse to a poetic world.
Or has he? For Nabokov the opposition between perversity and poetry is
constantly undergoing deconstruction: the existence of each can only be
verified by—indeed, is predicated on—its reflection in the other. When
Pnin is introduced as a speaker to an audience, his name is given as "Professor Pun-neen" (26), and we may think of him as a personification of a pun's
effects. What is a pun but a verbal squint, a distortion of meaning achieved
through the superimposition of two meanings, of a text and a shadow text?
Puns are poetry—often bad poetry—in miniature, and Pnin's name reveals
his essential, inescapable tie to art's necessary perversion: the novel's central
metafictive concern.

The relationship between art and perversity is posited with most force in
the treatment of Victor's painting and his effect on the narration of Pnin's
life. Victor's intervention in Pnin's story seems in retrospect to be the point
at which Pnin's narrator "friend" first loses control over his "subject." For a
while, Pnin literally escapes from the text as Victor takes center stage. The

---

23. The kidney also recalls an earlier moment in the mockery of Pnin—his claim that Tolstoy's
Ivan Ilyich died of "kidney of the cancer" (108). In this instance, too, an earlier joke at Pnin's expense
returns as part of the narrator's discomfiture.

24. The second sentence of the novel refers to Pnin's "infantile absence of eyebrows" (7). The
adjective is appropriate, for Pnin the character has just been born.

novel's telltale syllable continues to wriggle along the sentences of this chapter, but here—just as in the Cinderella story—glass begins to take over. Glass features prominently in several of the descriptions of Victor's art: "In the chrome plating, in the glass of a sun-rimmed headlamp, [Victor] would see a view of the street and himself comparable to the microcosmic version of a room (with a dorsal view of diminutive people) in that very special and very magical small convex mirror that, half a millennium ago, Van Eyck and Petrus Christus and Memling used to paint into their detailed interiors" (97–98). Victor prepares to paint by first placing "*vari*ous objects in *turn*" "behind a *glass* of water and studying their distortion (98, emphasis added). Glass is as important a characteristic image for Victor as the squirrel is for Pnin and is most marked in the "perfectly divine" bowl with its "pure inner blaze" (157, 153) that Victor gives his surrogate father.

The climactic scene in which Pnin drops a nutcracker into the sink and almost breaks the bowl may be viewed as a contest between creative forces—two phonic brothers (*vair/verre*) in translation. In *Pnin* these two markers of antagonistic versions of poetic control operate like malignant (or indifferent) and benign gods. The squirrel accords Pnin little pleasure, using him for her own purposes. Their earlier meeting by the water fountain reads like a one-sided sexual encounter, with Pnin striving to satisfy an unresponsive partner:

> He seemed to be quite unexpectedly (for human despair seldom leads to great truths) on the verge of a simple solution of the universe but was interrupted by an urgent request. A squirrel under a tree had seen Pnin on the path. In one sinuous tendril-like movement, the intelligent animal climbed up to the brim of a drinking fountain and, as Pnin approached, thrust its oval face toward him with a rather coarse spluttering sound, its cheeks puffed out. Pnin understood and after some fumbling he found what had to be pressed for the necessary results. Eyeing him with contempt, the thirsty rodent forthwith began to sample the stocky sparkling pillar of water, and went on drinking for a considerable time. "She has fever, perhaps," thought Pnin, weeping quietly and freely, and all the time politely pressing the contraption down while trying not to meet the unpleasant eye fixed upon him. Its thirst quenched, the squirrel departed without the least sign of gratitude. (58)

Victor's bowl brings Pnin a more pleasurable, nearly erotic experience, with a better outcome. While reading the following description of Pnin doing dishes, we should recall that Victor has "known the sensuous delight of a graded wash" (98) and that the last word we have read before encountering the paragraphs below is "pleasure":

> He prepared a bubble bath in the sink for the crockery, glass, and silverware, and with infinite care lowered the aquamarine bowl into the tepid foam. Its resonant flint glass emitted a sound full of muffled mellowness as it settled down to soak. He rinsed the amber goblets and the silverware under the tap, and submerged them in the same foam. Then he fished out the knives, forks, and spoons, rinsed them, and began to wipe them. He worked very slowly, with a certain vagueness of manner that might have been taken for a mist of abstraction in a less methodical man. He gathered the wiped spoons into a posy, placed them in a pitcher which he had washed but not dried, and then took them out one by one and wiped them all over again. He groped under the bubbles, around the goblets, and under the melodious bowl, for any piece of forgotten silver—and retrieved a nutcracker. Fastidious Pnin rinsed it, and was wiping it, when the leggy thing somehow slipped out of the towel and fell like a man from a roof. He almost caught it—his fingertips actually came into contact with it in mid-air, but this only helped to propel it into the treasure-concealing foam of the sink, where an excruciating crack of broken glass followed upon the plunge.
>
> Pnin hurled the towel into a corner and, turning away, stood for a moment staring at the blackness beyond the threshold of the open back door. A quiet, lacy-winged little green insect circled in the glare of a strong naked lamp above Pnin's glossy bald head. He looked very old, with his toothless mouth half open and a film of tears dimming his blank, unblinking eyes. Then, with a moan of anguished anticipation, he went back to the sink and, bracing himself, dipped his hand deep into the foam. A jagger of glass stung him. Gently he removed a broken goblet. The beautiful bowl was intact. He took a fresh dish towel and went on with his household work.
>
> When everything was clean and dry, and the bowl stood aloof and serene on the safest shelf of a cupboard, and the little bright house was securely locked up in the large dark night, Pnin sat down at the kitchen table, and, taking a sheet of yellow scrap paper from its drawer, unclipped his fountain pen and started to compose the draft of a letter (172).

This crucial scene leads in two directions, to two negatively charged scenes in related works. Pnin's dishwashing has muffled but nonetheless insistent echoes of Ophelia's death: he is gathering silverware "into a posy," the "melodious bowl" echoes the flower-gathering Ophelia's "melodious lays," even the silver may recall the treacherous "sliver" that breaks beneath Ophelia's weight. Pnin's "abstraction" may be a muted reminder of Shakespearean madness; the *Hamlet* connection is reinforced by a famous phrase that suffuses the surrounding words: "a mist of abstraction in a less methodical man." ("Though this be madness, yet there is method in't" [2.2.203–4]. As in *Hamlet,* this abstraction has its sexual elements: the melodious bowl, the leggy thing, the treasure-concealing foam, Pnin's moan of anticipation, the excruciating crack, the sting of glass, the uncharacteristic, subdued, largely monosyllabic postcoital calm of the last quoted paragraph ("the large dark night"). Here, though, the underwater disaster that would be the equivalent of drowning is prevented: the bowl is brought back whole from its watery grave and placed on the safest shelf. This safe conclusion to an erotically charged scene points in another direction—Humbert's tussle with Lolita on the davenport: "Absolutely no harm done. The conjurer had poured milk, molasses, foaming champagne into a young lady's new white purse; and lo, the purse was intact. Thus had I delicately constructed my ignoble, ardent sinful dream; and still Lolita was safe—and I was safe" (62). In this case, too, the ominous subtext for the scene has been undone, the squirrel's power has yielded to the glass, the homonym which, as in the Cinderella story, has emerged in "an obvious case of the survival of the fittest" (158). Now Pnin can pick up the pen and begin—"in his clear firm hand"—to write his own story.[25] His triumph is apparent on a first reading, but comprehension of the extent of Pnin's victory is dependent on the reader's willingness to leer at the passage and so glimpse the homonymic and intertextual forces hard bent on Pnin's story's corruption.

Perversion would seem to be condemned by the examples I have cited: the perversion of Ophelia's sad tale and the mistelling of Pnin's story are evil narrative deeds. But the irony is that Nabokov's texts *must* be perverted—read improperly—if their richness is to be properly appreciated. At one point Pnin seems vaguely cognizant of the narrative distortion to which he is subjected: "he was perhaps too wary, too persistently on the lookout for diabolical pitfalls, too painfully alert lest his erratic surroundings (unpredictable America) inveigle him into some bit of preposterous oversight" (13). "Preposterous" owes its meaning to an etymology of inversion; it is derived from the Latin

---

25. Pnin writes with a *fountain* pen a detail that serves as an echo and reversal of the earlier encounter with the squirrel by the fountain. His prose is eloquent, and he crosses out the one mistake "recaputilate" that still survives here as an incompletely effaced trace of his mockery: a hint that while the tide has turned, his struggle with the narrator is still not over.

praeposterus, meaning reversed or perverted, and its original English meaning is "having or placing last that which should be first, inverted in position or order." In Elizabethan drama the word was used bawdily—"hind-side before" to refer to anal intercourse (Henke, 202)—this is how Shakespeare uses it in *Troilus and Cressida*[26]—and we might extend this connotation to the narrator's chief source for anecdotes about Pnin: Jack Cockerell, evidently one of the people of the lunar light: "a rather limp, *moon*-faced, *neutr*ally blond English-man" (187, emphasis added). In a metafictive sense, this preposterous over-sight is the narrator's in that it absurdly, outrageously perverts Pnin's story. Yet preposterous oversight is not only a description of Cockerell's tale-telling; it is also the duty of the good reader. "True understanding" of *Pnin*—and of any novel by Nabokov—requires the reader to read the early portions of the book with knowledge derived from the book's latter end. An adequate reading of Nabokov can *only* be preposterous... and complicitly perverse.

Pnin's fate in many respects hinges on a battle between two preposterous constructions, and this struggle is often figured as a tug-of-war between left- and right-leaning versifiers. Pnin is unaware of the full dimensions of this contention, but he is repeatedly depicted in the process of left-right alterna-tion. On the bus to Cremona, he is tortured by anxiety: "Ever since he had been separated from his bag, the tip of his left forefinger had been alternating with the proximal edge of his right elbow in checking a precious presence in his inside coat pocket" (19). Pnin's "tussle with the wallpaper" contains a ter-rific example of Nabokovian misdirection... with the clue to a fundamental pattern disguised as "mere" hermeneutic process:

> He had always been able to see that in the vertical plane a combination
> made up of three different clusters of purple flowers and seven different
> oak leaves was repeated a number of times with soothing exactitude; but
> now he was bothered by the undismissable fact that he could not find
> what system of inclusion and circumscription governed the horizontal
> recurrence of the pattern; that such a recurrence existed was proved by
> his being able to pick out here and there, all along the wall from bed
> to wardrobe and from stove to door, the reappearance of this or that
> element of the series, but when he tried traveling right or left from any
> chosen set of three inflorescences and seven leaves, he forthwith lost
> himself in a meaningless tangle of rhododendron and oak. (23)

---

26. 5.1.16–19. According to Gordon Williams, in *Love's Labor's Lost* when "Armado describes an act of coition as 'that obscene and most preposterous event,' he means only that he discovered Costard performing arse-upwards." But in *Troilus and Cressida* "when Thersites [...] would have 'the rotten diseases of the south [...] take and take again such preposterous discoveries,' he has in mind the homosexual relationship between Achilles and Patroclus" (244). See also Rubinstein, 202.

Pnin's pedagogical pose has been described a few pages earlier in similar terms: "Feverishly, he would flip right and left through the volume, and minutes might pass before he found the right page" (12). Poor Pnin does not understand that the direction one travels is as important as one's destination; like all characters he lacks the ability to reread his life repeatedly until he gets it right.[27] If Pnin's enemies have their way, "Assistant Professor Pnin must be left in the lurch"—a phrase doubly connotative of sinistrality because "lurch" is derived from a Middle High German word referring to the left hand (*Webster's New International,* 1469).

Finding the *right* page would be akin to reversing the perverse narrator's bend sinister. And as in *Bend Sinister,* the heart is a particularly intense metafictive battleground, reflecting the emotional temptations and threats posed to Pnin from portside. A bad versifier, Liza is definitely a sinister— if still pathetic—force: "I haf nofing *left,* nofing, nofing!"[28] Pnin's narrator adopts cardiological precision when discussing Pnin's physical ailments (20); "a shadow behind the heart" might be a "good title for a bad novel"—the one the narrator is writing (126). Pnin is right to refuse to sleep on his left side and to refuse the narrator's offer—made in "the most *cor*dial" [or heart-y] of terms—to remain at Waindell as the narrator's assistant (186). "It warmed my heart, the Russian-intelligentski way he had of getting into his overcoat" (65), the narrator condescendingly writes, and this association of bad writing and sentimentality ought to give pause to readers who like *Pnin* for its uncharacteristic warmth.

The description of Mira's possible fates ("gassed in a sham shower bath with prussic acid") would seem to be the "heart" of a sentimental, emotionally charged reading of *Pnin.* Yet even here, a perverted, lewd reading is plausible, for in the sentence's Teutonic setting (the concentration camp, the prussic acid), the phrase "sham (*scham*) shower bath" provides a German "translation" of the *chat-eau*/douche theme discussed above. The memories of Mira are "conjured up" by "chatty madam Shpolyanski," the first in the chapter to mention her fate (134). Pnin finds he has to try to forget Mira's death at Buchenwald, located "in the cultural heart of Germany" (135) "because one could not live with the thought that this graceful, fragile, tender young woman with those eyes, that smile, those gardens and snows in the background, had been brought in a cattle car to an extermination camp and killed by an injection of phenol into the heart, into the *gentle heart* one

---

27. The left-right opposition, significant in many of Nabokov's books, is probably most marked in *Look at the Harlequins!* See Johnson, *Worlds in Regression,* 170–84.

28. "Nofing left" may be a nod to the conclusion of *Bend Sinister,* when "nothing" is similarly given a slight visual and phonetic twist: "A good night for mothing."

had heard beating under one's lips in the dusk of the past" (135, emphasis added). Indeed, if the evil aesthetic force in *Bend Sinister* transforms the heart into an arse, in an equally demeaning gesture those same "leftist" forces in *Pnin* threaten to turn it into vulva.[29]

In what Barabtarlo correctly terms a metafictive and textually self-descriptive comment (*Phantom of Fact*, 245), Joan Clements asks: "But don't you think—haw—that what he is trying to do—haw—practically in all his novels—haw—is—haw—to express the fantastic recurrence of certain situations?" (159). "Haw" is a cart driver's command to turn left, and here can be heard the narrator's attempt to steer this book in his own, perverted direction as he struggles with *his* driving instructor. We find the complementary command a page earlier: "Roy Thayer [...] had squandered a decade of gray life on an erudite work dealing with a forgotten group of unnecessary poetasters, and kept a detailed diary, in cryptogrammed verse, which he hoped posterity would someday decipher and, in sober backcast, proclaim the greatest literary achievement of our time—and for all I know, Roy Thayer, you might be *right*" (157, emphasis added). I don't mean to suggest that Thayer is the real author of *Pnin,* but I do want to stress that in its "cryptogrammed verse," Thayer's possibly dextral diary provides a model for the book's use of the squirrel and names the novel's fundamental device, albeit with a twist: as an idea and as a word, "verse" (*vers*) is cryptogrammed (in the squirrel, in glass) in prose. The novel has already linked Pushkin to the word "cryptogram" and we can see Thayer, who twists napkins into "all kinds of weird shapes" (171) as a lesser, latter-day incarnation of the great poet.[30] ("*Squandered*" and "gray life" may be further echoes of the squirrel; "detailed"(de-tailed?) may both invoke and work against that beast).[31] Thayer's name is pronounced by Pnin as "Feuer" and "Fire" (31); it may be that his name and the narrator's association with "fever" establish the two as pale if mutually antipathetic hypostases of authorial brilliance, as the forerunners of a later text's Shade and Kinbote. Just as important as Thayer's name and his penchant for cryptogrammed verse is his hope that "posterity would someday decipher and in sober backcast" acclaim his work. "Sober backcast" provides an apt description of the preposterous oversight required of Nabokov's necessarily perverse reader.

---

29. The epitome of this equation is Liza: "'There is nothing softer than your heart.' / And I lowered my gaze" (181). Just as he represents a kinder, more generous form of art, Victor offers the promise of a redemption of the image of the heart: his dream of an ideal father is redolent with this image: "at the heart of that heart sat the King" (85).

30. Bodenstein (1:223) and Barabtarlo ("Pushkin Embedded," 28–29) have noted the presence of poetic lines in Thayer's diary.

31. Victor's work is indebted to "Van Eyck and Petrus Christus and Memling," who used to paint magical mirrors "into their detailed interiors" (97–98).

"And now," Pnin's obsessive imitator Cockerell says in the book's final words: "I am going to tell you the story of Pnin rising to address the Cremona Women's Club and discovering he had brought the wrong lecture" (191). Readers should be taken aback—we thought we knew that Pnin had corrected his mistake (jumped off the bus, obtained his valise, secured the right paper)—yet the irony is that whether the novel becomes the right or the wrong *lecture* (in the French sense of the word, a reading) depends on the reader's having been sufficiently perverse to grasp the nature of the narrative pressures to which Pnin has been subjected. In this sense, important lectures are always cata-strophic.

Let us return to the scene of Pnin discovering his mistake: "Emitting what he thought were international exclamations of anxiety and entreaty, Pnin lurched out of his seat. Reeling, he reached the exit. With one hand the driver grimly milked out a handful of coins from his little machine, refunded him the price of the ticket, and stopped the bus" (19). Although we don't realize it at the time, this was Pnin's escape from the pervert's narrative world. *The Brothers Karamazov* has been comically invoked a few pages earlier—Eileen Lane has been told that when one masters the Russian alphabet, "one could practically read 'Anna Karamazov' in the original" (10)—and later Pnin will consider that "no conscience, and hence no consciousness, could be expected to subsist in a world where such things as Mira's death were possible" (135). The catalogue of deaths which might have befallen Mira in a concentration camp—"inoculated with filth, tetanus bacilli, broken glass, gassed in a sham shower bath with prussic acid, burned alive in a pit on a gasoline-soaked pile of beechwood"—is an updated version of Dostoevsky's novel's list of tortures which God ought not to countenance and which lead Ivan Karamazov to reject God's world: "Too high a price is paid for harmony [. . .]. And so I hasten to give back my entrance ticket" (226). We can't realize the significance of Pnin's exit from the bus until we reread it. Refusing to submit to a world of pain and suffering, Pnin has already done—in his novel's first chapter—what Ivan Karamazov only threatened to do, resisting narrative perversion—Nabokov's characteristically procedural version of Dostoevsky's notion of evil—by hastening to return his ticket. Many readers, on the contrary, may be sufficiently impressed with the creator to want another ride. Indeed, the pursuit of understanding virtually demands the purchase of a second (and a third, and a fourth) trip. Pnin's courageous and narratively blasphemous rejection of his author's vehicle allows us to take his place, preposterously. In this world no rereader can be an atheist, and were he to read *Pnin,* Ivan Karamazov might respond: "I know that I believe in God only when I read Vladimir Nabokov." That would be no mean concession, for if rereading is endless, so is belief.

❦ CHAPTER 4

Hermophobia

(On Sexual Orientation and Reading Nabokov)

What is to be done with the homosexuals who inhabit Nabokov's novels? These characters, whose sexual preference is so immediately legible, so caricatured, raise questions about the role of excess in the work of an author so famously focused on the control of every word in a highly organized aesthetic structure. Some readers may be tempted to look away, dismissing Nabokov's homosexuals as a sign of his times and a feature without fundamental importance to an appreciation of his work, but scholars have produced several attempts to address this issue. Most of the work falls into one of three categories: the political, which has revolved around alleged homophobia (Ohi); the philological, which traces Nabokov's use of homosexual imagery and characters back to Russian predecessors in prose, poetry, and philosophy (Etkind; Skonechnaia, "People of the Moonlight"; Rylkova); and the biographical, including Brandon Centerwall's suggestion that Nabokov was molested by his uncle and Anna Brodsky's more sensitively couched argument that *The Gift* was shaped in part by Nabokov's anguished response to the homosexuality of his younger brother, Sergei. Much of the writing on this question has been character-centered and thus fundamentally inadequate to the richness of Nabokov's metafictive concerns. Here I want to try to suggest a different way of approaching the question, one that is sensitive to some of the concerns of queer theory and to the quiddities of Nabokov's world. Recontextualizing criticism is often of limited value when directed at Nabokov; a generalizing ideological force obscures everything that makes Nabokov worth reading. Yet we may find surprising, productive compatibilities between critical work on sexual orientation and the study of Nabokov if we seek the overlap in the area of metafiction and pay attention not to characters but to the *process* of interpretation. Sexual and hermeneutic desires and anxieties are bound up in Nabokov's fiction, and the excitement of getting Nabokov right is shadowed by an interpretive panic that is part of the preprogrammed experience of mastering and being mastered by his texts.

In his reply to Edmund Wilson and other critics of his translation of Pushkin's *Eugene Onegin,* Nabokov expressed irritation over "the amount of unwillful deceit going on in the translation trade." "I recall once opening a copy of Bely's *Petersburg* in English, and lighting upon a monumental howler in a famous passage about a blue coupé which had been hopelessly discolored by the translator's understanding *kubovyy* (which means "blue") as cubic! [*kubovoi*] This has remained a model and a symbol" (*Strong Opinions,* 243). But most of the unwillful deceit here is, it turns out, Nabokov's. The word *kubovyi,* which is sufficiently rare as to be glossed for the educated Russian reader by the editors of the authoritative *Literaturnye pamiatniki* edition, is *not* used in the famous scene of Ableukhov's trip to his ministry, where Bely describes the carriage as black—*chernyi kub karety* (21). *Kubovyi* does appear once in *Petersburg,* where it modifies *vozdukh* (air).[1] In that instance, John Cournos, the author of the only English translation of *Petersburg* at the time of Nabokov's remark, correctly translates it: "the indigo air" (183). Yet this mistake by Nabokov has an interesting prehistory. In a letter to his friend, the émigré poet Khodasevich, written around twenty-five years earlier, Nabokov noted: "*Ia chital Peterburg raza chetyre—v upoenii—no davno*" (I've read Petersburg four times, with elation, but long ago), and he cited "*kubovyi kub karety*" as one of several puns he had particularly liked (Malmstad, 278). In other words, Nabokov himself came up with a pun on *kubovyi/kubovoi,* retrospectively—and inaccurately—inscribed it in *Petersburg* as an example of Bely's genius, and

---

1. I am grateful to Alexander Dolinin for pointing out the presence of *kubovyi* in *Petersburg* when I expressed my bewilderment at not finding it where Nabokov said it would be (See our two posts, both entitled "VN and Translating Bely.") Dolinin has subsequently gone on to publish an article on Nabokov's use of the word, tracing its appearance in *Drugie berega,* Nabokov's Russian version of his autobiography, to Bunin's employment of the word in his poetry and prose (*Istinnaia zhizn',* 338–45).

still later used the phrase as evidence of an inept translation. This nexus of bad translations, genius, and Nabokov's own wordplay is intriguing: if bad translations did not exist, did Nabokov have his reasons for inventing them? In at least one novel he did. In *Look at the Harlequins,* Nabokov's final, parodically autobiographical work, his hero enjoys similar sport with another translation mistake:

> I recall regaling the company with one of the howlers I had noticed in the "translation" of [Lermontov's poem] *Tamara.* The sentences *vidnelos' neskol'ko barok* ("several barges could be seen") had become *la vue était assez baroque.* The eminent critic Basilevski, a stocky, fair-haired old fellow in a rumpled brown suit, shook with abdominal mirth—but then his expression changed to one of suspicion and displeasure. After tea he accosted me and insisted gruffly that I had made up that example of mistranslation. I remember answering that, if so, he, too, might well be an invention of mine. (58)

Bad translators play a large role in Nabokov's oeuvre. Some are fictitious, others are real but achieve the status of mock-heroic characters in Nabokov's scholarship, such as his edition of *Eugene Onegin,* where, to my mind, at least, Nabokov's predecessors—"bluff," "Matter-of-fact Lt.-Col. Spalding," "the entomologically minded Miss Radin," "solecistic Prof. Elton," who "can always be depended upon for triteness and awkwardness," not to mention "alas, poor Brodsky"—are more vivid characters in Nabokov's commentary than Eugene or Tatyana in his translation (2:103, 116, 319, 464, 304). Indeed, the *Onegin* commentary is a monument to bad translators: many of the specimens of their work are presented with great flair that testifies to Nabokov's curatorial appreciation for what he had earlier called "the art of the gaffe" (*Sobranie sochinenii,* 4: 597). Nabokov relished inept translators just as he did examples from the larger, equally charming category of bad readers, for what is a bad translator but a bad reader who has publicly given himself away, a reader who is unambiguously wrong? Emma Bovary is a bad reader, Anna Karenina is another (*Lectures on Russian Literature,* 157), and in Nabokov's lectures that is probably a worse sin than adultery. Nabokov talked a lot about good readers, too. The volume *Lectures on Literature* opens with the essay "Good Readers and Good Writers" which includes Nabokov's famous quiz: which of the following ten characteristics define a good reader? On that list there are more items defining a bad reader (six) than a good one (four) (3). The distinction between good and bad readers seems so clear, so fundamental, so stable. The frequency with which scholars writing about Nabokov themselves employ these terms indicates their continued importance to the field and to the scholars' sense of professional identity.

But how stable is the distinction? And what practices are employed to keep it in place? We might start by considering the disciplinary function of a *quiz* to get at the essence of good reading. Tests might not necessarily entail right and wrong answers, but they certainly bring with them well-known power dynamics and the possibility of shame, humiliation, and—even for a student who gets things right—a certain uneasiness at having pleased the teacher by divining and responding to pedagogic desire. Nabokov's story "The Vane Sisters" has become something of a touchstone for the recent wave of writing preoccupied with Nabokov's interest in the next world, but we should not forget that the story works in many respects like a test. Sybil Vane, one of the work's hidden authors, kills herself after her midterm examination. The narrator-professor, who has broken up Sybil's affair with his colleague, D., and is evidently unhappy that D. "must have known [Sybil's] body down to its last velvet detail," has spent this exam feeling "acutely unhappy about my dutiful little student" and looking her over with such persistence that a reader might be reminded that an exam is a medical as well as pedagogical term (*Stories,* 622, 621). (Even his correcting of his student's paper is charged with libidinal energy: "Next day, having arranged the ugly copybooks alphabetically, I plunged into their chaos of scripts and came prematurely to Valevsky and Vane, whose books I had somehow misplaced" [621]. The reason for his coming prematurely is not only the different places of V in the Cyrillic and Latin alphabets.) The joke is that the narrator fails to discern the signs of the Vane sisters' ghost writing in his own universe, as do most readers when they fail to see the acrostic confirming the sisters' authorship in the last paragraph. The story begins on "a compunctious Sunday" not just because the narrator has not gone to church but also because even when the good reader pays attention he cannot help feeling that he might be giving this work of art more (619). Nabokov's revelation of his concluding acrostic in a subsequently written introduction to the work—"this particular trick can be tried only once in a thousand years of fiction" (*Stories,* 659)—establishes in today's reader a sense of both belatedness and hopelessness: this is now a story about reading practices that from a position halfway between interpellation and ogling dares its readers to come up to the mark while at the same time withdrawing the possibility of showing that they are *really* good.

For another insight into how bad reading necessarily subtends good reading of Nabokov, let us look at the article that closes his *Lectures on Literature:* "The Art of Literature and Commonsense." Common sense is common, the opposite of artistic imagination. "Commonsense," Nabokov writes, "has trampled down many a gentle genius whose eyes had delighted in a too early moonbeam of some too early truth; commonsense has back-kicked dirt at the loveliest of queer paintings because a blue tree seemed madness to its well-meaning hoof" (372). The good writer is always threatened by common sense: "the more brilliant, the more unusual the man, the nearer he is to the stake. *Stranger* always rhymes with *danger*" (372). Strangeness would seem unmistakably positive. But a few pages later, Nabokov reverses the terms when he turns his attention to "badness": "Now 'badness' is a stranger to our inner world; it eludes our grasp; 'badness' is in fact the lack of something rather than a noxious presence; and thus being abstract and bodiless it occupies no real space in our inner world" (375–76). The stranger, so clearly the emblem of good art, is also a figure used to describe bad art, though in the essay the two would seem to be polar opposites.

The fear of being a bad reader, of not measuring up to the master's high expectation, is a characteristic feature of Nabokov studies. This hermeneutic performance anxiety was effectively captured by a Wesleyan undergraduate who posted a query several years ago on NABOKV-L. Andrew Fippinger described himself as in the midst of "a cosmic crisis of sorts," which had "managed to blow way out of proportion" in his life. He felt that on some basic level he still did not understand *Lolita,* which he had read four times; the rest of Nabokov's oeuvre also held him in an enthralling but frustrating grip:

> The level at which VN requires his readers to read makes me feel as though I am at best an attentive reader, but nothing more. I question whether I have any future whatsoever in scholarly literary studies when books such as *Despair* (which I have also read four times) or *Sebastian Knight* (three times) continuously throw me for a loop and leave me feeling as though I understand the novel worse than after I had read the backcover for the first time. I love Nabokov, I love his style, his mastery of the language [...] and his deep grasp of subtextual complications and motif placement, but I still feel without reward or at least without comprehension having read and "reread," as he would require, most of his books. I have performed personal studies of word and theme motifs, I have read scholarly literature, I have even tried parodying him myself in order to gain some low level mastery of his work. And yet, I feel as though I haven't gotten much further than that low level mastery; I understand his themes and his general biography, of course, but do I really understand his novels on half the level that he would expect? [...] All I'm asking is: are these common symptoms of the young Nabokov reader, is Nabokov possibly just way beyond me, have I simplified literature too much to even understand it deeper than

the surface level? [...] Of course, you don't know me personally and thus cannot respond to me in particular, but I would like to know if these are common feelings of the young Nabokov scholar, or if I'm just out of my league. [...] I only request that you post this message, because I am looking for others who might have felt the same on the way up and can offer me some advice.

This post captures the anxiety that many readers of Nabokov experience but few scholars dare to put into print. Have I met the Master's expectations? On the surface, the electronically published query has nothing to say about sexuality and should not be read in any way as expressing anything about the author's libidinal desires. Its form, however, closely follows that found in appeals to sexual health experts and advice columnists, and it presents a fascinating example of how Nabokov's writing channels readers' anxieties about their interpretive performance into expressive forms frequently used to deal with worries about sexual performance and function. Is this simply because Nabokov writes so frequently about sex? Or are his texts doing something else to bring the circuits of interpretation and sexual desire into this sort of formal conjunction?

Let's look at one more instance of the anxieties represented by a specific reader. The most striking example of the energy that must be expended to keep good and bad apart is provided by Nabokov's treatment of William Woodin Rowe in that hostile 1971 review I have already sampled: "The purpose of the present review is not to answer a critic but to ask him to remove his belongings." Taking umbrage at Rowe's unearthing of sexual symbols in *Lolita* and *Ada*, Nabokov derided the scholar's "preposterous and nasty interpretations":

I wish to share with him the following secret: In the case of a certain type of writer it often happens that a whole paragraph or sinuous sentence exists as a discrete organism, with its own imagery, its own invocations, its own bloom, and then it is especially precious, and also vulnerable, so that if an outsider, immune to poetry and common sense, injects spurious symbols into it, or actually tampers with its wording (see Mr. Rowe's crass attempt on his page 113), its magic is replaced by maggots. (*Strong Opinions*, 305)

There is a strong sense of disgust in the passage, and we may feel that we've seen this scene before, in clichéd rejections and revulsed banishments of unwanted desire. ("How could you possibly think I meant that?!")

The phrases "crass attempts" and "preposterous and nasty" are often cited gleefully by Nabokov scholars, but the sexual orientation of their phonetics has not been taken into account. These words might be given a physical locus if mounted next to a few other similar phrases in Nabokov's fiction, some more overtly sexually evocative than others but all invoking anality in a condemnation of aesthetic taste: Kinbote's "cr*ass* b*anal*ities circulated by the scurrilous and the heartless" (*Pale Fire*, 85), Pnin's condemnation of "conventional neo-pl*a*sticism or b*anal* non-objectivism" (96), Cynthia Vane's description as "curiously frowzy, after a way I obscurely *ass*ociated with left-wing enthusiasms in politics and 'advanced' b*anal*ities in art" (*Stories*, 623), Humbert's disgust at seeing in the Haze household "that b*anal* darling of the arty middle cl*ass,* van Gogh's "*Arlé*sienne" (*Lolita*, 36), as well as two extended alliterative cruises in *Pale Fire*: "a haughty and morose captive, he was caged in his rose-stone pal*ace* from a corner turret of which one could make out with the help of field gl*ass*es lithe youths diving into the swimming pool of a *fairy tale* sport club, and the English amb*ass*ador in old-fashioned flannels playing tennis with the B*as*que coach on a clay court as remote as paradise" (119); "Proust's rough m*as*terpiece was a huge, ghoulish *fairy tale,* an *as*paragus dream, totally un*con*nected with any possible people in any historical France, a sexual *travestissement* and a colo*ss*al *farce*" (162, here, as elsewhere in this paragraph, emphasis added). (The compunctious reader should observe the way the sexualized French (*travestissement*) activates the in-this-case unconnected "*con*". She should note, too, the mirror effect in the last nine letters of the sentence—colossal farce—as well as the possible chiming in of the first syllable in colossal: *cul*). We'll come back to this matter of posteriority. Notice for now that Rowe is condemned for lacking—of all things—common sense.

Part of the savagery of Nabokov's response may reside in the anxiety that Rowe is the reader—a stranger to "common sense"—whom Nabokov has been courting for decades but whose disturbing emergence parallels that of many fantasies that come true in real life. In this respect, I think Rowe's sex mattered. Despite his work's appearance in the pages of *Playboy,* I probably cannot prove with any rigor that Nabokov's ideal reader was male or that Nabokov wrote chiefly for men. He dedicates nearly all of his novels to his wife, a thoughtful, protective first reader. But if we return to our initial association of translators with textual interpreters, it is worth recalling Nabokov's expressed preference that his translators be male:

> I need a man who knows English better than Russian—and a man, not a woman. I am frankly homosexual on the subject of translators. I would revise every sentence myself and keep in touch with him all the time, but I *must* have somebody to do the basic work and then to polish my corrections. The Gift was published serially in the

"Annales Contemporaines" (the great Russian review that appeared in Paris during 20 years, since 1920), but the war, or rather the complete destruction of Russian intellectual life in Paris by the German invasion, has made its appearance in book form impossible—naturally. (*Selected Letters,* 41)

Homosexuality here is frankly admitted...as a metaphor. In light of the callipygian passages quoted above, the placing of *The Gift* in the *Annales contemporaines*—a name more anatomically suggestive than the Russian title, *Sovremennye zapiski*—is part of a Nabokovian theme, and the adverb at the end of the passage—"naturally"—may have a normalizing, redemptive function that accounts for its seeming semantic inappropriateness in the sentence. The next day Nabokov followed up this missive to the publisher James Laughlin with further comments in which the themes of inversion and solicitation are marked:

Without a good deal of linguistic and poetical imagination it is useless tackling my stuff. I shall control the translation as to the precise meaning and nuance, but my English is not up to my Russian, so that even had I the necessary time I would not be able to do the thing alone. I know it is difficult to find a man who has enough Russian to understand my writings and at the same time can turn his English inside out and slice, chop, twist, volley, smash, kill, drive, half-volley, lob and place perfectly every word. [...] But difficult though it is, I think that such a person can be found. What about inserting an advertisement in some literary or professional review? (*Selected Letters,* 42–43)

Rowe's lack of common sense ought to have qualified him to be a good reader, but did he have *too much* imagination? I am less concerned with whether Nabokov was "right" than with the effect of Nabokov's criticism, with the way Rowe continues to serve as a howling object of disgust that allows *other* imaginative scholars to be good readers. By and large, Rowe-bashing and good reading of Nabokov go hand in hand. Attacks on Rowe function as a ritual gesture of identification with Nabokov—even (or especially) for the very best of Nabokov's readers:

although Rowe seems to have found himself in the right forest, his equipment is quite useless, for one does not hunt harlequins with an harquebus à croc (Barabtarlo, *Phantom of Fact,* 22).

Nabokov attacked Rowe's "preposterous and nasty" techniques of spotting sexual symbols in innocent contexts in his "Rowe's Symbols," *New York Review of Books,* October 1981, rept., *Strong Opinions*

(304–307). I criticize Rowe's identical techniques aimed at his new targets in my "Spectral Hypotheses": *Nabokov's Ada* (213–218). (Boyd, "The Problem of Pattern," 586)

Amazingly, Boyd's first book, *Nabokov's Ada: The Place of Consciousness,* contains a special fifteen-page appendix devoted to distinguishing his approach from Rowe's:

> The reader who has dipped into this book and knows William Woodin Rowe's *Nabokov's Spectral Dimension* may suppose Rowe and I are essentially in agreement. After all, we both note Nabokov's concern with an afterlife and both suggest that characters who die in the course of his stories may somehow come back into the action later, in ways that seem far from visible to the unwary reader. But it seems to me that not to make plain our disagreement would be a disservice to Nabokov. Rowe persistently trivializes his subject; were his findings true, Nabokov would be intellectually shallow and artistically cheap. Fortunately Rowe is quite wrong—wherever he does not merely muddy the self-evident. (237)

Nabokov's essay on good readers lays down guidelines for good reading, and it seems to suggest that there is such a thing as normative interpretation. Yet by tarring "common" as a negative characteristic, Nabokov strongly implies that good reading is always something special, that it must to some extent be abnormal and transgressive. The case of Rowe would seem to suggest that not all transgressions are permissible, a formulation that would undermine the very notion of transgression. There is, however, another way to view this dynamic. The community of Nabokov scholarship, by invoking the specter of Rowe, follows a road map charted by Nabokov's texts, which both encourage and chastise exceptionality. This dynamic can be observed in some of the most interesting works in the field, which simultaneously offer and ward off interpretations. Alfred Appel's *Annotated Lolita* contains "anti-annotations," necessary because "in a novel so allusive as *Lolita* it is only natural to be suspicious of the most innocuous references, and to search for allusions under every bush." "Anticipating the efforts of future exegetes," Appel offers "non-notes," which "simply state that Nabokov intended no allusion whatsoever" (334). The insertion of these notes denying allusions, however, serves in practice to bring to consciousness interpretations that would be wrong if the reader thought of them; they allow Appel to suggest readings for which he simultaneously disclaims responsibility. Gennady Barabtarlo's excellent book on *Pnin* is even more vociferous and conflicted in this regard. He responds as follows to the narrator's reference to a childhood toy, a monoplane with a rubber motor that would "change its manner of twist and develop fascinating thick whorls which predicted the end of its tether" (177):

> A simple allegoric parallel which crassly tempts the reader here should be gingerly brushed aside even if it lands on his lap of its own accord. Indeed, the "manner of twist" of the narration has perceptibly changed in this final chapter, having developed "fascinating thick whorls" of rapid recollections of N—'s previous encounters with Pnin. The end of the winding is near, the cord connecting them will snap soon, and the hooked hero will free himself from the ingenious puppeteer. But this kind of facile metatextual reading is too easy and too perilous even when it sounds true and promising. (*Phantom of Fact,* 269)[2]

Both Appel and Barabtarlo are particularly on the censorious alert when possible interpretations involve sex. We have already noted Barabtarlo's "Don't Even Think of Parking Here!" gloss on "douche." To this might be added Appel's annotation of Humbert's reference to the guards at Buckingham Palace as "beaver eaters": "Some have seen this as an obvious obscene joke, but Nabokov did not intend one. 'Moronic and oxymoronic,' he said, remembering the guard's old reputation for male prostitution ('beaver' is of the female gender, innocent reader)" (373).

Sarah Herbold has written insightfully about the ethical "double bind" in which Nabokov's readers find themselves as they are placed between different sets of "moral claims and aesthetic conventions" ("Reflections on Modernism," 147). In Nabokov studies this dynamic is also at work hermeneutically, with readers in an interpretive dilemma—they have to read imaginatively but not preposterously, without common sense and with it. They want to find things in the text but fear finding too much. A yearning for identity with the master has two faces: the desire to dazzle and the fear of seeming ridiculous or crude. The text simultaneously tempts the interpreter and threatens to expose him. With a little etymological license, one might call this state of affairs hermophobia. It encompasses a number of responses, including

---

2. Barabtarlo's *Phantom of Fact* is both a commentary and a narrative of temptation: he repeatedly yields to the desire to suggest readings that an internal, censorious agency then shuts down (see 181, 271, 276). That internal censor is most likely the phantom not of fact but of Vladimir Nabokov: "Such an interpretation would be, of course, neither here nor there, but Nabokov might have installed a yawning trap to which such an inviting possibility manoeuvres the blindfolded" (161). An important corollary to this rhetoric of temptation and correction is the commentator's continual delight in the deprecation of Rowe (22, 81, 111, 112, 194, 196), whose theories Barabtarlo applauds Boyd for "successfully exorcis[ing]" (192).

excessive caution, a fear of exposure, shame, and self-protecting (and, thus, self-intimidating) attacks on the interpretive excesses of others. To answer the query from Wesleyan: this condition *is* common to readers of Nabokov; it is the state of affairs that Nabokov's oeuvre works incessantly to produce.

It is worth noting that the quality of strangeness so often a part of queer narratives is for Nabokov a defining feature of art. "I trust the reader appreciates the strangeness of this," Kinbote writes, "because if he does not, there is no sense in writing poems, or notes to poems, or anything at all" (*Pale Fire,* 207). The words *strange, curious, queer,* and *odd* serve as crucial markers of aestheticization, doing the work lexically that is performed iconically by butterflies, wind, and squirrels. "*Lolita, or the Confession of a White Widowed Male,* such were the two titles under which the writer of the present note received the strange pages it perambulates" (3). "These heart-rending dreams transformed the drab prose of his feelings for her into strong and strange poetry" (*Pale Fire,* 209). "So this is all treacherous old Shade could say about Zembla—*my* Zembla? While shaving his stubble off? Strange, strange..." (*Pale Fire,* 272). Reviewing with Zina the history of their coincidental near-meetings in *The Gift,* Fyodor repeats "*Kak eto stranno*" (How strange it is)(*Sobranie sochinenii, 4: 362–63),* and Fyodor's world lights up with strangeness at the moment of their first near-kiss (*The Gift,* 182). Strangeness becomes the mark of fiction in a pair of lines from the *Onegin* translation:

> "Sit down—how queer it is!
> I'd swear this scene is from a novel!"
> (*Sadis'—kak eto mudreno!*
> *Ei bogu-, stsena iz romana....*) (1:270)

Nabokov's characters feel queer when they are aestheticized or when they become conscious of the author's presence or of being in an aesthetic, ordered world. "The Strange Case of Dr. Jekyll and Mr. Hyde" has become a staple of queer studies, and although Nabokov was among the first to ask why there are no women in the story and what all those well-to-do men are doing prowling deserted streets at all hours of the night, he closes his lecture on that work by showing the strange way in which Stevenson's death brings the author into his own work. (Earlier he has described the themes of wine and transformation as central to the story):

> [Stevenson] went down to the cellar to fetch a bottle of his favorite burgundy, uncorked it in the kitchen, and suddenly cried out to his

wife: what's the matter with me, what is this strangeness, has my face changed?—and fell on the floor. A blood vessel had burst in his brain and it was all over in a couple of hours.

What, has my face changed? There is a curious thematical link between this last episode in Stevenson's life and the fateful transformations in his most wonderful book. (*Lectures on Literature, 204*)

I don't think this is just a matter of *ostranenie* (the Russian Formalists' notion of defamiliarization or, more literally, making-strange as the essence of art) bared as device, nor is it merely a remainder of the Symbolist treatment of the noumenal world.[3] Rather, Nabokov's strangeness entails an aura of anxiety, of often disquieting supervision, of being observed, even stalked by the author.

Paranoia should not be an unexpected result of suddenly realizing that one is a character in somebody else's text. To be sure, for some of Nabokov's characters—Dreyer in *King, Queen, Knave,* Godunov-Cherdintsev in *The Gift,* at times *Ada*—the feeling that all is taken care of is reassuring. The world is well-ordered, beautiful, benevolent. For other characters, who have more in common with Ivan Karamazov than with his brother Alyosha, the absence of free will appears crushing. Nabokov's contemporary, the Russian literary scholar Mikhail Bakhtin, describes the creation of a hero by an author as the latter's loving bestowal of a gift of death: "Memory begins to act as a gathering and completing force from the very first moment of the hero's appearance; the hero is born in this memory (of his death), and the process of giving form to him is a process of commemoration (commemoration of the departed). [...] In this sense we could say that death is the form of the aesthetic consummation of an individual. [...] The deeper and the more perfect the embodiment, the more distinctly do we hear in it the definitive completion of death and at the same time the aesthetic victory over death. [...] Throughout the entire course of an embodied hero's life, one can hear the tones of a requiem" (*Art and Answerability,* 131).[4] The author's fatal love—and the agents who transmit

---

3. Leland de la Durantaye suggests that Nabokov's insistence on "strangeness" in his aesthetic pronouncement owes much to Walter Pater, whom Nabokov cites approvingly in his work on *Onegin* (*Style Is Matter,* 36–37).

4. Bakhtin compares aesthetic creativity, aesthetic closure or consummation, to the embracing or "overshadowing" of an other (*Art and Answerability,* 41), although at one point, he insists on the figurative nature of his analogy: "It should be evident, of course that we are abstracting here from the sexual features, which cloud the aesthetic purity of these irreversible actions" (Art and Answerability, 42). The disturbing power of Nabokov's writing comes from his willingness to have his characters occupy this cloudy territory where sexuality and aesthetics are firmly enmeshed in an author's rapport with his hero.

it—are a constant feature in Nabokov's world, which is why these agents bear names such as Phil (*Transparent Things*), Valentinov (*The Defense*), and Stranno-liubskii (literally: "Strange loving," *The Gift*) In *Pnin,* the antagonistic narrator arrives to displace Pnin on Valentine's Day (187).[5]

There is something perverse about the notion that creating a character is akin to immortalizing him by loving him to death. Fyodor, the hero of *The Gift,* "recalled his father saying that innate in every man is the feeling of something insuperably abnormal (*nepreodolimaia neestestvennost' krovno chu-vstuemaia chelovekom, strannaia i starinnaia obratnost' deistviia*) about the death penalty, something like the uncanny reversal of action in a looking glass that makes everyone left-handed: not for nothing is everything reversed for the executioner: the horse-collar is put on upside down when the robber Razin is taken to the scaffold; wine is poured for the headsman not with a natural turn of the wrist but backhandedly" (203). As Alexander Etkind has recently pointed out, lefties in Nabokov's fiction are often homosexual (403). All heroes in Nabokov's fiction are under a loving sentence of death, and in passages such as this one from *The Gift,* we see death assuming a homosexual and homosexualizing tinge, even if the executioner is not figured as clearly as *Invitation to a Beheading*'s creepily chummy M. Pierre.

Life in a Nabokov novel can be beautiful, but it can also drive a character mad, and although Nabokov tells us not to identify with characters in a novel, many Nabokovians do, not only in the sense of empathizing with, say, *Ada*'s Lucette but also in sharing characters' *hermeneutic* anxieties. Nabokov's world is charged with interpretive paranoia. No text is more developed in this sense than *Pale Fire,* which answers to many of Eve Kosofsky Sedg-wick's parameters for the hermeneutics of suspicion. Paranoia is anticipatory, demanding "a complex relation to temporality that burrows both backward and forward: because there must be no bad surprises, and because to learn of the possibility of a bad surprise would itself constitute a bad surprise, paranoia requires that bad news be always already known" ("Paranoid Reading," 10). While this burrowing is most obviously the reader's task in *Pale Fire,* it is an important model for good reading of any work by Nabokov. We come back to the beginning after reading the end first, we have not read unless we have reread, we are constantly wary of falling into traps, and we gleefully point out

---

5. An interesting variation on this notion of an author's fatal love for his character is suggested by *The Original of Laura,* in which Phillip Wild, a neurologist and author, practices his self-erasure in an auto-erotic exercise that provides the grounds for the work's parenthetic subtitle: *(Dying Is Fun).* Wild's pleasure, the particular intimacy that stems from the author and the hero being one and the same, is especially intense; Wild discovers that "the process of dying by auto-dissolution afforded the greatest ecstasy known to man" (171).

to our colleagues that they have fallen into them. According to Sedgwick: Paranoia is "reflexive and mimetic." It proposes both "'Anything you can do to me I can do worse' and 'Anything you can do to me I can do first'" ("Paranoid Reading," 10)—hence all Nabokov's texts' parodies and exaggerations of their own most impressive and flagrant hermeneutic practices. Indeed, one might say of *Pale Fire* that it exaggerates pathological interpretation and sexual activity to the point where any nervousness they inspire is overcome by delight. Kinbote is so obviously out as a homosexual and a bad reader—no closet can hold him, he literally goes right through them (125–27, 132–34)—that he clears a tremendous amount of space for readers to play in stylistic imitation without having to fear being called out for their mistakes. This novel that sets the standard for misguided interpretation paradoxically manages to free the reader from interpretive anxiety. *Pale Fire* may be the work by Nabokov that readers can enjoy with the least compunction about having missed something important. I return to the theoretical basis for this assertion below, but for now please register that the real hero of *Pale Fire* is interpretation in drag.[6]

Nabokov's polemical writing is so compelling in part because chastisement and *characterization* go hand in hand. Nabokovian derision surrounds an opponent with the trappings of fiction. Such a gesture is not unexpected when directed at Edmund Wilson, whom Nabokov knew well:

> A patient confidant of his long and hopeless infatuation with the Russian language and literature, I have invariably done my best to explain to him his monstrous mistakes of pronunciation, grammar, and interpretation. As late as 1957, at one of our last meetings, in Ithaca, upstate New York, where I lived at the time, we both realized with amused dismay that, despite my frequent comments on Russian prosody, he still could not scan Russian verse. Upon being challenged to read *Evgeniy Onegin* aloud, he started to perform with great gusto, garbling every second word, and turning Pushkin's iambic line into a kind of spastic

---

6. As part of his critique of alleged homophobia in Brian Boyd's reading of *Pale Fire,* Kevin Ohi argues that the novel inspires "ecstasies of panicked critical rebuke" (155). Ohi describes Kinbote as "strikingly uncloseted" but contends that Kinbote's "undisguised" and "flamboyant" (Boyd's terms) sexual orientation leads Boyd to "attribute a closet" so that "the reader can puncture it and deduce its hidden secret" (162). In many respects, Ohi projects onto Boyd moral judgments and tastes so as to keep them away from Nabokov, who emerges from Ohi's article morally unscathed and a perspicacious deconstructor of narcissism. Although Ohi raises fascinating questions about the role of narcissism in literary criticism and in this novel in particular, he overstates the degree of homophobic anxiety in critical readings of *Pale Fire.* Robert Alter has compared the contrast between Kinbote and Shade to the difference between Shakespeare and Pope, founding this insight on the richness and sweep of Kinbote's poetic universe (*Partial Magic,* 180–217).

anapest with a lot of jaw-twisting haws and rather endearing little barks that utterly jumbled the rhythm and soon had us both in stitches. (*Strong Opinions,* 248)

With his reputation at its height Wilson was a noble target. Even with lesser-known adversaries, one might be tempted to see these descriptions as paradoxically generous; after all, Nabokov's fame is such that everything his work touches turns to canonical gold.[7] Yet the condition of being a character is so limited, so subservient, that the transformation of a real-life person into a literally flat figure must be regarded as a form of divine vengeance (or, quite literally, character assassination), because in Nabokov's world no loss is more grievous than that of a dimension. Nabokov made this point bluntly in his English translation and reworking of *King, Queen, Knave* with an alteration in the text that has been discussed by Brian Boyd (*The American Years,* 523). Dissatisfied with the reviews he had been receiving from the British scholar Ronald Hingley, Nabokov bestowed Hingley's name on a hitherto anonymous mannequin: "an unresponsive young man of painted wood who had been changed recently into tennis togs" (169). (Nabokov immediately adds, "The shopgirls had dubbed him Ronald," covertly suggesting a causal link between the dummy's name and his unresponsiveness). Ronald comes in for much abuse and suffers the final indignity of being undressed by the novel's half-dead, ultra-German "hero," the shop assistant Franz:

Franz embraced the wooden corpse and started undoing its tie. As he worked at it, he could not help touching the stiff cold neck. Then he undid a tight button. The shirt collar opened. The dead body was a brownish green with darker blotches and paler discolorations. Because of the open collar Ronald's fixed condescending grin became even more caddish and indecent. Ronald had a dark-brown smear under one eye as if he had been punched there. Ronald had a pied chin. Ronald's nostrils were clogged with black dust. Franz tried to recall where he had seen that horrible face before. Yes, of course—long, long ago, in the train. In the same train there had been a beautiful lady wearing a black hat with a little diamond swallow. Cold, fragrant, madonna-like. He tried to resurrect her features in his memory but failed to do so. (170)

---

7. After the publication of *The Gift,* Nabokov was rebuked by the emigré author Mark Aldanov for his parodic inclusion of "reviews, which have such a limited life," into "a novel that will live forever." Nabokov punningly responded: "Smile, Mark Aleksandrovich! You say that *The Gift* [Dar] is designed to have a very long life. If that is so, then that is all the more reason for my courteous provision of free passage [*liubezno vziat' darom*] to the images of several of my contemporaries, who would otherwise have been left at home forever" (quoted in Dolinin, *Istinnaia zhizn',* 274).

Since Franz has been having an affair with this "madonna" from the train, the connection between Ronald and his undresser metonymically acquires a sexualized aura. A certain logic underpins this metafictive nightmare: if all characters are dead, the *reductio ad absurdum* of sexual contact between them must be a portrait of necrophilia. But let us not neglect the obvious homophobic and more subtle hermophobic dimensions of this scene. Hingley's fate—exposure to ridicule, being undressed by Franz—represents a worst-case scenario for the hermeneutically sensitive Nabokovian reader. As in a Gothic novel, where a character reading a ghost story—and thus serving as the reader's stand-in—is surprised by an intruder (Radcliffe, 563), so Nabokov's reader, enjoying a sense of Olympian aloofness from the stick figures on the page—is aware that interpretive engagement carries the risk of the collapse of the textual fourth wall.

Every good reader of Nabokov dreads being fooled like Luzhin, exposed like Albinus. And every good Nabokovian scholar *desires* the master's approval. Boyd concludes his acknowledgments to his recent book by thanking Vladimir Nabokov "for eventually making it possible to find a much more exciting explanation of what really happens and what is really at stake in *Pale Fire*. I wish he could read this centenary offering" (*Nabokov's "Pale Fire,"* xii). Much recent attention to Nabokov's interest in "the next world" may stem from the critical desire for the author's approval, an approval more likely to be bestowed now that death has rounded off the sharp edges. (*I wish he could read this—thank God that he can't!*)[8] The opposing side of this coin is the raising of the dead for the sake of imagining how Nabokov would foam at the mouth were he to read the remarks of some *other* scholar: "I venture to state that such an observation would have thrown Nabokov himself, with

---

8. The death of Nabokov has largely released scholars and critics from their fear that immediate negative consequences will follow a misreading, but it has also rendered impossible the bliss so evidently experienced—and shared—by Alfred Appel in his introduction to *The Annotated Lolita*. Appel recounts an attempt to put on a puppet show for his children that ended in a collapse of the theater and reminded him, he told Nabokov, of the response Nabokov sought to produce in his readers at the end of his novels: "'Exactly, exactly,' [Nabokov] said as I finished. 'You must put that in your book'" (xxxii). Now, with approval and chastisement more removed and mediated, submission entails a willingness to serve as the author's vessel in perhaps more profound ways: "The poetic epiphany [of understanding Nabokov] takes its temporal dimension from the intense sensation that the reader experiences in being suddenly in contact with this magician who has done all he can to remain inaccessible. To be sure, this is in part illusory, but that enhances rather than diminishes the intensity of the experience. I will never manage to have completely unmasked this magician and I will never be on an equal footing with him, and it is this which drives my desire to pursue my reading ever further, in the hope, always disappointed, to find myself in the presence, if not of the author himself, who is already dead, then at least of his desire, his frustrations and his anguished fears, which can become embodied only in me" (Couturier, *Nabokov, ou la tyrannie,* 153).

his amazing visual imagination, into an indescribable rage" (Dolinin, untitled review, 87). *The Gift*'s hero, Godunov-Cherdyntsev, wants to find somebody to thank for "all these gifts with which the summer morning rewards me- and only me" (328). One of the most erotically charged scenes in all of Nabokov's work occurs between Godunov-Cherdyntsev and his maker, as the two fuse into one:

> The sun bore down. The sun licked me all over with its big smooth tongue. I gradually felt that I was becoming moltenly transparent, that I was permeated with flame and existed only insofar as it did. As a book is translated into an exotic idiom so was I translated into sun. The scrawny, chilly, hiemal Fyodor Godunov-Cherdyntsev was now as remote from me as if I had exiled him to the Yakutsk province. He was a pallid copy of me, whereas this aestival one was his magnified bronze replica. My personal I, the one that wrote books, the one that loved words, colors, mental fire-works, Russia, chocolate and Zina— had somehow disintegrated and dissolved; after being made transparent by the strength of the light, it was now assimilated to the shimmering of the summer forest with its satiny pine needles and heavenly-green leaves, with its ants running over the transfigured, most radiant-hued wool of the laprobe, with its birds, smells, hot breath of nettles and spermy odor of sun-warmed grass, with its blue sky where droned a high-flying plane that seemed filmed over with blue dust, the essence of the firmament: the plane was bluish, as a fish is wet in water.
> One might dissolve completely that way. (333–34)

This is bliss, and far more ennobling than the authorial hand job given to Humbert, when after an hour's sleep he is "aroused by gratuitous and horribly exhausting congress with a small hairy hermaphrodite, a total stranger" (109).

Sarah Herbold suggests that in the famous davenport scene in *Lolita*, "the 'magic friction' between Humbert's penis and Lolita's thinly clad buttocks [...] is also occurring between reader and author," since "the reader is plea-surably and painfully rubbing himself or herself up against (and/or being rubbed by) the shifting layers of the story" ("'I have camouflaged every-thing,'" 83). Anxiety and fear are equally parts of this process. Nabokov's work obsessively figures the rapport between author and reader; the novels offer a variety of visions of metafictive relations, and it is disconcerting to realize that there is no particular assurance that one relationship will end well and another badly. One of Nabokov's signal lessons is that reading necessar-ily involves putting oneself in the control of another who, at least initially, operates from a position of greater knowledge and broader vision. The reader is always at risk of occupying the position of Albinus, the blind cuckold of *Laughter in the Dark* who lives in a false world dictated to him (through his deceitful lover) by the vulgar cartoonist, Rex. Virtually everything Albinus, formerly an art critic, now knows of the world around him has been narrated by Rex, just as everything we readers know about the narrated world has been communicated to us by Nabokov. In one of the novel's climaxes, Rex sits naked in front of Albinus, who looks with "agonized tension" in front of him, trying to discern if someone else is in the room. Rex decides to amuse himself by "one or two little tests": "Rex bent slowly forward and touched Albinus' forehead very gently with the flowering end of the grass stem which he had just been sucking. Albinus sighed strangely and brushed away the imaginary fly" (276–77).[9] Rex has earlier disguised his affair with Albinus's vulgar mistress by masquerading as a homosexual, and here, in this metafictive nightmare about the reader's fear of occupying a compromised position, the homoerotic orientation of the author's avatar seems particularly salient. Albinus's "strange sigh" serves as a mark of horribly misfounded aesthetic contentment.[10] He functions as a counterexample to Rowe, the other figure holding the double bind in place. Where Rowe, supposedly, saw sexual innuendo where there was none, Albinus cannot see the author's sex even when it is staring him in the face.[11]

An initially less troubling moment of aesthetic bliss occurs in *Lolita,* in a scene that Sarah Herbold intriguingly sees as a parallel to Humbert's sexual climax with Lolita on the davenport:

> And softly, confidentially, arching her thin eyebrows and puckering her parched lips, she emitted, a little mockingly, somewhat fastidiously, not

---

9. One of these "little tests" may be of the reader's recollection of *Anna Karenina*. Levin's epiphany at the end of the novel comes when he watches a little bug crawl up "a stalk of couch grass (stebel' pyreia)" (796). Rex puts this "long stalk of grass" to horrific, parodic use. Seifrid (1–12) and Alexandrov ("Nabokov and Tolstoy," 65–68) write in detail on *Anna Karenina's* significance in this novel (1–12).

10. The description of Rex's body is an explicit reprise of an earlier one, in which Albinus gazes with desire at his nearly naked mistress: "With nothing but deep blue above, Margot lay spread-eagled on the platinum sand, her limbs a rich honey-brown" (112). Compare: "[Rex] was stark naked. As a result of his daily sunbaths his lean but robust body with, on his breast, black hair in the shape of a spread eagle, was tanned a deep brown" (276). The echo of the earlier moment of sexualized contemplation compounds the erotic nature of the later scene between the men.

11. Of Rex's dumbshow Maurice Couturier observes: "Everything in this unbearable scene— Rex's nudity, his robustness, his hairiness, emblazoned in the form of a spread eagle, his tan, etc.— proclaims his desire to be the sovereign phallus imposing the sick law of its gaze on the other, whose desire he strives to humiliate and abolish. Here one might say the perverse artist achieves the peak of his phallic erection" (*Nabokov, ou la cruauté,* 127).

untenderly, in a kind of muted whistle, the name that the astute reader has guessed long ago.

Waterproof. Why did a flash from Hourglass Lake cross my consciousness? I, too, had known it, without knowing it, all along. There was no shock, no surprise. Quietly, the fusion took place, and everything fell into order, into the pattern of branches that I have woven throughout this memoir with the express purpose of having the ripe fruit fall at the right moment; yes, with the express and perverse purpose of rendering— she was talking but I sat melting in my golden peace—of rendering that golden and monstrous peace through the satisfaction of logical recognition, which, my most inimical reader should experience now. (272)

Noting that Humbert has used the expression "golden load" to refer to his excitement on the davenport, Herbold concludes that Humbert "is here implicitly comparing the male reader's hypothetical burst of pleasure at seeing his suspicions of 'Gustave von Trapp's' real identity confirmed to the orgasm he himself has experienced while fantasizing about Lolita. [...] Humbert's ecstasy is masochistic as well as sadistic: Lolita's revelation will enable him to pursue and eliminate his enemy, but it also represents sexual humiliation" ("'I have camouflaged everything,'" 86). The difference between this and the earlier scene, however, is as salient as the similarity, and it suggests that there is no reason to read this passage as representing a particularly male experience of pleasure. On the contrary, this moment of shared interpretive breakthrough— all the more humiliating if the reader still doesn't experience hermeneutic climax—is far more placid than that explosive moment on the sofa in Ramsdale: here Humbert just melts and melts—rendering also means to melt—in "my golden peace." Where the first orgasm was stereotypically male—"I crushed out against her left buttock the last throb of the longest ecstasy man or monster had ever known" (61)—this one has the clichéd hallmarks of female climax. Receiving the author's word, Humbert is the passive partner, and in this happy hermeneutic embrace he is depicted as something of a woman, a "perverse" transformation he is eager to share with his imagined, similarly satisfied "most inimical reader." The subsequent murderous assault—played for metafictive laughs—on Quilty may be read as a homophobically induced payback for Humbert's passive pleasure of understanding.

Let us go back to "Good Readers and Good Writers": "Up a trackless slope climbs the master artist, and at the top, on a windy ridge, whom do you think he meets? The panting and happy reader, and there they spontaneously embrace and are linked forever if the book lasts forever" (*Lectures on Literature*, 2). Who wouldn't want such a hermeneutically affirming experience: a face-to-face encounter with his favorite author? But in Nabokov's world author-reader bliss rarely occurs in the missionary position. Here is how Nabokov opened his lecture on *Bleak House:*

> We are now ready to tackle Dickens. We are now ready to embrace Dickens. We are now ready to bask in Dickens. In our dealings with Jane Austen we had to make a certain effort in order to join the ladies in the drawing room. [...] We had to find an approach to Jane Austen and her *Mansfield Park*. I think we did find it and did have some degree of fun with her delicate patterns, with her collection of eggshells in cotton wool. But the fun was forced. [...] With Dickens we expand. [...] Here there is no problem of approach as with Jane Austen, no courtship, no dillydallying. We just surrender ourselves to Dickens's voice. [...] All we have to do when reading *Bleak House* is to relax and let our spines take over. Although we read with our minds, the seat of artistic delight is between the shoulder blades. That little shiver behind is quite certainly the highest form of emotion that humanity has attained when evolving pure art and pure science. [...] I repeat again and again it is no use reading a book at all if you do not read it with your back. (*Lectures on Literature*, 63–64)

The difficulty in dealing with Austen is that she takes too much work in the form of contextualizing foreplay. Reversing the stereotype of female sexual response, Nabokov wearies of her because reading her work does not insure automatic hermeneutic arousal. With Dickens, receptivity is automatic, and the height of surrender to an author is to accord him a posterior position. This was a pose Nabokov insisted on temporally, too. In 1970 *Triquarterly* published a special issue devoted to Nabokov's seventieth birthday. Shortly afterwards, the journal published a special supplement to the issue, sixteen pages or so in which Nabokov graciously responded to most of the contributors, giving them, as it were, a pat on the behind, though George Steiner got more of a spanking (*Strong Opinions,* 284–303). This gesture of the author speaking after his critics is a temporal inversion of the usual order of things, but it is entirely in keeping with Nabokov's effort to inscribe good and bad readers into his texts, to preempt their posteriority, so that the author, not the commentator, always has the last word. The reader's job is to accord the writer this position. Mastery and being mastered by the author go hand in hand in a mixture of admiration (if not adulation) and submission, rendered all the sweeter by the compensatory bullying of Rowe in his original or in some latter-day incarnation.[12]

Reading with one's back is one of twin injunctions invoking a reverse gear. The other is reading backward. We have already examined the irony of "preposterous oversight" in *Pnin:* the term is a perfect description of the good reader's task, rereading so as to enlighten early material with a knowledge of what comes after. This hermeneutic stance, elsewhere identified in *Pnin* as "sober backcast" (157), in *The Defense* as "retrograde analysis" (10), and in *Ada* as directing "the searchlight of backthought" (*153*), is the readerly, procedural equivalent of nostalgia, as the reader obliged to look backward for words and images he vaguely remembers oscillates between the feelings produced by Proust's madeleine and Freud's uncanny: the pleasure of recapturing the past and the fear of being seized by the consequences of forgetting it.

Reading backward and reading with one's back entail a certain vulnerability, as Rowe discovered when his "crass attempts" were condemned as "preposterous and nasty." We should remember that the response of common sense to art is portrayed as an act of backward-moving revulsion: "Commonsense has trampled down many a gentle genius whose eyes had delighted in a too early moonbeam of some too early truth; commonsense has back-kicked dirt at the loveliest of queer paintings" (*Lectures on Literature,* 372). This caution is given in more sensuous terms in "Good Readers and Good Writers": "In reading, one should notice and fondle details. There is nothing wrong about the moonshine of generalization when it comes *after* the sunny trifles of the book have been lovingly collected. If one begins with a ready-made

---

12. Couturier also sees submission as part of the formation of Nabokov's reader. Claiming that Nabokov's reader has great difficulty undertaking a "specific interpretation" of a novel, by which, I think, Couturier means the application of an external critical methodology, he elaborates: "In obliging us to defer the work of interpretation, the searches undertaken by the reader constitute a perverse trap, in as much as they are never totally pursued to their end. To read is to enter from the first moment into the logic of the author, to submit oneself to his law without ever being able to escape it. That which incites us to bend ourselves to this authoritarian and perverse law is the hope, always illusory, to be able to one day understand the principals of this law so that we will be able to escape it; it is also the desire, partially satisfied, to develop with this maestro of genius an intense complicity through extensive play with him" (*Nabokov, ou la tyrannie,* 199).

Brian McHale, in a review of Couturier's book, charges that Couturier suffers from "an 'anxiety of interpretation'": "Time and again, whenever the possibility of attributing meaning arises, Couturier demonstrates how Nabokov's strategies deflect or pre-empt interpretation, rendering it useless or redundant. In doing so, he calls attention simultaneously to the temptation to interpret and to his own success in withstanding interpretation" (279). McHale here makes what might be called the field's first diagnosis of hermophobia (minus the sexual connotation of interpretive failure), but Couturier is the Nabokov scholar who has been most open and perceptive about the interpretive dilemmas that have shaped the enterprise of Nabokov studies, his own work included.

generalization, one begins at the wrong end and travels away from the book before one has started to understand it" (*Lectures on Literature,* 1). Yet the preposterous pleasure of good reading comes to the fore at the very end of the essay, and here the pleasures of the spine are surrounded by the phonetic connotations of physicality that marked Nabokov's references to homosexuality in *Pale Fire* and to Rowe's preposterous and nasty reading:

> In order to bask in that magic a wise reader reads the book of genius not with his heart, not so much with his brain, but with his spine. It is there that occurs the telltale tingle even though we must keep a little aloof, a little detached when reading. Then with a pleasure which is both sensual and intellectual we shall watch the artist build his castle of cards and watch the castle of cards become a castle of beautiful steel and glass. (6)

Caution signs are out everywhere, but so are temptations, and good reading of Nabokov entails the willingness to take preposterous hermeneutic risks, to realize that the fear of exposure, the possibility of humiliation, are essential in a world where perversity and poetry are inseparable. To read Nabokov insightfully, one needs to read him queerly, with a squint, an optical stammer, a leer, a posterior tingle, playing the game that Nabokov describes in *Speak, Memory* as "Find what the Sailor has Hidden" (*Speak, Memory,* 310). The injunction from "An Evening of Russian Poetry," "a poem where "every line is bent" is worth repeating here: "The other way, the other way. I thank you" (*Poems and Problems,* 158).[13]

An even more comic version of this sort of reading is performed by Luzhin in *The Defense:* "He read with a funny stammer, pronouncing some of the words oddly and at times going past a period, or else not reaching it, and raising or lowering the tone of his voice for no logical reason" (226). Luzhin's manner of reading is perverse rearticulation, and a critical reading adequate to the text's own queerness should be seen as the execution of a perverse task assigned by the author. For Nabokov, interpretation (as translation, university lecture or commentary) was first and foremost a mode of performance. At the podium, in interviews, behind his desk, he fused the roles of critic, teacher, and artist so as to set intoxicating and intimidating standards

---

13. See also Albinus's struggle to understand the world that "really" surrounds him: "He had the obscure sensation of everything's being suddenly turned the other way round, so that he had to read it all backward if he wanted to understand" (*Laughter in the Dark,* 220). "Obscure" is an aptly chosen word—the book that contains Albinus—and which he can never read—was originally entitled *Kamera obscura.*

for those who write about him. Van's vaudeville performance in *Ada,* his unexpected "acrobatic wonders" of inversion that frighten children (quoted in chapter 1), is a hyperbolic model not just for authorial creativity but for adequate interpretive performance of the Nabokovian text.

Performed "in a theatrical club that habitually limited itself to Elizabethan plays, with queens and fairies played by pretty boys" (181), Van's act indicates the important place of performativity in Nabokov scholarship. Nabokov's prose has much in common with Judith Butler's notion of "queering" in drag: "inhabiting the practices of [a norm']s rearticulation" (237). What Butler's drag does by exaggerating and rearticulating the "rules" of gender, Nabokov's novels do with the power dynamics of fiction. The role of a scholarly reader is often to facilitate the performance of perversion, ministering to Nabokov's text—fondling its details—so as to expose its constructed essence, to bare its methods and devices. Butler focuses on the use of exaggeration in drag:

> As an allegory that works through the hyperbolic, drag brings into relief what is, after all, determined only in relation to the hyperbolic: the understated, taken-for-granted quality of heterosexual performativity. At its best, then, drag can be read for the way in which hyperbolic norms are dissimulated as the heterosexual mundane. At the same time these same norms, taken not as commands to be obeyed, but as imperatives to be "cited," twisted, queered, brought into relief as heterosexual imperatives, are not, for that reason, necessarily subverted in the process. (237)

Not *necessarily* subverted. Insightful writing in queer theory often betrays a nervousness about political efficacy. Might not drag, like the more broadly sweeping term of carnival, sometimes—often—most often?—serve to limit the scope of subversion, to channel "abnormal" dissent, to further isolate its audience, even to collect that audience for surveillance? Can sexually obsessed or insistently gendered deconstruction move from critique to action in the real world? Butler predicates the legitimacy of queer theory on its willingness to yield to more traditional forms of political action: "If the term 'queer' is to be a site of collective contestation, the point of departure for a set of historical reflections and futural imaginings, it will have to remain that which is, in the present, never fully owned, but always and only redeployed, twisted, queered from a prior usage and in the direction of urgent and expanding political purposes. This also means that it will doubtless have to be yielded in favor of terms that do that political work more effectively" (228).

Nabokov had no such qualms about strangeness and political power. The political consequences of art are an unworthy subject for him: the only power that interests Nabokov is authorial and aesthetic, and this power is *reaffirmed* by queer reading. Queer reading of Nabokov invariably presents itself as authorized: rearticulating and twisting the text are means for arriving at an intended, hidden meaning. The joke is on the philistine reader, who misses it, but the interpreter is also placed in a subservient position, for his queer reading is performed with an eye toward authorial approval. This aspect of queer reading distinguishes the enterprise of deconstruction in and of Nabokov's texts from the mainstream of psychoanalytic or poststructural critique.

Eve Sedgwick comes very close to arguing for authorized queering in readers of Henry James. Criticizing Kaja Silverman's psychoanalytic treatment of James, she objects:

> I am very eager that James's sexual language be heard, but that it not be heard with this insulting presumption of the hearer's epistemological privilege—a privilege attached, furthermore, to Silverman's uncritical insistence on viewing sexuality exclusively in terms of repression and self-ignorance. When we tune in to James's language on these frequencies, it is not as superior, privileged eavesdroppers on a sexual narrative hidden from himself; rather, it is as an audience offered the privilege of sharing in his exhibitionistic enjoyment and performance of a sexuality organized around shame. ("Shame and Performativity," 229)

Sedgwick envisions a supportive relationship between author and reader, whom she sees as members of a shared community, rather than an author who indoctrinates the reader by encouraging the latter's submission to professional chastisement. James Creech makes a similar argument about Herman Melville's appeal to his "gay" audience (75–76, 96). Like Sedgwick, he imagines a perhaps desperately supportive rapport between a literary master and his homosexual readers. The power of literary mastery works differently in Nabokov's work, which provides not an escape from humiliation but an erotically charged tussle with it. Shame is already part of the common heritage of James and his queer readers; the perversely articulating reader of Nabokov exposes himself to it as part of his search for authorial approval. It may be that a good reading of Nabokov is one of which one ought to be ashamed. And while Sedgwick's notion of queer studies sees itself as examining and jubilating in an "open mesh of possibilities, gaps, overlaps, dissonances and resonances, lapses and excesses of meaning" (*Tendencies,* 8), queer reading in Nabokov aims at recovering hidden but nonetheless monolithic authorial intent and is beset by a reader's necessary fear of inadequacy. All those prefaces to translations and the carefully staged interviews do not so much wink supportively at the reader as trouble him. These paratexts turn

the reading of Nabokov's novels into something like master classes: seduc-
tively dismissive but highly educational lessons in good reading.

To what extent have I been using sex completely as a metaphor, appropriating the language and methods of queer theory without engaging with its
object? Do readers of Nabokov only have words—and no bodies—to play
with? Or might hermophobia be firmly tied to homophobia at some other,
not simply figurative level? Might Humbert's lament about the absence of
flesh in metafiction be the protective cloak of invisibility that allows a critic to
appeal to queer studies without engaging with real-world bodies? My argument has been that the tensions involved in reading "the other way" generate
interpretive anxieties and pleasures that are disquietingly similar to sexual
ones, and that in Nabokov's writing homosexuals serve as a marker of that
resemblance at least and, perhaps, by distraction, as the purposefully incomplete denial of those pleasures' relationship to the body. Nabokov does not
repress but exploits this relationship between good, perverse, nasty, preposterous reading and erotic desire; and he fosters it by his work's insistent linkage of
interpretation and sex. In *Ada* Marina always mispronounces "flashback" as
"fleshbeck" (201): looking back at earlier portions of the text—a vital mode
for good reading of Nabokov—is linked to the body's call. In the same novel
we read that "the mental in Van [or is that VN?] always rimmed the sensuous"
(373). We cannot entirely disregard the somatics of reading Nabokov.

One of the most extensive sexual rants in Nabokov's work occurs when
Humbert attempts to trace Lolita's abductor in hotel guest books: "His main
trait was his passion for tantalization. Goodness, what a tease the poor fellow
was! He challenged my scholarship. I am sufficiently proud of my knowing
something to be modest about my not knowing all; and I daresay I missed
some elements in that cryptogrammic paper chase. What a shiver of triumph
and loathing shook my frail frame when, among the plain innocent names
in the hotel recorder, his fiendish conundrum would ejaculate in my face!"
(250). We have seen this shiver of triumph before, in the Dickens lecture,
identified as a marker of aesthetic bliss. In *Lolita* that bliss is partnered with
the loathing and self-loathing that accompanies aggressive reading. Humbert
cannot so easily distance himself from Quilty. Put another way: when a reader
fondles the details of a text, it is not the text that is more likely to ejaculate. A
similar dynamic is at work in Humbert's disdain for the theater: "a form that
smacks of stone-age rites and communal nonsense despite those individual
injections of genius, such as, say, Elizabethan poetry which a closeted reader
automatically pumps out of the stuff" (200).

The interpretive climate surrounding Nabokov's texts is so fraught with
the energies of transgression and obedience that the reader's sexual orientation

is always at issue. Here the question is not so much—at least not initially—sexual preference but sexual orientation in general, the taking of the text as an object for the direction of sexual energy. Several works by Nabokov present the problem of oversexed interpretation in a nearly exclusively heterosexual context, although in Nabokov's best-known works, this energy is most effectively stigmatized and intensified by its figuration as homosexual.

"In place of a hermeneutics we need an erotics of art"—if the famous conclusion to Susan Sontag's "Against Interpretation" (14) seems so inapplicable to Nabokov it is because in Nabokov's metafictive universe a sensuous attitude toward the text is already part of the hermeneutic enterprise, and the reader's conflicted responses to libidinal and analytical energies provide much of the power for the sustained draw of Nabokov's work. The good reader should remember that one of the adjectives employed by Nabokov in his devastating inscription of Hingley into *King, Queen, Knave* was "unresponsive."

Here is a point that Nabokov scholars have taken great pains to deny. A fundamental tenet of Nabokov studies is that people who expect to get a rise out of reading Nabokov are *always* disappointed. (This has been perhaps the only area in which reader response has been deemed worthy of comment, and the tone is nearly always one of bemused detachment that forestalls further analysis).[14] The most famous example is Alfred Appel's description of reading *Lolita* in the barracks while stationed with the American army in France:

> I brought *Lolita* back to my base, which was situated out in the woods. Passes were hard to get and new Olympia titles were always in demand in the barracks. The appearance of a new girl in town thus caused a minor clamor. "Hey, lemme read your dirty book, man!" insisted "Stockade Clyde" Carr, who had justly earned his sobriquet, and to whose request I acceded at once. "Read it aloud, Stockade," someone called, and skipping the Foreword, Stockade Clyde began to make his remedial way through

---

14. Of particular interest here is Samuel Schuman's contribution to a series of postings archived on NABOKV-L under the title "My First Time with Lolita." Like Appel, Schuman's academic supervisor, who mentions how well his wife did in Nabokov's class and incorporates his (happy, laughing) children into his introduction (xxxi–xxxii, xlii), Schuman makes sure his readers understand his basic normalcy: "Like many another adolescent in the late 1950s my first time with Lolita was a major disappointment; I was looking for a dirty book and only found a great one. My first serious encounter with the novel came some years later. [...] My wife and young children and I spent a summer in Yorkshire, at the home of another Northwestern colleague, and I picked up *The Annotated Lolita* because I was curious about the scholarship of my supervisor. A few days later, I finished the book, dashed to the local bookshop, and purchased everything by Nabokov they had for sale."

the opening paragraph. "Lo...lita, light...of my life, fire of my...loins. My sin, my soul...Lo-lee-ta: The...tip of the...tongue...taking...a trip...."—*Damn!* yelled Stockade, throwing the book against the wall. "*It's God-damn Litachure!!*" ("Introduction," xxxiv)

The setting here is significant. Stockade Clyde's grabbing of the book has the homoerotic trappings of fantasized molestation, a potential abandoned at the moment that *Lolita's* pornographic potential is also denied. Albeit in more sober tones, in Nabokov studies such anecdotes are recounted so frequently, so apotropeically that their use ought to be examined more closely. Less colorful than Appel's anecdote, but perhaps more insightful, is a remark to Nabokov from his Cornell colleague Morris Bishop: "Some of your phrases are so good they almost give me an erection—and at my age it is not easy, you know" (Boyd, *The American Years,* 192). "Almost" is doing an extraordinary amount of work in that sentence, insisting on an all-or-nothing dynamics of male arousal to protect Nabokov's work from association with pornography and to disavow homosexual interaction between author and reader. But "almost" can also entail a gradation of sexual and homosexual response. We might not want to dwell on the image of an almost erect Morris Bishop, but we should recognize the subtleties, the continuum and the preposterous nature of readerly arousal. A good reader of Nabokov reads queerly, warily, with a strange mixture of aggression and submission, lashing out at his colleagues while fearing and welcoming the attentions of an author who thinks the best readers allow themselves to be taken from behind.

❧ PART TWO

*Setting Nabokov
Straight*

✹ CHAPTER 5

Reading Chernyshevsky in Tehran
Nabokov and Nafisi

Although neither Azar Nafisi nor any of her reviewers seem to have acknowledged it, by the standards of Nabokov's famous quiz about good readers, the word "well" could not be added to the title of *Reading "Lolita" in Tehran*. Nabokov begins his little test—"Select four answers to the question what should a reader be to be a good reader"—with six wrong responses, the first three of which are:

1. the reader should belong to a book club;
2. the reader should identify himself or herself with the hero or heroine; and
3. the reader should concentrate on the social-economic angle (*Lectures on Literature,* 3).

These three commandments are flagrantly broken by Nafisi's book, the back cover of which is topped by advance praise from Geraldine Brooks: "Anyone who has ever belonged to a book group must read this book."

Nabokov would have disliked book groups even more than he disliked book clubs. The newest incarnation of socialized reading, book groups make the act of reading subordinate to talking and communal bonding. (Recalling the Winds in *Pnin,* we might say that book groups are to literature what Planned Parenthood group counseling sessions were to sex). There is nothing intrinsically wrong with reading Nabokov as he would wish not to have been read, and such a position might be appropriate for a book that proudly sports its transgressive intent, but Nafisi portrays herself as embracing rather than defying Nabokov, enlisting him as an ally in a project to immure literature within the context of politics. Once literature and politics are explicitly and allegorically enmeshed, Nabokov may prove a troubling ally, for if we succumb to the temptation of drawing allegories between literature and politics, strong writers may have more in common with political dictators than with those dictators' victims. One might even start with pedagogy. A teacher in firm control of his material, Nabokov loved tests, he assigned marks to other writers who had never been his students (Boyd, *The American Years*, 459), and his best readers know that they are constantly under examination. For many participants, the beauty of a book club is that there are no exams and no grades.

We can appreciate Nafisi's memoir as a story about life under the tyranny of the mullahs; her book is particularly powerful in its tragic portrait of the Iranian intelligentsia, which got what it wished for—the overthrow of the shah—and then saw its freedoms and sense of personal autonomy rapidly erode. In this respect, one need not frame the issue as "Nabokov and Nafisi"; it is possible to read their works within the parameters of entirely different genres of writing. But rather than dismissing Nafisi as more or less irrelevant to Nabokov, as someone teaching and writing about Nabokov I want to dwell precisely on this question of relevance, because I think we can see Nafisi's book and its reception as an extreme but still instructive example of a tendency—indeed, an anxiety—that pervades writing about the author of *Lolita*. This anxiety revolves around the social, real-world usefulness of reading Nabokov. In this respect, *Lolita* may stand in for literature or fiction as a whole, but Nabokov seems especially to provoke this anxiety because he so firmly insisted that his work had no moral in tow, and because he deals so richly—on the level of content—with transgressive issues that often lead scholars to adopt redemptive, socially justifiable strategies for their reading and appreciation.[1] You become a better reader by reading Nabokov, and—as we know from one study, reading him in high school may make it more likely that you will be admitted to the college of your choice (Marjorie Schiff)—but

---

1. An exception to this tendency is Allen Barra's essay, "Reading *Lolita* in Alabama," which expresses great appreciation for Nabokov's writing but concludes by admitting that "accepting literature on his terms can negate what you loved about literature in the first place." Barra also notes the disparity between Nafisi's and Nabokov's approach to fiction: "Nafisi, I think, is wrong in seeing social and political intent in *Lolita*, but she is not wrong in wanting them to be there."

does reading Nabokov make you a better person? Does becoming a better reader of texts make you a more attentive reader of people? This is the central assumption behind Richard Rorty's "The Barber of Kasbeam" (141–68), and this idea has also been advanced forcefully in a recent essay by Leona Toker (136), but it appears more grandiosely in Nafisi's book and in that book's appreciative reviews. Suellen Stringer-Hye concludes her review in *Nabokov Studies* as follows:

> Borrowing from the rhetoric of Mike Gold and others who sought, however unsuccessfully or misguidedly, to overthrow societal unfairness by direct political action, Nafisi posted this directive at the website entrance to the Dialogue Project, an online forum she conducts to discuss Democracy in the Middle East: "Book Lovers of the World Unite!" For Nafisi, and maybe even Nabokov, good readers really can "save the world." (211)[2]

In this chapter, and in the two that follow, I look closely at several works that in very different ways seek to deal with disturbing aspects of Nabokov's poetics through recuperative readings. None of these actually goes so far as claiming that reading Nabokov well will save the world, but all are implicitly rooted in notions of empowerment, aimed at providing support to the victims of political, sexual, or hermeneutic coercion. I argue that all these readings are misreadings, some more sophisticated than others, but these misreadings are valuable because they are indicative of the pressures Nabokov places on his readers and can help us to see more clearly some of the essential features of his poetics.

One of the most distressing aspects of the Islamic regime in Iran is the way it has marginalized educated women, making many of them feel alienated from the fundamental values of their society. "People like me seemed as irrelevant as Fitzgerald was to Mike Gold, or Nabokov to Stalin's Soviet Union, or James to the Fabian Society, or Austen to the revolutionaries of her time. In the taxi I took out the few books I had paid for and surveyed their covers, caressing their glossy surfaces, so giving to the touch. [...] I decided I would stop going to the university until they expelled me. Now that I would have a great deal of time on my hands, I could read without any feelings of guilt" (166–67). Nafisi, however, is unable to play the role of the self-indulging or even meditative recluse. There are moments in her memoir when she

---

2. Mike Gold (1894–1967) was the editor of the American leftist literary journal *New Masses* and author of the article "Proletarian Realism." His short stories were published in Russian in 1925 under the title *Prokliatyi advokator.*

pretends to seek asylum in the realm of the sensual, describing the pleasure of exposing her skin, of drinking coffee, even of eating cream puffs. These passages, however, are some of the weakest, aesthetically, in the book: "Too excited to eat breakfast, I put the coffee on and then took a long, leisurely shower. The water caressed my neck, my back, my legs, and I stood there both rooted and light" (9).[3] Nafisi repeatedly abandons these clichéd scenes for the principal idea behind the book: that literature is relevant because it speaks so precisely to the situation of Nafisi and other women in Iran. She begins her memoir with a student recalling Nafisi's own advice:

> She reminded me of a warning I was fond of repeating: do not, under any circumstances, belittle a work of fiction by trying to turn it into a carbon copy of real life; what we search for in fiction is not so much reality but the epiphany of truth. Yet I suppose that if I were to go against my own recommendation and choose a work of fiction that would most resonate with our lives in the Islamic Republic of Iran, it would not be *The Prime of Miss Jean Brodie* or even *1984* but perhaps Nabokov's *Invitation to a Beheading* or better yet, *Lolita*. (3)

This passage sets the tone for the entire book, which is a struggle between the sensibility of a literary scholar who knows she should know better and a political protester who, having come of age with Mike Gold, keeps trying to make literature relevant and useful. If *Reading "Lolita" in Tehran* has a single lesson for readers of Nabokov, it is about the dangers of relevance. In this book politics prevails, so that *Lolita* becomes a parable about Nafisi's life in Iran:

> Our class was shaped within this context [of Iranian censorship], in an attempt to escape the gaze of the blind censor for a few hours each week. There, in that living room, we rediscovered that we were also living, breathing human beings; and no matter how repressive the state became, no matter how intimidated and frightened we were, like Lolita we tried to escape and to create our own little pockets of freedom. And like Lolita, we took every opportunity to flaunt our insubordination: by showing a little hair from under our scarves, insinuating a little color into the drab uniformity of our appearances, growing our nails, falling in love, and listening to forbidden music. (25–26)

---

3. Gideon Lewis-Kraus is one of the few to criticize the book on literary grounds: "Nafisi's emptily lyrical sentences ('It was evening. Outside, the sky was the color of dusk—not dark, not light, not even gray') are perfectly suited for the facile readings she presents of the texts at hand."

The word "like" bears a heavy burden in Nafisi's memoir, as the simile becomes the figure of speech most responsible for demonstrating literature's relevance to the real world. "Like the best defense attorneys, who dazzle with their rhetoric and appeal to our higher sense of morality, Humbert exonerates himself by implicating his victim—a method we were quite familiar with in the Islamic Republic of Iran. ('We are not against cinema,' Ayatollah Khomeini had declared as his henchmen set fire to the movie houses, 'we are against prostitution!')" (42). This continual use of literature to serve as a parable about Iranian life is the memoir's most essential—and most overplayed—rhetorical device:

> What we in Iran had in common with Fitzgerald was this dream that became our obsession and took over our reality, this terrible beautiful dream, impossible in its actualization, for which any amount of violence might be justified or forgiven. [...] When I left the class that day, I did not tell them what I myself was just beginning to discover: how similar our own fate was becoming to Gatsby's. He wanted to fulfill his dream by repeating the past, and in the end he discovered that the past was dead, the present a sham, and there was no future. Was this not similar to our revolution, which had come in the name of our collective past and had wrecked our lives in the name of a dream? (144)

These moments are so frequent that the few passages in which Nafisi switches back into a Nabokovian mode and denies that she is writing political allegory have the opposite effect of hammering home, very succinctly, what she in effect has been arguing all along:

> I want to emphasize once more that *we* were *not* Lolita, the Ayatollah was *not* Humbert and this republic was *not* what Humbert called his princedom by the sea. *Lolita* was *not* a critique of the Islamic Republic, but it went against the grain of all totalitarian perspectives. (35)

Rhetorically, this emphatic denial gives Nafisi license to proceed with a reading of *Lolita* as political allegory, and the disclaimer has had just as little impact on her reviewers' presentation of her book (see Allen, Yardley, and Hewett).[4] Nafisi several times asserts that the novels she discussed with her students offered her an avenue of escape, but these flights bear less of a

---

4. The shifts between the moments when Nafisi endorses reading *Lolita* as political allegory and those when she rejects such a reading are particularly jarring in the excerpts published in the *Chronicle of Higher Education,* where the abridgment of her text draws its contradictory sentiments into much closer proximity.

resemblance to Lolita's than to Cincinnatus's, which, until the end of *Invitation to a Beheading,* always lead him back into prison. "Curiously, the novels we escaped into led us finally to question and prod our own realities, about which we felt so helplessly speechless" (39). On Nafisi's own terms, *Lolita* fails to provide an escape that would not involve a real-world geographical exit over the border. Moreover, in some respects, Nafisi profoundly misunderstands the nature of escape in Nabokov's fiction. Twice she cites *Bend Sinister* for the proposition that in most of Nabokov's novels—and here she includes *Invitation to a Beheading, Ada,* and *Pnin*—"there was always the shadow of another world, one that was only attainable through fiction" (32). Yet *Bend Sinister* seems to me to stand for the proposition that the other, kinder world of "tenderness, brightness, and beauty" may be the world that actually exists *outside* the literary text. One can read *Bend Sinister, Ada,* and *Pnin* as a concession that on Nabokov's terms there is often nothing crueler than fiction.

In the aesthetic realm Nabokov gamely embraced the dictator's mantle. As we have seen, he proudly asserted that he was "the perfect dictator" in the "private world" of his fiction (*Strong Opinions,* 69). This did not mean that Nabokov liked real-world dictators, only that in life and in art the same terms can have radically different meanings and that the two realms do not necessarily have anything in common—one translates between them at one's peril. Yet Alfred Appel's interview question—whether Nabokov had ever experienced the problem of a character threatening to "dictate" the course of a book's action—was a good one, because in large measure Nabokov's fiction is *about* that peril, about the dangers and temptations of creating equivalencies between life and art.[5] That peril is often figured by the question of whether fiction offers characters room for freedom of choice or escape; the reader who empathizes with an oppressed character is brought up short by Nabokov's reminder that all characters are inevitably oppressed, though some never realize it and others, like Fyodor in *The Gift,* are thankful for the benign conditions of their terms of confinement. Nabokov's reader may initially resent the interruption of his empathetic relationship with a novel's characters, but that resentment is often succeeded by aesthetic and metafictive gratitude. Perhaps more than anyone else's readers, Nabokov's reader thinks, "Thank God I'm a reader"—a formulation that implies both appreciation and relief.

Midway through the teaching of *The Great Gatsby* in a university classroom, Nafisi is confronted by students claiming that the novel is immoral. She has a pedagogic inspiration: "Suddenly a mischievous notion got hold

---

5. Several scholars have discussed this point, none better than Alexander Dolinin ("Nabokov's Time Doubling," 21).

of me. I suggested, in these days of public prosecutions, that we put Gatsby on trial" (120). Although this idea, with its weighty ideological tradition,[6] does wonders for student participation, it is emblematic of the way Nafisi's defense of literature inevitably serves to undermine literature. While Nafisi reminds one of the students attacking Fitzgerald that *Gatsby* is "a work of fiction and not a how-to manual" (120), Nafisi essentially uses *Gatsby* and *Lolita* as "how-not-to manuals", and she never acknowledges that this blurring of fiction and real life has dangerous potential. Nafisi portrays Nabokov as the enemy of solipsizers: "Nabokov had taken revenge against our own solipsizers; he had taken revenge on the Ayatollah Khomeini, on Yassi's last suitor, on the dough-faced teacher for that matter. They had tried to shape others according to their own dreams and desires, but Nabokov, through his portrait of Humbert, had exposed all solipsists who take over other people's lives" (33). Nafisi never seems to realize that her entire book is an exercise in solipsism. The rhetoric of the following passage, which succeeds a critique of the mullahs' appropriation of Iran's past, also speaks to Nafisi's political refracting of the novel:

> At some point, the truth of Iran's past became as immaterial to those who appropriated it as the truth of Lolita's is to Humbert. It became immaterial in the same way that Lolita's truth, her desires and life, must lose color before Humbert's one obsession, his desire to turn a twelve-year-old unruly child into his mistress.
>
> When I think of Lolita, I think of that half-alive butterfly pinned to the wall. The butterfly is not an obvious symbol, but it does suggest that Humbert fixes Lolita in the same manner that the butterfly is fixed; he wants her, a living breathing human being, to become stationary, to give up her life for the still life he offers her in return. Lolita's image is forever associated in the minds of her readers with that of her jailer. Lolita on her own has no meaning; she can only come to life through her prison bars.
>
> This is how I read *Lolita*. Again and again as we discussed *Lolita* in that class, our discussions were colored by my students' hidden personal sorrows and joys. Like tearstains on a letter, these forays into the hidden and the personal shaded all our discussions of Nabokov. And more and more I thought of that butterfly; what linked us so closely was this perverse intimacy of victim and jailer. (37)

---

6. On the genre of the ideological trial, see Cassiday and Wood.

Nafisi does not unpack the last sentence, but it may imply more than she intends. If there is perverse intimacy here, it is between the solipsizing Humbert and the politicizing Nafisi. That "again and again," referring to Nafisi's interpretation of *Lolita,* resembles the iteration of Humbert's solipsistic desire to possess Lolita ("oh, no, not again!") as his own sexual property and as the reincarnation of his first love (*Lolita,* 192). In Nafisi's hands, much of Nabokov's unruly text disappears. It is inevitable that *any* interpretation condenses and distorts its original object, but what I want to draw attention to now is that if *Lolita* functions as a parable in Nafisi's book, that parable may be not only about the political oppression of women in Iran but also about the oppression of literature by politics.

As we have seen, Nabokov confessed to a certain thematic repetitiveness in his work (*Strong Opinions,* 95), and in the work of some Nabokov scholars there is a tendency to take this dictum too literally, to choose one novel as a master text through which to read the others. For Nafisi the primary text is not *Lolita* but *Invitation to a Beheading.* The analysis of literature in the section of her book entitled *Lolita* begins and ends with *Invitation to a Beheading.* Indeed, Nafisi's attention keeps slipping from *Lolita* to this novel, which she says was one of her students' favorites. The appeal of *Invitation* should be obvious: it is one of the most easily allegorized works written by Nabokov. Many of Nabokov's other works may be read as allegories about literature, but this one has an obvious attraction for politically minded readers. Toward the end of the *Lolita* section, Nafisi writes, "there was not much difference between our jailers and Cincinnatus's executioners. They invaded all private spaces and tried to shape every gesture, to force us to become one of them, and that in itself was another form of execution" (77). The next and final paragraph lovingly evokes Cincinnatus's escape and the disintegration of both "the sham world around him" and his executioner, but by insisting on political allegory, Nafisi in effect carries out the execution, reinforcing the sham world and preventing Cincinnatus's escape.

The centrality of *Invitation to a Beheading* to *Reading "Lolita" in Tehran* raises an intriguing possibility. As we know from Brian Boyd's biography, *Invitation* was essentially spun off from Nabokov's efforts to write the fourth chapter of *The Gift* (*The Russian Years,* 408–17), which contains the hero's biography of the Russian nineteenth-century progressive icon and martyr, Nikolai Chernyshevsky. Not only that chapter, but all of *The Gift* was written to debunk many of the values for which Chernyshevsky stood, most notably utilitarianism and the subjugation of poetry to politics. In some respects, however, Nabokov has made Chernyshevsky sympathetic while emphasizing his responsibility for conditions in 1930s Russia, where the goal of enlightenment led to the "light [...] burning in the window of a prison overseer" (*The Gift,* 175). As Irina Paperno has demonstrated, aesthetically Fyodor does Cherny-shevsky a favor, coloring in the drab details of his existence and giving his life story "a poetic ring" ("How Nabokov's *Gift* is Made," 306; *The Gift,* 298). Nafisi's book can be seen as a sort of parodic reversal of the aestheticizing process in *The Gift:* having escaped from confinement in that novel's fourth chapter, the now somewhat postmodern Nikolai Gavrilovich picks up Lolita and has his de-aestheticizing way with Nabokov's most famous creation.

Chernyshevsky's novel and Nafisi's memoir offer several strange moments of contact. The most obvious point of comparison is the reading group, a sort of domestic class for ego-reinforcement and consciousness-raising. Vera Pavlovna's sewing workshop begins as an economic collective, but it rapidly evolves into a nineteenth-century book group that serves as a sentimentalized substitute for the formal education these girls could not have:

> From the very first Vera Pavlovna had begun to provide books. After giving the seamstresses instructions, she began to read aloud to them. [...] Needless to say, from the very beginning the girls conceived a liking for reading; some had been avid readers even before. Within two or three weeks this reading during work hours had become a regular institution. After three or four months several excellent readers emerged from the group. [...] Once Vera Pavlovna had been relieved of her obligation to read aloud, she began to relate more tales of her own devising. [...] Gradually her tales began to resemble light lectures on various fields of knowledge. Then—and this was a very large step— Vera Pavlovna saw the possibility of establishing a regular course of instruction. The girls were so eager to learn and their work was going so well that they decided to take a long break in the middle of the day just before dinner to conduct their lessons. (Chernyshevsky, 195–96)

Like Chernyshevsky, Nafisi uses the young women in the reading group to tell stories about the oppressive reality of everyday life. Chernyshevsky's tale of Mashenka Pribytkova, who is accosted on the street and then accused of prostitution, finds its corollary in the story of Sanaz, one of a group of girls caught in a raid of a boy's villa who are jailed, forced to sign confessions. and subjected to virginity tests. As part of her teaching of Jane Austen, Nafisi asks her students to dance. The chapter describing the sewing collective also leads to a dance—and the tonality is reminiscent of *Reading "Lolita" in Tehran:*

> They're delighted: they dance a gallop or a waltz, chase each other about, play the piano, chat, and laugh, but most of all, they sing. But all this

chasing, laughter, and everything else in no way prevent these young people from idolizing Vera Pavlovna totally: unconditionally, and boundlessly. They respect her more than most people respect their older sisters, as even a good mother isn't always respected. Moreover, the songs they sing aren't pure nonsense, although sometimes there's some of that, too. [...] Vera Pavlovna really enjoys this free, open, and active life, which is not without its sybaritic side—luxuriating in her soft, warm bed, as well as savoring real cream and pastries with cream. (Chernyshevsky, 202)

"We would walk to our favorite pastry shop, where they had amazing cream puffs, made with real cream. We bought the cream puffs and went back out into the snow, in whose protective gleam we ate them as we talked nonsense and walked and walked" (Nafisi, 145). That both these books pair female consciousness-raising with cream pastries might seem an extraordinary coincidence, but both spring from the marriage of ideology and sentimentalism. "We talked about creating a clandestine group and calling it the Dear Jane Society. We would meet and dance and eat cream puffs, and we would share the news. [...] I now remember that it was that day as Mahshid, Nassrin, and I walked to my office that quite suddenly, without thinking of it, I asked them to join in my secret class. [...] What will be required of us? Mahshid asked. *Absolute* commitment to the works, to the class, I said with an impetuous air of finality. More than committing them, I had now committed myself" (266). Nafisi's seminar emerges as a kind of conspiracy-light, merging this sort of collective responsibility (*krugovaia poruka*) with excessive reliance on pastries, stilted dialogue, and other markers of the ideological idyll. Change the names and translate the terms of endearment (sweetheart would become *milen'kii*) and the following passage might appear in either novel:

> That morning, we were waiting for Sanaz. Mitra, her dimples making a temporary appearance, had informed the class that Sanaz wanted us to wait for her—she had a surprise. All our wild speculations were met with a reticent smile.
>
> "Only two things could have happened," Azin speculated. "Another row with her brother and she's finally decided to leave home and move in with her wonderful aunt." She raised her hand with a tinkling of gold and silver bangles. "Or she's marrying her sweetheart."
>
> "The sweetheart seems the more likely of the two," said Yassi, straightening herself up a little, "judging by Mitra's expression."
>
> Mitra's dimples widened, but she refused to respond to our provocation. (258)

Nafisi's memoir contains many moments that refer consciously to *Lolita,* either by motif or quotation. But in its tonality and style, it probably owes more to the tradition of ideological fiction, perhaps as channeled by Mike Gold and the other American writers Nafisi read during her leftist, prerevolutionary phase. A curious example of a figure that straddles both traditions before toppling into the ideological one is the man Nafisi calls her "magician." This fellow—an older, reclusive scholar whom Nafisi first introduces as coming from a fictitious Nabokov story before acknowledging his "real" existence—has an interesting status in the novel. On one hand, this "inimitable, incorrigible Mr. R"—a name that nods to Nabokov's author-agent in *Transparent Things*—is given many of the memoir's most insightful lines. In fact, many of the comments I have been making here can be seen as extrapolations of his remarks to Nafisi: "I don't belong to their club, but I am also paying a big price. I don't lose, and I don't win. In fact, I don't exist. You see, I have withdrawn not just from the Islamic Republic but from life as such, but *you* can't do that—you have no desire to do that" (181). He rebukes Nafisi for being too engaged with the political culture around her: "Because the regime won't leave you alone, do you intend to conspire with it and give it complete control over your life?" (280). She seems to concede his point, but then returns to her solipsism, continuing to relate everything to the Iranian political scene (282). Mr. R even criticizes her penchant for the maudlin, giving the lie to Gloria Emerson's later praise in *The Nation* that Nafisi is incapable of writing a trite sentence:

> As he carries in the two mugs of tea, I tell him, You know, I feel all my life has been a series of departures. He raises his eyebrows, placing the mugs on the table, and looks at me as if he had expected a prince and all he could see was a frog. Then we both laugh. He says, still standing, You can say this sort of crap in the privacy of these four walls—I am your friend; I shall forgive you—but don't ever write this in your book. (Nafisi, 338)

There is much that is Nabokovian about this figure, who provides the sort of preemptive self-critique we might expect on a more profound literary level from *The Gift's* Koncheyev. Yet the magician, too, ultimately sinks down into the memoir's rapidly accumulating Chernyshevskian register. Most tellingly, Nafisi turns him into a sort of psychiatrist's psychiatrist. Nafisi portrays herself as a sort of therapist—"They came to my house in a disembodied state of suspension, bringing to my living room their secrets, their pains, and their gifts" (58)—and when she is in a moment of doubt herself, she turns to the magician:

> He finished my sentences for me, articulated my wishes and demands, and by the time I left, we already had a plan. This was what was good about him: people who went to see him somehow ended up with some plan or another, whether it was how to behave towards a lover or how to start a new project or structure a talk. I don't remember too clearly the exact nature of the plan I went home with, but he does, I am sure, for he seldom forgets. (175)

Obviously, there is the tradition of the confessor at work here, as well, and Vera Pavlovna, too, is ready to fulfill that role for her girls, but we can find a much closer parallel in the literature Chernyshevsky helped inspire: the consultation with the wise party mentor to whom the hero turns in moments of confusion or doubt. Chernyshevsky provides his protagonists with the superhuman figures of Rakhmetov and Bozio, model figures who help guide lesser mortals to personal and ideological epiphanies in the nineteenth-century equivalents of talking cures.

The most interesting point of comparison between Nafisi's and Chernyshevsky's work may be their use of intertextual parallels. In *What Is to Be Done,* these texts are Vera Pavlovna's four dreams, virtually self-interpreting, which provide opportunities for fantasies and conscience-raising and which she uses as touchstones for making sense of the real world. Nafisi follows a similar pattern, except that the heroic hermeneutics of dream interpretation ostensibly give way to literary criticism. The method, though, is the same: the application of texts encountered by the characters to the political situation around them.

It isn't clear in *Invitation to a Beheading* to what sort of world Cincinnatus is escaping. All we know is that "Cincinnatus made his way in that direction where, to judge by the voices, stood beings akin to him" (223). We do know, however, the kind of world into which Nafisi escapes. She now teaches at Johns Hopkins and has become a bestselling author in the United States. Although she portrays literature as offering the victims of totalitarianism an escape from ideology, hers was not an escape through literature but through real-world travel. We, her American readers, may be tempted to see ourselves as beings akin to her, and one of the ways her book succeeds is by transferring her own anxieties about relevance onto us, her readers. Behind the book's popularity may be the imagination of a spectacular sort of regime change—what if we had dropped five hundred thousand copies of *Lolita* onto Baghdad—that would demonstrate the importance of Western values to the Islamic world.[7] The book depicts Western literature as a triumphant institution; indeed, one of the greatest points of similarities between Nafisi's work and Nabokov's is that both represent attempts of established literary traditions to stake a claim to relevance in new soil (Russian literature comes to America in *Lolita,* the Western canon travels to Iran in *Reading "Lolita" in Tehran*). *Lolita* listens more closely to indigenous discourses, incorporating them in a way that makes them the hero of the book. For Nabokov, *Lolita* was the ultimate career move; the novel had to make its mark—even scandalously—on natives of the New World. Nafisi, however, writes not for Iranians—for whom the Western canon is claimed to be relevant—but for those same New World natives, who are now older, less susceptible to scandal, and less certain of their place in the world after the end of the American Century. Ironically, the *Lolita* she returns to us has been altered in transit; transformed into political allegory, it comforts rather than shocks and thus is suitable for book groups across the country.

My point is not that regime change in Iran would necessarily be a bad thing; I want, rather, to stress that celebration of the real-world power of writing has a cost. The price of literature's relevance may be the diminution of its literary value. Rejoicing in this sort of relevancy, we may experience something akin to Alice's horror when the baby in her arms turns into a pig. "Look at what *Lolita* can do," we cry, triumphantly, before examining the book in our hands and realizing that it is Vera Pavlovna's fifth dream. Liberated from Nabokov's prison of metafiction by Nafisi's emancipatory memoir, Nikolai Chernyshevsky has followed Nabokov—via Tehran—to America, to shape the understanding of Nabokov in our living rooms and to demonstrate that when literary characters gain the upper hand on their creator, we are no longer reading literature.

---

7. Nafisi's role in affirming the value of the Western canon is discussed at length in Hamid Dabashi's critique of Nafisi as a "comprador intellectual."

❧ CHAPTER 6

Lolita in the Real World

A few years ago, in one of the first senior seminars I offered on *Lolita,* we spent a few days discussing critical works employing a feminist approach to the novel. In the course of debating the merits of a chapter by Linda Kauffman that focuses on the silencing of Lolita, the students considered whether the novel was participating in or critiquing the suppression of women's speech. Several noted that the answer to this question depended on what a reader brought to the novel, both in terms of worldview and method of reading. One expressed the opinion that *Lolita* was a misogynistic book, but not because it justified child abuse. Rather, she said, the book was hostile to women because Nabokov could not bring himself to represent female sexual pleasure.

Were *Lolita* to portray its heroine enjoying her sexual encounters with Humbert, the novel would risk toppling into the genre of at least soft-core pornography. Adrian Lyne's generally faithful movie departs most strikingly from the novel in the scene where it depicts Lolita's experiencing an orgasm while she reads the funny papers on Humbert's lap. (According to Humbert, her reaction to this coitus is total indifference: "On especially tropical afternoons, in the sticky closeness of the siesta, I liked the cool feel of armchair leather against my massive nakedness as I held her in my lap. There she would be, a typical kid picking her nose while engrossed in the lighter sections of a newspaper, as indifferent to my ecstasy as if it were something she had sat upon, a shoe, a doll, the handle of a tennis racket, and was too indolent to remove" [165]). Seeing Lyne's movie, or reading *Lo's Diary,* Pia Pera's novelistic reconstruction of the plot from Lolita's point of view, one is constantly reminded of the extent to which the novel leaves the character of Lolita a blank page, a screen on which Humbert projects his fantasies and desires. Pera's description of Lolita as a young woman enjoying her body and in control of her own destiny is not a pleasant picture for all readers of *Lolita* to contemplate; in his legally negotiated preface to the English translation of Pera's novel Dmitri Nabokov claims that "feminists had mixed feelings about the calculating harpy that emerged" (viii). In a similar vein, Leland de la Durantaye is outraged by Sarah Herbold's suggestion that Lolita—"a trashy little girl"—enjoys her encounter with Humbert's lap on the davenport ("Lolita in *Lolita,*" 175). That phrase, however, is not Herbold's but de la Durantaye's; Herbold never uses the epithet "trashy" to describe Lolita as a girl. Rather, she says that when Humbert eventually finds an older Lolita at the novel's end, she has become "a diminished version of herself [. . .] a white-trash married mother-to-be whose defective and unliterary partner is no threat to Humbert" ("'I have camouflaged everything,'" 83). Herbold describes the young Lolita as an "elusive and sassy nymphet," but de la Durantaye's symptomatic transformation of (Herbold's) Lolita from sassy to trashy is the evident corollary of his reaction to a reading that acknowledges female sexual pleasure. Since readers have no way of knowing what sort of person Humbert prevents from speaking her mind, those who want to imagine Lolita as a real-world girl (or, at least, as a real girl's representation), have to construct the character themselves or attack the constructions of others. In the process, they are required to emulate Humbert, creating Lolita in a way that inevitably makes her reflect their own anxieties and desires.

Of course, the elaboration of any argument about the meaning or even about the poetics of a literary work provides an opportunity for projection, because a scholar inevitably adds something and by necessity subtracts a great deal from the text. Pera flaunts her imagination: that is the basis for her argument that *Lo's Diary* was an original work of fiction. Dmitri Nabokov sees the book not only as derivative but as a work that uses copying as a point of (untalented) departure: the treatment of VN by "PP" (as DN calls her) should be considered unauthorized because it takes too much license. To his mind, Pera did not have the right to re-create his father's characters.

Literary scholarship, whatever new paradigms it invents, is inherently a secondary enterprise, and thus this question of re-creation is particularly fraught, because a critical or scholarly interpretation is supposed to be accurate, adequate to its object of study. Even the simplest of paraphrases offers difficulties. What phrases are to be used to describe what Humbert and Lolita do with each other's verbally constructed bodies: "make love," "have sex," "bed"? And what is entailed in making only one of them the subject of the governing verb or, on the contrary, putting them both in the nominative?

Kauffman's operative assumption is that Humbert works by ellipses, leaving out Lolita's experience and suppressing her voice. When Humbert encounters Dolores Schiller near the novel's end, Lolita says (or, to put it more precisely, Humbert says she says—this is reported speech) "this world was just one gag after another, if somebody wrote up her life nobody would ever believe it" (273). One can take this "gag" in two (or even three) senses, since Lolita's words have been stopped up by Humbert's wit. Yet this restriction of speech is a feature of any writing that seeks to critique, summarize, or analyze a work of literature. Humbert's final meeting with Lolita is often cited as evidence of his reformation and transformation, and it is interesting to observe how Humbert's prose is quoted selectively by scholars. Leona Toker's approach is emblematic of those who see this scene as suffused with "genuinely beautiful emotion": "For the first time in his life Humbert really loves the woman who is no longer a 'nymphet' and can therefore generously renounce her" (*Nabokov*, 207). She continues:

> his lust for Dolly has been replaced by a belated yet genuine compassion and love: "There she was...hopelessly worn at seventeen...and I looked and looked at her, and knew as clearly as I know I am to die, that I loved her more than anything I had ever seen or imagined on earth, or hoped for anywhere else.... What I used to pamper among the tangled vines of my heart, *mon grand péché radieux,* had dwindled to its essence: sterile and selfish vice, all *that* I cancelled and cursed. (207, Toker's ellipses)

Ultimately, Toker distrusts the completeness of Humbert's transformation because, she points out, he would have written the first half of the book differently had he really repented. But she is able to present the Coalmont scene as exculpatory in large measure because she herself cancels part of it. Here is the entire paragraph from which her quotation is excerpted, with the omitted portions in italics:

> *She closed her eyes and opened her mouth, leaning back on the cushion, one felted foot on the floor. The wooden floor slanted, a little steel ball would have rolled into the kitchen. I knew all I wanted to know. I had no intention of torturing my darling. Somewhere beyond Bill's shack an afterwork radio had begun singing of folly and fate, and* there she was *with her ruined looks and*

her adult, rope-veined narrow hands and her goose-flesh white arms, and her shallow ears, and her unkempt armpits, there she was (my Lolita!), hopelessly worn at seventeen, *with that baby, dreaming already in her of becoming a big shot and retiring around 2020 A.D.*—and I looked and looked at her, and knew as clearly as I know I am to die, that I loved her more than anything I had ever seen or imagined on earth, or hoped for anywhere else. *She was only the faint violet whiff and dead leaf echo of the nymphet I had rolled myself upon with such cries in the past; an echo on the brink of a russet ravine, with a far wood under a white sky, and brown leaves choking the brook, and one last cricket in the crisp weeds...but thank God it was not that echo alone that I worshipped.* What I used to pamper among the tangled vines of my heart, mon grand péché radieux, had dwindled to its essence: sterile and selfish vice, all that I canceled and cursed. *You may jeer at me, and threaten to clear the court, but until I am gagged and half-throttled, I will shout my poor truth. I insist the world know how much I loved my Lolita, this Lolita, pale and polluted, and big with another's child, but still gray-eyed, still sooty-lashed, still auburn and almond, still Carmencita, still mine; Changeons de vie, ma Carmen, allons vivre quelque part où nous ne serons jamais séparés; Ohio? The wilds of Massachusetts? No matter, even if those eyes of hers would fade to myopic fish, and her nipples swell and crack, and her lovely young velvety delicate delta be tainted and torn—even then I would go mad with tenderness at the mere sight of your dear wan face, at the mere sound of your raucous young voice, my Lolita.*

Toker has omitted not only Humbert's continuing obsession with Lolita's body but also his repeated expressions of proprietariness, as well as the breathless, anaphoristic style that continues to cruise around her body. How scholars cite this passage—what parts of it they retain and what they omit—can frequently be used as a shorthand gauge of their interpretation of the novel's "message" and of the relative weights of moral and aesthetic factors in their analysis. Michael Wood cites the final sentence of this passage as he concludes that style still makes the man:

> The wan face, the raucous voice, the eyes like myopic fish, the velvety delicate delta are the notations of desperate love, and Humbert writes here the purest, most precise Nabokovian prose. What we question is not his passion but its supposed new respectability. The whole of this book has been asking us to trust Humbert's obsession, even as we are repelled by it. We can't leave off trusting it now, especially when it speaks in these accents, so lyrically mourning what it claims it won't miss. (141)

Especially striking in Toker's presentation of the passage is her use of terms of reality: "genuine compassion," "genuinely beautiful emotion," "really loves." Humbert's masterful command of language (and Nabokov's near-total control of his text's every word) leads to a readerly gesture toward the real world that, many critics claim, Nabokov intends to foster. The lesson of *Lolita,* Brian Boyd and Richard Rorty, among others, have argued, is the necessity of noticing the sufferings of others and, especially, our role in producing them. For them *Lolita* does indeed have "a moral in tow" (Rorty 164, quoting Nabokov's afterword to the novel). As Boyd puts it, "By making it possible to see Humbert's story so much from Humbert's point of view, Nabokov warns us to recognize the power of the mind to rationalize away the harm it can cause: the more powerful the mind, the stronger on guard one must be" (*The American Years,* 232). Boyd also sees the novel as running against a valorization of confession and repentance: "Humbert demonstrates how easy it is to let moral awareness turn into sincere regret after the fact, but how much more difficult to curb the self before it tramples others underfoot" (254). Rorty views the book's message not so much as an injunction against causing suffering as a warning about insensitivity to the pain of others: "the moral is not to keep one's hands off little girls but to notice what one is doing, and in particular to notice what people are saying. For it might turn out, it very often does turn out, that people are trying to tell you that they are suffering" (164). In both cases, the argument hinges on the novel's production of a real-world impact: the good reader of the book will become not just a better reader but a better person in his everyday life. Toker joins this position, arguing in a later article for the salutary effect of Nabokov's work more generally: "Nabokov is recognized as a master of uniquely elaborate imagery and sophisticated patterns of motifs: the implicit ethical function of this facet of art lies precisely in the refinement of the careful reader's sensibilities; the sensibilities that can later be directed to human relationships" ("Nabokov and Bergson," 136). Even just noticing things in a book will lead us to notice them in the world around us.

There are a few things to note about this position. First, it allows the reader to be both resistant and submissive—we condemn Humbert's actions but allow ourselves to succumb to the beauty of his prose after all. Second, such an approach permits us to combat the anxiety, explored in earlier chapters, of becoming a Nabokovian character. Rather than being written *into* the text, readers can export the text into their extratextual lives. This kind of desire for real-world relevance accounts, I believe, for Boyd's treatment of the characters as if they lived among us: "Lolita is a real child who leaves things around the house, like any preteen American girl" (235); "[Humbert's] book may possibly immortalize Lolita, but his conduct has quite certainly hastened her death. The girl he pretended he might have killed as his Carmen he has indeed killed young by thrusting her so early into the adult world" (250). Even when Boyd's own language approaches that of the coming attractions Lolita would have seen in the cinema, he is serious about the novel's mimetic properties: "Nabokov knew the odds for someone debauched at twelve, subjected to Humbert's apprenticeship in sex for pay, sodomized by Clare Quilty, but he also wanted to show Lolita as an extraordinary young girl who triumphs over her fate in the only way left to her" (237). A telling moment comes when Boyd examines Humbert's repentance:

> She is no longer a nymphet, no longer a projection of his fancy, but a real person whom he loves just as she is. As the love theme soars, so does the theme of guilt. On his way to Ramsdale in search of Quilty's address, Humbert reviews his case: "Alas, I was unable to transcend the simple human fact that whatever spiritual solace I might find, whatever lithophanic eternities might be provided for me, nothing could make my Lolita forget the foul lust I had inflicted upon her . . . a North American girl-child named Dolores Haze had been deprived of her childhood by a maniac." (ellipsis in original, 249)

The cutting here is as problematic as Toker's. Boyd has omitted the start of the second sentence, which reads in full: "*Unless it can be proven to me—to me as I am now, today, with my heart and my beard, and my putrefaction—that in the infinite run it does not matter a jot that* a North American girl-child named Dolores Haze had been deprived of her childhood by a maniac *(and if it can, then life is a joke), I see nothing for the treatment of my misery but the melancholy and very local palliative of articulate art*" (283, emphasis added). The parenthetical conditional is troubling, not only because in Nabokov's fiction parentheses often contain a sentence's most crucial, only seemingly incidental information, but because, as we have seen, in this novel the word *life* is, indeed, a joke.

Kaufman's chapter is also problematic because her desire to "reinscribe" Lolita's body as a means of recognizing her suffering and damaged subjectivity leads the critic to betray her own methodological principles. A chapter that begins by proclaiming its loyalty to intertextuality and deconstruction and its defiance of "the representational fallacy" proceeds to conclude—after a distracting detour through literary predecessors—that the novel is "an uncannily accurate" and even "clinically verifiable" depiction of father-daughter incest (161, 166). While asserting the importance of "symptomatic reading," Kaufman hobbles that practice by transforming it from the analysis of a text's unintentional, often libidinal slippages to a straightforward reading of the symptoms of a character. This redefinition of an aggressive form of reading allows her to stand with Nabokov as a psychological realist critical of child abuse. Ultimately she comes to the realization that—quoting Michèle Barrett—"representation *does* bear a relation to something which we can know previously existed" (166). Although in her final paragraph she keeps using words like defamiliarization, agency, deconstruction, and *jouissance,* it is with the desperation of someone trying to hold onto critical tools going up in smoke; the attempt to reinscribe Lolita's body has led Kaufman to rewrite herself as a positivist.

The most impassioned engagement with *Lolita* from a real-world perspective is that provided by Elizabeth Patnoe, in an article first published in 1995 and expanded for publication in an anthology seven years later. Patnoe emphatically places *Lolita* in the context of the trauma suffered by victims of childhood sexual abuse. She argues that the novel has been misinterpreted because it has been co-opted by a hegemonic paradigm that insists on both the invisibility of child abuse and the evil of female sexuality. The text of *Lolita,* she writes, "offers evidence to indict Humbert," but it is "subtle enough that many readers overlook its critique of the misogyny illustrated in and purveyed by the rest of the text" (113). *Lolita* must be read carefully, so as not to miss the depravity of Humbert's character. Her quotation of the final meeting scene is radically different from Toker's:

> I had no intention of torturing *my* darling…there she was with her ruined looks and her adult…hands…(*my Lolita!*), hopelessly worn…and…I knew…that I loved her more than anything I had ever seen or imagined on earth….She was only the…dead leaf echo of the *nymphet* I had rolled myself upon with such cries in the past…but thank God it was not that echo alone that I worshipped….I will shout my poor truth. I insist the world know how much I loved *my* Lolita, this Lolita, pale and polluted…*still mine.*…No matter, even if…her lovely *young velvety delicate* delta be tainted and torn—even then I would go mad with tenderness at the mere sight of your dear wan face, at the mere sound of your raucous *young* voice, *my* Lolita. (emphasis added [by Patnoe])(129)

This method of reading, albeit toward a different end, is something like that of the "perverse articulation" which I have been plying elsewhere in this book, which is why, I suppose, I find it so unsettling here. But reaccentuation of the text is insufficient for the goals of Patnoe's reading; she urges that the only way the novel can be read with adequate proximity, with an eye for its "covert, intratextual messages," is to preface that reading with an awareness of the extratextual, highly personal dimensions of individual readers: "if we can understand the part of the extratextual realm that influences the personal part of the extratextual, then perhaps we will better access and understand the interplay of our culture, ourselves, and the texts that become our texts" (115).

Patnoe's project is indebted to a position of feminist defiance; she seeks to inhabit and render harmless textual areas of misogynistic practice—to take back the text: "I would like to see those of us who have been excluded from the hegemonic readings of *Lolita* resuscitate the character, reclaim the book, and insist upon our experiences with and around it so we can at least begin to counter the Lolita myth distortions, to resist some of the cultural appropriations of female sexuality" (115). *Lolita*'s principal danger is that many readers will fail to grasp the violence hidden beneath the narrative. Patnoe attempts, therefore, to bring that violence to the surface, in part by referring to real-life experiences of child abuse and the reaction of abuse victims to Nabokov's novels: "While Nabokov avoids sustained, graphic descriptions of Lolita's violations, his words throw some readers into ripping, detailed memories of their own molestations" (133–34). Patnoe has opened her analysis with epigraphs from a book about the treatment of abuse victims (*Working with Adult Survivors of Child Sexual Abuse* by Elsa Jones), but the adjective "ripping" strikes a very different note and raises distinctly literary questions of style and genre. The sentence I have just quoted is from a footnote attached to two paragraphs of text that provide the principal evidence of *Lolita*'s "hegemonic" danger. The passage begins in a sentimental milieu—similar to Nafisi's—but quickly switches gears:

> I witnessed how this book is not "just a book" for some people when, nestled into a booth one afternoon, some women and I began discussing the implications of *Lolita*. Three of us were especially passionate as we discussed its narrative strategy, its characterization, our responses. Our fourth colleague occasionally nodded her head, but remained quiet. About fifteen minutes into our talk, she abruptly rose to go home. The closest of her friends among us walked her to her car and upon her return told us why our colleague had gone: when she was a child, her father woke her, carried her from her bed to the bathroom, made her bend forward over the tub, and raped her. When she cried out, her father stuffed a washcloth in her mouth. With blood dripping down her legs, he forced her to perform fellatio on him. When she refused to swallow his semen, he squeezed her nostrils shut until she did. When he was finished, he picked her up by the elbows, held her face to the

mirror, and said, "Do you know why Daddy did this to you? Because you are such a pretty pussy."

Is this shocking to you? Do you feel that in my writing it and your reading it, this person's trauma has been re-enacted? It has—through her, through and for me, and for you. And I imposed this trauma on you, thrust it into your eyes without your consent. If you feel upset, then perhaps you can imagine how our fourth colleague felt and how others might respond to texts and discussions that catapult them into chasms of deep, secret pains—including discussions less vivid and texts far less shocking than this one. (116–17)

Patnoe portrays this description of a rape as an abrupt departure from the "passionate" discussion of the novel's "narrative strategy, its characterization, our responses." But the story of the rape is equally impassioned, and replete with details that accentuate its potential as a pornographic narrative. Whose recitation is this? The victim's? Her closest friend's? Patnoe's? What determines whether the precise details are gratuitous, useful, or essential? The technique employed in reporting her colleague's rape will be put to use by Patnoe in countering the traumatic impact of *Lolita*. Patnoe condemns "countless critics" who "focus on the book's pleasure and neglect its trauma." In so doing, "they also neglect many of [*Lolita's*] readers and enable the violator's pleasure, reinforce it, invite it to continue without confrontation." "Thus," she continues, "in addition to particular critical comments that purvey the Lolita myth, the collectivity of Lolita criticism in some way becomes complicit in the aestheticization of child molestation perpetuated by individual people and by the culture at large" (117).

Patnoe's own diction—"enable the violator's pleasure, reinforce it, invite it"—bespeaks a fascination of her own, and she seems unaware that she herself may be participating in the enabling discourse. The core of her analysis is a close reading of the scene at the Enchanted Hunters, the first scene of sexual intercourse between Humbert and Lolita. The final paragraph of that chapter of *Lolita* begins with Humbert's refusal to provide explicit details and ends with a disclaimer of interest in the topic of sex:

However, I shall not bore my learned readers with a detailed account of Lolita's presumption. Suffice it to say that not a trace of modesty did I perceive in this beautiful hardly formed young girl whom modern co-education, juvenile mores, the campfire racket, and so forth had utterly and hopelessly depraved. She saw the stark act merely as part of a youngster's furtive world, unknown to adults. What adults did for purposes of procreation was no business of hers. My life was handled by little Lo in an energetic, matter-of-fact manner as if it were an insensate gadget unconnected with me. While eager to impress me with the world of tough kids, she was not quite prepared for certain discrepancies between a kid's life and mine. Pride alone prevented her from giving up; for, in my strange predicament, I feigned supreme stupidity and had her have her way—at least while I could still bear it. But really these are irrelevant matters; I am not concerned with so-called "sex" at all. Anybody can imagine those elements of animality. A greater endeavor lures me on: to fix once for all the perilous magic of nymphets. (133–34)

In many respects, the scene is oddly anticlimactic, particularly in comparison with the davenport chapter earlier in the novel. Patnoe, however, after quoting over a page of the novel's text, endeavors to slow down the speed of the narrative to consider in seven pages of her own who might have meant what and what the two characters desired at each moment. (Her basic conclusion is that Lolita's notion of an amorous game included fondling, not intercourse: "Surely Lolita does not think that sexual intercourse is common among youngsters—while it would be quite likely that she would believe kissing or petting games are" [123]).[1] In the process, however, Patnoe offers her readers a text that claims to recapture but in essence *produces* a graphic moment of sexual contact. Patnoe, having noted that in the passage just quoted "life" must mean "penis," provides a three-page gloss, focusing on what each character probably wanted to happen. She concludes:

However, what if, in a kind of reversal of Humbert's narrative trend to be strategically symbolic and indirect, we pull back his covers and consider

---

1. This question of what Lolita—and Nabokov's readers—consider usual in the course of sexual development also bedevils Eric Goldman's attempt to read the novel within the context of the Kinsey reports. Beginning with a deconstructive stance that credits the novel for "interrogating the boundary between sexual 'deviance' and 'normality'" and exposing "the volatility of the subjective, social constructs of 'deviance' and 'normality'," Goldman ultimately cannot help himself from subscribing to a prescriptive notion of normativity when it comes to the sexual practices of twelve-year-old girls. The scare quotes disappear, they flicker back, and by the end of the article they are firmly present again, although in the interval we have learned that Humbert is "bizarre" and "perverse," while Lolita's sexual development prior to her departure from camp is characterized as "patently normal." At one point in the middle of the article, the word normal is not only stripped of scare quotes but highlighted in italics: "Lolita's juvenile sexual experiences, which, for Humbert, are evidences of her 'depravity,' can be viewed, in light of such contemporaneous studies as Kinsey's 1953 *The Sexual Behavior of the Human Female,* as the *normal* sexual awakening and sex play of girls Lolita's age (barring her experience with Humbert of course)" (94). Goldman does not refer in any specific way to the activity engaged in by Lolita with Charlie, and thus his readers never learn whether he—or Kinsey—consider sexual intercourse for twelve-year-olds normal. The article is fascinatingly conflicted in moral and methodological terms, and in conjunction with Kaufman's chapter may lead one to conclude that Nabokov does to practitioners of deconstruction what Humbert seeks to do to psychiatrists—induce in them the problems they seek to identify in others.

life more literally. Within this reading, these lines suggest that, when they pet, Lolita obviously alters the direction of Humbert's future life, that she makes out with him as if their behavior is in no way going to affect Humbert's future [...] Furthermore, the second use of *life,* considering its literal definition based in length of time (not anatomy), reiterates that a youngster may be satisfied with petting games while an adult may not be. Merging both meanings of *life* and both meanings of *stark act,* and considering that *harsh, blunt,* and *grim* are synonyms for *stark* (*Webster* and *American Heritage*), this passage underscores that Lolita is at once not prepared for Humbert's size or his ejaculatory stamina during fondling, that her pride compels her to continue petting, that Humbert goes along with her game, feigning stupidity about her limitations and her intentions, and when her way—the way of a kid's life, either the kissing or the fondling—is no longer enough for him, in an abuse of both her body and her "pride,"[2] he, without her consent, directs the stark activity *his* way: he penetrates her, and, as he rapes her, feigns ignorance about her pain while he thrusts to ejaculation. (125–26)

The point Patnoe makes in the long, final sentence, culminating in "ejaculation," is an imagining and enabling of Humbert's abuse. Humbert has asked his reader, earlier in the chapter, to help him conjure the scene into being: "Imagine me; I shall not exist if you do not imagine me" (129). Patnoe provides that necessary imaginary force, supplementing it as she believes Nabokov would want a good reader to do (127). Oddly, she does not take into account the short chapter which immediately follows the scene: Humbert's description of the mural he would have painted at the Enchanted Hunters had he been commissioned to redecorate the dining room:

There would have been a lake. There would have been an arbor in flame-flower. There would have been nature studies—a tiger pursuing a bird of paradise, a choking snake sheathing whole the flayed trunk of a shoat. There would have been a sultan, his face expressing great agony (belied, as it were, by his molding caress), helping a callipygian

---

2. Patnoe may well be misunderstanding "pride" ("Pride alone prevented her from giving up") as an attribute of Lolita rather than of Humbert. In the tradition of Elizabethan bawdy, "pride" could refer to the state of erection, predicated on a resemblance with "the proud man, puffed up with self-conceit" (Schroeder, 157). As evidence Schroeder cites Shakespeare's Sonnet 151 ("Love is too young to know what conscience is"): "flesh stays no farther reason; / But rising at thy name, doth point out thee / As his triumphant prize—proud of this pride / He is contented thy poor drudge to be, / To stand in thy affairs, fall by thy side, / No want of conscience hold it that I call / Her love for whose dear love I rise and fall."

slave child to climb a column of onyx. There would have been those luminous globules of gonadal glow that travel up the opalescent sides of juke boxes. There would have been all kinds of camp activities on the part of the intermediate group, Canoeing, Coranting, Combing Curls in the lakeside sun. There would have been poplars, apples, a suburban Sunday. There would have been a fire opal dissolving within a ripple-ringed pool, a last throb, a last dab of color, stinging red, smearing pink, a sigh, a wincing child. (134–35)

Here Humbert recaptures his experience of intercourse, returning at the final moment to the "reality" of the victim of his pleasure. This is a fully aes-theticized, even meta-aestheticized view of sex, and it draws the reader into its orbit in a perniciously rich fashion: not only does the alliteration entice the reader to echo the text phonetically, to read with his tongue as in the opening, "light of my life" passage, it also makes Humbert's pleasure depen-dent on a recollection of the preceding text. Sexual release is here predicated on a rereader's fondling of details, including sexually charged lexical elements (nature studies, gonadal glow, the alphabetical striptease of the entries in the *Girl's Encyclopedia*); if the reader is going to reject the pleasure offered by this passage, he must also reject the pleasures and methods that make *Lolita* worth reading. Patnoe's approach to the morning at the Enchanted Hunters is de-aestheticizing, but it may be no less in debt to a rhetoric of frenzied enjoy-ment. And while Lolita, the character in Nabokov's novel, remains a cipher, the "real" Lolita bodied forth by Patnoe has wound up in a graphic, nearly pornographic narrative.

Patnoe is not certain whether she is reading with or against Nabokov. She admits that in her first version of the chapter she was "not ready to exculpate Nabokov, the text, or the likes of Lionel Trilling" (127). Several years later, her opinion has softened: "I still cannot know for certain how Nabokov intended this passage to be read, but now I feel more sure that he would support my reading. After all, his text does support it" (127). Patnoe's tone toward the end of her reading of *Lolita* becomes oddly reminiscent of Dr. John Ray's: "While it might be simpler to slap the book shut, this will not silence its echoes. Instead of retreating from its trauma, I believe we—students and teachers, women and men—should confront its messages and challenges, should address its personal and cultural implications" (130). This call to arms is one of the most pronounced efforts in Nabokov criticism to enlist read-ers and scholars in a cause that might best be described as Applied Nabokov Studies. In many respects, Patnoe represents something of an extreme case of resistance to the notion that literature should be no more than "just a book."

Yet this resistance is shared by many Anglophone and, particularly, American readers of Nabokov; Patnoe's reading of *Lolita* presents a symptomatic, if exaggerated, instance of this inclination. (In Russia, this phenomenon is far less common, in part because the philological tradition of annotation and commentary is so strong that the impulse to find a subtext overrides the desire to change the world, in part because the notion of literature's ability to shape extratextual reality has been so discredited by the failure of the Chernyshevskian line in Russian letters.)[3]

With his complaint that he has "only words to play with" Humbert has anticipated—indeed, appealed for—the sort of reading practiced by Patnoe. Unable to achieve contact with physical flesh, Humbert beseeches the reader to transcend the realm of the merely verbal for him. Patnoe, seeking to make *Lolita* useful in the real world, obliges, but in the process she becomes Humbert's pander by reinscribing not only Lolita's body but his. Her traumatized colleague was not driven from the restaurant by *Lolita* itself; she fled during Patnoe's discussion of the novel's "implications." Patnoe's approach to *Lolita* offers a cautionary tale of how the beauty of Nabokov's prose—along with the richness of his patterning and his insistence that readers not identify with his characters—offers the possibility of an aesthetic sublime so pleasurable that it leads some readers to worry whether literature has a point, and then to seek that point in extratextual applications which result in slighting or devaluing the powerful aesthetic that triggered the search for usefulness in the first place.

---

3. On this point, see Etkind, 471. A recent attempt to apply Nabokov to Russia is Nina Khrushcheva's effort to depict Nabokov as the creator of "practical Weberian" heroes. Supposedly, Nabokov explains "how going over to a capitalist way of thinking—understood as growing pragmatism, efficiency, personal success, and a sense of individual responsibility—should change the benevolent, slothful and impractical Oblomov-like Russian attitude to life" (19). Purportedly speaking on behalf of Russians, Khrushcheva writes: "He is our textbook, and our road map for today's transitional period from a closed and communal terrain to its Western alternative, one open and competitive" (20). A political commentator based in the West and with American graduate degrees, Khrushcheva is essentially attempting to import Applied Nabokov Studies back into Russia.

❧ CHAPTER 7

Blackwell's *Paradox* and Fyodor's *Gift*

A Kinder and Gentler Nabokov

In 1999 Brian Boyd delivered two addresses in honor of Nabokov's one-hundredth birthday. Conflated, they were published a few years later as "A Centennial Toast." Boyd begins with a story. After his truck breaks down in Utah, a biology student with an interest in lepidoptery notices an older man walking down the road with a butterfly net. The student attempts to engage the collector in a conversation, but the man introduces himself (as Vladimir Nabokov) only after the student has responded correctly to his request that he identify several species of butterfly. The two stay in contact and eventually Nabokov sends him many of his field notes. Boyd sees the story as emblematic:

> What strikes me about Nabokov's encounter with Downey in Cottonwood Canyon is the demands he makes, the conditions he imposes, on this grimy truck driver: You can walk with me, but I will test you a little. If you pass the test, I will let you see who I am, and I will even offer you all that I have found, so that you can go on to make *your* discoveries in turn. [...] T]he story suggests Nabokov's demanding but ultimately generous relationship to his readers, which reflects his sense of the demanding but ultimately generous world that life offers us. (10)

If generosity is a meaningful measure of aesthetic quality, Nabokov's works certainly have it. All readers should, indeed, be thankful to Nabokov, but

Boyd's relating of this anecdote is as reflective of Nabokov studies as it is of that field's object of analysis and appreciation. The story is representative of a tendency in Nabokov scholarship: the desire to idealize the relationship between author and reader and to neutralize its troubling complexities. Nabokov *never* ceases testing his readers, there is no such thing as a definitive pass, and he never lets his reader see who he is or offers us all he has found. Boyd's italicization of "your" implies that Nabokov's work offers us discoveries that would not be the author's; yet Boyd's work, like nearly all insightful analyses of Nabokov's prose, is very much committed to the recovery of authorial intention. Even Patnoe, who finds Nabokov's work disturbing, cannot dispense with the idea that she is reading in accordance with his will.

So how open are Nabokov's texts to readers' *own* discoveries? Nabokov delights his readers, causes them pleasure and anxiety. All these reactions are part of the process of scaling the peak, at the top of which we will find ourselves in the author's embrace. The routes that we take—the "tacit tunnels" (to use a different Nabokovian topographical metaphor [*Stories,* 156]) between seemingly isolated moments in the text that, when connected, allow us to see the work's design—have all been engineered by the author.

One of the most interesting books written to date on Nabokov's rapport with his readers is Stephen H. Blackwell's *Zina's Paradox: The Figured Reader in Nabokov's "Gift."* The first monograph on Nabokov's most technically complex and most overtly modernist novel, it contains many wonderful insights produced by inspired close reading. Its central thesis, however, strikes me as quite interestingly mistaken and serves as a telling example of a scholar doing his utmost to depict Nabokov's relation to his readers in reassuring terms. Essentially, Blackwell draws an analogy between the rapport of reader to writer and that of couples happily or at least securely in love.

Succinctly stated, Blackwell's argument is that *"The Gift* is a novel formed not by an author's omnipotent will, but by a reader's creative reception" (1). He sees Zina, the hero's beloved, as a coauthor: the novel is "constantly mediated for us by Zina's creative reception" (10). Zina's paradox is that "the reader forms the text" (5).

The Gift is the story of a young poet's evolution into a great artist. As first-time readers of the novel quickly discover, the work is extremely disorienting. In his excellent chapter on "problematic reading" Blackwell reviews these complexities. The novel shifts repeatedly from first- to third-person narrative, and the temporality constantly oscillates, so that sometimes the book is told from the perspective of the hero as he was at the moment of the described action, sometimes from a more omniscient position, as if the hero were looking back at the action from well into the future. The prose shifts into poetry—sometimes obviously, sometimes maintaining the form of prose and not breaking the lines into stanzas. Frequently the prose is about poetry; at one point Marx is put into verse to make him "less boring" (245). As the reader returns repeatedly to the text, the gap between "the actual narrative" and "the reader's perception of it" narrows: "In essence the narrative waits for the reader to catch up, during subsequent readings" (Blackwell, 85). As those who have taught the novel know, there is a danger that part of the class will just give up; the teacher's task is to focus on the beauty of the language and the breathtaking but confusing transitions to convince students that reading and rereading will be worth the effort.

Of all Nabokov's novels, this is probably the one where the hero's universe is the most benign. And Fyodor deserves this benignity—he inflicts no harm on others and is clearly a budding literary genius entirely adequate to functioning in the world around him. He has had loving, exemplary parents, and he knows the Russian literary tradition better than the back of his hand. Although Nabokov, in his introduction to the English version of the novel, warns against identifying Nabokov with Fyodor, the similarities are obviously there, and they are not given a sinister twist as elsewhere in Nabokov's fiction.

Zina and Fyodor meet only halfway through the book—in the third of five chapters—although since the book is written in retrospect, it can be argued that the lovers know each other all along. Fyodor rents a room in the apartment occupied by Zina, her mother, and her stepfather. A devotee of his poetry, she asks him to autograph her copy of his lone book. Their romance takes off: as Blackwell says, "she *reads* her way into his life" (101). She becomes the first audience for Fyodor's *Life of Chernyshevski;* and, Blackwell argues, her role in the novel is to provide the loving reading that overcomes the divide between writer and reader:

> Zina's reading is not extensively presented, but in fact the entire novel is saturated with its significance. Not only does her reading result, indirectly or directly, in her union with Fyodor, but of course her reading, or more precisely, listening, gives shape to Fyodor's "The Life of Chernyshevski": "There was an extraordinary grace in her responsiveness which imperceptibly served him as a regulator, if not as a guide" (205/R231). The chosen expression, of course, opens up the possibility that Zina is his guide, at least some of the time, and at least to an extent. She is Fyodor's first and ideal reader and helps give final shape to his artistic perceptions (which she too somehow senses, there can be no doubt). Thus the book is not the product of a single mind's work: it is a voice

and its sympathetic echo all at once. As a result, Fyodor's every word is saturated with Zina's responsiveness and complicity. If we recall again that Fyodor is the author of *The Gift,* as well, then we must consider Zina as a presence not just thematically through the unobtrusive recurrence of her name, and not simply as inspiration, but exactly as first reader, as a shaping echo that guides the artistic expansiveness of the novel. As a reader, she has the rare privilege to change the words of the text she faces, but in fact, this too is but a variant of ordinary reading, made possible by her intuitive knowledge of the vision Fyodor seeks to express. Zina's personal, emotional love for Fyodor is an extension of her loving relationship to his artworks; in *The Gift,* Nabokov proposes an analogous relationship between author and reader generally. Only by reading lovingly (in order to meet what has been lovingly written) can a reader breach the isolation of the object. (100-101)

The length of this quotation is necessary not only because it contains the crux of Blackwell's argument but because it reveals several problematic slippages: we see him trying to read Zina into a compositional role, and we can also trace the difficulties his argument meets. Is Zina a regulator or a guide? What force is contained in the qualification "at least some of the time and at least to an extent"? More fundamentally, just how much influence does Zina have over the text? Is she a contributor or an appreciative echo? If she is a stand-in for Nabokov's readers, how empowered should we feel?

A look at the passage from *The Gift* quoted by Blackwell at the start of the paragraph I have reproduced above should intensify doubts about his interpretation:

At his evening trysts with Zina in an empty little café where the counter was painted an indigo color and where dark blue gnomelike lamps, miserably posing as vessels of coziness, glowed on six or seven little tables, he read her what he had written during the day and she listened, her painted lashes lowered, leaning on one elbow, playing with a glove or a cigarette case. Sometimes the proprietor's dog would come up, a fat mongrel bitch with low-hanging bubs, and would place its head on Zina's knee, and beneath the stroking and smiling hand that smoothed back the skin on its silky round forehead, the dog's eyes would take on a Chinese slant, and when she was given a lump of sugar, she would take it, waddle in a leisurely manner into a corner, roll up there, and very loudly start crunching. "Wonderful, but I'm not sure you can say it like that in Russian," said Zina sometimes, and after an argument he would correct the expression she had questioned. Chernyshevski she called Chernysh for short and got so used to considering him as belonging to Fyodor, and partly to her, that his actual life in the past appeared to him as something of a plagiarism. Fyodor's idea of composing his biography in the shape of a ring, closed with the clasp of an apocryphal sonnet (so that the result would be not the form of a book, which by its finiteness is opposed to the circular nature of everything in existence, but a continuously curving and thus infinite sentence), seemed at first to her to be incapable of embodiment on flat, rectangular paper—and so much the more was she overjoyed when she noticed that nevertheless a circle was being formed. She was completely unconcerned whether or not the author clung assiduously to historical truth—she took that on trust, for if it were not thus it would simply not have been worth writing the book. A deeper truth, on the other hand, for which he alone was responsible and which he alone could find, was for her so important that the least clumsiness or fogginess in his words seemed to be the germ of a falsehood, which had to be immediately exterminated. Gifted with a most flexible memory, which twined like ivy around what she perceived, Zina by repeating such word-combinations as she particularly liked ennobled them with her own secret convolution, and whenever Fyodor for any reason changed a turn of phrase which she had remembered, the ruins of the portico stood for a long time on the golden horizon, reluctant to disappear. There was an extraordinary grace in her responsiveness which imperceptibly served him as a regulator, if not as a guide. (204–5)

This passage, one of those many moments in *The Gift* that prove Fyodor's value as a writer even as it describes his writing, contains in the Russian a few porticos not present in the English (i.e., the dog, in her "gastronomic" attitude to reading, approximating Chernyshevsky's approach to literature and love of sweets, chews with a "terrifying crunch" [*gryzla so strashnym khrustom*]).[1] But if the passage describes Nabokov's vision of an ideal reader, it seems an enormous exaggeration to say that Zina "forms the text" or influences it by "creative reception." The ideal reader here listens, admires,

---

1. Blackwell is excellent on the relation of Chernyshevsky's reading to food (105). The scene with the dog gnawing on sugar "*gryzla...sakhar*" will be echoed in the depiction of Chernyshevsky gnawing on things as he reads: "*za knigoi nepremenno chto-nibud' gryz: s priannikami chital "Zapiski Pikvikskogo Kluba," s sukhariami—'Zhurnal de deba'*" (219, *398*). All references to the Russian-language text refer to *Sobranie sochinenii russkogo perioda,* vol. 4. When both texts are referenced, I give the page numbers for the English version first, followed by the Russian page number(s) in italics.

remembers, is kind to animals, and occasionally insists on textual emendation. This reader's gift for memory and her love of repetition (echoing) do not come close to encroaching on the sole responsibility of the author. In fact, it may be that Fyodor has actually kept the phrase that he claims to have struck out: can one say *"prinimat' razrez"* ("take on a slant") in Russian?

Identification with Zina may well be the least troubling of all the cases in Nabokov's oeuvre where the reader finds himself in Nabokov's text. It should, however, still give us pause, if we seek to credit ourselves with giving shape to Nabokov's fiction. Fyodor's courtship of Zina is one of four erotic relationships in which he participates in the novel. Each one informs a chapter—the "Life of Chernyshevski," written by Fyodor but from which he is absent as a character, is the odd man out. In the first chapter, Fyodor engages in a love affair with his own poems, the second is dominated by his passionate attachment to his mother, the third by his relationship to Zina, and the fifth by his erotic proximity to the Big Author himself.

Chapter 1 of *The Gift* is devoted mostly to Fyodor's reading his own newly published verses and imagining the review that his friend Alexander Chernyshevski—as part of an April Fool's joke—has told him has just appeared. Blackwell sees this act of reading and rereading as a powerful gesture—as he returns to his poems, Fyodor reads "in three dimensions," reconstructing the past which has given the poems life: "Over the course of twenty pages, Fyodor's reading refracts into several different readings, perspectives and times. [. . . T]he passage describing Fyodor's perusal of his book encompasses a rich mixture of narrative perspectives, and these also reflect a kind of shattering of the crystal of time" (Blackwell, 94). This understanding of the chapter is in keeping with one of Blackwell's larger points—that the narrative complexity of the book is a way of transcending the self: "by refusing to create a stable narrative voice or perspective, Nabokov tries to escape the egotistical fallacy derived from over-confidence in one's own point of view; by exploding traditional narrative form, he resists the illusion that the world can be encapsulated or represented 'truthfully' by human conception and narration" (4). The fallacy here is, I believe, the same one attacked by D. A. Miller in his analysis of *The Moonstone,* a novel with many different narrators whose versions of the truth are remarkably compatible. Miller demonstrates that formal complexity or variation does not necessarily amount to conceptual profundity or a diverse range of competing views on the same issue (35–57). In *The Gift* the various narrative perspectives are entirely complementary and effectively serve to make the reach of the narrating, creative self ever wider. Particularly in chapter 1, the narrator's engagement with his own work is intensely narcissistic (a word

Blackwell avoids). The first mention of the volume of poems occurs in the following paragraph:

> He walked on toward the shop, but what he had just seen—whether because it had given him a kindred pleasure, or because it had taken him unawares and jolted him (as children in the hayloft fall into the resilient darkness)—released in him that pleasant something which for several days now had been at the murky bottom of his every thought, taking possession of him at the slightest provocation: my collection of poems has been published; and when, as now, his mind tumbled like this, that is, when he recalled the fifty-odd poems that had just come out, he would skim in an instant the entire book, so that in the instantaneous mist of its madly accelerated music one could not make any readable sense of the flicking lines—the familiar words would rush past, swirling amid violent foam (whose seething was transformed into a mighty flowing motion if one fixed one's eyes on it, as we used to do long ago, looking down at it from a vibrating mill bridge until the bridge turned into a ship's stern: farewell!)—and this foam, and this flickering, and a separate verse that rushed past all alone, shouting in wild ecstasy from afar, probably calling him home, all of this, together with the creamy white of the cover, was merged in a blissful feeling of exceptional purity.... What am I doing! [*Chto ia sobstvenno delaiu!*] he thought, abruptly coming to his senses and realizing that the first thing he had done upon entering the next shop was to dump the change he had received at the tobacconist's onto the rubber islet in the middle of the glass counter, through which he glimpsed the submerged treasure of flasked perfumes, while the salesgirl's gaze, condescending toward his odd behavior, followed with curiosity this absentminded hand paying for a purchase that had not yet been named.
>
> "A cake of almond soap, please," he said with dignity. (7)

The long first sentence, with its syntactic flow, ecstasy, foam, and creamy white cover, ends with a verbal ejaculation and the tried and true sexual ellipsis as Fyodor comes to his senses. His exclamation is a rephrasing of the title of Chernyshevsky's most famous book (*What Is to Be Done?*), and as such this is just one of many moments that link Fyodor to the somewhat abject target of his own work—either by direct opposition or through parodic similarity. The adverb *sobstvenno* ("as a matter of fact," but literally meaning "properly," with reference to the self, *sebia*) emphasizes further that here the action is all Fyodor's; this is not, as with Chernyshevsky's title, a question for everyone.

Chernyshevsky referred to masturbation in the diaries that Nabokov used as a source, and the onanistic quality of Fyodor's relationship to his poems is one of the opening chapter's principal themes. Returning home to his room, Fyodor receives a telephone call from a latter-day Chernyshevski (Alexander), who tells him to "get a firm grip on yourself" (*voz'mite sebia v ruki*) (8, *196*) just before informing him of a new laudatory review of his poems that has supposedly just been published; this phrase will be repeated by Fyodor many pages later, when, frustrated by Zina's amatory reluctance, he drifts off to sleep: "Take oneself in hand: a monastic pun" (*Vziat' sebia v ruki: monasheskii kalambur*) (326, *501*). When Alexander Chernyshevski declines to read him the review until they meet later in the evening, Fyodor goes into his room and, after a fashion, continues the activity engaged in at the shop: "And having locked his door, he took out his book, and threw himself on the couch [*on upal s nei na divan*, lit., he fell with her onto the couch]—he had to reread it right away, before the excitement had time to cool, in order to check the superior quality of the poems and fore-fancy all the details of the high approbation given them by the intelligent, delightful, as yet unnamed reviewer" (9). (Blackwell seems to see the possible sexual connotation of this scene, but he doesn't want to think about it: "Skipping over the fact that Fyodor's first bed-partner in the novel is his book "Poems," the first authentic, interpersonal love to be found in *The Gift*'s pages is that of the Chernyshevskis for their deceased son Yasha" [128].) Many pages later, Fyodor completes his rereading: "having squeezed the final drop of sweetness from it, Fyodor stretched and got up from his couch" (29).

Blackwell portrays Fyodor's penchant for imagining the reviews of others as a generous attempt to move beyond his self: "at least as far as his own works are concerned, reading is an area of thought that allows him to expand the horizons of his consciousness, allows him to practice sitting in the souls of hypothetical others. [...] That ability to recreate, resurrect, or simply discover a new consciousness seems—for Fyodor at least—to be of supreme value" (100). At several times in the novel, occasionally through technically brilliant narrative fades, Fyodor occupies the minds of others, and he presents their hypothetical thoughts as part of his narrative. Again, Blackwell sees this as an ethically praiseworthy trait: "While Fyodor's activity does not amount exactly to love [...], it does demonstrate something particular about his sense of his relationship to others in the world: he is already willing to posit the total existence of others with the same 'absolute central significance' as he automatically perceives in his self" (123). Fyodor's forays into the souls of others, however, are a kind of compositional exercise that Nabokov referred to in another story as "recruiting" (*Stories*, 401–5). These are *appropriative* gestures, even when they are tinged by a certain compassion, and Fyodor's basic impulse is to aestheticize, not to comfort or console: "And when Fyodor moved over into Mme Chernyshevski he found himself within a soul where not everything was alien to him, but where he marveled at many things, as a prim traveler might marvel at the customs in a distant land: the bazaar at sunrise, the naked children, the din, the monstrous size of the fruit" (36). This is not the respect of one person for another's concretely individual thoughts and feelings ("love"), but an author's exploration of his characters, preliminary work of the sort that when it comes to Chernyshevsky Fyodor will eventually call "firing practice" (196).

Fyodor's maturation as an artistic talent unfolds as a developmental drama with a succession of other readers who seem as erotic objects. Just after finishing his reading, Fyodor recalls his mother and thinks about how happy she will be to read his poems: "He imagined her joy upon reading the article about him and for an instant he felt maternal pride toward himself; not only that but a maternal tear burned the edge of his eyelids" (29). The second chapter of *The Gift,* devoted to Fyodor's attempts to imagine what it must have been like to have been his father, has at least muted Oedipal dimensions: the reunion of mother and son at the train station is one of the most passionate encounters in all of Nabokov's fiction:

> She had come to him for two weeks, after a three-year separation, and in the first moment when, powdered to a deathly pallor, wearing black gloves and black stockings and an old sealskin coat thrown open, she had descended the iron steps of the coach, glancing with equal quickness first at him and then at what was underfoot, and the next moment, her face twisted with the pain of happiness, was clinging to him, blissfully moaning, kissing him anywhere—ear, neck—it had seemed to him that the beauty of which he had been so proud had faded, but as his vision adjusted itself to the twilight of the present, so different at first from the distantly receding light of memory, he again recognized in her everything that he had loved: the pure outline of her face, narrowing down to the chin, the changeful play of those green, brown, yellow, entrancing eyes under their velvet brows, the long, light stance, the avidity with which she lit a cigarette in the taxi. (86)

In light of what Fyodor has said about his maternal attitude toward himself, however, this may be another instance of self-love: to be sure, incest can always be considered a kind of love for the self as broadly conceived within the original family. In *The Gift,* the intense love between mother and son becomes the basis for collaborative research for Fyodor's book, but

Fyodor's abandonment of the project indicates that he realizes the improper nature of the project. Here the Oedipal taboo merges with an acknowledgment that the process of aestheticization is inherently an expansion of the self in disregard to others:

> If you like I'll admit it: I myself am a mere seeker of verbal adventures, and forgive me if I refuse to hunt down my fancies on my father's own collecting ground. I have realized, you see, the impossibility of having the imagery of his travels germinate without contaminating them with a kind of secondary poetization, which keeps departing further and further from that real poetry with which the live experience of these receptive, knowledgeable, and chaste naturalists endowed their research. (139)

This privileging of chastity is interesting. As Anna Brodsky has noted, the aesthetics of *The Gift* are characterized by an insistence on purity that she attributes to a biographical imperative: Nabokov's "wish to purge unclean elements from [his] own family life"—the homosexuality of his brother, Sergei (112). Polina Barskova sees in the novel's insistence on chastity a reprise of Hamlet's conflicted, incestuous hesitations and his consequent desire that his "too, too solid [or sullied] flesh would melt, / Thaw and resolve itself into dew" (200), lines that manage to merge hatred for the flesh with a sensuous appreciation of the self's potential for sexual release. The novel's many references to chastity and cleanliness are too numerous to list—what does Fyodor buy in that first erotic scene? Soap!—but we should note here the most salient mention of the theme, with reference to the species that bears the hero's last name:

> [M]y father discovered the true nature of the corneal formation appearing beneath the abdomen in the impregnated females of Parnassians, and explained how her mate, working with a pair of spatulate appendages, places and molds on her a chastity belt of his own manufacture, shaped differently in every species of this genus, being sometimes a little boat, sometimes a helical shell, sometimes—as in the case of the exceptionally rare dark-cinder gray *orpheus* Godunov—a replica of a tiny lyre. And as a frontispiece to my present work I think I would like to display precisely this butterfly—for I can hear him talk about it, can see the way he took the six specimens he had brought back out of their six thick triangular envelopes, the way he lowered his eyes with the field magnifier close to the abdomen of the only female—and how reverently his laboratory assistant relaxed in a damp jar the dry, glossy,

tightly folded wings in order later to drive a pin smoothly through the insect's thorax, stick it in the cork groove of the spreading board, hold down flat upon it by means of broad strips of semitransparent paper its open, defenseless, gracefully expanded beauty, then slip a bit of cotton wool under its abdomen and straighten its black antennae—so that it dried that way forever. (112)

This representation of artistic chastity is also a guarantee of a kind of eternal, floating sensuality, incapable of achieving satisfaction but always *aesthetically* aroused. The comparison of the *orpheus* Godunov with "the present work" should be taken as a figure for an authorial injunction to appreciate without tampering. The moment of aesthetic satisfaction or consummation belongs to the author and is analogous to his completion of the book.

As both Brodsky and Barskova observe, desire for the body, and the female body in particular, is marked in *The Gift* by disgust. Fyodor knows that his desire for a woman will always fail to meet his expectations, and it may lead him into stylistic triteness or laughable Chernyshevskian formulations: "Down the helical stairs of the bus that drew up came a pair of charming silk legs: we know of course that this has been worn threadbare by the efforts of a thousand male writers, but nevertheless down they came, these legs—and deceived: the face was revolting" (163). When Fyodor looks at any passing girl, "he imagined simultaneously both the stupendous possibility of happiness and repugnance for its inevitable imperfection" (165). He finds one of his students cheaply arousing, but he knows "that their reading of Stevenson would never be interrupted by a Dantean pause [...] that if such a break should take place he would not experience a thing, except a devastating chill because the demands of the imagination were unfulfillable, and because the vacuousness of a gaze, forgiven for the sake of beautiful, moist eyes, inevitably corresponded to a defect as yet concealed—the vacuous expression of breasts, which was impossible to forgive" (165-66). One has to work as hard to find examples of bad writing in Fyodor's texts as Fyodor does to collect material of interest from Chernyshevsky, and I would like to suspect that "the vacuous expression of breasts" (*tupoe vyrazhenie grudi*) has been coined to provide a formal equivalent to the lack of attraction of the object.

Zina escapes this dynamic of problematic corporeality by not having much of a body. Indeed, given Fyodor's penchant for imagining conversations with Koncheyev, another poet whom he envies and respects, one might wonder—although this is a dangerous game, because no character ever truly exists—whether Zina is alive at all or whether she is Fyodor's projection of an idealized reader. Blackwell takes great pains to insist on Zina's individuality and distinctness: "once they do find each other, their individuality remains intact" (116). He seems especially troubled by Fyodor's observation that "not only was Zina cleverly and elegantly made to measure for him by a very painstaking fate, but both of them, forming a single shadow, were made to the measure of something not quite comprehensible, but wonderful and benevolent and continuously surrounding them" (*The Gift,* 177). Admitting that the passage is highly ambiguous, Blackwell insists that "even here there is no hint of complete merging, the two identities lost within the larger whole; rather, it seems the whole formed by their love depends absolutely on their enduring individuality" (118). The problem is that in comparison with Fyodor, Zina has little individuality, and it is hard to see what sort of a life she will have outside of his. (Her job in a law firm has little merit; its chief function, as Barskova demonstrates, is to provide fodder for Nabokov's first parodic reworking of *Hamlet* [193–97]). The corporeal component of Zina's relationship with Fyodor is particularly problematic. Blackwell's assertions that there is a physical dimension to their love rests on little evidence other than his own desire for "clarity": "their love clearly is not passionless and their physical attraction, while unconsummated during the novel, seems tightly bound to their spiritual love, equally elevated to the status of an ideal. Although Zina's beauty is idealized and elusive, this unmistakably carnal aspect of their love clearly challenges the body/spirit duality which underlies platonic thought about love, beauty, and truth" (115). The instability of Blackwell's position, and his persistent desire to believe in the reality of a balanced, incarnate love that will insure Nabokov's reader a creative role, is evident in his frequent hesitations in the following passage, which throw into relief the conscientiousness of a scholar unable to discard evidence that does not support his conclusion:

> Given Fyodor's extensive negative portrayal of the carnal side of love, it should not be surprising that when he finally describes his talks with Zina he emphasizes the spiritual. And yet it cannot be said that he eschews or denigrates the physical: when she arrives at their appointed spot, Fyodor kisses her "soft lips," unlike the other's "waxy" ones, just as on the first occasion he had kissed her "burning, melting, sorrowing lips" (184/R206). Still, Zina's physical being is almost tentative, almost ghostly (as Anna Brodsky has observed), described repeatedly using words like "pale" [...] "darker," "narrowness," "weakness." [...] In his semi-delirious dreams, he first imagines or hallucinates her presence nearby, then "reveled in the temptation, in the shortness of the distance, in the heavenly possibilities, which, incidentally, had nothing of the

flesh (or rather, had some blissful replacement for the flesh, expressed in semi-dreamlike terms)..." (179/R201). This dreamy disembodied-ness with its "blissful replacement for the flesh" hints at something beyond the carnal without explicitly denying the role of sexual love in the achievement of loving transcendence. Notwithstanding these ambivalent gestures, it is clear that Fyodor is just as attracted by Zina's physical beauty (which represents, after all, spiritual beauty) as by her metaphysical perfection for him. (133)

At the end of the novel, when Zina's mother and stepfather leave Berlin, and Fyodor and Zina return to her family's now empty apartment to con-summate their love, only the reader and the author know that neither Fyodor nor Zina has the key. Blackwell considers this detail relatively insignificant "[Their being locked out] is not really the important part: of course they will eventually find their place together. It is enough to know that their love has triumphed, and the triumphal Onegin-style stanza announces their continuing love in the spirit of creativity and art; there, it will engender Fyo-dor's novel, 'The Gift'" (128). On the contrary, the final irony of the novel *is* important because Fyodor's very nature tends against engagement in physical relations—the chastity belt remains in place. (Moreover, the Onegin-style stanza might be taken as a hint that just as Onegin and Tatyana never con-summate their love, physical intimacy will remain elusive for Fyodor and Zina.) "Fate," rather than working to bring Fyodor and Zina together, takes pains to keep them physically apart. As if to highlight the aesthetic stakes of this renunciation of the flesh, in the pages leading up to the nonconsumma-tion of Fyodor's and Zina's love, Nabokov gives us an example of the type of prose the flesh produces: "He imagined what he had constantly been imag-ining during the past two months—the beginning (tomorrow night!) of his full life with Zina—the release, the slaking—and meanwhile a sun-charged cloud, filling up, growing, with swollen, turquoise veins, with a firey itch in its thunder-root, rose in all its turgid, unwieldy magnificence and embraced him, the sky and the forest, and to resolve this tension seemed a monstrous joy incapable of being borne by man" (345-46). In both the Russian and the English this passage reads as though it had been written by an epigone of Lawrence. It is meant, I believe, to be an example of how writing suffers aesthetically when the author is unduly under the influence of the demands of the flesh.

Concluding his examination of Fyodor's and Zina's romance, Blackwell refers to Irving Singer's discusion of Rousseau's *Pygmalion* and proposes that Zina be seen as Nabokov's version of Galatea. This is a surprising suggestion in light of what Blackwell has been saying, and it makes a great deal of sense, but Blackwell immediately backs away from it:

> While not espousing the same degree of total merging found in Rousseau's play, *The Gift,* too, offers a picture of love in which the artist finds love by means of his creation, and that love enables the fullest blossoming forth of his spiritual—and hence artistic—being. For aside from Zina's independent existence, she can also be seen as Fyodor's creation: authors create their readers [...], and Zina is, most essentially, Fyodor's reader even before he meets her. She is also an independent human being, and it is the preservation of this fate that allows Nabokov to step beyond the original Pygmalion story's implications: in *The Gift's* plot, Zina is both created and independent, and the tension between these aspects of her being [...] looks paradoxical until we recognize that what the novel really implies is that together, in their love, Fyodor and Zina create each other. (139–40)

The overstatement of Zina's freedom and individuality—"an independent human being"—should lead us to question how far Fyodor (or Nabokov) has gone beyond the figure of the traditional Galatea. Fyodor's love for Zina strikes me as just a more complex version of his love for his own poems.

The final chapter of *The Gift* brings the culmination of Fyodor's narcissistic eroticism—his loving encounter with his creator. The novel has been populated by several figures who serve as lesser versions of Nabokov—Koncheyev, who shares some of Nabokov's views about art, and Vladimirov, who shares some of his biography (and is *do strannosti neprivlekatelen,* literally "unattractive to the point of strangeness") (321, *346*). Sunbathing in the Grunewald, Fyodor is licked by the sun and, surrounded by birds, butterflies, a squirrel, and the "spermy odor of sun-warmed grass," "almost dissolve[s] completely." Here the narcissistic erotic dynamic reaches its climax through reversal: now Fyodor is in the position of the work of art receiving his author's loving attention.

Several scholars have written of the importance in *The Gift's* preoccupation with the literature and philosophy of the Russian Silver Age and, in particular, of that era's preoccupation with sex. Late nineteenth- and early twentieth-century philosphers transformed the early materialistic asceticism of Chernyshevsky into an eroticized but still often ascetic program for idealistic transcendence of the human condition. At the same time, the Silver Age saw a rise in interest in alternative forms of sexuality, although some of this interest was ascetic in practice as well (Matich, passim). Initially, it would seem that there was a dramatic gap between Chernyshevsky and the later Silver Age philosophers of love—Vladimir Solov'ev and Nikolai Berdiaev—as well as the writers most closely associated with the new sexuality: Mikhail

Kuz'min, Zinaida Gippius, and Dmitrii Merezhkovsky. Vasilii Rozanov, the Russian philosopher whom Nabokov most frequently cites—though often covertly (Etkind, 393–99)—insisted, however, on a continuum of views on sexuality in Russian culture, linking together all nonprocreative sexual acts (not only homosexuality and masturbation but also abstinence and even the use of birth control) under the category of "sodomy," which he used to chacterize both Christianity and the Russian intellectual tradition.

The two scholars who have focused on sexuality specifically in *The Gift* have reached fundamentally different conclusions. Olga Skonechnaia portrays Nabokov as siding with Rozanov's attack on the "sodomy" of excessive idealism. For her Nabokov's position is that "the artist sees heaven only by intently examining the earth" (44). She does not deal, however, with Fyodor's rejection of the flesh. Anna Brodsky, on the other hand, focuses precisely on Fyodor's demand for purity and his asceticism, but because she sees the Silver Age as characterized by "pervasive" sexuality, she situates Nabokov in diametrical opposition: "a rejection [...] that verged on the rejection of sexuality itself" (104). The book's position on sexuality is actually more complex. On one hand, Nabokov disparages homosexual attraction and new, collective approaches to sexuality, making Yasha Chernyshevski's love triangle with his friends Rudol'f and Olya seem pathetic and ridiculous. He also derides Nikolai Chernyshevsky as effeminate and inept in his relations with the opposite sex. In contrast to the ascetics of the 1860s and the mystics of the 1900s who were willing to sacrifice the flesh or even this fallen world for the sake of political or spiritual transcendence, *The Gift* seems to be a life-affirming text. Nabokov certainly portrayed it as such to his cousin Zinaida Shakhovskaia, when he wrote to her in 1936 that the title of his next novel had "grown longer by a letter, not *Da* [Yes] but *Dar* [Gift], thus transforming the initial affirmation into something blooming, paganistic, even priapic" (Dolinin, *Istinnaia zhizn'*, 260). (Compare this to Chernyshevsky's remark in his diary about the gift that he would like to return—his penis: "It is disgusting that we have been given this thing [*Skverno, chto nam dana eta veshch'*] [1:82]). In effect, though, the novel plays a double game, mocking both Chernyshevsky and the Silver Age but also subscribing to and combining aspects of their sexual values in its own sexual aesthetic. Had he lived to review *The Gift*, Rozanov would probably have had no problem identifying it as the work of a "Sodomite."[2] The work is deeply, indeed programmatically

---

2. Etkind writes: "Nabokov's beloved heroes, handsome young fellows from Ganin to Van, constantly take pleasure in their own bodies, and the author and reader share this pleasure. The heroes are explicitly heterosexual, but the admiration of them from afar is of a different nature. For the reader the autoerotic nature of the text is difficult to distinguish from homoeroticism" (358).

narcissistic, and its pleasures amount at times to metafictive onanism. Right after he squeezes "the final drop of sweetness" from his book of poems, Fyodor notices that "the hands of his watch had lately begun to misbehave, now and then starting to move counterclockwise" (29). Initially this seems like a simple reference to nostalgia—Fyodor's poems have taken him back to his childhood—but a passage in Fyodor's "Life of Chernyshevski" raises suggestive doubts: "It is sad to read in his diary about the appliances of which he tries to make use—scale-arms, bobs, corks, basins—and nothing revolves, or if it does, then according to unwelcome laws, in the reverse direction to what he wants" (218). Is the reverse action of Fyodor's watch hands a reference to the "sodomic" (in Rozanovian terms) nature of his art? Does this novel seek to accomplish aesthetically an idealistic task akin to Chernyshevsky's goal in politics and Vladimir Solov'ev's in religion?[3] Fyodor's early reading of his poems might be seen as a first, early step in a developmental arc—a masturbatory relation to his own verse gives way to Oedipal passion, then to "normal" heterosexual attraction outside the family, and finally to a spiritual overcoming of the flesh. In all cases, though, there is a foregrounding of the self and a brilliantly productive appropriation of the surrounding world.

To some extent we are back in the territory we examined in *Bend Sinister*—the composition of which was still a decade away. The uselessness of art can be figured as nonreproductive, even disincarnate sexuality. (Otto Weininger had trumpeted the notion of the incompatibility of reproduction and genius, and Russians knew his work well [Bershtein, 208–16].) In this respect, the rapport of sexuality to art is as central to *The Gift* (and not only to its Chernyshevski sections) as to any of Nabokov's subsequent, American works.

It might seem that in the novel's final erotic scene, when Fyodor is licked by the sun in the Grunewald, Nabokov dispenses with the reader altogether. That may be true within the text—any bliss with Zina will fall far short of Fyodor's meeting with his true father—but the book's reader, I think, shares this moment of the central character's luxuriation in his creator's pride. We, too, have been appreciating "the sparkle, the thick green grease paint of the

---

3. Blackwell invokes Solov'ev as a model for Fyodor's and Zina's love, but to my mind he overemphasizes the importance of "psychological discreteness" to Solov'ev's doctrine of *sliianie* (mystical merger). Solov'ev's occasional attention to the importance of human incarnation is belied by his insistence on the "spiritualization" of flesh. Moreover, the passage in which Fyodor "loses himself completely and finishes his book," which Blackwell sees as an example of the hero's "temporarily abandoning his time-dependent 'egoism'" (121), strikes me as an example to the contrary: Fyodor's all-consuming push to complete his book elevates his egoism and leads to his forgetting Zina and her desire to meet him at the ball.

foliage" (328). We perceive the beautifully precise, magical images Fyodor has been noticing and refracting throughout the novel, we marvel at the deftness and inventiveness of the transitions, and we would join Fyodor in "want[ing] to offer thanks" for "the list of donations already made: 10,000 days—from Person Unknown." (328). In the novel's final twist, when Fyodor and Zina head toward her apartment without a key, the reader suddenly finds himself alone with the author, in the know. The reader, if he has been paying attention, does have the key to the ending that Fyodor and Zina lack. That key, the understanding of the novel's patterns and structure, permits a kind of intimacy with the author that may surpass whatever the characters can experience together.

Perhaps the two single most important motifs in *The Gift* are those of keys and connections. Both appear in numerous hypostases, some rather humorous, and ultimately refer not only to characters' erotic adventures but also to the reader's task of interpretation and to the pleasures of making a connection to the author through what the narrator, ostensibly speaking about chess but baring his own method calls "the cleverly hidden mating device" (175).[4] As we achieve ever greater intimacy with the text, we don't re-create it or enter into a rapport with it from our own perspective as real individuals, we read as Nabokov would want us to. This is intimacy on his terms. And each time, when we reach the end, Nabokov takes his leave of the book, with nary a word of fairwell for us. In a privileged position vis-à-vis the characters, we remain aware that Nabokov's affection for his creation is far greater than that for his audience.

One of the great pleasures of reading is being able to forget we exist. With the classics of realist fiction, this happens through identification with the characters—it is as if their world were both real *and* ours, something we can sink into. Maintaining a sense of individual discreteness, as Blackwell suggests is the case for Fyodor's readers, probably is a prerequisite for a good, sustaining romantic relationship in real life, but it is not necessary for the reading of fiction. With *The Gift,* this readerly forgetting happens not so much through identification with the characters, a dynamic of which Nabokov emphatically disapproved, but through the reader's effort to achieve ever greater understanding of how the text works, so that, eventually, she might begin to merge with the author (albeit on his terms). But why should this be a tragedy? In the world of metafiction, equal relationships are vastly overrated: "One might dissolve completely that way." Once we've read this

---

4. *Sviaz',* the word frequently used for "connection" in *The Gift,* is also the common colloquial term for a sexual "affair."

novel several times, we almost do. The reward for reading *The Gift* well is the absence of the anxiety that necessarily characterizes "good reading" of other novels by Nabokov. The "price" is a loss of self. As Zina says in the novel's final quoted line of dialogue, uttered as she and Fyodor prepare to leave a café, "We have to pay. Call him over" (365).

Part Three

Reading Preposterously

✌ CHAPTER 8

Litland

The Allegorical Poetics of The Defense

Much scholarly work written on Nabokov in the past twenty years has its root in the nervous desire that Nabokov prove more than a master of metafiction. Fearing that metafiction is not a sufficient engine to drive an author's canonization, scholars have urged us to move beyond that initial phase and accept Nabokov as a philosopher of subjectivity and personal relations, as an occult, even religious thinker, or as a moral prophet asserting the compatibility of art with humanitarian values. Although these approaches have significantly expanded the scope of Nabokov studies, they rest upon the assumption that the metafictive interpretive game has been adequately played out. As far as *The Defense* is concerned, this assumption is unfounded, in fact, so unfounded that the novel's central poetic device has not, I believe, been named in its scholarly treatments. While it may be that no novel by Nabokov can ever be read closely enough, *The Defense,* in particular, requires a closer reading than it has hitherto received.

The Defense is one of the least sexual of Nabokov's novels; while there are a few double entendres, the action is relatively chaste and, unlike in *The Gift,* this chastity does not work in service of an all-encompassing aesthetic eroticism. This is the first novel, however, where Nabokov begins to insist on the method of reading that will later be so closely tied to thematic issues of sexual perversity. Looking back at *The Defense* after reading *Bend Sinister, Lolita,* and *Pnin* offers a return to origins; in its connotative tricks and literary allusions the novel serves as a training ground for the perverse reader and as an arena where he can pursue authorized deconstructive readings without the attendant sexual anxieties that shadow and shape the interpretation of Nabokov's later work. In some respects this novel is Nabokov's most explicit in terms of methodology. Overtly and covertly, the novel's author comments on how to read it. In one of *The Defense*'s several self-reflexive moments, Mrs. Luzhin overhears a conversation "about a new novel." One character asserts that "it was elaborately and subtly written and that every word betrayed a sleepless night." A woman's voice asserts: "Oh, no, it reads so easily" (232, *243*). Both responses are crucial to understanding Nabokov's success as an author. Some of his work's susceptibility to "easy reading" may account for its appeal to naïve audiences who would not pass Nabokov's famous quiz, but the pleasures of a Nabokovian text are founded as well on the painstaking care entailed in their production. They can—but never should—be read "easily."

Ultimately, the interpretation of the novel I offer here builds on that well formulated by Pekka Tammi and Julian Connolly. *The Defense* explores the fundamental differences between the perspectives of character and author; it is about the struggle between "the hero's attempt to order the design of his life" and "the superior order imposed by the [author]" (Tammi, 136). I want to go further, though, and use a dirty word in Nabokov criticism, one that has nothing to do with sex. My argument will be that the work is intended as an *allegory* about the relationship prevailing between author and character in all fiction. Fundamental to allegory is the extent to which virtually all events in a text are reducible to an abstract idea or set of ideas relentlessly pursued. According to an unsigned article in the Russian version of the *Brokgauz Encyclopedia* (1890), the authoritative general reference work for the intelligentsia both before and well after the Revolution, allegory is characterized by a continuous rapport between a general concept arising from philosophical reflection and that concept's "cleverly conceived individual shell"; it may be defined as "the artistic description of abstract concepts by means of concrete representations" (1:461). Northrop Frye writes that allegory occurs "when the events of a narrative obviously and continuously refer to another simultaneous structure of events or ideas, whether historical events, moral or philosophical ideas, or natural phenomena" (12). To use the language of Nabokov's novel itself—drawn from a passage that ostensibly deals with the description of an apartment—allegory materializes "when a strictly problem idea, long since discovered in theory, is repeated in a striking guise on the board in live play" (133, *143–44*).

This section of the book takes us further into the territory of work first written in Russian and later translated into English. I refer to both the Russian and English texts of *The Defense,* and at certain points an argument rests on a nuance present in only one of them. Nabokov did not always find exact interlinguistic equivalencies for the precise, often paronomastic presence of his allegorical theme, but this theme is unceasingly pursued in both versions. The English version compensates in some places for allusions it could not capture in others. For the sake of conciseness, I cite only the English text in my examples except where the presence or absence of paronomasia in the Russian version is at stake; where an English pun is not supported by the Russian, I provide both versions for the sake of scholarly fair play. It is essential to observe that a stream of verbal playfulness—often to quite serious effect— nourishes both the English and Russian versions of *The Defense,* even though it bubbles to the surface in different places.

In her study of the translation of Nabokov's work, Jane Grayson takes W. W. Rowe to task for failing to distinguish between the work of Nabokov and that of Michael Scammell, who translated *The Defense* "in collaboration with the author." On the basis of Scammell's manuscript, she asserts that Rowe is "quoting Scammell and not Nabokov[;] Nabokov certainly gave these passages his approval, but they are not his own" (180). Brian Boyd notes that Nabokov worked hard at correcting Scammell's translation, "practically rewriting entire paragraphs" (*The American Years,* 475). I proceed from the assumption that the entire English text of *The Defense* was authorized by and can thus be read as the verbal work of Nabokov himself. Some of the English wordings that I discuss may have been entirely fortuitous, others may have arisen from Scammell's partial or complete understanding of the novel's allegorical meaning. Nevertheless, I do not think it is possible to detach Nabokov from even a single word of any of his English or Russian texts; if ever translations were author-ized, they are Nabokov's. In a few cases, a particularly effective pun seems to have been the most natural translation for a particular word, but I can easily imagine Nabokov noticing and savoring his good luck.

An approach to *The Defense*'s allegorical nature requires an appreciation of *the* central structural opposition in the novel: the conflict prevailing between registers of two and three dimensions. This theme has not escaped the attention of scholars, but its significance—and in particular the inversion of the expected dimensional relationship between chess and the characters' "real" world—has not been adequately explored. Essentially, the society through which Luzhin moves in both Russia and Germany is portrayed as governed by only two dimensions. Words drawn from plane geometry characterize this world. The use of such lexical items is not limited to this Nabokovian text, but the density of their use in *The Defense* is remarkable.[1] Circles, squares, arcs, rectangles, and words that contain or stem from them appear repeatedly. It has frequently been pointed out that Luzhin sees—and the text describes—the world in terms of a chess board—but squares are only a part of the planar landscape through which the characters move.

In general, two-dimensional geometrical figures are most often used in *The Defense* to describe the world of prosaic tedium Luzhin must endure when he is not playing or thinking about chess; they describe either the actions of characters who sur*round* (*okruzhit'*—a key two-dimensional word in the Russian) Luzhin, or they characterize Luzhin's actions when he immerses himself in that world and—via marriage—succumbs to its tawdry attractions. Just before he makes his marriage proposal Luzhin strides "all around the room" (*krugami zashagal po komnate*) (102, *112*); Luzhin's parents move around him "in apprehensively narrowing circles" (15, *23*), and his mother is "surrounded by cheats" (*okruzhena obmanom*) (53, *61*). Luzhin is told that he will go far if he continues "on the same lines" (*v tom zhe dukhe*—lit., "in the same spirit") (56, *64*); his father's book has "still to find a definite design, a sharp line" (*naiti opredelennyi risunok, rezkuiu liniiu*) (82, *90*); talking to her mother, Luzhin's wife tries "to keep all her words on the same level" (*derzhat' slova na tom zhe urovne*) (107, *116*). Characters other than Luzhin reduce their vision of the world to silhouettes: Luzhin's wife frequently sees him in profile,[2] and Luzhin and his wife are playfully flattened in their marriage application, which "will hang on the wall for two weeks" (172, *182*). When Mrs. Luzhin asks Smirnovsky, a friend of her parents, to bring "interesting, free-thinking people" to meet Luzhin, he replies that he "did not revolve in such circles and then began to censure such revolving and quickly explained that he revolved in other circles in which revolving was essential, and Mrs. Luzhin's head began to spin as it used to in the amusement park on

---

1. D. Barton Johnson provides a fascinating discussion of Nabokov's uses of geometric shapes and concepts in *Bend Sinister* and "Solus Rex," the Russian novel Nabokov left unfinished when he emigrated to America (*Worlds in Regression,* 203–14). In particular, he suggests that the source for Nabokov's working title for *Bend Sinister* (Game to Gumm) refers to volume 10 of the *Encyclopedia Britannica,* which contains articles on "God" and "Geometry" that have left their imprint on the novel.

2. "An artist, a great artist, she frequently thought, contemplating his heavy profile" (*gliadia na ego tiazhelyi profil'*")(88, *97*); "'Luzhin is well,' she said with a smile, looking at his ponderous profile (the profile of a flabbier Napoleon)" (*gliadia na ego tiazhelyi profil', profil' obriuzgshego Napoleona*) (162–63, *173*) (N.B. the exact repetition disappears in translation); "She bent her head to one side, looking at her husband's profile surrounded by the bulges in the pillow" (*gliadia na profil' muzha, okruzhennyi vzdutiem podushki*)(236, *247*). An artist sketches Turati and Luzhin in profile at the chess tournament (125, *135*). "Silhouette drawings in black frames" grace the entry hall in the Luzhins' apartment (172, *183*).

the revolving disk" (227, *238*). The epitome of superficial circularity is the Revolution itself, which Luzhin's poor father considers an inescapable topic for anyone writing a novel about contemporary Russians—and which in his own novel Nabokov manages almost entirely to elide: "With the revolution it was even worse. The general opinion was that it had influenced the course of every Russian's life; an author could not have his hero go through it without getting scorched, and to dodge it was impossible. This amounted to a genuine violation of the writer's free will" (80, *88*). One should read this passage as indicating not only the antithesis between the Russian Revolution and art but also between two-dimensional circularity and the free will of a great artist. The absence of a definite article in Russian permits the question that immediately follows—"Actually how could the revolution affect his son?" (*Mezh tem, kak mogla revoliutsiia zadet' ego syna?*) (80, *88*)—to be read as also meaning "how could revolution affect his son?" This query is emblematic of much of Luzhin's interaction with what Russian philosophers at the turn of the century called the "bad infinity" (*durnaia beskonechnost'*) of the two-dimensional world around him.[3] This association of revolution with two-dimensional, superficial life is perhaps most strongly intimated in the description of the mechanical game that Luzhin finds at the train station in the opening chapter: "five little dolls with pendent bare legs awaited the impact of a coin in order to come to life and revolve" (*ozhit' i zavertet'sia*) (20, *27*). Here the cheap superficiality of revolution is compounded (the round coin makes the dolls rotate), and the phrase "come to life" sounds ironic or banal.

Nabokov often raises the theme of two-dimensionality through clever paronomasia. Luzhin's wife "outlines" the couple's schedule for the week (*ona nametila* plan *etoi nedeli; plan* means either "schedule" or "plane") (240–41, *252*). Later, she reads the émigré newspapers to her husband while he surreptitiously solves the chess problems he has spied in their pages:

If in this respect," she continued, "nothing is respected. . . ." (Oh, splendid! exclaimed Luzhin mentally, finding the key to the problem—a bewitchingly elegant sacrifice). *"Esli v etom* plane,*"—prodolzhala ona,—rassmatrivat' ikh dalneishie* plany. . . ." *"Akh, kakaia roskosh',"—myslenno voskliknul Luzhin, naidia kliuch k zadache—ocharovatel'no iziashchnuiu zhertvu.* [lit., "If on this plane . . . we examine their further plans (or planes)"]. (224, *235*)

3. For one example of the term's use, see Solov'ev, 2:547.

Ostensibly the "problem" to which Luzhin finds the key in this scene is a chess problem, but the passage also contains the key to the two-dimensional theme and ought to be found by the reader, who must apply it to the proper homonymic lock.

The book's obnoxious Soviet visitor to Berlin is almost a phrase book of Russian two-dimensional speech. She declares that "one has to be broad-minded" (*nuzhno shiroko myslit'*)—in subtle opposition to thinking *profoundly*— (210, *221*); and, shortly before telling Mrs. Luzhin that she will "take advantage" of her (*Ia vas voz'mu v oborot*—lit., "I will take you into circulation") (213, *224*), she rages against the newspapers: "I opened the paper and began to read, and there was such slander printed there, such lies, and everything so crude. [...] It is a conspiracy." (*[O]tkryvaiu gazety, chitaiu, i takaia tam napechatana kleveta, takaia lozh', tak vse plosko* [lit., "everything is so flat"]. [...] *Krugovaia poruka* [lit., "a circular guarantee"]) (211, *222*).

The novel's English version is no less playful. Luzhin's mother-in-law "sincerely loved the daubed, artificial Russia she had rigged up a*round* her, but sometimes she became unbearably *bored,* not knowing exactly what was missing" (*kotoruiu vokrug sebia ponastroila, inogda skuchala nevynosimo*) (104, *114, emphasis added*); the sideboards in her and her daughter's apartments are mentioned more than once; "the more closely [Luzhin's wife] read the news-papers, the more *bored* she grew. [...] But when she turned to the newspapers of the other world, Soviet newspapers, her *boredom* then knew no bounds" (*tem ei stanovilos' skuchnee, skuke ne bylo granits*) (224, *235, emphasis added*). The *board* (*pravlenie*) of the Union of Émigré Writers honors the memory of Luzhin's father with a minute of silence (82, *90*); the émigrés in Berlin live in petty-bourgeois "*flats,*" one of which is described in such detail that the reader can barely resist making a two-dimensional floor plan of it. It is hardly a compliment when Nabokov writes that Luzhin's future mother-in-law "was *flattered*" (*ei bylo lestno*) by Luzhin's asking her for her daughter's hand (115, *125, emphasis added*).

Nabokov is particularly insistent on the two-dimensionality of bad or vulgarized art. Luzhin's father imagines himself descending with a candle "to the drawing room where a Wunderkind, dressed in a white nightshirt that came down to his heels, would be playing on an enormous black piano"; later, as several critics have noted (Boyd, "The Problem of Pattern," 580; Tammi, 140), we see this image in a woodcut in the Luzhins' apartment. This reduction of a character to a two-dimensional image—a process of reductive "framing" insightfully explored by Connolly (*Nabokov's Early Fiction,* 97–98)—is a textual operation also performed on Luzhin's wife. Con-templating herself emerging from the bath, she declares "Turkish beauty"

(183, *193*), a phrase that ought to recall the reproduction of "Phryne Taking Her Bath" twice mentioned as hanging in Luzhin's parents' apartment (38, 40; *46, 48*). When Luzhin first meets his future wife, "he recalled quite irrelevantly but with stunning clarity the face of a bare-shouldered, black-stockinged young prostitute, standing in a lighted doorway in a dark side street in a nameless town" (99, *108*). The "stunning clarity" (*s potriasaiushchei iasnost'iu*) of this memory should bring back to mind the reader's own earlier glimpse of the picture of Phryne—a Greek courtesan most famous as the legendary model of Praxiteles' Cnidan Aphrodite, sculpted for the Anatolian city of Cnida (in modern Turkey)—who "was particularly vivid as a result of the intensified light" (*kotoraia, blagodaria usilennomu osveshcheniiu, byla osobenno iarka*) (40, *48*).

The two-dimensionality of Mrs. Luzhin's character is most exposed by her identification with literary texts disparaged by Nabokov. The passage that dwells in greatest detail on her personality is worth quoting at length:

> The young Russians who visited them in Berlin considered her a nice but not very interesting girl, while her mother said of her (in a low-pitched voice with a trace of derision) that she represented in the family "the intelligentsia and avant-garde literature"—whether because she knew by heart a few poems of the "Symbolist" Balmont that she had found in the *Poetry Reader* or whether for some other reason, remained unknown. Her father liked her independence, her quietness, and her particular way of lowering her eyes when she smiled. But nobody yet had been able to dig down to what was most captivating about her: this was the mysterious ability of her soul to apprehend in life only that which had once attracted and tormented her in childhood, the time when the soul's instinct is infallible; to seek out the amusing and the touching; to feel constantly an intolerable, tender pity for the creature whose life is helpless and unhappy; to feel across hundreds of miles that somewhere in Sicily a thin-legged little donkey with a shaggy belly is being brutally beaten. Whenever she did come across a creature that was being hurt, she experienced a kind of legendary eclipse—when inexplicable night comes down and ash flies and blood appears on the walls—and it seemed that if at once, at once, she did not help, did not cut short another's torture (the existence of which it was absolutely impossible to explain in a world so conducive to happiness), her heart would not stand it and she would die. Hence, she lived in perpetual, secret agitation, constantly anticipating a new delight or a new pity, and it was said of her that she adored dogs and was always ready

to lend money—and listening to these trivial rumors she felt as she had in childhood during that game where you go out of the room and the others talk about you, and you have to guess who said what. And among the players, among those whom she joined after a stay in the next room (where you sat waiting to be called and conscientiously sang something so as not to overhear, or else opened a chance book—and like a Jack-in-the-box a passage from a novel would spring up, the end of an unintelligible conversation), among those people whose opinion she had to guess there was now a rather taciturn man, difficult to budge and thinking completely unknown things about her. (105–6, *114–16*)

Several scholars adopt a sympathetic stance toward Luzhin's wife and accept the pathos of her sentimentality for true coin (Connolly, *Nabokov's Early Fiction,* 291; Toker, *Nabokov* 74–75), but this ostensibly laudatory passage strikes me as a collage of moments from literary works that Nabokov did not respect.[4] *Crime and Punishment* peeks out from the tormented donkey; the future Mrs. Luzhin's inability to accept torture even in a world "so conducive to happiness" recalls Ivan Karamazov's rejection of God's "ticket"; her later worry about Luzhin's prospective visits to her parents' drawing room, "imaginary calls" that will end in the "monstrous catastrophe" of Luzhin knocking down "the scenery" (*eti voobrazhaemye poseshcheniia konchalis' chudovishchnoi katastrofoi*)(104, *113*), should trigger associations with Prince Myshkin (Meerson, 28–33).

Mrs. Luzhin's most sustained association is with the heroine of one of Turgenev's less successful novels—*On the Eve*'s Elena Stakhova. As in the passage cited above, the chapter introducing Elena emphasizes her early pity for the suffering of others. The defiant relationship of Luzhin's future bride with her dense, superficial parents is strikingly similar to Elena's, as is her decision to marry without their permission. Both Elena and Luzhin's fiancée nurse their future husbands back to health after a devastating illness. Like Luzhin's intended, Elena boldly (and more unconventionally) makes an

---

4. The award for panegyric treatment goes to S. V. Sakun: "Her love is not egoistic, not erotic, not blind; she is inseparable from pity, perceptive and tragically realistic. Her love is altruistic. This woman is much better than the other people who surround Luzhin, she senses the secret of his gift and even feels her own belonging. It is precisely her perception of Luzhin that endows the main hero with that attractive and tender-tragic charm, which is somehow felt in this sullen, alienated, clumsy and inconvenient man" (14). Brian Boyd is cautious, appreciating Mrs. Luzhin's "compassion and self-abnegation," but admitting this may be the sort of stereotype "that a writer of Luzhin Senior's mediocre stamp would rush to for a happy ending" ("The Problem of Pattern," 603, 595). Elsewhere, he is more sanguine: Mrs. Luzhin is an "attractive and sympathetic woman" whose "ability to see Luzhin for what he is and her determination to protect him from life's sharp edges are deeply moving" (*The Russian Years,* 322, 323).

unchaperoned visit to the man she will eventually marry; in both cases, the man imagines that the encounter is a dream. Another visit by Elena leads to the physical consummation of the romantic relationship (*"Tak voz'mi zh menia,"—prosheptala ona chut' slyshno* ["'Then take me,' she whispered so softly he could barely hear" (6:268)]); during his fiancée's visit to his hotel room Luzhin has an orgasm without her noticing it.[5] Mrs. Luzhin calls her husband by his surname; when her mother objects, she responds: "Turgenev's heroines did it. Am I worse than they?" (113, *123*). Later, an elderly member of the intelligentsia is "unable to look at Mrs. Luzhin without emotion, for in her he found a resemblance to the clear-eyed, ideal maidens who had worked with him for the good of the people" (231–32, *243*).[6] In brief, Luzhin's wife, this representative of "the intelligentsia and avant-garde literature," is kinder but no less clichéd than the regular guests at the Chernyshevskis' literary evenings in *The Gift*.

When we read closely the passage quoted at length above, we see hidden in the parenthetical clause a subtle baring of the character's constitutive principle: "[from] a chance book [...] like a Jack-in-the-box a passage from a novel would spring up." Here intertextuality serves not to introduce allusive depth but to flatten a character with a pastiche of the intelligentsia's literary greatest hits.

---

5. In the English text the sexual connotation of the scene is heightened by a double entendre: "'Let me go,' she demanded in a shrill voice. 'Notes on various games, notes ...' repeated Luzhin, pressing her to him, his narrowed eyes looking up at her neck. A sudden spasm distorted his face and for an instant his eyes lost all expression; then his features relaxed oddly, his hands unclenched of themselves, and she moved away from him, angry without knowing exactly why she was angry, and surprised that he had let her go. Luzhin cleared his throat and greedily lit a cigarette, watching her with incomprehensible mischievousness. 'I'm sorry I came,' she said" (109, *119*). The delayed attribution of the line of dialogue ("she said" following rather than preceding the quotation) encourages a momentary flicker of lewd connotation. There is at least one other place where the English is lewd and the Russian chaste: Mrs. Luzhin's actor acquaintance tells her that he is now making movies: "Big parts with close-ups." Compare: *"Bol'shie roli, i vo vsiu mordu"* (233, *244*). An early passage also is capable of being read as a double entendre, particularly in light of the subsequent eroticization of Luzhin's wife as the next Phryne: "'Stark naked again,' sighed the editor of an art magazine, taking a passing look at Phryne, who was particularly vivid as a result of the intensified light. At this point young Luzhin cropped up under his feet and had his head stroked. The boy recoiled. 'How huge he's grown,' said a woman's voice from behind." (*"Opiat' vyshla nagishom",—so vzdokhom skazal izdatel' khudozhestvennogo zhurnala, vzglianuv mimokhodom na Frinu, kotoraia blagodaria usilennomu osveshcheniiu, byla osobenno iarka. Tut malen'kii Luzhin popalsia emu pod nogi i byl poglazhen po golovke. Luzhin popiatilsia. "Kakoi on u vas stal ogromnyi," skazal damskii golos szadi*) (40, *48*).

6. The relevance of *On the Eve* to Nabokov's novel is reinforced by the borrowing of a name from a secondary character in that novel. Turgenev's "Bersenev" appears at the start of his novel as one of a pair of young men lying on the bank of the Moscow river. "Bersenev" surfaces in Nabokov's novel as one of a pair of odious schoolmates invited to young Luzhin's birthday party.

Not all the novel's two-dimensional literary allusions involve Luzhin's wife. At other points Nabokov introduces clichéd literary material in parodic ways that emphasize the shoddy material's compatibility with characters who inhabit a two-dimensional world. A long passage describing a sultry day in the country during Luzhin's youth is a parodic amalgam of the likes of Artsybashev (Luzhin spying on the naked girls in the river) and Maupassant (Luzhin's mother plying him with *boules-de-gomme* and stroking his hand from under her bedclothes). Toward the start of this passage—just before Luzhin hears "ecstatic squeals" and spies "naked bodies" in the river—Nabokov refers to soaring swallows ("their flight recalled the motion of scissors swiftly cutting out some design") (59–60, 67) in terms that not only emphasize authorial presence but hint at the mechanistic production of this cut-and-paste passage.[7] A similar moment comes when Valentinov describes his plan for a film in which a young man from a good family will ravish a girl who has dozed off in his train compartment: "She falls asleep and in her sleep spreads her limbs. A glorious young creature. The young man—you know the type, bursting with sap but absolutely chaste—begins literally to lose his head. In a kind of trance he hurls himself upon her" (*On v kakom-to transe nabrasyvaetsia na nee*) (247, 259). The scene described by Valentinov is a reworking of Andreev's sensationalistic story "The Abyss" ("Bezdna"), in which a young man and his beloved are attacked by hooligans; discovering her unconscious and the victim of a gang rape, he loses his mind and throws himself on her in a sexual frenzy.[8] Prior to this scene there have been many references in *The Defense* to chess chasms and metaphysical abysses; Nabokov has used the word *bezdna* (and—less frequently—its denotative twin *propast'*) in the Russian. The references to abysses intensify in this final chapter, and just prior to learning the plot of Valentinov's movie Luzhin comes across film journals on Valentinov's table with "photographs of frightened women and ferociously squinting men" (247) who might have emerged from Andreev's pages. Next Luzhin sees a picture of an actor, probably Harold Lloyd (Appel, *Nabokov's Dark Cinema,* 161) "hanging by his hands from the ledge of a skyscraper—just about to fall off into the abyss." (Here the Russian word used—*propast'*—refers to Andreev's title only by synonym.) The identification of Valentinov's scenario with Andreev's story not only hints at Luzhin's

---

7. Particularly hard working here is the adverb "swiftly": a pun on the nominal and adjectival meanings of "swift."

8. Andreev, as Ol'ga Skonechnaia points out ("Primechaniia," 711) has already made an appearance in the novel as the "celebrated writer, a very pale man with a very conspicuous goatee," whom the future Mrs. Luzhin has seen in Finland (90, 99).

coming fate but also serves as yet another instance of Nabokov's parodic pasting of a vulgar text onto his own. Valentinov's scenario, like Andreev's "Abyss," has no aesthetic depth.

Quite early in the novel, in a moment that should be read as an invocation of the paronomastic muse, Nabokov describes little Luzhin's dictation exercises: "'Being *born* in this world is hardly to be *borne.*' And his son wrote, practically lying on the table and *baring* his teeth" (17, *25, emphasis added*).[9] Luzhin finds that being born into this two-dimensional world is indeed difficult to be borne. When the light in his study goes off suddenly, he does not realize "what was going on around him" (*Luzhin ne ponial, chto krugom proiskhodit*) (219, *229*). (This is just one of many moments where a statement ostensibly directed at a specific scene in the novel has far-reaching metaphysical significance; here, as elsewhere in Nabokov's work, the reader must read an adverbial construction with reference to both a specific context and the novel as a whole.) Luzhin's desire to escape is expressed as a yearning to flee two-dimensionality—he dreams of "voluntarily committing some absurd unexpected act that would be outside the systematic order of life" (*sovershit' kakoe-nibud' nelepoe, no neozhidannoe deistvie, kotoroe by vypadalo iz obshchei planomernosti zhizni* [or "fall away from the general planar order of life"]) (242, *254*). These efforts are marked by the novel's attention to depth, a focus that tantalizingly hints at the possibility of Luzhin's transcendence of everyday, nonchess life and, more generally, at a character's hope of rising above the surrounding text. As a child, Luzhin has "a painful inner life of some sort" (32, *40*), he is drawn to activities and objects that hint at a third dimension, such as the globe in his room and magic tricks: "He found a mysterious pleasure, a vague promise of still unfathomed delights, in the crafty and accurate way a trick would come out" (*On nakhodil zagadochnoe udovol'stvie, neiasnoe obeshchanie kakikh-to drugikh, eshche nevedomykh naslazhdenii, v tom, kak khitro i tochno skladyvalsia fokus*)(36, *44*). Luzhin's potential for profundity is what makes him "the most unfathomable [*zamyslovateishii*] of men" (110, *120*) for his wife and other characters. Far more representative of the novel's two-dimensional world is Luzhin's father, who, having spent the day with his lover, experiences "a residue of shame it was better not to investigate" (*chuvstvo styda, v kotoroe luchshe bylo ne uglubliat'sia*—lit., "into which it was better

---

9. The Russian is different—"'*Eto lozh', chto v teatre net lozh.*' *I syn pisal, pochti lezha na stole*" (lit., "it is a lie that in the theatre there are no loges")—but in both cases, the wordplay spills out of the exercise into the larger narrative, an example of the porous boundaries prevailing between texts and among characters in this world where the illusion of reality is constantly subordinated to the insistent marking of the artistic text.

not to go deep") (65, *72–73*). Nabokov makes Luzhin's extradimensionality painfully clear when Luzhin's fiancée wonders "how she could show this man to her father and mother, how could he be visualized in their *drawing room* [*gostinaia*] [N.B. the two-dimensionality in the English text]—*a man of a different dimension,* with a particular form and coloring that was compatible with nothing and no one" (103, *113, emphasis added*).

The Defense contains many passages in which the three-dimensionality of Luzhin, with his "heliced crown" (*s zavitkom na makushke*) (17, *25*) and his "tender, concave temple" *(nezhnyi, vpalyi visok)* (31, *39*), comes into play. "How ill-bred he is" (Kakoi *neotesannyi,* or "how unpolished, how unsmoothly cut")—thinks Luzhin's future wife, using a word that implies Luzhin's resistance to being reduced to a flat surface (100, *109*). We should note in particular Luzhin's attachment to three-dimensional geometric figures. When Luzhin begins to draw as a pale substitute for chess, his wife in profile does not turn out well, but his pictures concerned with depth or three-dimensionality are far better: these include a train on a bridge spanning an abyss, a bas-relief done in charcoal, a cube casting shade, and "a confidential conversation between a cone and a pyramid." Luzhin's mother-in-law compliments him, saying, "You're a real cubist" (*priamo futuristika*) (208, *218–19*).

Images of three-dimensionality mark Luzhin's slippage back into the world of chess: for example, when a *lining* suddenly develops the additional dimension of a hole which opens on to internal space containing a chess board and, perhaps most prominently, when Luzhin attends a *ball*. The scene at the ball with Petrishchev is remarkable for the playful subsurface tension between two and three dimensions. When Luzhin first says the word "ball" he imagines something superficial, in two dimensions: "lots and lots of circling couples" (*mnogo kruzhashchikhsia par*) (193, *205*). The circling motif is repeated several times until Luzhin slips into a "a deep armchair not far from the staircase" (*glubokoe kreslo nedaleko ot lestnitsy*) (196, *207*), a phrase that suggests space lying both below and above the diegetic plane. A man approaches him and Luzhin complains to him that he doesn't understand the world around him: "Who knows what it all means? It surpasses my conception." The man replies: "Particularly when you work, as I do, on a Brazilian plantation [plan*tatsiia*]." "Plantation [Plan*tatsiia*]," repeated Luzhin after him like an echo. "You have an odd way of living here," continues the stranger, as he evokes a flat, two-dimensional conception of geography: "The world is open on all four sides" (196–97, *208, emphasis added*). Yet when Petrishchev's memories of their shared past begin to drag Luzhin back into the chess world, the third dimension takes over: "The ball's in full swing, and we're sitting here talking about the past. You know, I've traveled the whole world. . . . What women in *Cuba!*" (199, *210,* emphasis added).

Particularly marked in the Russian but even more so in the English is the application to Luzhin of imagery and words of spherical proportions. Luzhin's wife hopes that within her fiancé "some kind of still unfathomed forces would come into play and he would blossom out and display his gift in other spheres [*v drugikh oblastiakh*] of life as well" (129, *139*). On their wedding night, Luzhin's wife understands that "the limits of her feminine competency were now in sight and [. . .] there was one sphere [*oblast'*] in which it was not her place to lead" (182, *193*). Later, she reproaches herself "for the narrowness of her mental vision and her inability to find the sphere [*oblast'*], the idea, the object which would provide work and food for Luzhin's inactive talents" (222, *233*).[10] Her marriage to Luzhin amounts to an attempt to reduce him to two dimensions. The world in which the couple is to travel after their marriage is depicted on an atlas in which the world is portrayed "first as a solid sphere, [. . .] then it was rolled out flat, cut into two halves and served up in sections" (185, *196*). When she first meets Luzhin, his future mother-in-law complains about Luzhin's small talk. "'There's a nice atmosphere here.' Atmosphere! Quite a word, eh?" (*Tut priiatnaia atmosfera. Atmosfera, a? Slovtso-to?*) (108, 118). This word is emphasized again after Luzhin and his wife attend a film in which actors are playing "this unfortunate game of chess, which that fool of a director had seen fit to introduce for the sake of 'atmosphere'" (*dlia nastroeniia*) (192, *203*). These wordplays on "sphere" provide an equivalence for a large number of puns in the Russian text on the Russian word for the same figure, *shar.* As Luzhin walks along a path, touching objects with his cane, he is forever groping in his pocket—*Vse sharil v karmane*—and when he sees that the pocket's lining is deficient he denigrates it as "poor material" (*skvernaia materiia,* with a possible pun on *skver* meaning "square") (86, *95*). After Petrishchev mentions the women in Cuba, Luzhin begins to grope in his pocket—"*stal sharit' v karmane*" (201, *211*)—again.

There is a wonderful irony here. Luzhin's world of chess creativity is anchored to a board that literally has two dimensions, yet this "real chess life" (133, *144*)—because of its link to art—is often accorded an extra dimension relative to the "real" world of Nabokov's characters. Luzhin plays chess "in a celestial dimension" (*v nezemnom izmerenii*) (92, *101*); he experiences "deep enjoyment" (*glubokoe naslazhdenie*) when he abandons the board and plays in his mind (91, 101). Luzhin's wife understands little of chess, because she

---

10. In all three of these cases, the word "sphere" in the English adds a dimension not present in the original Russian.

cannot comprehend it on her even, two-dimensional plane: "she knew nothing at all about chess" (*o shakhmatakh ona ne znala* rovno *nichego*—lit., "she knew nothing *evenly* about chess") (88, 97). Luzhin's sight of his first chess game follows a strange, seemingly irrelevant question by Petrishchev:

> Gromov was telling some story in a hoarse voice, pronouncing strange obscene words with gusto. Petrishchev begged everyone to explain to him how we know that they are equal to two right-angled ones [*pochemu my znaem, chto oni ravniaiutsia dvum priamym*]. And suddenly, behind him, Luzhin distinctly heard a special sound, wooden and rattly, that caused him to grow hot and his heart to skip a beat. (48, *56*)

The odd, unconnected second sentence has a pronoun (they) with no clear antecedent. Coming after the previous sentence, "they" would presumably refer to "words," but on reflection the reader should see that in fact "they" must refer to the angles of a triangle, the sum of which in Euclidean geometry must equal two right angles. This sentence is doubly significant. First, its unfixed pronoun binds together two types of figures (verbal and mathematical). Second, the answer of non-Euclidean geometry (indebted to Lobachevsky, Bolyai, and Riemann) to Petrishchev's question is that the angles of a triangle are *not* necessarily equal to two right angles if they are located on the surface of a three-dimensional body (such as a sphere) rather than on a plane.[11] That this breakthrough occurs in a geography class should be taken as evidence of its global importance for the novel's world: Petrishchev's question, its answer and the ensuing chess match hint that there is another dimension beyond the characters' flat world.[12]

---

11. For a discussion of the importance of the sphere in the transcendence of Euclidean axioms, see Smith, 180–210, and Coxeter, 7:1112–20. In an 1888 article in *Severnyi vestnik*, Akim Volynsky cited Spinosa's summary of the Euclidean axiom: "*Kogda ia izuchal Evklida, to ia prezhde vsego uznal, chto tri ugla treugol'nika ravny dvum priamym*" ("When I first studied Euclid, I learned first of all that the three angles of a triangle are equal to two right angles"). These lines were cited by P. D. Uspensky, who popularized non-Euclidean geometry in Russia for his own mystical purposes; Uspenskii had already informed his readers that "in geometry on a sphere the sum of the three angles of a triangle will be greater than two right angles, while in geometry on a concave surface, it will be less than two right angles (136, 52). In *The Gift*, Fyodor writes of Chernyshevski's hostility to Lobachevsky: "all Kazan was of the unanimous opinion that the man was a complete fool.... What on earth is the curvature of 'a ray' or 'curved space.'" (240). Perhaps as a form of poetic punishment, in which the geometric sins of the father are visited on his progeny, Chernyshevski's son is "afraid of space, or, more exactly, he was afraid of slipping into a different dimension—and in order to avoid perishing he clung continuously to the safe, solid—with Euclidean pleats—skirt of Pelageya Nikolaevna Fanderflitt" (240).

12. When the geography teacher is sick, he is replaced by "the predatory little mathematics teacher" (48, *56*). This substitution should be read as connoting the essential geometric aspects of the novel's "world." This linkage between geography and mathematics is reinforced by the similarity between the titles of a collection of problems, "Merry Mathematics" (*Veselaia matematika*) (36, *44*), and the game of "jolly geography" (*veselaia geografiia*) (190, *201*) played by Luzhin and his wife.

Ultimately, the power of chess to redeem two-dimensional life proves illusory, and Luzhin, after his match with Turati has been interrupted, finds himself becoming "flatter and flatter" *(on kak budto spliushchivalsia, spliushchivalsia, spliushchivalsia)* (143, *153*). Luzhin discovers that a character in a novel cannot escape the relentless two-dimensionality of literary existence: at the novel's end he is able to flee only to imprisonment on yet another plane. The chessboard that opens up beneath him connotes endless planar repetition: not a three-dimensional abyss but an infinitely two-dimensional mise en abyme.

In his chapter on *The Defense,* Julian Connolly discusses Luzhin's "inability to establish intimate contact with any of the more tangible others in his world" and criticizes Luzhin's "decision to lie to his wife" as if it were a character fault *(Nabokov's Early Fiction,* 83). Let us take this critique in another direction and note that Luzhin suffers from the ultimate, allegorical character fault—the fault of being a character.

Nabokov repeatedly emphasizes not only that Luzhin is a literary character but that his suffering springs from his placement within a novel that is about *being* a literary character. The genius of the novel arises from the tension inherent in this paradoxical condition. Realist fiction relies on readers forgetting on some level that characters are not living people; modernism foregrounds the created, fictive nature of fiction, and modernist characters are more likely to be perceived as constructs, verbal figures to which the word "being" is less apt to be applied. The power of Nabokov's best novels resides in their ability to be read as both premodernist and modernist works. *The Defense* provides us with a sympathetic, potentially premodernist, "warm" character who begins to perceive what modernism has done to the denizens of fiction. The reader who identifies with Luzhin and struggles with him against the cruel, encroaching pattern of plot is essentially suffering from the palpable advent of modernism. To the extent that nostalgia operates as a guiding principle in Nabokov's fiction, it is nostalgia for a premodernist fictive world from which the author and reader have been exiled. The reader may yearn for that paradise, but the author more than compensates by making its loss his theme. Unless he is completely inured to the charms of realism, the reader suffers from the triumph of modernism even as he delights in the brilliance that makes that suffering so acute.[13]

---

13. Tammi formulates this dynamic similarly: *"The Defense* causes its reader to vacillate between two interpretations, either of them valid to a point, but tending to cancel out one another when brought together. In the first instance the novel is regarded as a more or less "realistic" narrative. [...]

Allegory demands continued reference to an underlying theme. In many allegories, such as Dante's, the presentation of these references is facilitated by an episodic structure. In a first encounter, the allegory is examined from one perspective; in the next it is embodied through the hero's acquaintance with new characters who pose the allegorical problem in a different way. *The Defense* has its equivalent structure: Nabokov provides his readers with a series of seemingly unconnected, richly *descriptive* scenes that repeatedly pose the problem of author-character relations. The episodic nature of this structure is concealed because the reader is apt to appreciate these scenes purely as a matter of style and to miss their allegorical substance. These scenes are not merely descriptive flourishes; rather, they are the plot's equivalent of parentheses, and it is within parentheses and their equivalents that the meaning of Nabokov's fiction is often to be sought.[14] One of the most interesting of these allegorical descriptions occurs at the start of chapter 11:

> In a rudimentary [*zachatochnym*] jacket minus one sleeve Luzhin, who was being renovated, stood in profile before a cheval glass, while a bald-headed tailor either chalked his shoulder and back or else jabbed pins into him, which he took with astonishing deftness from his mouth, where they seemed to grow naturally. From all the samples of cloth arranged neatly according to color in an album, Luzhin had chosen a dark gray square, and his fiancée spent a long time feeling the corresponding bolt of cloth, which the tailor threw with a hollow thud onto the counter, unwrapped with lightning speed, and pressed against his protruding stomach, as if covering up his nakedness [*slovno prikryvaia nagotu*]. She found that the material tended to crease easily, whereupon an avalanche of tight rolls of cloth began to cover the counter and the tailor, wetting his finger on his lower lip, unrolled and unrolled. Finally a cloth was chosen that was also dark gray, but soft and flexible, and even just a bit shaggy; and now Luzhin, distributed about the cheval glass in pieces, in sections, as if for visible instruction (... here we have a plump, clean-shaven face, here is the same face in profile, and here we have something rarely seen by the subject himself, the back of his head, fairly closely cropped, with folds in the neck and slightly protruding

---

The second reading in effect verifies the hero's suspicions: the universe contained in the novel *is* a stylized game, the function of which can be only partially grasped by the fictive mind" (142). See also Stephen Koch's claim that "all Nabokov's work is gripped by a tension between modernity and nostalgia" (184).

14. Duncan White describes parentheses in *Lolita* as "windows into a deeper reading of the novel, small holes delicately torn by Nabokov in Humbert's flamboyant screen" (49).

ears, pink where the light shines through . . .) looked at himself and the material, failing to recognize its former smooth, generous, virgin integrity. "I think it needs to be a bit narrower in front," said his fiancée, and the tailor, taking a step backward, slit his eyes at Luzhin's figure, purred with the polite trace of a smile that the gentleman was somewhat on the stout side [*portnoi, otoidia na shag, prishchurilsia na luzhinskuiu figuru, promurlykal s vezhlivym smeshkom, chto gospodin neskol'ko v tele*], and then busied himself with some newborn lapels [*novorozhdennye otvoroty*], pulling this and pinning that, while Luzhin in the meantime, with a gesture peculiar to all people in his position, held his arm slightly away from his body or else bent it at the elbow and looked at his wrist, trying to get accustomed to the sleeve. In passing, the tailor slashed him over the heart with chalk to indicate a small pocket, then pitilessly ripped off the sleeve that had seemed finished and began quickly to remove the pins from Luzhin's stomach. (169–70, *180–81*)

The theme of incarnation is by turns obvious—*zachatochnyi*, with associative links to *zachatie*, "conception," can also mean "embryonic," and "newborn" speaks for itself—and subtle: rather than "somewhat on the stout side" *neskol'ko v tele* might also be read to mean "slightly embodied," signifying that the process of character creation is not yet complete. We should note how much is flat or flattened in this scene of creation: the choice of a square, the mirrors showing Luzhin in profile and in their multiplicity creating the illusion of depth, the material which is rolled out flat. Particularly ingenious is the biblical resonance of this creation scene: the phrase "as if covering up his nakedness" (*slovno prikryvaia nagotu*) has a whiff of the garden of Eden. We should pay special attention to what we might call the "literally figurative" meaning of *slovno* (translated "as if" but formed from the root meaning "word"). The tailor is a figure for the author covering nakedness with words; accordingly, the instruments employed to pin Luzhin to the two-dimensional board of fictive life are taken from his mouth. In this passage the reference to Luzhin's "figure" ought to be particularly noted. *Figura* is a crucial word in the Russian version of *The Defense;* the word appears at least forty-four times and most often refers to chess pieces, but it can also refer to geometrical figures, as well as to characters; in Nabokov's text it is twice used to refer to Luzhin's appearance. Moreover, in a verbal artifact, and in particular in allegory, almost everything is a "figure": a figure of speech and a figure of the underlying idea. The rich meaning of this word establishes Luzhin's identity as an artistic construct, as an actor in a world shaped by notions of geometry, and, perhaps most important, as a verbal plaything. The etymology of Luzhin's name, to which Nabokov calls attention in the English introduction by comparing its sound to that of "illusion," supports this interpretation of Luzhin as a piece in a verbal game. Deprived of the prefix necessary for its appearance in English, "lusion" (from the Latin *ludere*), might mean something like "an act of play" or "play" itself. Twice Nabokov has Luzhin obliquely comment on the ludic nature of his character. The first occurs when Luzhin is seeking to amuse his young Soviet visitor: "'A toy would do it,' he said to himself" ("*Igrushku by,*"—"*skazal on pro sebia,*" which can also mean "about himself") (217, *228*). Earlier, when Petrishchev overhears Luzhin's last name, he asks "Is your name Luzhin?" Luzhin, denying the name's significance, says "it's of no importance" (*eto ne igraet znachenie*)(197, *208*). This response literally means "it does not play any significance," but the name's significance is that it will soon lead Petrishchev to remember that Luzhin played chess.

The metafictive theme is frequently sounded with reference to the production and maintenance of the fictive environment around Luzhin. There are numerous veiled references to various types of "management"; in virtually all of these one should see a nod toward authorial presence. "In general, life around him was so opaque and demanded so little effort of him that it sometimes seemed someone—a mysterious, invisible manager—continued to take him from tournament to tournament" (95, *105*). Luzhin "felt dimly grateful to an obliging memory [not necessarily his own—E.N.] that indicated the necessary resort so aptly, took all the trouble on itself and put him into a ready-made, ready-waiting hotel" (98, *108*). Upset by the cold, the polar bears in the zoo find "that the management had overdone it" (*chto direktsiia pereborshchila*) (205, *216*). Occasionally, the management seems to have been careless, as if the writer has forgotten to fill in some of the decor or neglected to insure the character's transportation from one place to the next. Luzhin, trying to reach his match with Turati, opens his hotel room door and instead of seeing Turati in front of him finds himself looking at a hotel corridor which would, of course, exist in real life but need not exist in a novel. "They removed it," Luzhin says of the café and its expected *narrative* proximity, "How was I to know that everything would be removed?" (135–36, *146*). Luzhin is comforted by the way in which the world seems to take care of him, "but at unavoidable moments of solitude during his engagement, late at night or early in the morning, there would be a sensation of strange emptiness, as if the colorful jigsaw puzzle done on the table had proved to contain curiously shaped blank spots" (177, *187–88*).

The author's presence as producer often may be discerned if the reader probes passive and impersonal constructions or looks closely at moments where words or actions are not clearly attributed to a specific, visible actor.

(Nabokov may be paying himself a sly complement when he describes the obnoxious Soviet visitor as "a slim, animated, nicely made-up, nicely bobbed lady" ["*udachno nakrashennaia i ostrizhennaia dama*" (209, *220*)]). The penultimate paragraph of chapter 11 contains a passive construction that should be read as a parody (or generic transposition) of Symbolist poetic discourse, with the crucial distinction that in Symbolist poetry such indefinite language (*some, somewhere, someone, unknown, shadow*) would be taken as a sign of a higher, nouminal world. Here, this higher world is the realm of the author:

> Before going to bed she moved back the window curtain to see if the blind had been lowered. It had not been. In the dark *depths* of the courtyard the night wind rocked a shrub and in the faint light shed from *somewhere unknown something* glistened, perhaps a puddle on the stone path that skirted the lawn, and *in another place the shadow* of *some* railings fitfully appeared and disappeared. And *suddenly everything went dark and there was only a black chasm.*
>
> *Pered tem, kak lech', ona otodvinula shtoru okna, chob posmotret', spush-cheno li zhaliuzi. Ono ne bylo spushcheno. V temnoi* glubine *dvora nochnoi veter trepal* kakie-to *kusty, i pri tusklom svete,* nevedomo otkuda *livshem-sia,* chto-to *blestelo,* byt' mozhet—*luzha na kamennoi paneli vdol' gazona, i v* drugom meste *to poiavlialas', to skryvalas'* ten' kakoi-to *reshetki.* I vdrug vse pogaslo, i byla tol'ko chernaia propast'. (183–84, *194*; emphasis added)

This passage brings together in very condensed fashion several of the images that in this novel—and elsewhere in Nabokov's oeuvre—indicate authorial presence: depth, wind, shadow, the attribution of sensory stimuli to an unseen source, and the sudden illumination or extinction of lighting on the book's "set." Here these images are highlighted by both the Symbolist lexicon noted above and by Blokian syntax: the marked reliance on "and" (*i*) to string images together.[15]

Frequently, authorial presence is indicated by voices from unseen or initially unseen sources. Such a voice breaks in when Petrishchev is about to provide Luzhin with details of his relations with women in the jungles of Cuba:

---

15. See, inter alia, the conclusion to Blok's 1906 poem "Peredvecherneiu poroiu," where eight of the final sixteen lines begin with *I*. Dolinin observes that the phrase *tusklyi svet* (faint light) recalls Blok's famous poem "Noch', ulitsa, fonar', apteka" with its *tusklyi svet* and the partnered rhyme *iskhoda net* ("there is no escape") (I *stinnaia zhizn'*, 68).

"It's all lies," sounded a lazy voice from behind. "He was never in any jungle whatsoever. . . ."

"Now why do you spoil everything?" drawled Petrishchev, turning around. "Don't listen to him," continued a bald, lanky person, the owner of the lazy voice. "He has been living in France since the Revolution and left Paris for the first time the day before yesterday." "Luzhin, allow me to introduce you," began Petrishchev with a laugh; but Luzhin hastily made off, tucking his head into his shoulders and weaving strangely and quivering from the speed of his walk. (199, *210*)

It may be that Luzhin has just avoided a meeting with his maker, who is, presumably, the "friend" who has "dragged" Petrishchev to the ball (*menia siuda zatashchil priiatel'*) (196, *206–7*).[16]

Valentinov is the novel's most specific incarnation of the author as manager, and he is presented as a kind of intermediary, an "evil spirit" (166, *176*) sent to inscribe a particularly visible trace of the author's will on the text's two-dimensional surface. Valentinov reenters Luzhin's life through the telephone, an apparatus that is often a sign of author-character (mis)communication in Nabokov's fiction. One of the most significant references to Valentinov occurs when Mrs. Luzhin telephones an actor friend to follow up on his earlier statement that he is acquainted with Valentinov:

Luckily the actor turned out to be at home and immediately launched into a long account of all the frivolous and mean actions committed at one time or another by the lady he had been talking to at the party. Mrs. Luzhin heard him out impatiently and then asked who Valentinov was. The actor said "Oh yes!" and continued: "You see how forgetful I am, life is impossible without a prompter" [*bez suflera ne mogu zhit'*]; and finally, after giving a detailed account of his relations with Valentinov, he mentioned in passing that, according to him, he, Valentinov, had been Luzhin's chess father, so to speak, and had made a great player

---

16. Nabokov was certainly lanky in his youth, and photographs from the 1930s show him to have had less and less hair throughout the decade. By no means totally bald when writing *The Defense,* he may have seen himself as balding and thus have used the word "bald" when referring to himself in ironic, self-deprecating tones. In *The Gift,* Godunov-Cherdyntsev sits next to his colleague, Vladimirov, obviously an ironic copy of a Nabokov a few years younger than the author of *The Defense.* "At twenty-nine [Vladimirov] was already the author of two novels" and so has not yet written his "Defense." Vladimirov's hair is already "receding": "*ubyl' volos po bokam lba preuvelichivala ego [t.e., lba] razmery*" (320, *359*). See Tammi on Nabokov's use of his own "physiognomy" as a metafictive code (320–23).

out of him [*Valentinov, po ego, valentinovskim, slovam, byl shakhmatnym opekunom Luzhina i sdelal iz nego velikogo igroka*]. (238, *250*)

The phrase *po ego, Valentinovskim, slovam* is worth pausing over. Initially, it appears to mean simply that Valentinov has said he was Luzhin's chess father. But this construction may also be read instrumentally: Valentinov is Luzhin's chess father (and has made a great player out of him) *by virtue of his own words.* To put it differently, pursuing the literal meaning, Valentinov is Luzhin's verbal creator. This subtle use of *po ego, Valentinovskim, slovam* is heightened by the apparently unrelated aside that life is impossible without a prompter. If this self-deprecatory statement refers to the actor's relation to Valentinov, it may be read as a virtually ontological statement about the status of characters, who cannot act independently but must be prompted by the author.[17] Moreover, the word *sufler* ("prompter," from the French *souffleur* [prompter] and *souffler* [to blow]) seems particularly significant in the context of author-character relations, because an author may be seen as breathing a kind of limited life into his characters. There are many references to the shortness of Luzhin's breath (73, *80;* 95, *105;* 113, *123;* 118, *128;* 142, *152;* 172, *183*); the theme is so pronounced that it, too, should give rise to a meditation on the status of literary characters, who must all suffer from a relative shortness of breath, since their existence is confined to the pages of a book and to the life blown into them by their author.

Valentinov, the authorial agent, is linked to respiration at several points in the novel. In an apparently extraneous detail, Mrs. Luzhin is bothered by the heavy breathing of her maid—an irritation that leads immediately to her recollection of the telephone call from Valentinov:

> The silence was such that the maid's breathing was clearly audible as she served the tea. Mrs. Luzhin several times caught herself with the impossible thought that it would be a good idea to ask the maid why she breathed so loudly, and could she not do it more quietly. She was not very efficient in general, this pudgy wench—telephone calls were particularly disastrous. As she listened to the breathing, Mrs. Luzhin recalled briefly how the maid had laughingly informed her a few days beforehand: "A Mr. Fa...Felt...Felty. Here, I wrote down the number." (232, *243*)

---

17. The most obvious self-referential use of the prompter image occurs at the conclusion of *The Real Life of Sebastian Knight:* "The bald little prompter shuts his book, as the light fades gently" (203).

The description of Valentinov as an evil *spirit* (*zloi dukh*) also hints at his role as a literal *inspirer* of Luzhin, as does a strange interposition from a suddenly obtrusive narrative voice that erupts immediately after the description of Luzhin's tailor: "His fiancée did not dare to ask why Luzhin had formerly needed a tuxedo and an opera hat, fearing to arouse chess memories, and therefore she never learned about a certain big dinner given in Birmingham, where incidentally Valentinov....Oh well, good luck to him" (*Bog s nim—lit.,* "God is with him") (170, *181*). This final remark should be read as an indication of Valentinov's proximity to the novel's divinity, the author, who appears demonic to those whose life he must inevitably bring to an ordered close. Similar import may be assigned to the recollections of Luzhin's father: "All three of them were in Switzerland when the Austrian archduke was killed. Out of quite casual considerations (the notion that the mountain air was good for his son... Valentinov's remark that Russia now had no time for chess, while his son was kept alive solely by chess... the thought that the war would not last for long) he had returned to St. Petersburg alone" (*poleznyi synu gornyi vozdukh, slova Valentinova, chto teper' Rossii ne do shakhmat, a syn tol'ko shakhmatami zhiv, da eshche mysl', chto voina ne nadolgo—lit.,* "the mountain air that was beneficial to his son, Valentinov's words that...") (79, *87;* ellipses in the original). If, following Luzhin's method of reading, we fail to follow through to the sentence's end, we may see an apposition established between Valentinov's words and purer, more invigorating Olympian air.

The theme of breathing is present on the final pages of the novel as well. Luzhin tries in vain to flee the two-dimensional world of his text; another plane awaits him at the moment he escapes from his present "life." Even the promised abyss loses its verticality, and as a new board is arranged "obligingly and inexorably," Luzhin feels "icy air gush[ing] into his mouth" (256, *267*), as if authorial inspiration and intention (*stremitel'nyi, ledianoi vozdukh*) is insisting once again that he experience fictional life. (As Luzhin prepares his plunge, he hears several people, including Valentinov, on the other side of the door. "Someone was puffing and someone was greeting someone else" [253, *265*]. This puffing may be part of the preparations for Luzhin's inspiration on another plane.) The word "obligingly" is wonderfully double-edged (unlike *ugodlivo,* the Russian adverb it replaces); what initially sees to be a service performed by the novel for its hero can also be read as an act of compulsion.

Valentinov plays an important role, too, in the imposition of the patterns and repetitions that serve to remind Nabokov's reader of the imposed design and structure without which there can be no such thing as plot. Luzhin begins to understand the tremendous threat represented by repetition; his predicament is close to that of Freud in "The Uncanny," who demonstrates, as Anne Nesbet has argued, the terror that comes from finding oneself in someone else's text (2). For Freud that "someone else" is one's own sub-conscious, for Nabokov, that other is the creative author, but in either case the protagonist is beset by an uncanny awareness of operating within the contours of an opaque, repetitive design. Many critics have stressed the rep-etition of particular images as *The Defense* reaches its conclusion, but lexical and paronomastic repetition have been much less appreciated.[18] Lexical rep-etition occurs in several cases where specific combinations of words from the opening chapters of the novel reappear in similar combinations toward the novel's end. Thus, when hanging up the phone after talking to Valentinov and apparently removing him from Luzhin's life, Mrs. Luzhin fails to realize that she has helped replay an earlier scene and that the author's switchboard has connected her directly to the novel's first paragraph.[19] More important, in this very conversation with Mrs. Luzhin, Valentinov has punningly bared the novel's reliance on repetition: "Every second is precious. I'll expect him today at exactly twelve o'clock. Please tell him. Every second" (*Kazhdaia sekunda doroga. [...], kazhdaia sekunda*) (237, 249). The repetition inherent in the etymological root of the word "second" is here brought to the fore by the word's seconding within this quotation. Later Nabokov doubles this play on "second" when Luzhin's father-in-law attempts to instruct him about "life":

> "Life, my friend, is so arranged," it was said in this conversation, "that every second costs a man [*Zhizn' tak ustroena [...] chto za kazhduiu sekundu chelovek dolzhen platit'*], at the very minimum estimate, 1/432 of a pfennig, and that would be a beggar's life; but you have to support a wife who is used to a certain amount of luxury." "*Yes, yes,*" said Luzhin with a beaming smile, trying to disentangle in his mind the complex computation that his interlocutor had just made with such delicate deftness. "For this you need a little more money," the latter continued,

---

18. Boyd has called attention to lexical repetition in the passage dealing with the adjournment of Luzhin's match with Turati: "Normally [Nabokov] avoided proximate repetitions as the coarsest of authorial sins. I can recall nothing in Nabokov's entire oeuvre comparable with this scene, where in one third of a chapter ten musical images [...] are succeeded by another row of eleven phantomic images" ("The Problem of Pattern," 583–84). Yet, as we shall see, lexical repetition is marked through-out *The Defense,* reaching its apogee at the novel's end.

19. Compare: "Replacing the receiver on its hook she listened again, and hearing only the beat-ing of her own heart she then sighed and said '*ouf*!' with boundless relief. Valentinov had been dealt with. Thank goodness she had been alone at the telephone. Now it was over. And soon they would depart" (239–40, *251,* emphasis added). And "'*Ouf*...that's a real weight off my shoulders.' 'How nice ...' said his wife. Slowly drawing the silk blanket over her. 'Thank goodness, thank goodness ...' It was indeed a relief" (15, *23,* emphasis added).

and Luzhin held his breath in expectation of a new trick. "A second will cost you...dearer. I repeat: I am prepared at first—the first year, let's say—to give you generous assistance, but with time...(176, *187*)

These words bespeak a wisdom about the importance of repetition in *arranged* lives, an importance of which Luzhin, as he naively repeats himself ("Yes, yes"), is still blessedly ignorant.

Nabokov's plays on "seconds" illuminate other uses of doubling toward the novel's end: Luzhin realizes that he must "redouble his watchfulness and keep track of every second of his life, for traps could be everywhere" (*udvoit' bditel'nost', sledit' za kazhdoi* sekundoi *zhizni*) (228, *239*). Anaphoric constructions abound, *"No vsegda byt' na cheku, vsegda napriagat' vnimanie"*) (228, *239*), as do the repetitions of individual words: "It was difficult, extremely difficult to foresee the next repetition in advance, but just a little more and everything would become clear and perhaps a defense could be found" (242, *253*). (That is, *The Defense* will be completed, sealing Luzhin's confinement in a fictive, two-dimensional world.) A passage describing Luzhin's attempts to escape from the pattern of repetition is a masterpiece in its author's display of the very device that his character is trying to flee:

> But the next move was prepared very slowly. The lull continued [*prodolzhalos' zatish'e*] for two or three days; Luzhin was photographed for his passport, and the photographer took him by the chin, turned his face slightly [*chut'-chut'*] to one side, asked him to open his mouth wide and drilled his tooth with a tense buzzing [*zhuzhzhaniem*]. The buzzing [*zhuzhzhanie*] ceased, the dentist looked for something on a glass shelf, found it, rubber-stamped Luzhin's passport and wrote with lightning-quick [*bystro-bystro*] movements of the pen. "There," he said, handing over a document on which two rows of teeth were drawn, and two teeth bore inked-in little crosses. There was nothing suspicious in all this and the cunning lull continued [*zatish'e prodolzhalos'*] until Thursday (*chetverga*). And on Thursday (*chetverg*), Luzhin understood everything.
>
> Already the day before he had thought of an interesting device [*priem*], a device with which he could, perhaps, foil the designs of his mysterious opponent. The device [*priem*] consisted in voluntarily committing some absurd unexpected act that would be outside the systematic order of life, thus confusing the sequence of moves planned by his opponent. It was an experimental defense [*zashchita*], a defense [*zashchita*], so to say, at random—but Luzhin, crazed with terror before the inevitability of the next move, was able to find nothing better.

So on Thursday afternoon, while accompanying his wife and mother-in-law round the stores, he suddenly stopped and exclaimed: "The dentist [*dantist*]. I forgot the dentist [*dantist*]." "Nonsense, Luzhin," said his wife. "Why, yesterday he said that everything was done." "Uncomfortable [*nazhimat'*]," said Luzhin and raised a finger. "If the filling feels uncomfortable. [*nazhimat'*]. . . . It was said that if it feels uncomfortable [*nazhimat'*], I should come punctually at four. It feels uncomfortable [*nazhimaet*]." (242–43, *253–54*)

The Formalists' notion of a "baring of the device" is put to brilliant literal and metapoetic use here by making the word "device" one of the words that bares the importance of repetition. A similar dynamic is at work much earlier in the novel, when Luzhin's mother, upset that the memory of her deceased father, a great piano player, is being ignored, complains that it was all "intrigue, intrigue, intrigue" (*intrigi, intrigi, intrigi*) (40, *48*), thus reinforcing the notion that plot (intrigue) is all about repetition.

This is not the only triple repetition in the novel. At the end of chapter 8, Luzhin's chess match is adjourned and he is told to go home: "it was as if he were becoming flatter and flatter, and then he soundlessly dissipated" (*[Luzhin] kak budto spliushchivalsia, spliushchivalsia, spliushchivalsia, i potom bezzvuchno rasseialsia*) (143, *153*). (The triple repetition in the Russian becomes just a double in the English.) This process of character flattening is inevitable in a novel; characters live on the flat surface of paper. It is amusing to see that Luzhin himself has delighted in other instances of the flattening process of which he is perforce constantly the object. As a child, Luzhin has found "illusory relief in jigsaw puzzles" (*skladnye kartiny*) (37, *45*). He has also been amused by a book of magic tricks:

He found a mysterious pleasure, a vague promise of still unfathomed delights, in the crafty and accurate way a trick would come out. [. . .] The complicated accessories described in the book irritated him. The secret for which he strove was simplicity, harmonious simplicity, which can amaze one far more than the most intricate magic. *On nakhodil zagadochnoe udovol'stvie, neiasnoe obeshchanie kakikh-to drugikh, eshche nevedomykh naslazhdenii, v tom, kak khitro i tochno skladyvalsia fokus [. . .] Slozhnye prisposobleniia, opisannye v knige, ego razdrazhali. Taina, k kotoroi on stremilsia, byla prostota, garmonicheskaia prostota, porazhaiushchaia pushche samoi slozhnoi magii.* (36, *44*)

Remarkable in this passage is the play on a literal, basic meaning of the verb *skladyvat'* / *slozhit'*: to compress, to lay out flat, to compose. In the composition and production of a book (*slozhit' knigu*), an author performs a cognitive and perceptional trick capturing the illusion of three-dimensionality on the page. Not only may the trick that comes out right be read as a flattening of focus, but the word *slozhnyi* (complicated) may itself be understood etymologically as connoting the condensation of a great deal of artistic power onto a two-dimensional plane.

The final pages contain many more (and more obvious) doubled words, including "a trap, a trap" (249, *260*), "home, home" (244, *255*), "*gluboko, gluboko*" (254, *266*—translated in the English as "far below"), and most prominently the final pieces of dialogue in the novel: "Luzhin, Luzhin" (255, *266*) and "Aleksandr Ivanovich," "Aleksandr Ivanovich" (256, *267*), when Luzhin is given a first name for the first, second, and last time.

Some of the most striking and creative images illuminating the characters' relations to their creator in *The Defense* occur in a series of scenes involving various sorts of machines that represent different hypostases of the process of writing. I have already mentioned the "marionettes" at the station, a rather vulgar form of "art" in which deposited coins ought to make puppets come to life (but do not because the machine is broken). Chess is twice figured by a similarly mechanical image. The old man against whom Luzhin plays is willing to take back advantageous moves, "as if disclosing the mechanism of an expensive instrument he would show the way his opponent should have played in order to avert disaster" (55-56, *66*). When they draw, he moves his queen "back and forth a few times the way you move the lever of a broken machine" (56, *64*). An elevator functions as a mechanical device by which the author is able to extract characters from his narrative; Luzhin's governess ascends and disappears: "Goodness knows what had happened to her (*Bog vest', chto sluchilos' s nei*—lit., *God* knows) (164–65, *175*)). A literal—albeit travestied—parallel to the compositional machine controlled by Nabokov is the "typewriter"—*pishushchaia mashinka,* literally "writing machine"—belonging to Luzhin's father. The machine has been acquired "second-hand"—*po sluchaiiu,* that is, from the author (76, *84*)[20]—and on its keys one can spy "reflected light" (78, *86*). Later Luzhin himself becomes fascinated

---

20. The verb "*sluchit'sia*" (to occur or happen to) and the noun "*sluchai*" (a chance occurrence) provide rich opportunities for the oblique communication of authorial agency. See, for instance, the passage just quoted: *Bog vest, chto sluchilos's nei.* See also "out of quite casual considerations" (*po soobrazheniiam, sovershenno sluchainym*)(79, *87*); "or else opened a chance book" (*sluchainuiu knigu*) (106, *116*); and "thanks to a chance phrase that had come flying out of the next room" (*blagodaria sluchainoi fraze*)(213, *224*). Paradoxically, the word "chance" often marks the total absence of chance in Nabokov's fiction (Liuksemburg and Rakhimkulova, 146), largely because Nabokov's reader should know that in his writing there is no such thing.

by a typewriter and uses it to try to write randomly and unpredictably so as to demonstrate his freedom from overarching control.

At least twice in the novel Nabokov allows Luzhin to penetrate the core of the novel's "writing machine." In an attempt to show his future wife the hall in which he played a tournament as a child, Luzhin becomes lost and finds himself moving desperately about the hotel, nearly frantic in his inability to locate the remembered room. Seemingly abandoned by his hitherto obliging "manager," Luzhin spies a strange device: "Corridor. Window giving on garden. Gadget on wall, with numbered pigeonholes. A bell whirred. In one of the pigeonholes a number popped up awry. [*V odnom iz okonets krivo vyskochil nomer*—lit., "in one of the little windows a number jumped out awry")] He was bemused and troubled, as if he had lost his way in a bad dream— and he quickly walked back, repeating under his breath: 'Queer jokes, queer jokes'"(100–101, *110*). Luzhin, I think, is so disturbed because he has seen the inside of the fiction-machine, with the little squares—characters/figures— being called up by the author's ring.[21] (The figure of Luzhin will later disappear from the text through another, larger window.) A similar moment occurs when the match between Luzhin and Turati is adjourned, and Luzhin is, in effect, about to be temporarily put away with the novel's other "figures": "A phantom went by, stopped and began swiftly to stow the pieces away in a tiny coffin" (*Proshla ten' i, ostanovivshis', nachala bystro ubirat' figury v malen'kii grob*) (140, *150*). When Luzhin resists, he is allowed to see—in the form of shades and ghosts—beings from a dimension beyond his,[22] and finally he encounters a "gently revolving glass radiance" (139–41, *150–51*). Here Luzhin is in effect reduced to a two-dimensional being; it is as if he is experiencing the third dimension—that of authorship—from the perspective of the second and can see only spectral shadows cast on his plane from above. Voices speak to Luzhin, directing him in an authoritative manner to "go away" and go "home, home" (141, *151*). This last word refers to the place of the author

---

21. This scene in the hotel will be reprised in the novella *The Enchanter*, when the unnamed protagonist becomes lost in a hotel at night: "he went down only to lose his way in some faintly lit storage rooms where stood trunks and, from the corners, now a cabinet, now a vacuum cleaner, now a broken stool, now the skeleton of a bed protruded with an air of fatality. He swore under his breath, losing control, exasperated by these obstacles" (68). As Gennadi Barabtarlo notes in his wonderful article on this work, these items are "fatal" because they have already been encountered, albeit obliquely, in the novel (100). One might go further and say that the hero has discovered—and become lost in—the novel's prop room.

22. At several points in the novel, the author assumes the ghostly presence of a higher being: "And old Luzhin mentally invited his future biographer (who as one came nearer to him in time became paradoxically more and more insubstantial [*vse prizrachnee*], more and more remote) to take a good close look at this chance room (*sluchainuiu komnatu*) where the novella *The Gambit* had been evolved" (77, *85*).

(from which all characters come) and to everything intimately connected with him. These orders should be read as the author's instruction to his characters. The author may also be heard in the instruction to leave pronounced by a "gyratory kind of voice" (139, *150*) emanating from an unseen source. The Russian word *vertliavy* recalls the puppets in the "glass case" (*stekliannyi iashchik*) who are supposed to revolve (*zavertet'sia*) (20, *27*).[23]

The prevalence of mechanical images in the novel is so great that it should not be a surprise to see Nabokov ultimately describing Luzhin as winding down:

> And suddenly Luzhin stopped. It was as if the whole world had stopped [*slovno ostanovilsia ves' mir*]. It happened in the drawing room, by the phonograph.
>
> "Full stop [*Stop-mashina*]," she said softly and burst into tears. (251, *263*)

The originally nautical term used by Luzhin's wife seems odd in this scene until it is put into the context of the theme of the mechanics of text production that we have explored above. The machine coming to a full stop is the one that has been continually generating representations of the author-character relation. One of the most far-reaching comments about the novel proves to have been D. Barton Johnson's assertion that "notwithstanding Luzhin's ineffectual charm, *The Defense* is one of Nabokov's most mechanistic works" (*Worlds in Regression,* 83). All allegories have a mechanical aspect to them: the often tedious, excessive reproduction of a central idea. The genius of *The Defense* resides in its author's ability to disguise the workings of the machine, to display its products in such a wide variety of unexpected settings that repetition produces not tedium but aesthetic delight.

In moments of limited epiphany, Luzhin begins to grasp the nature of the two-dimensional fictive world in which he lives. The clearest comprehension

---

23. It is amusing to see that in this flattening encounter with the ghostly, authorial world, Luzhin meets one of his author's future creations: "A pale light sailed past and disintegrated with a mournful rustle" (*Proplyl* bletnyi ogon' *i rassypalsia s pechal'nym shelestom*)(141, *152*). Nabokov would later use these words in their literal English translation as a title for an English book. Tammi has noted that in the English version of *The Defense,* Nabokov has inserted the (inverted) title of a story—"Signs and Symbols"—written long after the Russian text was first published (344). The appearance of *bletnyi ogon'* appears to be an extraordinary case, since the phrase appears decades before the writing of *Pale Fire.* The significance of the phrase's presence is not that Luzhin is clairvoyant in some sort of extratextual sense (the supreme irony of a character foreseeing his author's future!) but that Nabokov has been struck by the phrase and is already associating it with the concept of a character's subordination to (and resistance against) an author. Cf. Fyodor's remark in *The Gift:* "Where shall I put all these gifts with which the summer morning rewards me—and only me? Save them up for future books?" (328).

comes at the novel's end ("he saw exactly what kind of eternity was obligingly and inexorably spread out before him" [256, *267*]), but Luzhin earlier
has had inklings about the nature of an author's creative love, a love that is
necessarily lethal because totalizing authorial vision necessarily sums up and
puts an end to all that it creates. "Everything was wonderful, all the shades
of love, all the convolutions and mysterious paths it had chosen. And this
love was fatal" (*Vse bylo prekrasno, vse perelivy liubvi, vse izluchiny i tainstvennye*
tropy, izbrannye eiu. I eta liubov' byla gibel'na) (246, *258*). Here, as elsewhere,
Nabokov hides an important truth about his novel in a seemingly unessential
grammatical apposition. In the English version of the sentence quoted above
one might well substitute "tropes" (*tropy*) for "paths" (*tropy*): this fatal love
works through the employment of poetic figures.[24]

There is a striking affinity between Mikhail Bakhtin's aesthetic metaphysics of the early 1920s (not published until 1979) and those of Nabokov's novel. Bakhtin viewed the attitude of an author toward a hero as a
form of love: "Lovelike sympathy accompanies and permeates aesthetic co-
experiencing throughout the entire duration of the act of aesthetic contemplation of an object, transfiguring the entire material of what is contemplated
and co-experienced" (82–83).[25] An essential difference between Nabokov
and Bakhtin, though, is that Bakhtin views the process of aesthetic consummation through the eyes of the author.

> Artistic vision presents us with the whole hero, measured in full and
> added up in every detail; there must be no secrets for us in the hero
> with respect to meaning; our faith and hope must be silent. From the
> very outset, we must experience all of him, deal with the whole of him:
> in respect to meaning, he must be dead for us, formally dead. In this
> sense we could say that death is the form of the aesthetic consumma-
> tion of an individual. (131)

A character has no future because for him everything has already been
decided: "The aesthetic embodiment of the inner man anticipates from the
very outset the hero's hopelessness with respect to meaning [on his own
terms]" (*Art and Answerability,* 131). A hero, Bakhtin emphasizes, is someone
whose life has been put into rhythm. Bakhtin insists on the beauty of such

---

24. Alexander Dolinin notes a similar pun on *tropa* in Nabokov's next novel, *Podvig* (Glory)
(*Istinnaia zhizn',* 188).

25. Stephen Blackwell also cites this passage, as a model of the reader's relationship to the author
in *The Gift.* In keeping with his interpretation of author-reader relations, he sees this love as benign
and "analogous to love between two people" (102).

poeticization—"To be sure, the unfreedom, the necessity of a life shaped by rhythm is not a *cruel* necessity [...]; rather, it is a necessity bestowed as a gift, bestowed by love: it is a beautiful necessity" (*Art and Answerability*, 119).

In *The Defense*, Nabokov views this process from the standpoint of a character who does not want to be consummated (i.e., does not want to be a character), who is terrified by the sepulchral tones which must inevitably sound all around him in the unfolding of "a bewitchingly elegant sacrifice" (*ocharovatel'no iziashchnaia zhertva*") (224, *235*). Alexander Dolinin identifies an important factor in Luzhin's inability to appreciate repetition: "Luzhin does not correctly understand the very nature of "repetitions," for they are not exact doubles, but variations, like harmonies in an inexact poetic rhyme. [...] In a word, the repetitions have in no way a chess but a poetic character, but Nabokov's hero, who, as his wife says, finds rhymes a burden, is not capable of evaluating or comprehending their harmony" (*Istinnaia zhizn'*, 66–67). To put it differently, Luzhin fails to value the aesthetic trappings of his own demise.

An early moment of metafictive understanding for Luzhin comes when he overhears a conversation between his wife and the Soviet visitor. Luzhin cries out, apparently because the visitor has just mentioned his aunt: "there was really something to celebrate. The combination he had been struggling to discern since the ball had suddenly revealed itself to him, thanks to a chance phrase that had come flying out of the next room" (213, *224*). Nearly all scholars who mention this moment accept at face value that the combination "country house...town...school...aunt" (214, *225*) is significant here, yet no one has closely examined the overheard and quoted dialogue for clues to Luzhin's mini-epiphany. Following Nabokov's direction, we should look more closely at that conversation and search for moments of resonance between "a chance phrase" and the earlier scene at the ball. Shortly before Luzhin cries out, the Soviet visitor says: "yes, yes, I know he's a chess player. But what is he? A *reactionary*?" (*Reaktsioner?*) (211, *222;* emphasis added). This last word is crucially important. Earlier, speaking to Petrishchev at the ball, Luzhin has tried to ignore the lure of the past: "'...just don't react,' Luzhin said quickly to himself" ("*...prosto ne reagirovat'—bystro skazal pro sebia Luzhin*") (198, *209*). Here *pro sebia* should again be read as meaning both "to himself" *and* "about himself." Later we learn that Luzhin "was indignant with himself for [...] not taking the initiative, but with trustful blindness letting the combination unfold" (214, *225*). Unfortunately for Luzhin, a character's essential problem is that he can only be a *react*ionary, he lacks the creative power to make his own rules, to create the board or even—in metafictive terms—to play white. To the extent that he relates directly and consciously to his creator, that relation must always be in the nature of reaction and response. And while the character's reactions may be aimed at warding off aesthetic consummation (*zavershenie*), the result is inevitable. Indeed, Luzhin's defeat (*porazhenie*) is already announced by the novel's first sentence: "What struck him most was the fact that from Monday on he would be Luzhin" (*Bol'she vsego, ego porazilo to, chto s ponedel'nika on budet Luzhinym;* the Russian might also be translated, less idiomatically, "what defeated him most") (15, *23*). A character's entry into a novel already entails that character's eventual defeat.[26]

A page or two later it appears that Luzhin has understood. Here is a scene that makes much more sense, I think, to readers who understand Russian:

> Ivan sat on the couch and scratched his knee, trying not to look at Luzhin, who also did not know where to look and was thinking how to occupy the flabby child. "Telephone!" exclaimed Luzhin finally in a high voice, and pointing to it with his finger he began to laugh with deliberate astonishment. But Ivan, after looking sullenly in the direction of Luzhin's finger, averted his eyes, his lower lip hanging. "Train and precipice!" tried Luzhin again and stretched out his other hand, pointing to his own picture on the wall. Ivan's left nostril filled with a glistening droplet and he sniffed, looking apathetically before him. "The author of a certain divine comedy!" bellowed Luzhin, raising a hand to the bust of Dante. (216, *227–28*)

What is going on here? To grasp Nabokov's purpose, the reader must understand that although this scene appears to provide evidence of Luzhin's insanity, Luzhin is quite reasonably attempting to entertain the lad with a parlor game. Nabokov, however, has not supplied the conventional riddling formula—"My first is X, My second is Y, and my whole is Z"—where even Z may be a pun for the hidden term.[27] (Here Nabokov is using a technique he would later ascribe to Sebastian Knight, who is "constantly playing some game of his own invention, without telling his partners its rules" [179]). The telephone signifies *Allo,* the impending accident hints at *gore* (misfortune), Dante is Alighieri—the whole is *allegoriia* (allegory), the stuff of which *The Defense* is made. It is particularly appropriate that Dante himself was an allegorist.[28] And—although this may be going too far for the paronomastically

---

26. See also the first line of *Invitation to a Beheading:* "In accordance with the law the death sentence was announced to Cincinnatus C. in a whisper" (11).

27. In *The Gift* Fyodor and his sister are nocturnal devotees of this game. The text provides a specimen of one of her riddles, which are less "fantastic" and "silly" than Fyodor's and adhere to the "classical model": "mon premier est un métal précieux / mon second est un habitant des cieux / et mon tout est un fruit délicieux" (16, *23*). See also a similar exercise in *Despair,* 50; *Otchaianie,* 49.

28. In *The Defense* Dante's name surfaces in several guises, peeking out from *Dantès* and dentist (*dantist*). (It is ironic that Luzhin attempts to use the *dantist* as an excuse for an escape from the allegory in

faint of heart—in Russian the name of this parlor game—charades *(sharada,* from the French *charade)*—itself refers to the hell *(ad)* in which the spherical *(shar)* Luzhin finds himself.

Terming *The Defense* an allegory will probably raise the hackles of some read-ers, since the term was anathema to Nabokov himself. "Ignore allegories," he instructed his readers in a 1966 interview. "Ask yourself if the symbol you have detected is not your own footprint" *(Strong Opinions,* 66). Keeping this statement in mind, we should nevertheless appreciate that if *The Defense* is an allegory, it departs in one significant respect from traditional allego-ries. Nabokov's allegory in *The Defense* is intrinsic to its own medium; he is not applying a psychological or religious allegorical model—the "footprint" of another discipline—to literature but rather providing literature with a model about itself. Allegory is both the subject and the device of *The Defense.* To a certain extent, this is true of much of Nabokov's writing. In his intro-duction to *The Annotated Lolita,* Alfred Appel describes Nabokov's fiction as "involuted": "An involuted work turns in upon itself, is self-referential, conscious of its status as a fiction, and *allégorique de lui-même*—allegorical of itself, to use Mallarmé's description of one of his own poems" (xxiii).[29] *The Defense* is probably the most thoroughgoing of Nabokov's allegories, but the allegorical element, while constant, always remains slightly beneath (or in the shadow of) the novelistic plot. An allegorical reading of the sort proposed here would not fall within the purview of "the learned loonies who find sexual or religious allegories in my fiction" and to whom Nabokov's books were pointedly "not addressed" *(Strong Opinions,* 196).

To appreciate the nature of Nabokovian allegory in *The Defense,* it may be instructive to consider two of that allegory's possible sources. *The Defense* bears a playful resemblance to a whimsical English allegory that was influential at the end of the nineteenth century and has enjoyed a renaissance in our own day: *Flatland,* by the educator, theologian, Shakespeare scholar, and Cambridge

---

which he finds himself!) The bust of Dante appearing in the parlor scene is itself a repetition: Nabokov has ingeniously encoded an early mention of "Dante's bust" *(biust Dante)* in the novel's second paragraph: "Poor, poor *Dantès* [the hero of *The Count of Monte Cristo*] did not arouse any sympathy in him, and observing her educational sigh he merely slitted his eyes and rived his drawing paper with an eraser, as he tried to portray her protuberant *bust* as horribly as possible" (16, *24,* emphasis added). Like *The Defense,* Dante's allegory is built on a contrast between horizontal and vertical movement: the inhabitants of his allegory are locked into their levels, which only the poet and his guides are permitted to transcend.

29. Appel was not the first to call Nabokov's work allegorical. P. M. Bitsilli termed Sirin's work allegorical in a more traditional, metaphysical sense in 1935 (191–204).

graduate E. A. Abbott. First published in 1884, *Flatland* is narrated by "a square" who inhabits a two-dimensional world in which all the characters are "figures." Some are circles, others rectangles, lines, polyhedrons, or triangles. (This is indeed a world in which geometric figures can have "confidential conversations"!) The narrator explains in great detail what it means to see in two · dimensions—how the world looks and how figures live on a plane: "Imagine a vast sheet of paper on which straight Lines, Triangles, Squares, Pentagons, Hexagons, and other figures, instead of remaining fixed in their places, move freely about, on or in the surface, but without the power of rising above or sinking below it, very much like shadows—only hard with luminous edges—and you will then have a pretty correct notion of my country and countrymen" (1). On December 31, 1999, the square is visited by a strange, incomprehensible being: a sphere. The sphere gradually proves to the square that a third dimension exists and takes him out of Flatland's plane into three-dimensional space. The square then has the insight that there must be a fourth dimension and a fifth, but the sphere refuses to accept his own relativity and hurls the square back to the latter's flat earth. There the square attempts to spread his multidimensional gospel, but he is arrested and put on trial, during which he twice refers to his narrative—the story of what he has just experienced—as his "defence" (117–18).

Flatland was published in 1884 and precipitated a boom of interest in the fourth dimension. Part social satire (the various figures approximate the British class structure) and part geometric treatise, the book was popular in the United States, where many unauthorized copies were published, but it remained out of print in England until 1926.[30] It is possible that Nabokov learned of it while at Cambridge, or that he became acquainted with the book after the appearance of the second edition. Abbott's death, which also occurred in 1926, may have served to bring the book to Nabokov's attention. Abbott's name is even obliquely inscribed in *The Defense*. Luzhin, having appropriated an object that he may hope is *the* writing machine but which is only a typewriter, bangs out a crazy note that cannot escape the allegorical pattern: he signs it "the Abbé Busoni" (*Abbat Buzoni*) (189, *200*). This alias, which is used as a disguise by Edmond Dantès in *The Count of Monte Cristo*,[31] may also be providing cover for the author of *Flatland*.

---

30. For an introduction to the publication history, sources, background, and legacy of *Flatland*, see Banchoff, 364–72.

31. The mention of Busoni serves as yet another repetition: *The Count of Monte Cristo* and the name Dantès have appeared in *The Defense*'s second paragraph. The reader might well assume from the context (the novel is being savored by the stout French governess) and, perhaps, from the exact similarity in Russian of the character's last name, Dantès, to that of Pushkin's assassin, d'Anthès (in a Russian novel, the words *bednyi, bednyi Dantes* would seem to border on blasphemy!), that Nabokov's

The name of at least one other figure who used the example of a two-dimensional world as an analogy for transcending the limitations of three-dimensional life also appears in *The Defense.* J. J. Sylvester, a preeminent nineteenth-century scholar of algebra and geometry, employed this conceit in "A Plea for the Mathematician," an address published in *Nature* in 1869: "for as we can conceive beings (like infinitely attenuated bookworms in an infinitely thin piece of paper) which possess only the notion of space of two dimensions, so we may imagine beings capable of realising space of four or a greater number of dimensions" (quoted in Smith, 181). Whether Nabokov knew of this speech, which argued that mathematics "affords boundless scope for the exercise of the highest efforts of imagination and invention," is a matter for speculation; assuming that the name of Luzhin Senior's publisher, Silvestrov, alludes to J. J. Sylvester, it may do so simply as part of the work's geometric theme.

Abbott and Sylvester were not alone in their use of the playful two-dimensional model. In his *Scientific Romances* (1884), C. H. Hinton—an English mathematician with a wide-ranging career in England, Japan, and the United States—asked his readers to imagine how inhabitants of a two-dimensional world would perceive three-dimensional bodies; such an exercise, like playing chess blindfolded, would, he suggested, help to enable his readers to visualize a fourth dimension (18). Hinton's work was cited at length by the Russian mystic and philosopher P. D. Uspensky, whose views on mimicry and the fourth dimension, Vladimir Alexandrov has suggested, may have influenced Nabokov. (*Nabokov's Otherworld,* 227–30). Like Hinton, Uspensky discusses—but does not turn into allegory—the perceptions of two-dimensional beings (*Tertium Organum,* 40–49). The examples of influence offered by Alexandrov are intriguing, but Uspensky's mysticism seems far removed from Nabokov's sense of measure and play. Much more striking, I would submit, are Nabokov's affinities with the English tradition on which Hinton (and through him, Uspensky) drew. This tradition encompasses not only Abbott and Sylvester but also Lewis Carroll, whose pamphlet *The Dynamics of a Particle* (1865) begins in mock-novelistic fashion: "It was a lovely Autumn evening, and the glorious effects of chromatic aberration were beginning to show themselves in the atmosphere as the earth revolved away from the great western luminary, when two lines might have been

---

attitude toward the French classic is dismissive, yet Nabokov seems to have been fond of the novel, with which he demonstrates an intimate familiarity in a letter written in 1923 to his future wife (quoted in Stacy Schiff, 11). Dumas's novel also makes an implicit appearance in *Invitation to a Beheading;* the sounds heard by Cincinnatus through his cell wall are a parodic echo of the digging discerned by Dantès as he contemplates suicide in his dungeon.

observed wending their weary way across a plane superficies") and tells of these lines who, observing that they have been intersected by a straight line that has made two interior angles together less than two right angles, exclaim: "Yes! We shall at length meet if continually produced!" (*Works,* 907).

Carroll's point was no more elevated than to provide "a striking illustration of the advantage of introducing the human element into the hitherto barren region of Mathematics" (*Works,* 907), but Abbott followed Carroll's lead by using geometrical figures to write an allegorical romance, and Nabokov went further still, using these figures as the basis for a metafictive novel. Nabokov's novelization of the theme introduces a degree of "the human element" not envisioned by Carroll or Abbott, but it retains, albeit at the hidden level we have been examining, the spirit of playfulness that characterizes their work. It is worth noting, too, that the interest in geometrical punning that charac- terizes Carroll's book is preserved by Nabokov, although in the latter's work puns function to ominous rather than humorous effect. Carroll's "General Considerations" begin with a definition that puns on geometric terms: "Plain Superficiality is the character of a speech, in which any two points being taken, the speaker is found to lie wholly with regard to those two points" (*Works,* 908). The book continues in the same spirit. (Carroll was also the author of *A Tangled Tale* [1885], a book of humorous arithmetic, algebra, and geometry problems that may have been the inspiration for the collection of "Merry Mathematics" in *The Defense*).

Since Abbott was a theologian, his work has been read as a spiritual alle- gory, but what is more striking is its status as an allegory for relativity—for every sphere there is always a higher sphere, as it were. It is here that Nabokov essentially parts company with Abbott, for though there are various planes of perceptual power in *The Defense,* the reader should have no doubt about who stands at the top.

How many dimensions are there in Nabokov's novel? Most of the char- acters live on a two-dimensional plane, although there are hints that Luzhin (and the game of chess) have three-dimensional potential. The author and reader exist in a fourth dimension, the inhabitants of which enjoy a tran- stemporal position in relation to the events described in the text.[32] In effect, the experience of existing outside a text is akin to having a divine rapport to time in which all events are contemporaneous. Andrei Bely made a related

---

32. Vladimir Alexandrov concludes that Luzhin's final act is "an unconscious and desperate attempt to achieve timelessness, or in the context of the novel's hidden [occult or even gnostic] meaning, to transcend the physical world and move into another dimension of being" (*Nabokov's Otherworld,* 66–67). See also his elegant formulation of the hermeneutics of "atemporal insight" in Nabokov's fiction (ibid., 7).

observation in 1912: "A book is truly a four-dimensional creature; this is so evident as to be a banality. The fourth dimension, intersecting the third, forms, so to speak, a cube in the shape of a book in octavo, where the page is the flat surface, and the line—linear time" (quoted in Skonechnaia, "Cherno-belyi kaleidoskop," 696). Nabokov himself refers in *The Defense* to this tran-stemporal power of reading; Luzhin's grandfather is remembered perusing a score: "now smiling, now frowning, and sometimes turning back like a reader checking a detail in a novel—a name, the time of the year" (56–57, *64*).

With his "limited field of vision" (246, *257*) Luzhin does not share the reader's position outside of time.[33] One of Luzhin's chief enemies is time; he cannot escape it even when playing chess. "Time is merciless in the universe of chess" (138, *148*); both the two-dimensional and the three-dimensional worlds (life outside of and within chess) run on clockwork.

The flatness and hostility of temporality provide the basis for a number of puns, some of which play on the similarity in several grammatical cases of *vremennyi* (temporary) and *vremennoi* (temporal) and would require in the English that the word "temporary" be replaced by "temporal." Luzhin's wife hopes that he will find "a temporary diversion" (*vremennoe razvlechenie*) in politics (227, *237*), but Luzhin disappoints her: "something would temporar-ily weaken inside him" (*chto-to vremenno oslabevalo v nem*) (228, *239*). Luzhin's first attempt to kiss his future bride, which occurs immediately after his proposal of marriage, ends as a symbolic embrace of temporality: "He seized her by the elbow and kissed something hard and cold—her wristwatch" (103, *113*). The best such plays may be on colloquial uses of *chas* (hour): Luzhin's future mother-in-law claims that "Luzhin was going out of his mind not by the day but by the hour" (*Luzhin ne po dniam, a po chasam skhodit s uma*) (129, *139*). These are metafictive puns: Nabokov refers to the temporal predica-ment of literary characters who are forced to experience time linearly and cannot emulate the (good) reader by moving back and forth to check details in the novel that contains them.

---

33. The reference to Luzhin's "limited field of vision" (*ogranichennoe pole Luzhinskogo zreniia*) comes during Luzhin's meeting with his former manager: "At this moment someone called Val-entinov in an agitated voice, and after pushing an open box of cigars into Luzhin's limited field of vision he excused himself and disappeared" (*ischez*) (246, *258*). Here again we see a relatively frequent Nabokovian device at work: a metafictive, general truth about the plight of characters in literature is concealed within the precise decor of an individual scene. (In addition, the verb "disappear" deserves our notice. Valentinov doesn't just go out through the door, he suddenly vanishes from the characters' plane.) See also the comparison of Krug's scope of comprehension with that of the author: "O yes— the lighting is poor and one's field of vision is oddly narrowed [...] but a closer inspection [...] reveals the presence of someone in the know" (*Bend Sinister,* 64).

We might read Nabokov's dismissive words about allegory as defensive. To some extent it is true that throughout his career, Nabokov essentially wrote different versions of the same allegory, toward the end of his career trying to disguise this propensity with increasingly Joycean trappings that never transform the core of his writing.[34] Yet *The Defense* occupies a unique place in Nabokov's oeuvre because it is such a single-minded meditation on the author-character relationship; later works are more diffuse and have a wider range of concerns. Moreover, *The Defense*'s exploration of the allegory of fiction is exceptional because it works by taking the symbolist discourse of allegory and deploying it on a metafictive plane. The symbolist worldview—from Merezhkovsky to Bely—was subtended by a distinction between allegory and symbol—the former being a dead version of the latter, dead because it had lost its opacity, become too conventional, predictable, too clear. As Bely's Aleksandr Ivanovich Dudkin warns in *Petersburg*, "Don't confuse allegory with symbol. Allegory is a symbol that has become common currency" (*Petersburg*, 184; *Peterburg*, 263). The affinities between Bely and Nabokov have been explored by D. Barton Johnson, Alexandrov, and Skonechnaia, but those discussions have centered on novels other than *The Defense*.[35] Once we perceive the basic geometric axis of Nabokov's text, its relation to Bely's geometrically obsessed novel demands close attention. Although Bely's Apollonian hero is comforted by all sorts of geometric figures, there is always the danger (and the hope) that the plane will crack and allow the Dionysian abyss to erupt and destroy ordered life: "We often drink coffee with cream while suspended above the abyss" (249, *364*). Nabokov provides a metafictive parallel—there is always the inevitability that life on the narrated plane will be tampered with by its creator; the board may crack (as has the first chessboard mentioned in *The Defense* [23, *31*]), or the pieces may be put away at any time.

The Defense contains many references, some extremely subtle, to Bely's novel. Luzhin's protruding ears are similar to those physical trademark appendages of Senator Ableukhov, and his love of travel folders—"Very attractive things—folders" (*Ochen' voobshche privlekatel'naia veshch'—prospekty*) (197, *208*) serve as Nabokov's geometric and geographic nod to Ableukhov's

---

34. For example, the theme of dimensionality surfaces in nearly all of Nabokov's work. (See, for instance, Sebastian Knight's knowledge that "his slightest thought or sensation had always at least one more dimension than those of his neighbours" and his awareness that he is "a crystal among glass, a sphere among circles" (64).

35. *The Gift* has received the lion's share of the attention devoted to this question. See D. Barton Johnson, "Belyi and Nabokov"; Alexandrov, *Nabokov's Otherworld*, 218–23; Alexandrov, "Nabokov and Belyi"; and Skonechnaia, "Cherno-belyi kaleidoskop."

comfortingly straight avenues (*prospekty*). The folders are associated on their first mention with the Nile and with a tourist strolling about "in his white suit" (*v belom kostiume*) (187, *198*). Bely's *nom de plume*—Bely means "white"—makes concealing and, perhaps, finding his name almost too easy. The playful sentence that prefaces Luzhin's rediscovery of the jacket, which with its concealed chess set will trigger his renewed descent into the abyss of chess, also contains a veiled reference to Nabokov's predecessor: "The winter that year was a white, St. Petersburg one" (*Zima byla v tot god belaia, peterburgskaia*) (192, *203*).

A seemingly superficial conversation between Mrs. Luzhin and her Soviet visitor may be read as a contestation over *Petersburg* and Bely's legacy:

> "How is it, St. Petersburg? It must have changed a lot?" asked Mrs. Luzhin. "Of course it's changed, replied the newcomer jauntily. "And a terribly difficult life," said Mrs. Luzhin, nodding thoughtfully. "Oh, what nonsense! Nothing of the sort. They're working at home, build-ing. Even my boy—what, you didn't know I had a little boy?—well, I have, I have, a cute little squirt—well, even he says that at home in Len-ingrad 'they wuk, while in *Bellin* the boulzois don't do anything.'" [*u nas v Leningliade liabotaiut, a v Belline bul'zui nichego ne delaiut*]. (210, *221*)

The transformation of Berlin to "Bellin," especially following a reference to Petersburg's new name, establishes an affinity not only between the two cities but between this book and Bely's. Lecturing at Cornell on *Bleak House,* Nabokov drew the attention of his class to the connotative uses to which a lisp could be put:

> Sitting in the midst of the mist and the mud and the muddle, the Lord Chancellor is addressed by Mr. Tangle as "Mlud." At the heart of the mud and fog, "My Lord" is himself reduced to "Mud" if we remove the lawyer's slight lisp. My Lord. Mlud, Mud. We shall mark at once, at the very beginning of our inquiry, that this is a typical Dickensian device: wordplay, making inanimate words not only live but perform tricks transcending their immediate sense. (*Lectures on Literature,* 72)

In *The Defense,* Nabokov is using a lisp to perform a similar trick. St. Peters-burg may have become Leningrad but thanks to the boy's speech defect Berlin emerges as Bely's new city and this novel as *Petersburg*'s metafictive heir.[36]

---

36. On Nabokov's use of *Petersburg* and of the St. Petersburg literary and iconic tradition, see Dolinin, *Istinnaia zhizn',* 346–62.

Most of the examples I have cited would align Luzhin with Senator Apollon Apollonovich Ableukhov. But Luzhin's name and patronymic—Aleksandr Ivanovich—so marked by their first and only appearance at the very end of the novel, are those of the Dionysian Dudkin, who states the symbolist creed on allegory and whose madness most approximates Luzhin's.[37] We should note, too, that both their surnames contain that central, chaotic *Petersburg*ian vowel—y—a sound to which Nabokov calls attention in the very first sentence of his foreword to the English text: "the name rhymes with 'illusion' if pronounced thickly enough to deepen the 'u' into 'oo'" (7). It is particularly significant that Bely's Aleksandr Ivanovich voices *Petersburg*'s most extended discussion of dimensionality: "Petersburg is the fourth dimension which is not indicated on maps, which is indicated merely by a dot. And this dot is the place where the plane of being is tangential to the surface of the sphere and the immense astral cosmos. A dot which in the twinkling of an eye can produce for us an inhabitant of the fourth dimension, from whom not even a wall can protect us."[38] In *The Defense,* the author has a propensity for emerging most unexpectedly "in the twinkle of an eye" in the midst of seemingly unambiguous words. No diegetic "wall" can keep him away from any of his characters. Yet Nabokov's Aleksandr Ivanovich differs in one fundamental respect from Bely's hero of the same name. Dudkin is destroyed by chaos; Luzhin goes insane as a result of being ravished by order.

Luzhin's relation to Dudkin raises the question of the rapport between allegory and symbols in Nabokov's work. Luzhin rises enough above the herd to perceive the presence of symbols—the chess board is the "material symbol" (219, *230*) of his obsession—but he never fully understands what these symbols mean.[39] For God, and the Nabokovian author, however, omnipotent vision necessarily renders all of the created world transparent. (As Abbott's square says when he rises up into the third dimension: "Behold, I am become as a God. For the wise men of our country say that to see all things, or as they express it, *omnividence,* is the attribute of God alone" [95]). Symbols are sensitive humanity's compensation for the limitations of its cognition;

---

37. I would like to thank Lina Ilic for first pointing this similarity out to me in an unpublished paper.

38. Bely, *Petersburg,* 207, *298*. In expressing his admiration for Belyi to Edmund Wilson, Nabokov used a word particularly marked in *The Defense:* "The 'decline' of Russian literature in 1905–1917 is a Soviet invention. Blok, Bely, Bunin, and others wrote their best stuff in those days. [...] I am a product of that period, I was bred in that *atmosphere*" (*The Nabokov-Wilson Letters,* 246, emphasis added).

39. See Connolly's insightful suggestion that Luzhin "experiences life in a manner recalling Baudelaire's vision in the poem 'Correspondances': the world has become a 'forest of symbols' which observe him 'with a familiar gaze.' For Luzhin, everything in the world is a material signifier of an immaterial yet oppressive higher consciousness" (93).

God's knowledge, though, is something of a curse, for symbolic beauty gives way to complete legibility. Reading—and understanding—Nabokov has its price, for the process of comprehension involves illuminating the text's most opaque moments; to reach the author on the summit, the reader is required to transform symbols into allegories. Once there, and enveloped in the author's somewhat patronizing embrace, the reader may exult in his triumph, but he may also yearn nostalgically for the innocence and beauty made possible by limited vision.

The Costs of Character

The Maiming of the Narrator in "A Guide to Berlin"

Why does an author cripple a character? This question acquires poignancy only for readers with feet firmly planted on both sides of the modernist divide, readers simultaneously old-fashioned *and* textually aware. Violence inflicted on a character matters only when we identify with him or, at the very least, attribute to him a meaningful subjectivity and the capacity to suffer. Readers of nineteenth-century fiction do this all the time, but the illusion of realist fiction precludes its readers from holding the author responsible for the misfortunes of characters. Readers of modernist and postmodernist fiction will focus more on the presence of the author, but the pain of characters will seem less compelling as a result.

The consumers of realism rarely think to blame the author for bad things that happen in the narrated world, because these things also happen or are thought to have happened in real life. There is little point in rebuking George Eliot for deforming Philip Wakeham—she is, instead, to be credited with empathy. When Ivan Karamazov berates God for allowing a child to suffer and retells in detail horrible things done by Turks, it is probably not our first response to note that these poor victims are suffering in perpetuity thanks to Dostoevsky. Nor do we tend to accuse authors of cruelty to characters when injuries are sustained before the first page is turned: we implicitly presume that a physical defect was obviously always part of the hero's fate and nature. It is not surprising that the surname of J. M. Barrie's captain was Hook even before he lost his hand. But with a writer who insists on making the reader aware of his presence, the stakes are different. One of the unique features of Vladimir Nabokov's work is its penchant for oscillating on the boundary of modernism; the reader who toggles in and out of modernism regrets all the more keenly the loss of a time when characters were people and when the happening of bad things was not the fault of the author. This reader shares the characters' sorrow—not because he identifies with them but because he no longer can.

Even in Nabokov's most sentimental, humanly generous fiction this issue of authorial responsibility for damage inflicted on characters is particularly fraught. Pnin refuses to accept the fate of his beloved, Mira, who has been killed at Buchenwald: "No conscience, and hence no consciousness, could be expected to subsist in a world where such things as Mira's death were possible" (135). Of course, no conscience or consciousness *actually* exists within *Pnin* or any other text; this knowledge may be reassuring because the alternative is to admit that if characters *live* on the page, their suffering never ends: even if Mira's precise form of death had been recorded, she would keep "dying a great number of deaths in one's mind, and undergoing a great number of resurrections, only to die again and again" (135). If a character has a heart, that heart becomes a site of particular vulnerability, one cannot forget that "this graceful, fragile, tender young woman [...] had been brought in a cattle car to an extermination camp and killed by an injection of phenol into the heart, into the gentle heart one had heard beating under one's lips in the dusk of the past" (135). In Nabokov's mature work there is nearly always "a shadow behind the heart," a shadow cast by the author (*Pnin,* 126). And, as we have seen, the reader's awareness of this presence has led to a variety of recuperative enterprises, where the notion of authorial cruelty or lust is parried by the insistence that the text has a real-world mission: to use cruelty's depiction to prevent cruelty in our extratextual world.

A particular case of author-character violence is posed by Nabokov's early story "A Guide to Berlin." The work has not been treated in these terms. Rather, it has been seen as a kind of technical credo, and I do not mean to say that it is not also that.

A first-person narrator enters a pub with his "usual pot companion" or *postoiannyi sobutyl'nik.*[1] The narrator begins to talk about where he has been that day and what he has seen: he speaks about utility pipes in the street, his

---

1. All references to the English version of the story, "A Guide to Berlin," refer to *The Stories of Vladimir Nabokov;* all references to the Russian text, "Putevoditel' po Berlinu," refer to *Sobranie sochinenii russkogo perioda,* vol. 1.

ride in a streetcar, various sorts of workers, and his trip to the Berlin zoo. In the pub, his friend objects that this is "a very poor guide." "'It's of no interest,' my friend affirms with a mournful yawn. 'What do trams and tortoises matter? And anyway the whole thing is simply a bore. A boring, foreign city, and expensive to live in, too'" (159). The narrator looks through a wide passageway at a small boy eating soup beneath a mirror. He realizes that what the boy sees in the mirror—the room in which the narrator sits and the narrator himself—will be something the child will always remember. "'I can't understand what you see down there,' says my friend, turning back toward me. What indeed! How can I demonstrate to him that I have glimpsed somebody's future recollection?" (160).

The story has been the subject of insightful commentary by several scholars, most notably D. Barton Johnson ("A Guide"), Maxim Shrayer (75–81), Omry Ronen, and Jacob Emery. Johnson argues that this story is "the first of Nabokov's writings to show the ingenious integration of theme and device that marks his mature work" (360). In one of the best pieces of formal analysis performed on a story by Nabokov, Johnson focuses on the concluding sentence in the section on pipes:

> Today someone wrote "Otto" with his finger on the strip of virgin snow and I thought how beautifully that name, with its two soft *o*'s flanking the pair of gentle consonants, suited the silent layer of snow upon that pipe with its two orifices and its tacit tunnel. (155)

Johnson proposes that the word on the pipe and, indeed, the shape of the pipe itself provide the work's dominant verbal device—the palindrome. He also demonstrates that the English translation of the story does a magnificent job in reproducing the Russian palindromes, though he has to admit that at some places the palindrome gives way to partial metathesis and other sorts of letter transposition.

Given the admirable closeness of Johnson's reading of the original and translation, it is odd that he does not mention one of the most striking differences: the addition of several sentences that draw attention to the narrator's having suffered physical trauma. The narrator now walks with a "thick rubberheeled stick" (155). The first paragraph of the "Work" section has been altered—from "*Vot obrazy raznykh rabot, kotorye ia nabliudaiu iz tramvainogo okna*" (here are examples of various kinds of work that I observe from the tram window [*178*]) to "here are examples of various kinds of work that I observe from the crammed tram, in which a compassionate woman can always be relied upon to cede me her window seat—while trying not to look too closely at me" (157). Johnson attributes the difference to sound:

"the corresponding English passage has been markedly expanded in order to incorporate equivalent anagrammatic elements[. . . . The] syllable doublings and inversions iconically evoke the dual nature of the street car with its two, reversible, cars in tandem. Even were it not for its divergence from the Russian text the new material in the English might well call attention to itself simply by its Baroque and gratuitous nature" (359). Johnson is so intent on admiring the way in which Nabokov achieves equivalence through difference that he seems almost willfully to avoid commenting on this instance of a difference with no equivalence, although perhaps the word "gratuitous" may hint at an opinion that the narrator's deformity has been unnecessarily inflicted. In the final section, the boy's future recollection includes more than the billiard table and pool player, the cigar smoke, the din of voices, and his father filling a mug of beer; the translation adds the information that the mug is being filled for the narrator, now equipped with an "empty right sleeve and scarred face" (160).

Johnson is not alone in his reluctance to tackle the maiming of the narrator. Maxim Shrayer quotes the final passage with the empty sleeve but does not comment on that detail or its addition (80). Marina Naumann, one of the first scholars to write about the story, observes in a footnote that Nabokov has "added rather horrifying details to the child's recollection," quoting the final paragraph without analysis (233). Roy Johnson, who evidently read the story only in English, notes in his electronic commentary archived on NABOKV-L that Nabokov "invents for no immediately obvious reason a first person narrator with one arm, a scar, and a walking stick—a post-war veteran who speaks of his enthusiasm for Berlin life to his 'friend and usual pot-companion' in the pub" (online posting).

Ronen was the first scholar to attempt an explanation, but I find his conclusion far from convincing. Like Shrayer, he asserts that the story is a response to the Russian Formalist author and critic Viktor Shklovsky. This claim makes a great deal of sense. Shrayer eloquently argues that in "Putevoditel' po Berlinu" Nabokov has emended Shklovsky's notion of *ostranenie* (making strange, or defamiliarization), first put forward in the Formalist's famous manifesto of 1917, "Art as Device," by transferring the agency of defamiliarization from "the writer's creative consciousness" to the principle of (imagined) temporality (79). But Ronen goes further and asserts that in his English translation Nabokov was responding to Shklovsky's 1964 somewhat abbreviated republication of his 1923 novel *Zoo, or Letters Not About Love.* Ronen notes that in the revised, 1964 version of *Zoo,* Shklovsky removed from the text references to Turks mutilated and killed by blows to the right arm and the head. He argues that Nabokov, "who never curtailed his internal conversation with those who remained in Russia," created in the revision of "A Guide to Berlin" "a monument" to the "moral mistake" of Viktor Shklovsky's accommodation with Soviet power (172). The mutilated narrator is a reference to the writer Shklovsky had become. This solution strikes me as ingenious but unlikely. Would Shklovsky have been on Nabokov's mind in the 1960s and 1970s? Would Nabokov have cared enough about Shklovsky even to read the republication of his earlier work? Nabokov does not mention Shklovsky in his correspondence with Edmund Wilson, and while it is not impossible that he would repress an influence, I am doubtful that he would have been sufficiently curious to follow Shklovsky's career with the degree of close attention necessary to make Ronen's hypothesis correct.

One explanation might refer to the very process of translation. The story concludes with a reference to somebody's "future recollection" (160), and this phrase might be taken as a metafictive pun—the story now has been re-collected in the future. It has been reprinted, though, in another language; and it is conceivable that this process has taken its toll on the text itself, particularly since it is a story that wears its poetic qualities on its now-empty sleeve. In a perceptive article Jacob Emery attributes the narrator's mutilation to the author's double exile. The writer of "Putevoditel′ po Berlinu" had lost his native land; the author of "A Guide to Berlin" has lost his native tongue. In support of his claim Emory quotes a line from a 1965 interview: "My complete switch from Russian prose to English prose was exceedingly painful, like learning anew how to handle things after losing seven or eight fingers in an explosion" (303, quoting *Strong Opinions,* 54). Yet as D. Barton Johnson has shown, the translation of this story is a tour de force that manages to preserve the phonetic and paranomastic games of the original. Nabokov appended the following note to the story's translation:

> Written in December 1925 in Berlin, "Putevoditel′ po Berlinu" was published in *Rul′,* December 24, 1925, and collected in *Vozvrashchenie Chorba, Slovo,* Berlin, 1930. Despite its simple appearance, this "Guide" is one of my trickiest pieces. Its translation has caused my son and me a tremendous amount of *healthy* trouble. Two or three scattered phrases have been added for the sake of factual clarity. (648, emphasis added)

Indeed, in translation the story seems to have gained in coherence in the tight relationship between signifiers and signifieds that do similar things on parallel planes. In the Russian version of the story, Nabokov emphasizes "depth" as the mysterious source of poetic inspiration. The word "Otto" is said to go surprisingly well with the snow, the pipes and their openings' *tainstvennaia glubina* (mysterious depth) (177), a phrase echoed with reference to the aquarium (*v siiaiushchikh uglubleniiakh* [in its shining depths]) (*179*) and the boy glimpsed *Tam, v glubine* (There, in the deep) (*181*). The English text, however, refers to the pipe's two orifices and "its tacit tunnel" (156), a phrase that fits the pipes into a large number of other hollow or capacious images in the book and emphasizes the way that words—and sounds, too—can be tacit tunnels, tacit not because they are silent but because they do not at once reveal themselves as linkages. When laid into the fabric of the story, these tunnels establish all sorts of phonetic and thematic connections. Here it is important to note that right from the beginning Nabokov sets the tone with the reference to his "usual *pot* companion," a phrase that sets up both the thematic notion of holes and containers—a pot may be a pit or a vessel—as well as the dominant phonetic cluster of the story:

> In the morning I visited the zoo and now I am entering a pub with my friend and usual *pot* companion. Its sky blue sign bears a white inscription, "Löwenbräu," accompanied by the *port*rait of a lion with a winking eye and mug of beer. We sit down and I start telling my friend about utility pipes, streetcars, and other im*port*ant matters. (155, emphasis added)

We will later be referred to the "*pot* bellied blue tram" in St. Petersburg (157) and to writers who wish to "*port*ray our time" (157), as well as to the sense of literary creation: "to *port*ray ordinary objects as they will be reflected in the kindly mirrors of future time" (157). (The rendering of *laskovyi* [affectionate, tender] with *kind*ly does justice to the final image of the mirroring gaze of a Berlin child.) The crescendo of both these themes occurs in the fourth section, "Eden":

> Rows of illuminated displays behind glass in the dimly lit hall resemble the portholes through which Captain Nemo gazed out of his submarine at the sea creatures undulating among the ruins of Atlantis. Behind the glass, in bright recesses, transparent fishes glide with flashing fins, marine flowers breathe, and, on a patch of sand, lies a live, crimson five-pointed star. This, then, is where the notorious emblem originated—at the very bottom of the ocean, in the murk of sunken Atlantica, which long ago lived through various upheavals while pottering about topical utopias and other inanities that cripple us today. (158)

D. Barton Johnson has noted the appearance of OTTO in this "bottom" (354), and it is worth noting that in these lines we can see OTTO emerging as the *story*'s emblem, picked up in the line immediately following just below: "Oh, do not omit to watch the giant tortoises being fed" (158). We should further observe that in the English, this passage also captures the phonetic pot refrain along with references to depth and containment—"portholes, recesses, bottom, pottering"—as if a tacit tunnel has led from the story's opening to this marine view. A port itself is a kind of aperture—in this sense, every port is a porthole—and each appearance of the grouped consonants *pt* and *prt* serves as another opening on to the story's principle of construction. (Note, too, the theme's presence in the last section: "the only sad part," "divided into two parts," "part of the publican's humble little apartment" [159]). To reflect the increased prominence of this tunnel theme, Nabokov has loosely translated the "usual pot companion's" rejection of the story he has just heard. "It's of no interest.... What do trams and tortoises matter? And anyway the w*hole* thing is simply a *bore*" (159, emphasis added). Perhaps not the best pun, and here definitely not to be taken in the sexual connotation evoked in *Lolita* and *Pnin,* but it may render another pun from the Russian: *Neinteresno...Delo vovse ne v tramvaiakh i cherepakhakh. Da i voobshche...Skuchno, odnim slovom (180)* ("It isn't interesting. The trams and turtles don't matter. And in general...it's boring, in a word.") That is, the text is boring to the pot companion because it has no plot, and because the texture takes over, with the *word* playing the starring role alone.

If the translation does not mutilate the story, it is important to think about the way in which it *changes* the experience of reading the work. One of the striking differences between Shklovsky's version of defamiliarization and Nabokov's is not only the latter's attention to temporality but also the tone of gentleness and placidity in "Putovoditel' po Berlinu." In "Art as Device" Shklovsky is attracted to images of violence and, in particular, sexual violence as examples of defamiliarizing practice. This is particularly true of the second (1919) and third (1925), more widely published versions of the article, which added striking details from erotic folklore ("naïve" descriptions of copulation) and were in keeping with the rhetorical violence of the revolutionary era, as was Roman Jakobson's definition of verbal art as "the violated word" (32).[2] Shklovsky concludes his author's preface in *Zoo* with a reference to Aleksandr Afanas'ev's *Forbidden Tales* (Zavetnye skazki), which, he says, have given him the essential metaphoric device for the work. In Nabokov's defamiliarized world, on the contrary, all the potential for violence seems to have been drained out—workers hammering are compared to a carillon, and even slaughtered animals are described in aestheticized terms. Images of coupling lack any sort of erotic charge and seem to have been selected as part of a polemic with the

---

2. For a comparison of the versions of "Art as Device," see Naiman, "Shklovsky's Dog," 333–52.

Formalists and revolutionary aesthetics in general; the pipes that will have to
be fitted together (in the English the word "Otto" has been written on the
"virgin snow" covering it [155]); the tram pole (or pen, *pero*) which has to be
manipulated to bring it into its proper place; and the tramcars themselves—
one like "a submissive female"—which require recoupling at the end of the
line (157) are all part of a gentle, placid mating game.

Indeed, although the narrator pokes fun at the Soviet star as the emblem
of "topical utopias" (158), he himself has created a kind of paradise. Like the
zoo, it is a "man-made Eden" (158). Perhaps it is even more halcyon than the
menagerie itself, since in the zoo lions still have to be prevented from devour-
ing does (*lev pozhral by lan'* [179]), while in Nabokov's Berlin a lion frequents
the narrator's pub, amiably winking from a Löwenbräu advertisement. It
would seem that nobody can be hurt in a world where all the animals are
"tropical" (158, 179).

The sense of reigning aesthetic harmony is so strong that we should probably return to the date of the story's publication (December 24) and think
seriously about its possible status as a "Christmas story." Within this rubric,
the visit to the zoo might serve—along with the Löwenbräu lion gracing
the poster of the pub—to provide the inhabitants for an urban manger; the
final scene's vision of the young child and his mother, "with faded looks and
big breasts," who is feeding him soup would correspond to a glimpse of a
contemporary Madonna and child. In this parallel, the narrator and his companion would take the role of the Magi, who here come to admire a future-
oriented notion of art.[3] Nabokov wrote two other Christmas stories for
Rul' in the 1920s ("Christmas" [*Rozhdestvo*], published on January 6 and 8,
1925, and "The Christmas Story" [*Rozhdestvenskii rasskaz*] on December 25,
1928). In the second of these, an aspiring Soviet writer suggests to an older
colleague that he write a communist Christmas story that would include a
tree with a red star; in "Putevoditel' po Berlinu" Nabokov takes that star and
drops it to the bottom of the ocean, where it nevertheless lights the way to the
writing of his guide. The innovative boldness of Nabokov's guide, though,
resides not in its thematic or spiritual deployment of the Christmas story, but
in Nabokov's projection of the Christmas genre from the thematic (ethical)

---

3. The Magi may make at least one other, soup-oriented, appearance in Nabokov's work of
this time. In *Mary*, published in early 1926, the poet Podtiagin is visited by an old friend, Kunitsyn,
who used to write cribs for him in school. In several respects, Kunitsyn is something of an authorial
agent, and there is something of a magical quality to his visitation: "That evening Anton Sergeyevich
had a visitor. He was an old gentleman with a sandy moustache clipped in the English fashion, very
dependable-looking, very dapper in his frock coat and striped trousers. Podtyagin was regaling him
with Maggi's bouillon when Ganin entered. The air was tinged blue with cigarette smoke" (38).

to the compositional (aesthetic) plane: the sense of well-being that suffuses "Putovoditel' po Berlinu" relates to the work's materials and methods rather than to its plot. (In its simultaneous attention to formal concerns *and* its pacification or even conversion of the violent ethos of Formalist defamiliarization, the story might be considered "Shklovsky's Christmas").[4] This would be further justification for Johnson's claim that the story is an early harbinger of Nabokov's best work, in which the dynamics of literary composition take priority over psychological or ideological motivation.

The maiming of the narrator introduces a disturbing note to this paradise. With his explicit reference to the scarred face and the empty sleeve, Nabokov leads the reader—no longer in immediate anticipation of Christmas—to reflect on what she has just read earlier in the story. In "A Guide"'s most programmatic statement, Nabokov writes that "the sense of literary creation" is "to find in the objects around us the fragrant tenderness that only posterity will discern" (157). In a metafictive sense this posterity is represented by the rereader who knows what the narrator has suffered and may read his tender appreciation of detail as a response to trauma. A layer of psychological complexity has been added, but by inflicting these injuries on the narrator, and by turning attention from the work of composition to the narrator as emergent character, Nabokov has not only moved much closer to Shklovsky's version of making strange but has—at least for me—made the story less audacious, less strange as a work of art.

From today's perspective the maiming of Nabokov's narrator functions to inscribe the story into the vision of Weimar Berlin that we have inherited from Georg Grosz, Max Beckmann, and Fritz Lang. In 1925 Nabokov could not have known the iconic portrait that would eventually take shape in the West; in translation the maimed narrator fits easily into this retrospective image. Was crippling the narrator a gesture at this convention? Nabokov is not a writer to fall easily for a cliché, although World War II certainly increased his hostility to Germany, hostility we find surfacing only as irony in many works written in the 1920s and 1930s. In this respect, the tainting of the German utopia has something in common with the slightly earlier rewriting of *King, Queen, Knave* (1968), in which Nabokov retrospectively gave one of the heroes, Franz, traits suggestive of a proto-Nazi.

Whether or not the story has been discolored by Nabokov's heightened, postwar disgust with Germany, in its English version it certainly reflects a

---

4. At the start of his article Ronen calls the story Nabokov's "Berlin Christmas story of 1925" (*berlinskii rozhdestvenskii rasskaz 1925 goda*) (164), but with this formulation he seems to refer exclusively to the story's date rather than its genre. On Nabokov's use of holiday genres, see Syrovatko, 126–44.

blurring of various levels of narrative, as the boundaries between the narrator, the things he describes, and the reader become more porous. In the Russian version, the narrator has virtually no relationship with the things he describes or, more precisely, he has no lasting impact on them nor they on him. Even in the zoo, he does not mention that the absence of bars would put *him* at risk. (Compare *Lev pozhral by lan'* ["the lion would devour the doe"] to the more threatening English version: "the very first dingo would savage me" [158]). In Russian the narrator floats above the text, describing what he sees, preserving images for literature's museum of the future, just as he preserves the child's future memories. The child's memories do not necessarily include him, and they are formed on the basis of habit alone. This would seem to be the capstone of Nabokov's disagreement with Shklovsky—the child *ko vsemu etomu davno privyk* (*181*) ("has long grown used to this scene" [159])—yet this oft-repeated, familiar rather than defamiliarized scene will be the basis of artistic beauty. In the Russian, the things the child will forever remember do *not* include the narrator. In the English version, the child's recollections have been scarred—perhaps by the intervening "future" that is now the past, perhaps by the narrator's presence, perhaps by the reader's having read the story. Memory has itself become a distorting mirror and, when compared with the original version, the translation may serve as a parable about the unreliable, distorting vision—the creative trauma—of the kindliest of mirrors.

Taking these observations one step further, we might see the translation as serving also as a parable about the fate of characters, even the least defined characters, in art. While recognizing that the narrator's presence has had an impact on the world he describes, scarring—and fixing—the child's future memory, we should also recognize that in the story's narrative logic, the narrator is damaged—and fixed—by the child's vision, for his injury is described most fully in terms of how the child sees and remembers *him*. Both are damaged by what seems to be the narrator's insistence on narrative control: "He has long since grown used to this scene and is not dismayed by its proximity. Yet there is one thing I know. Whatever happens to him in life, he will always remember the picture he saw every day of his childhood from the little room where he was fed his soup. He will remember the billiard table and the coatless evening visitor who used to draw back his sharp white elbow and hit the ball with his cue, and the blue-gray cigar smoke, and the din of voices, *and my empty right sleeve and scarred face,* and his father behind the bar, filling a mug *for me* from the tap" (159–60). (The italicized words have been added in translation and do not correspond to the Russian original.) In the English version we witness a narrative struggle—however short—that inscribes itself well in Nabokov's more mature narratological and characterological concerns, as the collector of urban, picturesque details is himself collected—and infinitely recollected—"he will always remember"—by the object of his caressing gaze.

There is one more factor to consider—the role of the author. A hallmark of Nabokov's late work is the punishing of the narrator, disciplined for the hubris of attempting to tell a tale. In *Lolita* and *Pnin* the punishment is morally deserved: these narrators are developed characters eventually undone by the material of which they seemed to be in control. The position of the narrator of *Pnin* is in some ways analogous to that of "A Guide to Berlin": his voice has been heard throughout, but he materializes as a character only as the novel comes to an end and he is hoisted on his own narrative petard. The narrators of "The Vane Sisters" and Herman in *Despair* are also undone by their own material. (This is true as well for the boy who cried "wolf," despite Nabokov's unconvincing assertion that "the poor little fellow's" fate—being finally eaten up by a real beast because he lied too often—is quite incidental," *Lectures on Literature,* 5.) In the translation of "A Guide to Berlin," the narrator has not done anything unethical, with the possible exception of not allowing the child or the reader the freedom of memory. (Like Humbert Humbert, who nearly chose the self-referential "Otto Otto" as a pseudonym [*Lolita,* 308], the narrator is using a child to immortalize himself.) If the narrator is not punished for this solipsizing transgression, he seems to be damaged merely as a matter of course, caught between the gazes of his narrative object and his real author. Although Roy Johnson says the narrator is a war veteran (online posting), there is no evidence for that conclusion. He might better be considered a veteran of the battles of metafiction, where the "healthy trouble" of the author may be inversely proportional to the protagonist's control over his world. We should pause on the one sentence in the story where Nabokov discusses a cause of crippling. Where the Russian refers to the star bequeathed to us *"s samogo dna okeana—iz temnoty potoplennykh Atlantid, davnym-davno perezhivshikh vsiakie smuty—opyty glupovatykh utopii—i vse to, chto trevozhit nas"* (*180*) ("from the very bottom of the ocean, from the darkness of sunken Atlantises, which long ago lived through various times of trouble—the experiments of silly utopias—and everything that troubles us"), the English has "at the very bottom of the ocean, in the murk of sunken Atlantica, which long ago lived through various upheavals while pottering about topical utopias and other inanities that cripple us today" (158). The phrase "topical utopias" is much more ambiguous—and interesting—than the *glupovatye utopii* ("silly utopias") of the Russian, and I think we should pay attention to its complex meaning—and not see it merely as a kind of phonetic filler for the alliterative pot theme. The more obvious meaning of the word "topical" is its dismissive sense of *trendy, fleeting, in demand*. But the word may also refer, of course, to a place rather than a time, and in this sense we might understand it as a description of the original "Putevoditel'po Berlinu" itself, a quite literally topical utopia where literature never harmed anybody. We can see the maiming force of "topical utopias and other inanities that cripple us today" as a nod to the later Nabokov's understanding about what it means to be "most artistically caged" (*Pale Fire,* 37) in literature. This reading would not be out of keeping with other metafictive carceral images in Nabokov's work, including his 1956 reference to "the first little throb" of *Lolita,* which "was somehow prompted by a newspaper story about an ape in the Jardin des Plantes, who, after months of coaxing by a scientist, produced the first drawing ever charcoaled by an animal: this sketch showed the bars of the poor creature's cage" (*Lolita,* 311). While in some places in Nabokov's oeuvre a life of confinement in an aesthetic prison can be gloriously fulfilling, replete with unexpected developments and coincidences that inspire reverence, in other works the experience is nightmarish. *Ada* probably presents the most extreme, auto-parodic example of this view of punishment as an essential part of the creation of a fictional, character-inhabited world; the co-narrator, Van, explicitly predicates his existence on his capacity to inflict pain on others:

> Van felt that for him to survive on this terrible Antiterra, in the multicolored and evil world into which he was born, he had to destroy, or at least maim for life, two men. (301)

Unlike its first, Russian incarnation, "A Guide to Berlin" is informed by the later Nabokov's concern with the inescapable relationship between pain and beauty, between the inflicted deformity and crafted order in what Humbert calls the "very local palliative of articulate art." Humbert continues: "The moral sense in mortals is the duty / We have to pay on mortal sense of beauty" (*Lolita,* 283). In "A Guide to Berlin" the "mortal sense of beauty" has a cost not charged in "Putevoditel' po Berlinu."

CHAPTER 10

The Meaning of "Life"

Nabokov in Code (King, Queen, Knave *and* Ada)

Driving away from Ardis after his first summer with Ada, Van stops at the Forest Fork, where he plans to meet her for one last tryst before catching the train:

> Van plunged into the dense undergrowth. He wore a silk shirt, a velvet jacket, black breeches, riding boots with star spurs—and this attire was hardly convenient for making *klv zdB AoyvBno wkh gwzxm dqg kzwAAqvo a gwttp vq wifhm* Ada in a natural bower of aspens; *xliC mujzikml,* after which she said:
>
> "Yes—so as not to forget. Here's the formula for our correspondence. Learn this by heart and then eat it up like a good little spy." (157)

Characteristically, Nabokov gives us the details of the code only in the next chapter (26), at which point we are to take a backward look at the coded passage. We expect, of course, something that could not otherwise have made it past the censor, but upon deciphering the passage, all we get is "his way through the brush and crossing a brook to reach...they embraced." A disappointment—these jumbled letters have proved far less erotic than, say "nictating" in *Lolita* or the names of various types of butterflies or orchids mentioned throughout *Ada*.[1] Chapter 26, which contains the key to this and later codes, is one of the shortest in the book, and Ada, in a note at its end, suggests deleting it. Even Van, who disregards Ada's suggestion, apologizes: "Codes are a bore to describe; yet a few basic details must be, reluctantly, given" (160).

At this point the reader of *Ada* is probably thankful that more explanations have not been provided and that more words have not been put into code. The entire "genre" of code seems to have been dismissed. The brevity of this chapter—while not unparalleled in *Ada*—contrasts notably with the length of the novel as a whole. (In a book that has struck many readers as too long, it is characteristic that an internal editor—Ada—suggests dropping one of the shortest chapters.) The sheer ugliness, visually and phonetically, of the code we have been shown contrasts with the lush beauty of the writing that characterizes the entire text. Some of the other codes used by the lovers but not—so far as I can tell—actually employed in the novel are based on Marvell's "The Garden" and Rimbaud's "Mémoire"; their choice emphasizes just how much damage a code does to literature when the beautiful original is put to work to produce cacophonous combinations of letters or monotonous number chains. And yet . . . when Nabokov dismisses an interpretive practice, he often reincorporates it. What is the place of code in *Ada*?

A code is a collection of laws. It can also be "a system of signals for communication" (*Webster's New International,* 517). In Nabokov's writings, the weight placed on both correct interpretation and the process of reading is so high that the two definitions of code come close to meaning the same thing. For both definitions of code, economy is crucial; if a code is too cumbersome, it ceases to be of much use. And use, above all things, is central to the value of code. A useless code might still be an object of play, but whether it could ever reach the level of art would depend on its variability and on the possibility that its imaginative deployment might triumph over the dull utility of its origins.

As a way of approaching the question of code in *Ada,* I want to look at another project on which Nabokov worked while he wrote his longest work of fiction: the translation of his second novel, *King, Queen, Knave. Ada* surfaces, obliquely, in that translation's preface as the "new novel that has now obsessed [the author] for five years" (ix–x), and the two works reflect similar concerns. Jane Grayson, who has written one of two detailed considerations

---

1. As Bobbie Mason notes, the sentence containing the code is more sexually evocative if the coded phrase is simply skipped: "Van is 'making Ada' in the trees" (63). Including the code uncharacteristically limits the physical content of these lovers' meeting to an "embrace" and deprives "after" of its traditional suggestiveness as a postcoital cliché.

of the changes made to *King, Queen, Knave* in the process of translation, notes that there are similarities between those revisions and the poetics of *Ada:* chiefly the "profusion of minor characters" with comic names, the extent of literary allusions, and the new "humorous treatment of sex" (113). A detour through the revised *King Queen, Knave* provides insight into the concerns and strategies of Nabokov as a writer in the mid-1960s. How Nabokov rewrote a novel of his youth can help us to understand the reader's stakes in the more complicated text.

In the preface to the English translation of *King, Queen, Knave,* Nabokov writes:

> I foresaw having to make a number of revisions affecting the actual text of a forty-year-old novel which I had not reread ever since its proofs had been corrected by an author twice younger than the reviser. Very soon I asserted [*sic!*] that the original sagged considerably more than I had expected. I do not wish to spoil the pleasure of future collators by discussing the little changes I made. Let me only remark that my main purpose in making them was not to beautify a corpse but rather to permit a still breathing body to enjoy certain innate capacities which inexperience and eagerness, the haste of thought and the sloth of word had denied it formerly. Within the texture of the creature, those possibilities were practically crying to be developed or teased out. I accomplished the operation not without relish. The "coarseness" and "lewdness" of the book that alarmed my kindest critics in émigré periodicals have of course been preserved, but I confess to have mercilessly struck out and rewritten many lame odds and ends. (ix)

Nabokov's choice of imagery here is intriguing. As its title indicates, one of the central themes of *King, Queen, Knave* is the notion of convention. In reducing his characters to playing cards, Nabokov gestures toward their stereotypicality as figures in a drama of adultery. Grayson has aptly termed the novel a story of "dehumanization" and cites Mikhail Tsetlin's original review of the Russian novel: "The author wanted to show us the mechanicalness, the soullessness, the automatism of contemporary people.... As if not trusting readers to understand this, the author has used symbolism to make his meaning clear" (90). Tsetlin's comment reflects both his insight and his misunderstanding: "mechanization" is certainly a theme in the novel, but Nabokov is not engaged in social critique. Rather, he seems to have set himself a double task. First, he is posing himself a challenge: how much of the mechanics of fiction can I show the reader and still have him care what happens to the characters? Second, he uses the novel as a kind of laboratory to explore the meaning of fictional life. Since no living beings exist on the page, where does life in literature begin and end?

The department-store automata financed by the entrepreneur Dreyer are just the most obvious example of a marked theme: in this novel normally animate and conventionally inanimate objects die or come to life with astonishing frequency. On his way to Berlin in the first chapter, Dreyer's poor relation Franz has in his wallet "an inviolate month of human life in reichsmarks" (3). "Pious popular prints that had frightened him in childhood came to life again" (11). Dreyer understands that every new fashion of suit has "a pathetically short life" (9). One of the novel's basic narrative techniques is to "cut" from one character's perspective to another's; it oscillates just as prominently between life and death. The following passage, which begins with Franz imagining his life in Berlin, exemplifies the novel's fascination with transitions in both narrative perspective and to and from animacy:

> [I]n a brilliantly lit-up emporium, among gilded dummies, limpid mirrors, and glass counters, Franz strolled about in cut-away, striped trousers, and white spats, and with a smooth movement of his hand directed customers to the departments they needed. This was no longer a wholly conscious play of thought, nor was it yet a dream; and at the instant that sleep was about to trip him up, Franz regained control of himself and directed his thoughts according to his wishes. *He promised himself a lone treat that very night.* He bared the shoulders of the woman that had just been sitting by the window, made a quick mental test (*did blind Eros react? Clumsy Eros did, unsticking its folds in the dark*) [*vzvolnovan li on?*]; then, keeping the splendid shoulders, changed the head, substituting for it the face of that seventeen-year-old maid who had vanished with a silver soup ladle almost as big as she before he had had time to declare his love; but that head too he erased and, in its place, attached the face of one of those bold-eyed, humid-lipped Berlin beauties that one encounters mainly in liquor and cigarette advertisements. Only then did the image come to life: the bare bosomed girl lifted a wine glass to her crimson lips, gently swinging her apricot-silk leg as a red backless slipper slowly slid off her foot. The slipper fell off and Franz, bending down after it, plunged softly into dark slumber. He slept with mouth agape so that his pale face presented three apertures, two shiny ones (his glasses) and one black (his mouth). Dreyer noticed this symmetry when an hour later he returned with Martha from the dining

car. In silence they stepped over a lifeless leg. Martha put her handbag on the collapsible window table, and the bag's nickel clasp with its cat's eye immediately came to life as a green reflection began dancing in it. (14, *139*)[2]

In addition to raising the theme of the characters' status as minor creators, the passage animates the clasp on Martha's handbag and kills off Franz's leg. Franz's success in bringing to life the image of a woman who can provoke his lust also enlivens his loins. This scene sets the tone for many others in the novel, which in its metaphoric demography—the per-page average of figurative births and deaths—may well set a record for Russian or American fiction. "Pious popular prints that had frightened him in childhood came to life again" (11, *138*), "a succulent omelet and a bit of liver revived her" (122, *210*),[3] Dreyer's jacket seems alive (267, *302*), Dreyer's affairs attain "a certain independent existence" (*kakuiu-to samostoiatel'nuiu zhizn'*) (195, *256*), his new club "comes to life in April" (168, *240*), snails "come to life after the rain and stick out of their round shells a pair of sensitive yellow little horns *that made no less sensitive Franz's flesh creep*" (231, *279*).[4]

As the last sentence suggests, an important factor in characterization is the attitude of the characters to life. Dreyer is constantly delighted by what the world offers him: "What fun it was to be alive" (*Kak veselo zhit', kak vse liubopytno v zhizni*—lit., "How merry to be alive, how interesting everything in life was") (205, *263*). This love of life motivates him to fund the development of the automata, whose progress he animatedly follows: *oni uzhe ozhivali, ozhivali* [lit., "they were already coming alive, alive"] (not in the English 205, *263*), but it also enables him to endow virtually anything with animacy. Visiting a courthouse museum, Dreyer thinks critically of all who would murder their neighbors: "How much those simpletons were missing!

---

2. I quote only the English when it is seems substantially similar (connotatively and denotatively) to the Russian. When the texts differ substantially, the translation's new interpolations are put in italics, and I provide the Russian text replaced—if any—either in a footnote or in text. Russian page citations are to *Sobranie sochinenii russkogo perioda, vol. 2*. Even when the English text is entirely new, I cite the Russian page where the absence of the added text is retrospectively to be noticed.

3. "*Ogromnyi neznyi omlet, podernutyi ryzhim krapom, srazu ee ozhivil.*" There is a little less life in the original, since the omelet, while huge, is not accompanied by *liver*.

4. Jürgen Bodenstein provides an interesting analysis of Nabokov's use of "transferred epithets," a device that "signifies that the natural relations between two components of an idea are exchanged so that the adjective qualifying the subject (usually a person) comes to qualify the object of a sentence (usually a thing or activity)." The result is a tendency toward personification and "imaginative anthropomorphic metaphors which transfer human characteristics to inanimate things" (1:258). Bodenstein describes their use as prevalent throughout Nabokov's prose, but in *King, Queen, Knave* they play a particularly important role supporting the novel's investigation of the artificiality of life.

Missing not only the wonders of everyday life, the simple pleasure of existence, but even such instants as this, the ability to look with curiosity upon what was essentially boring" (207, *264–65*). This "look with curiosity" is in many respects the delighted attitude of the novel as it seizes on details from daily existence. Dreyer is described as more of an artist than a businessman, and it is one of the originalities of the book to portray an entrepreneur so positively; in very few places in European fiction of the 1920s would one find a capitalist depicted in such bright colors. Dreyer's appetites, which would be so caricatured in contemporary German and Russian depictions of his profession, are shown to be part of his affirmation of life. Even a selfish moment, such as when he tells his wife that he is in too much of a hurry to get her a glass of water but proceeds to sit down on the terrace to "two rolls with butter and honey"—and then, having consulted his watch, eats a third—even this works to his benefit, since his failure to notice Martha's sickness probably hastens her death and, as a result, prevents her from killing him (257, *293*). (This thoughtless, indulgent repast and its happy result suggests that *King, Queen, Knave* may be *Anna Karenina,* as retold by Stiva Oblonsky.)

Both Martha and Franz are repelled by Dreyer's excess of life. "There he was, *big as life,* tawny-mustached and ruddy, eating at one table with her and sleeping in the adjacent bed" (113, *204*).[5] Martha complains about "*the injustice of life*" (142, *224*). "All my life I've been unhappy," she says, justifying her adultery with Franz (111, *202*). She grows "unusually animated" when thinking about murdering Dreyer (212, *267*).

Franz's attitude toward life is the most complex. On one hand, he is driven by his sexual desires, which seem to constitute a basic life force. He looks lustfully at Berlin's "*animated* boulevards" (73, *178*);[6] he thinks of Martha with "unbearable clarity" (*tak nesterpimo-zhivo*"—lit., "unbearably vividly") (78, *182*); the adverb *zhivo* aptly describes the intensity of his desire for her. But those snails make his flesh crawl, dogs disgust him, Martha reminds him of an old toad, and even his own tongue feels "repulsively alive" (3, *132*).

Since *King, Queen, Knave* emphatically embraces the category of "novel of adultery," it is not surprising that the novel links life and sex. Grayson draws attention to the extent to which Nabokov has added sex in the English translation. One of Nabokov's aims in both works, she writes, was "not to ape pornography, but to parody it, and to parody the image of himself as a pornographic writer" (116). (The difference between pornography and the parody of pornography, however, is difficult to fix. To some, pornography

---

5. "Big as life" replaces *tut kak tut* (lit., "just there") and "ruddy" replaces *shumnyi* ("loud").
6. *nochnaia ulitsa*—lit., "street at night."

probably always seems a parody. For others, pornography becomes a parody when it fails to achieve or is no longer needed to achieve its object.) Nabokov's statement in his preface—his nervousness about not beautifying a corpse—suggests that he was especially concerned about the novel's vigor and keeping "a still breathing body" alive. The theme of life had already been present in the original, now it was "crying to be developed or teased out." Nabokov's statement that the original "coarseness" and "lewdness" of the book had "of course been preserved" is a classic gesture of misdirection: in the revised novel the lewdness has been dramatically heightened, as if the author has been smoking the characters' cigarette of choice, "Libidettes" (86—they were just "Viennese cigarettes" in the original). As Carl Proffer puts it: "The profusion of new private parts calls to mind a madman merrily decorating a Christmas tree with male genitalia" ("A New Deck," 302). Sex was a large part of keeping the novel alive.

Between the 1920s and the 1960s, Nabokov, perhaps through Shakespeare, had discovered a new meaning of "life." "Stirred by Cleopatra," Antony paws verbally at his beloved:

> Now, for the love of Love and her soft hours
> Let's not confound the time with conference harsh.
> There's not a minute of our lives should stretch
> Without some pleasure now. What sport tonight?
> (1.1.46–49)

and, in another example collected by Frankie Rubinstein (148), Jessica says in *The Merchant of Venice:*

> It is very meet
> The Lord Bassanio live an upright life,
> For, having such a blessing in his lady,
> He finds the joys of heaven here on earth.
> (3.5.63–66)

By the early 1950s Nabokov had discovered the play on "life" in Ronsard (*vie/vit*) and, as we have seen, used it in *Lolita* repeatedly before its most florid deployment yet, in *Pale Fire,* where Nabokov puts actual magazine advertisements to ribald use. Kinbote copies out two clippings from "the family magazine *Life,* so justly famed for its pudibundity in regard to the mysteries of the male sex":

> The first comes from the issue of May 10, 1937, p. 67, and advertises
> the Talon Trouser fastener (a rather grasping and painful name, by the

way). It shows a young gent radiating virility among several ecstatic lady-friends, and the inscription reads: "You'll be amazed that the fly of your trousers could be so dramatically improved." The second comes from the issue of March 28, 1949, p. 126, and advertises Hanes Fig Leaf Brief. It shows a modern Eve worshipfully peeping from behind a potted tree of knowledge at a leering young Adam in rather ordinary but clean underwear, with the front of his advertised brief conspicuously and completely shaded, and the inscription reads: *Nothing beats a fig leaf.* (114–15)

Now we understand why, just before the quotation of Ronsard, Nabokov has Lolita ask Humbert if he is through with *"Glance and Gulp"* (47). *Look*—here just hiding behind *Glance* ("glans")—is an appropriate rival for *Life*.

In revising *King, Queen, Knave,* Nabokov took pains to inject as much new life as possible. Life has been added to a description of Franz's room: *"It gave on a pleasant by-street with a delicatessen shop. A palace-like affair that the landlord said would be a movie house was being built on the corner, and this gave life to the surroundings. A picture above the bed showed a naked girl leaning forward to wash her breasts in a misty pond"* (48, *161*). The description of the newly employed Franz walking through the Berlin streets and looking at prostitutes has been dramatically enlivened in the English version:

> The luster of the black asphalt was filmed by a blend of dim hues, through which here and there vivid rends and oval holes made by rain puddles revealed the authentic colors of deep reflections—a vermilion diagonal band, a cobalt wedge, a green spiral—scattered glimpses into a humid upside-down world, into a dizzy geometry of gems. The kaleidoscopic effect suggested someone's jiggling every now and then the pavements so as to change the combination of numberless colored fragments. Meanwhile shafts and *ripples of life (stolby sveta*—lit., "columns of light") passed by, marking the course of every car. Shop windows, bursting with tense radiance, oozed, squirted and splashed out into the rich blackness. (74, *178*)

Martha is particularly bothered by her husband's vivacity: "And you know," she says to Franz, "lately he's been so terribly alive. *Is he stronger than we? Is he more alive than this, and this, and this?"* (204, *263*). The text does not specify what Martha is touching, but Dreyer's life has been so explicitly portrayed in sexual terms that it is not difficult to guess: "Her husband was in the bathroom; she saw him through the open door. Naked, *full of ruddy life, various parts of his anatomy leaping,* he was giving himself a robust rub-down, and yelling every time he touched his red-blotched shoulders" (250, *288*). Martha and Franz have different conceptions of Dreyer: "Martha's subject was deafeningly loud, intolerably vigorous and vivacious; *he threatened her with a priapus that had already once inflicted upon her an almost mortal wound*, smoothed his *obscene* moustache with a little silver brush, snored at night with triumphant reverberations; while Franz's man was lifeless (*blednyi*) and flat" (178, *246*). In the Russian Dreyer was already "intolerably alive" (*nevynosimo zhivoi*), but now Nabokov has filled in explicit physical detail and added "life" even to its absence—in Franz's mind Dreyer was originally pale (*blednyi*), he is now "lifeless." References to birth control have been inserted, again activating "life" through its Gallic etymology:

> This pair of slippers (his modest but considerate gift) our lovers kept in the lower drawer of the corner chest, *for life not unfrequently imitates the French novels. That drawer contained, moreover, a little arsenal of contraceptive implementa, gradually accumulated by Martha, who after a miscarriage in the first year of her marriage had developed a morbid fear of pregnancy.* (102, *197*)[7]

Nabokov even gestures toward the new definition of this crucial term by seeming to give Martha insight into the novel's revamped vocabulary: her interest in Dreyer's business "did not combine organically with the new piercing, *moaning and throbbing* meaning of her life" (114, *204*).

Is this, perhaps, more life than the novel can bear? The bawdy play with "life" in *Lolita* works because there are so many levels of interpretation at stake. The sexual uses of "life" frequently appear there at emotionally "inappropriate" moments and work against the ostensible meaning of the lines. If the reader perceives them, he is forced to reevaluate the initial reading, but that reading is never canceled out. ("*He* broke my heart. *You* merely broke my life" [279].) The flatness of the characters in *King, Queen, Knave*, however, fails to supply the coded meaning of "life" with a weighty counterpart: life as a reader imagines it to be lived by characters who matter.

Sex is not the only area where Nabokov has repainted the scenery in *King, Queen, Knave* with a very thick brush. Several features stand out much more prominently in the translation than in the original. First, Nabokov has made himself far more present. As the photographer Vivian Badlock, he takes Dreyer's picture in Switzerland and casts a shadow over the photo; later, along

---

7. Martha refers to the condom she washes for Franz's reuse as "your macky," a parodic reworking of an image that Nabokov had made a symbol of art in *Mary* and which he later associated with Joyce (*Lectures on Literature*, 318–20).

with an avatar for Vera, he forms part of the couple at the shore for whom Franz conceives an envious hatred. This pair made a brief appearance in the Russian original, but now the man has been handed a butterfly net (254, *291*) and, as if there were any doubt about his identity, Nabokov writes in the preface that this is he, moving through the text on one of his "visits of inspection" (viii). Second, as Grayson notes, there are "a full dozen more references to lavatories" in the English (112). This is not only a matter of increased attention to physical functions. Rather, Nabokov here is reinforcing with a vengeance the motif of excremental creation that he has been urging with augmented intensity in the years since 1928. If toilets were a place where Humbert's destiny was likely to catch, Franz is even more their prey. Where the Russian text simply has him walk out of his train compartment into the corridor, the English dispatches him to the lavatory to contemplate his fate: "*As he stood there holding on to an iron handle, he found it strange and dreadful to be connected to a cold hole where his stream glistened and bounced, with the dark head-long-rushing naked earth so near, so fateful*" (16–17, *141*). Plumbing is even offered as a key to a metafictive metaphor that might offer competition to the lifeless, lifelike automata: in the translation Dreyer's American customer must decide whether he wants to buy the robots or to invest in "running water in luxury hotels," which will "produce recognizable tunes," an "orchestra of faucets" (263, *297*). The water theme reaches its apogee with the death of Martha; in her demise water, like a toilet, purifies, washing away filth. (As a foreshadowing of the musical alternative to robots, in the translation Dreyer hears "a veritable orchestras of wheezes tuning up" in Martha (140, *223*).[8] The theme of waste is given a much stronger linkage to the production of art. At the criminal museum, unaware that he himself is in a crime novel, Dreyer expresses his dissatisfaction with the narrative of murder: "all this trash expressed the very essence of crime" (207, *264*).[9] Just a few pages before, Martha's possible response to the idea of the robots—"*Zanimaesh'sia chep-ukhoi*" and Dreyer's imagined retort—"*Da,—no kakaia chudesnaia chepukha*" (lit., you're spending your time on trifles." "Yes, but marvelous trifles")—has been replaced by "'You're spending your time on rubbish.' 'Yes, but what marvelous rubbish'" (205, *263*). Nowhere in Nabokov's fiction is this meta-aesthetic conceit presented with more clarity than in the enhanced portrait of

---

8. *Ia otsiuda slyshu, kak u tebia vnutri vse posvistyvaet* (lit., "from here I can hear how everything inside you whistles").

9. In the Russian the "trash" still has not been discovered—*vse eto, v predstavlenii Draiera, vyrazhala samuiu sushchnost' prestupleniia*—lit., "all this, in Dreyer's opinion, expressed the very essence of crime."

Enricht, Franz's landlord, who believes he has created his tenant. At the end of chapter 4, Franz hears a chuckle in Enricht's room and peeps in: A single sentence in the Russian—"*Starichok-khoziain, vo odnom nizhnem bel'e, stoial na chetveren'kakh i, nagnuv sedovato-bagrovuiu golovu—gliadel—promezh nog—na sebia v triumo*"—(the old landlord, in only his underwear, stood on all fours and, bending his hoary head—looked through his legs at himself in the pier glass) has been elaborated to highlight the notion of excremental creation:

> Old Enricht, clad only in his nightshirt, was standing on all fours with his wrinkled and hoary rear towards a brilliant cheval glass. Bending low his congested face, fringed with white hair, like the head of the professor in the "Hindu Prince" farce, he was peering back through the archway of his bare thighs at the reflection of his bleak buttocks. (87, *187*)

References to wind, often a marker of authorial inspiration in Nabokov's prose, have also been heightened, with such intensity that they, too, approach a kind of code. In the Russian we could already hear the "hurricane-like clatter of typewriters" in Dreyer's office (88, *187*); Franz had "fantastic difficulties with the vol-au-vent" (37, *154*); the landlord held a paper fan in his hand when informing Franz that he no longer existed (229, *278*); and the toilet door banged in the wind (159, *234*). In the boat, planning to row Dreyer to his death but about to catch her own from cold, Martha felt that "an odd, cool, not unpleasant emptiness was in her chest, as if the breeze had blown right through her, cleaning her inwardly, removing all the trash" (245, *285*). In a pun that Nabokov could not translate, both Franz and Martha worried about being fooled—the Russian used is *naduvat'*—literally "blown up" (12, *138; 230, 261*). In the English Franz is forced to work in an "*over-ventilated*" department (78, *182*), but the most notable and precise injection of authorial air comes when the characters reach the beach resort and a photographer announces the advent of the author: "Weaving his way among the ramparts of sand [...] an itinerant photographer, ignored by the lazy crowd, walked with his camera, yelling *into the wind:* "The artist is coming! The divinely favored, *der gottbegnadete* artist is coming" (234, *280;* first emphasis added). In scrambled form, Nabokov's name has been included with aeolian force in the resort's guest list; the wind picks up and Martha's teeth begin to chatter as Dreyer reads out "Blavdak Vinomori" (239, *282*).

One of the major differences between the earlier and later versions of *King, Queen, Knave* is the expanded role given to Tom, the Dreyers' dog. In *Nabokov's Spectral Dimension*, Rowe notes the new prominence accorded to this animal (95–101), the only being whose murder Martha successfully arranges, but whose bark seems to haunt Martha from the next world at the moment of her death.[10] Rowe rightly focuses on one of Franz's dreams, in which Dreyer is winding a phonograph, and Franz feels with horror that "in a moment the phonograph would bark the word that solved the universe after which the act of existing would become a futile, childish game" (202, 260–61). As Rowe points out, in English this word must be "bark"—for by the end of the novel the characters will row in the "fatal bark" from which Martha will emerge mortally chilled (99). I suspect that Nabokov has hidden a pun in the Russian, as well, which the bark/bark homonym has replaced. It is possible that the key word in the Russian is *pes* (dog). "*Frants vdrug zamechal, chto tut obman, chto ego khitro naduvaiut, chto v pesenke skryto imenno to slovo, kotoroe slyshat' nel'zia*" ("Franz would understand that it was all a ruse, that he was being cleverly fooled, that within the song lurked the very word that must not be heard" [203, 261].) *Pes* is hidden in *pesenke* (song, *v pesenke skryto imenno to slovo;* "within the *song* lurked the very word"), as it is in *pesok* ("sand"), the milieu of Martha's death and a word which appears marked in the Russian at the moment when Dreyer climbs into the boat: "*Ona prodol-zhala ozirat'sia. Pesok, dal'she peschanyi skat, obrosshii lesom. Ni dushi krugom*" (lit., "She continued to look around. Sand, further off the sandy slope, covered by forest"]. Nabokov has translated this in the English so as to reinscribe the hound: "She continued her survey. Sand, rocks, and further on, heathery slopes and woods. Not a soul, *not a dog ever came here*" (244, *285*).

Rowe claims that "if Martha had not had Tom killed, his spirit would not have prompted her death" (100). Although his dynamics of causation here do not seem quite warranted, Rowe's reading nicely draws attention to the close link between Tom and the forces of authorial creation. Tom's favorite objects are spheres: the balls that dot both texts. The dog attempts to lead Dreyer to Martha when she is hiding in Franz's room, until, in a duel of authorial demiurges, Dreyer and the dogs are stopped by the landlord. Franz feels as strong an antipathy to the dog as he does to the net-wielding Nabokov. When Tom breathes on Franz, Franz feels enveloped in "an unendurable odor": "That is how my childhood smells" (83, *184*). Most telling is the final line of dialogue in the English translation, as Martha in her final delirium, scolds her absent maid:

> And then—*with her good old familiar sharpness: "Frieda, why is the dog here again? He was killed. He can't be here any more."* (271, *305*)

---

10. Earlier, Rowe already noted the prominence of dogs throughout Nabokov's work: "dogs may be seen as the author's fateful agents—inconspicuously prefiguring, promoting, or presiding over key episodes in Nabokovian 'reality'" (*Nabokov and Others,* 118).

The word "familiar" has been used earlier with reference to Tom—when Martha is waiting for Franz in his room and suddenly hears Tom's "horribly familiar bark" (220, *272*). In the Russian the bark is described as abrupt (*otryvistyi*)—it is Dreyer's voice which is *znakomyi* (familiar). By transferring the epithet from Dreyer to his dog, and then repeating it later, Nabokov is getting particular mileage out of the substantive English meaning of "familiar," here identifying the dog as a spirit-servant and as his own sign within the text. Nabokov had experimented with introducing ghosts as authorial figures in "The Vane Sisters," and including a spectral dog in this novel would make sense as an extension of an already existent theme, for if life doesn't really exist, only partly exists, or can flicker on and off several times in the course of a page, death should have no dramatic power over the presence of a character in fiction. The dog's final "appearance" is reminiscent of the fateful marker of narrative closure provided by the reappearance of the blind man at the moment of Madame Bovary's death. (Both the blind man and the dog take their final bows offstage; they are heard by the characters but not seen by the reader.) The relevance of Flaubert's novel has been signaled by a disparaging comment about Martha added to the translation: "She was no Emma, and no Anna" (101). In another added line, Dreyer recalls a remark by his former mistress: "You are touched not by the blind man but by his dog" (235, cf. *280*).[11]

These changes were meant to give *King, Queen, Knave* more complexity—Nabokov had sought to "develop" its "texture" in his rewriting (ix). But might not they have a contrary effect, making the novel too simple by overwhelming it with overlapping authorial codes, the blatancy of which, once they are glimpsed, swamps all other aspects of the text? This is a question that already loomed at the conclusion of my reading of *The Defense,* but even in that "mechanical" novel, the allegorical focus of reference is hidden in a variety of contexts, and the overall impression, at least for me, is more one of repetition with difference than of reemployment of the same metafictive shorthand.

Toward the end of the novel, Dreyer attempts to sell the rights to the automata to an American investor. During the demonstration for this potential buyer, Dreyer realizes that he has lost interest in the project: "The automannequins had given all they could give. Alas, they had been pushed

---

11. Emma's final laugh—"an atrocious, frantic, despairing laugh" (quoted in *Lectures on Literature,* 170)—has been given in slightly modified form to Franz—laughing uncontrollably at the close of the novel "in a frenzy of young mirth" (272). The laugh was already present in the Russian, but the "frenzy" was added to the English, perhaps to "tease out" the similarity to Emma's "rire atroce, frénétique" (Flaubert, 383).

too far. Bluebeard had squandered his hypnotic force, and now they had lost all significance, all life and charm. He was grateful to them, in a vague sort of way, for the magical task they had performed, the excitement, the expectations. But they only disgusted him now" (263). In the original Russian, this passage was much longer; in fact, this is one of the few places in the greatly rewritten chapter 13 where the original passage occupied more space than in the revision:

> *I vdrug Draieru stalo skuchno. Ocharovanie isparilos'. Eti elektricheskie luna-tiki dvigalis' slishkom odnoobrazno, i chto-to nepriiatnoe bylo v ikh litsakh,— sosredotochennoe i pritornoe vyrazhenie, kotoroe on videl uzhe mnogo raz. Konechno, gibkost' ikh bylo nechto novoe, konechno, oni byli iziashchno i miagko srabotany,—i vse-taki ot nikh teper' veialo skukoi,—osobenno iunosha v belykh shtanakh byl nevynosim. [...] I Draier ponial, chto vse, chto mogli dat' eti figury, oni uzhe dali,—chto teper' oni bol'she ne nuzhny, lisheny dushi i prelesti, i znacheniia. On im byl smutno blagodaren za to volshebnoe delo, kotoroe oni vypolnili. No teper' volshebstvo strannym obrazom vydokh-los'. Ot ikh nezhnoi sonnosti tol'ko pretilo. Zateiia nadoela. [...] Figury umerli (296–97).*

> And suddenly Dreyer became bored. The enchantment had evaporated. These electrical lunatics were moving too monotonously, and there was something unpleasant in their faces—a concentrated and cloying expression which he had already seen many times. Of course, their flexibility was something new, of course they were elegantly and dexterously made, but all the same now they induced boredom. The young man in white trousers, especially, was unbearable. [...] Dreyer understood that these figures had already given all that they had to give now they were no longer needed, they had been deprived of their souls, charm and significance. He was dimly grateful for the magical service they had performed. But now, strangely, the magic had died out. Their tender lassitude only disgusted him. The conceit had grown boring. [...] The figures had died.

In the translation, the scene describing the demonstration has a few added piquant details—the lack of a bosom makes one robot seem like a "female impersonator," and the inventor now has a couple of effeminate assistants—but this reference to monotony is repressed, although it is arguable that the English version, by relying on far more intrusive, more predictable codes, is the more monotonous text, thus "developing" or "teasing out" the theme of boredom suggested by the end of the Russian version. In both cases, of course, Nabokov is signaling the reader that it is time for the characters in his novel to go. This works well in the Russian, where "the *figures* have died," but there is something paradoxical about the idea of these three figures having a second life in the English text. By the end of the novel the characters have become corpses—either literally (in Martha's case) or metafictively, by being dismissed from the text (Franz and Dreyer). Despite his insistence to the contrary in the preface, Nabokov's task in the English translation has indeed been to raise the dead. He tries to do it with "life," but it may be that in this revised novel life is overkill.

Perfectly appropriate that Nabokov should mention "teasing out" themes in his preface to *King, Queen, Knave.* Teasing was very much on his mind as he wrote *Ada.* (" "Oh, Van, oh Van, we did not love her enough. [. . .] We *teased* her to death!" [586]). Teasing is the defining poetic mode of that novel. But *Ada* also gave Nabokov the opportunity to develop and tease out a theme that had preoccupied him for at lest thirty years. He had translated Gertrude's recitation of Ophelia's death in 1930, and, as we have seen, his poetic preoccupation and investment in that scene only intensified upon his becoming an English-language author. Ophelia's death lies at the heart of *Bend Sinister,* and she floats through the entire narrative of *Pnin,* serving as a model for the narrator's harsh metafictive treatment of the hero. *Pale Fire*'s Hazel is to some extent an Ophelia figure, collateral damage in Kinbote's narrative duel with Shade, and Brian Boyd has made a strong case for her role as an inspirational force behind both those characters' work (*Nabokov's "Pale Fire,"* 149–87). In *Ada,* though, Ophelia attains her most overt presence, as the character "teased to death."

Ophelia is named explicitly five times in the novel—in reference once to Marina, twice to Ada, and twice to Lucette—but the first three mentions merely put the theme on the table. By the end of the novel, the reader knows that Ophelia has been reincarnated (and drowned again) as Lucette. Van makes this quite clear in a letter after her death:

As a psychologist, I know the unsoundness of speculations as to whether Ophelia would not hove drowned herself after all, without the help of a treacherous sliver, even if she had married her Voltemand. Impersonally I believe she would have died in her bed, gray and serene, had V. loved her; but since he did not really love the wretched little virgin, and since no amount of carnal tenderness could or can pass for true love, and since, above all, the fatal Andalusian wench who had come, I repeat, into the picture, was unforgettable, I am bound to arrive, dear

Ada and dear Andrey, at the conclusion that whatever the miserable man could have thought up, she would have *pokonchila s soboy* ("put an end to herself") all the same. (497–98)

For Boyd, who has written a monograph on the novel and who continues to annotate it online, Lucette stands at the novel's moral core. She dies because she has loved her "cousin" Van passionately since girlhood, but he has repeatedly spurned her in favor of his lifelong love for their sister, Ada. She has been an onlooker of their trysts, and though she has been instructed in all sorts of Sapphic pleasures by Ada, she and Van have never engaged in intercourse. According to Boyd, the novel's principal lesson is that one can injure others by blindly pursuing one's own passion. Van and Ada "have reveled quite magnificently in the infinity of their own emotion for each other—as if the privilege of an infinity of emotion for another person could exist without one's also being interconnected with other lives and without one's being responsible for each of those interconnections" (144). They—and Ada in particular—have ignored Lucette's feelings; worse, they have subjected her to a form of sexual abuse: "Lucette is initiated too early and for that reason becomes tragically fixed on the idea of Van's deflowering her" (123). This is the essence of their fatal "teasing." The reader, admiring Van's and Ada's cleverness, perhaps envying the intensity of their passion, can be seduced by their seeming attractiveness, but Lucette's death is a reminder of "the mortal price of beauty"—in this sense the novel's ethical force is much like *Lolita*'s. Commenting on what he sees as Nabokov's implicit rebuke of Van and Ada for rudeness toward their mother, Marina, Boyd writes: "there would be very few indeed who would read *Ada* without being lulled into any such moral lapses, and those few obviously do not need Nabokov's sudden correctives. For the rest of us, though, Nabokov's fiction can prove to be a healthy lesson—and it makes us keep on learning, usually about lapses far more serious than mere conversational rudeness" (59).

For Boyd, *Ada* succeeds because it is both a beautiful and a subtly didactic work. Nabokov's ethics and metaphysics "offer a tentative promise of successive enrichments of reality and at the same time an insistence that the world of real, responsible life is the only one we know and the only one in which we act" (236). At times immoderately effusive in his praise—"Has masturbation ever been rendered so artfully, so lyrically" (*Ada* online)—he portrays the novel as the height of Nabokov's artistry, comparing it to *King Lear* and Beethoven's Ninth Symphony (257). Boyd's appreciation of the text's virtues reaches a crescendo in his book's final chapter, "Ada's Allure": "Never before has a novel made the accumulation of human experience over a lifetime seem so richly romantic, never, not even in Proust, has the shock of the present been so amplified by the repetition, recollection, anticipation, regret, remorse, amusement, and rapture. Never before has a novel suggested quite how inexhaustible a story a life can build up in time" (315–16).

Boyd does not mean to channel Humbert—"Never in my life—not even when fondling my child-love in France—never"—but I think it might be worthwhile thinking about what "life" in that last sentence ("Never before has a novel suggested quite how inexhaustible a story a life can build up in time") would mean if Humbert or Van had spoken it.

In the sexualized, punning sense there are very few novels as "alive" as this one. Just as in *Lolita* Humbert occasionally tries to insert as many bawdy words into a sentence as would be grammatically possible, so in *Ada* Nabokov appears to be striving for new quantitative and qualitative records in the inventiveness of verbal sexual positionings. How inexhaustible a story *can* "life" build up in novelistic time? What is the perverse reader's lexical stamina? Will we measure up to the characters and keep from becoming exhausted ourselves?

Boyd writes compellingly about the deployment of "crosses" in the novel. One of its appearances is in the novel's coined word for Lucette's clitoris— her little cross, or *krestik*. Boyd suggests that Lucette is a victim of a kind of sexual torture (182–83). Michael Wood, who likes the novel far less, hints at a different sort of torture:

> What has happened here is that the "idiotically sly novelist" of old has become the idiotically friendly punster; but behind both of them lurks a more interesting figure, a writer who cannot hear a word as saying only one thing if there is a chance that it can be got to say more, by whatever contortions of tongue or syntax. (211)

Wood is not speaking here about sex, but so many of the quibbles in *Ada* are sexual that in its own attitude toward language the narration captures the avidity of its heroes for intercourse. The issue is not so much sex scenes in the conventional sense of the term—although there is no shortage of those—rather, sex is playfully suggested virtually everywhere; the book sets impressive standards for lexical nymphomania and satyriasis. We will look at some of these moments of innuendo—to do more would be to come close to rewriting *Ada* without Nabokov's skill—but as we pursue this path, it is well to bear several considerations in mind. The first is the question of excess. At what point does the constant punning sexual banter become a form of pathology? On one hand, the play between author and reader is one of gamesmanship. Is our French, our lexical libido, the voraciousness of our attention to language, the tenderness and dexterity of our fondling of details, up to the level of the author? On the other hand, when we do miss something, when we do tire, is that a sign of weakness or of health? Some readers may find that even when we stick with Nabokov, we begin to enjoy the game less; the fun—as Nabokov said about Austen—is forced, and it takes a specially inventive turn of phrase to reinvigorate us, so that even if we groan, we then find something wonderful.

A second, related question concerns the aesthetic value of such play. If the play becomes repetitive enough, it begins to approach code, so that a reader, attuned to it, finds that solving the puns can become like the cliché of "tired" sex engaged in too often with the same partner. The sheer size of *Ada*— especially as compared to the brevity of the one chapter which does explicitly discuss codes—would seem to weigh against Ada's belonging to that genre, yet the essentially binary nature of the items continually referred to by the lush linguistic play raises the question of whether the "timelessness" of *Ada*'s paradise might not be reducible to an endless series of verbal transpositions of the male and female sex organs. In an early, measured, but still appreciative reading of *Ada,* Robert Alter suggested that one could look past the verbal gamesmanship, which he also characterized as code:

> Fortunately, the code-games and allusions in *Ada* are merely pointers to the peculiar nature of the novel's imaginative richness, which does not finally depend on the clues. Despite its incidental annoyances and even its occasional *longeurs,* few books written in our lifetime afford so much pleasure. ("*Ada,* or the Perils of Paradise," 118)

How separable, though, are the novel's pleasures from its code? And in what do the pleasures consist? Alter, like the aesthetically more reproving Wood after him, suggests that the pleasures are stylistic—he compliments the richness of the writing and the density of the allusions. Given the thoroughgoing eroticization of the work's verbal texture, an appreciation of the language may entail approval of stylistic wantonness and "exuberance." Alter prizes above all the work's "lyrical" qualities, though he realizes this may make it less successful as a novel: "Van and Ada sometimes seem to be more voices and images in a lyric poem than novelistic characters; the excess of formal perfection they must sustain makes them less interesting individually, less humanly engaging, than many of Nabokov's previous protagonists" (112). Caring less about the characters, Alter necessarily devotes much less time than Boyd to Lucette, mentioning her just four times in his fifteen-page article. As I think Boyd implicitly realizes, once you decide that the characters matter less than the verbal texture (which is what, after all, Nabokov said about

Shakespeare), the eroticism suffusing the novel becomes poetically dominant and the lesson of Lucette's fate matters less. If the reader doesn't care about the characters, the sex scenes and the sex in the scenery begin to take over, and we are left with a highly stylized work that in its consecutive and nearly constant coupling is indebted to the poetics of pornography. Indeed, since the lexical sex can occur nearly anywhere, we can see all the action on the microlevel of the text as the equivalent of the "big parts and close-ups" in pornographic film.

There are many places in *Ada* where Nabokov calls attention to the smallest units of sexual code. Several instances of this device baring are particularly worthy of notice. The night of the burning barn, *Ada's* equivalent of *Lolita's* davenport scene, Ada and Van's first coupling is described through a lexicographer's detour: "For the first time in their love story the blessing, the genius of lyrical speech descended upon the rough lad, he murmured and moaned, kissing her face with voluble tenderness, crying out in three languages—the three greatest in all the world—pet words upon which a dictionary of secret diminutives was to be based and go through many revisions till the definitive edition of 1967" (121). Boyd rightly suggests that this dictionary is *Ada* itself (*Ada* online). Throughout the novel, the characters find words exciting, and this is obviously a thrill Nabokov hopes his reader shares. Moments where words are defined, discussed, and fondled are offered as the good reader's equivalent of voyeur scenes in pornography, where a character within the story or film serving as the viewer's or reader's stand-in watches sexual activity and becomes aroused.

> Speaking as a botanist and a madwoman, she said, the most extraordinary word in the English language was "husked," because it stood for opposite things, covered and uncovered, tightly husked but easily husked, meaning they peel off quite easily, you don't have to tear the waistband, you brute. "Carefully husked brute," said Van tenderly. The passage of time could only enhance his tenderness for the creature he clasped, this adored creature, whose motion was now more supple, whose haunches had grown more lyrate, whose hair-ribbon he had undone. (267)

The implicit Ophelia reference here ("a botanist and a madwoman") establishes the connection between libidinal flower picking (or any other form of erotic collecting) and word gathering. Another, equally important code-defining moment comes with Van's lecturing:

> Now the mistake—the lewd, ludicrous and vulgar mistake of the Signy-Mondieu analysts consists in their regarding a real object, a pompon, say,

or a pumpkin (actually seen in a dream by the patient) as a significant abstraction of the real object, as a bumpkin's bonbon or one-half of the bust if you know what I mean (scattered giggles). There can be no emblem or parable in a village idiot's hallucinations or in last night's dream of any of us in this hall. In those random visions nothing— underscore "nothing" (grating sound of horizontal strokes)—can be construed as allowing itself to be deciphered by a witch doctor who can then cure a madman or give comfort to a killer by laying the blame on a too fond, too fiendish or too indifferent parent—secret festerings that the foster quack feigns to heal by expensive confession fests (laughter and applause). (363–64)

Although Van seems to be rejecting the idea of interpretive codes altogether, his enthusiastically received lecture should be read as the privileging of a Shakespearean code over a Freudian one. In effect, Van is arguing against an iconic, Freudian code in favor of a verbal, Shakespearean one—even if, in fact, Freud appreciated wordplay and Shakespeare made use of obvious anatomical symbolism. Both relied on sexual codes, but Shakespeare's use of language was playful, literary, and focused on the conscious deployment of language, while Freud's was pseudoscientific and always had the unconscious in its sights. Van's comments indicate an awareness that the two codes are, in a way, competitors.

On the basis of the hints offered in these two passages, it would not be difficult to put together a glossary of secret diminutives, indebted to Shakespeare, French erotic poetry, and a few choice Russian obscenities. Indeed, computer search engines make this sort of thing all too easy, once one chooses the right terms and employs the right mental filter.

One could start with "spirit," meaning "erection" or "semen" (Booth, 441–42): "Details of the L disaster [...] are too well-known historically, and too obscene spiritually, to be treated at length in a book addressed to laymen and lemans" (17). "A billion of Bills, good, gifted, tender and passionate, not only spiritually but physically well-meaning Billions, have bared the jillions of their no less tender and brilliant Jills" (70). We can move by relay to the vaginal "case": "A diligent student of case histories, Dr. Van Veen never quite managed to match ardent twelve-year-old Ada with a non-delinquent, non-nymphomaniac, mentally highly developed, spiritually happy and normal English child" (219). The concordance entry for case would be quite long: Lucette provides "a gripping and palpitating little case history" (381), "another case (with a quibble on *cas*) engaged his attention subverbally" (484), "conceived, *c'est bien le cas de le dire*" (26). Ada says menstruation "would certainly not occur in her case" (80). We could continue this sort of pudendal variation on *Pale Fire*'s game of "word golf" by having "case" pass off to another monosyllable, "*con*": "*Per contra,* the omission of panties was ignored by Ida Lariviere, a bosomy woman of great and repulsive beauty (in nothing but corset and gartered stockings at the moment) who was not above making secret concessions to the heat of the dog-days herself; but in tender Ada's case the practice had deprecable effects" (77–78). The next sentence in *Ada* immediately takes us to the "Shattal apple tree," for the name of which Boyd provides all sorts of complicated geographic explanations when phonetics alone (*chatte*) would suffice; we will later have another suggestively named tree—in Kim's pornographic album, which opens with "preparatory views" of "the colutea circle, an avenue, the grotto's black O, and the hill, and the big chain around the trunk of the rare oak, *Quercus ruslan* Chat" (398). This last chain of verbal combinations (circle, grotto, O, Chat), may provide as much justification for Kim's blinding as anything else he photographs, for here he does to "Ruslan and Liudmila"'s opening lines—"A green oak grows by the cove; / On the oak is a golden chain; / And day and night a learned cat / Keeps walking around it on the chain"—what Mariette did to Pushkin's nickname in *Bend Sinister.* And we shouldn't forget that "*nick*names" itself is the category we have been tracking, as Ada notes in her criticism of poor Fowler's inept poetry translations: "The forged *louis d'or* in that collection of fouled French is the transformation of *souci d'eau* (our marsh marigold) into the asinine 'care of the water'—although he had at his disposal dozens of synonyms, such as mollyblob, marybud, maybubble, and many other nicknames associated with fertility feasts" (65). Souci d'O indeed! The problem with Fowler's asinine translation might not be what he does with "souci" but with what he doesn't do with "eau."

Further items in the Concordance:

Chose: 1. "'tell him about your success in London. *Zhe tampri* (please)!' 'Yes,' said Van, 'it all started as a rag you know, up at Chose'" (271–72); 2. "la force des choses ('the fever of intercourse')" (405); 3. "Van, in whom the pink-blooming chestnuts of Chose always induced an amorous mood" (470); 4. "the time he had refused to show her some silly Chose snapshots of punt girls and had torn them up in fury and she had looked away knitting her brows and slitting her eyes at an invisible view in the window. Or that time she had hesitated, blinking, shaping a soundless word, suspecting him of a sudden revolt against her odd prudishness of speech, when he challenged her brusquely to find a rhyme to 'patio' and she was not quite sure if he had in mind a certain foul word and if so what was its correct pronunciation" (297).

Nature: 1. "'Nature, as I informed you once, has been kind to me. We can afford to be careless in every sense of the word'" (442, referring to Ada's inability to become pregnant); 2. "Her drawing teacher, Miss Wintergreen, respected him greatly, though actually her *natures mortes* were considered incomparably superior to the works of the celebrated old rascal who drew his diminutive nudes invariably from behind— fig-picking, peach-buttocked nymphets straining upward, or else rock-climbing girl scouts in bursting shorts" (111); 3. "'Naturally,' continued Demon, 'there is a good deal to be said for a restful summer in the country. . . .' 'Open air life and all that,' said Van" (244); 4. Mlle Larivière, on being told by Ada that normal girls no longer menstruate, wonders if "the progress of science had not changed that of nature" (81).[12]

Nothing: 1. "'we were just ordinary sisters, exchanging routine nothings'" (376); 2. "'There is nothing to know,' retorted Van. 'Nothing, nothing has changed! But that's the general impression, it was too dim down there for details, we'll examine them tomorrow on our little island'" (192).

Life: 1. "'All in all, I suppose I have had her about a thousand times. She is my whole life'" (440); 2. Kim, the pornographic photographer, "'lectures, if you please, on the Art of Shooting Life'" (397); 3. "'But girls— do you like girls, Van, do you have many girls? You are not a pederast, like your poor uncle, are you? We have had some dreadful perverts in our ancestry but—Why do you laugh?' 'Nothing,' said Van. 'I just want to put on record that I adore girls.' [. . .] 'How strange, how sad! Sad, because I know hardly anything about your life, my darling'" (233).

---

12. On the basis of lines from *Pale Fire* that we have already looked at once: "But like some little lad forced by a wench / With his pure tongue her abject thirst to quench, / I was corrupted, terrified, allured." Jim Twiggs has suggested in a posting on NABOKV-L that John Shade was sexually abused as a child by his aunt Maude. In several earlier lines he finds further evidence of one of her abusive sexual practices: "How fully I felt nature glued to me / And how my childish palate loved the taste / Half-fish, half-honey, of that golden paste!" Twiggs comments: "Any grown man with a lick of worldly experience ought to be struck, on a first reading, by the strong sexual connotations of the words 'honey,' 'fish,' and 'taste.' Then he might decide that what's being talked about here is merely the liquid glue that children use for pasting items in scrapbooks. But then, when he reaches lines 161–62, he may once again want to reconsider. If he does, the image that comes to mind—Aunt Maud's pudenda plastered to a small boy's face—might seem as funny, in a very Nabokovian way, as it is appalling." The frequent plays on "nature" in *Lolita* and *Ada* would seem to lend support to Twiggs's suggestion, but rather than adopting a psychoanalytic explanation on the basis of very little evidence and concluding that Shade's poetry is a response to trauma, it makes more sense to see these lines as another erotic flicker, a wink at the reader, and an indication of the presence of erotic elements in Shade's attitude toward nature (rather than to any one person's "nature" in particular). See Jerry Friedman's response to Twiggs in this vein.

Idiot (via the secondary meaning of *con*): 1. "'*Je ne peux rien faire,*' wailed Lucette, '*mais rien*—with my idiotic Buchstaben'" (227); 2. "Her spectacular handling of subordinate clauses, her parenthetic asides, her sensual stressing of adjacent monosyllables ('idiot Elsie simply *can't read*')— all this somehow finished by acting upon Van, as artificial excitements and exotic torture-caresses might have done, in an aphrodisiac sinistral direction that he both resented and perversely enjoyed" (67). *Monosyllable* was lexicographer-talk for 'cunt' into the twentieth century. (Grose, 235) Cf. "I derived some fun from that nuptial night and had the idiot in hysterics by sunrise" (*Lolita,* 26).

Is this any way to read a novel? In a small article entitled "D'O You Get the Joke?" Boyd expresses his appreciation for Nabokov's sense of humor in *Ada.* For all his past attention to the name of the character "Baron d'O" (Onegin, the real Baron d'Onsky, Don Juan), Boyd good-humoredly notes that he has only recently noticed "the extra joke in d'O's name": *d'eau,* meaning "of water." The irony, which Boyd appreciates, is that he has written extensively (and well) of the significance in *Ada* of water ("the element in which Lucette drowns," "the element which holds Antiterra" together). Now that he sees that joke, he grins at his earlier blindness:

> Nabokov allows us inexhaustible discoveries as we reread, but from the first he offers humor that stays funny *even* as we reread. When the two combine, so that we discover after many rereadings a joke that had been staring us in the face, and that at the same time links with other discoveries we have already made, we can almost imagine we see him twinking with pleasure at the pleasure he was hiding for us to find. (9)

The joke, here, however, is also that Boyd, even as he writes this article, does not see anything bawdy in "O." And although he is certainly willing to discuss sex in his annotations, many of the obvious glossary terms mentioned above slip by his closely reading eyes. There is a reason, I think, for this lack of perspicacity in someone who is in many other respects a brilliant interpreter. When the canvas becomes too sexually saturated, when it begins to sink into repetitive code, and when the genitalia become too visible, the characters count less as people, and the moral message begins to slip away. The fault may be the perversity of the reader, or it may be the design of the text—or it may be both if the perverse reader is the product of the text. This was the crux of the problem surrounding Boyd's extended attack on Rowe, the scholar who, in many ways, has been the heroic Pnin of my book. In his monograph on *Ada,* where he devotes sixteen pages—an entire appendix—to

Rowe, Boyd takes as his model of Rowe's ineptitude a passage mentioned in passing by Nabokov in his own attack on that scholar. In this section of his book Rowe analyzes the scene of Ada's literal "fall" from the Shattal tree. (Ada will tumble from a branch and Van ends up with his head in her crotch. She is not wearing underwear and the result causes even punctuation to come undone: "his expressionless face and cropped head were between her legs and a last fruit fell with a thud—the dropped dot of an inverted exclamation point" [94]). Rowe begins by quoting Nabokov:

> Van, in a blue gym suit, having worked his way up to a fork just under his agile playmate...betokened mute communication by taking her ankle between finger and thumb as *she* would have a closed butterfly. (*Ada,* 94; Rowe, *Nabokov's Deceptive World,* 112–13)
>
> "Butterfly," in Nabokov's works, can often be seen to symbolize the female private parts. Above, one has only to read the word *as* as *when* (or especially as *since*) to effect the transformation, which is carefully screened, but not at all encumbered, by the italics of "*she*." (Rowe, 113)

The stakes in Boyd's refutation make it worthwhile to pay close attention to his argument:

> Rowe does not explain *why* we should change the words a writer has settled on after long deliberation. But in any case he seems too excited by the possibility of having a vagina in the sentence to think what happens if we do take his suggestion. If we substitute *when* for *as,* we might momentarily construe the meaning to be that Van took Ada by the ankle between finger and thumb when she would have a closed vagina. The subordinate verb however now has a conditional and recurrent value, while the action of the main clause happens only on one occasion. So in fact with the proposed transformation the sentence becomes the impossible: he took her ankle (once), when(ever) she would have a closed vagina. Hmm. Shall we try *since*? He took her ankle since she would have taken a closed vagina. Sigh.

In this scene Van and Ada though each in love with the other are still far from being lovers and have had no sexual contact of any kind, so that when they tumble and Van's mouth accidentally presses against Ada's naked crotch, it seems as if gravity itself were conspiring to promote their relationship. So far as I understand it, Rowe suggests that there is some playful implication that Van signals to Ada by pinching her ankle, only because her vagina is closed; if it were open, he would signal by pinching her there. Even if this worked grammatically, which it doesn't, Rowe's suggestion of such a signaling at this stage of Van and

Ada's relationship simply destroys the whole point of the scene: that the kiss on Ada's crotch is an undreamt-of advance on their previous intimacy. (242)

Boyd's insistence on reducing the text to pure denotation, on straightening out the meaning into a paraphrase, not only reflects a fundamental misunderstanding of how erotic suggestion works but also misses what Nabokov specifically mentions in Rowe's symbols as irritating him in this instance: Rowe's "tamper[ing]" with the passage's wording. If we return to the original passage, we see that it is even more suggestive than Rowe realized:

> Van, in blue gym suit, having worked his way up to a fork just under his agile playmate (who naturally was better acquainted with the tree's intricate map) but not being able to see her face, betokened mute communication by taking her ankle between finger and thumb as *she* would have a closed butterfly. (94)

This scene, set as they climb "the glossy-limbed Shattal tree at the bottom of the garden" is coded, even overcoded with pudendal synonyms, including the parenthetical "*naturally* . . . better a*cquaint*ed." (In addition, Van is working his way up to a *fork*). In this lexical environment a twisted reading of "as she would have a closed butterfly" is entirely warranted. It has nothing to do with a signal Van is sending to Ada—it is entirely about Nabokov's teasing of the reader.

Boyd's hostility to Rowe rests partly on the consequences of Rowe's approach for an ethically oriented, character-centered reading, partly and less interestingly on questions of priority—who saw what first. Most significant of all, however, is the import of Rowe's method for an understanding of *all* Nabokov's work. By insisting that all of Nabokov's work could be read through attention to shorthand, to consistently applied verbal symbols (for pudenda, for ghosts), Rowe broke down the barriers between distinct works. Applying the same codes to book after book, he could, especially in *Nabokov's Spectral Dimension,* race through Nabokov's oeuvre with speed offensive to a scholar devoting an entire monograph to a single novel. In comparison with the care Boyd devotes to a specific text, Rowe's readings are extraordinarily quick connections.

But is this Rowe's fault? In regard to *Ada's* defects, Alter writes: "At the book's weaker moments, one feels that the novelist permits himself too much, inadvertently unraveling threads in his own rich tapestry through his eagerness to pursue every linguistic quibble, every gratuitous turn of a sexual or literary double meaning" (104). One could go further. As Rowe's example proves, *Ada* provides the basis for an unraveling of just about everything

Nabokov ever wrote. Virtually any novel can now be read through *Ada;* the temptation to use Nabokov's longest novel as a crib for the earlier master-pieces is hard to resist. Sexual meanings which might be regarded as artful when latent can tip a work into crudeness or predictability if too many of them are seen as overt.

Boyd is upset that Rowe does not dwell longer over each text. He is appalled by the proliferation of examples cited by his colleague. His principal objec-tion to Rowe is that in both his books "Rowe simply does not know where to stop" (240). Perhaps in the late 1960s neither did Vladimir Nabokov.

In *Bend Sinister* Nabokov depicted a world shaped by a sinistrally inflected dictatorship of art. *Ada* can be read as another novel about art's wanton potential. Robert Alter wonders if in *Ada* Nabokov meant "to suggest that there is something ultimately monstrous about the artistic imagination itself; that, given absolute freedom, it will conjure up not only beautiful birds of paradise but the most fearful monstrosities as well" (117). What does this mean for the good reader? Is it possible to recuperate the sexual excess of the novel into a metafictive, if not a moral fable? Such an approach might start with a rereading of the novel's version of Scrabble:

> Pedantic Ada once said that the looking up of words in a lexicon for any other needs than those of expression—be it instruction or art—lay somewhere between the ornamental assortment of flowers (which could be, she conceded, mildly romantic in a maidenly headcocking way) and making collage-pictures of disparate butterfly wings (which was always vulgar and often criminal). *Per contra,* she suggested to Van that verbal circuses, "performing words," "poodle-doodles," and so forth, might be redeemable by the quality of the brain work required for the creation of a great logograph or inspired pun and should not preclude the help of a dictionary, gruff or complacent.

> That was why she admitted "Flavita." The name came from *alfavit,* an old Russian game of chance and skill, based on the scrambling and unscrambling of alphabetic letters. (222)

D. Barton Johnson has provided an exemplary analysis of the novel's Scrabble games in an article memorably subtitled "Taking Nabokov Clito-rally" (*Worlds in Regression,* 51–59). He doesn't comment on the name of the game (alfaVIT) or the necessity of a "lexiCON" to play it, but he does note that whether or not one agrees with Ada's sentiments on brainwork may reflect what one thinks of the novel as a whole.

Flavita offers the lexical equivalent of an extreme pornographic close-up. At first, it isn't clear what one is looking at or reading, until there is a focal adjustment. The discussion of Flavita in the novel revolves around the letters Lucette puts in her "groove" and her initial difficulties deciphering them. She has trouble finding MERKIN in REMNILK—"*Je ne peux rien faire, mais rien*—with my idiotic Buchstaben"—or KLITOR (Russian for clitoris) in LIKROTL. Lucette, though, is a quick study, and soon she is engaging in bawdy sexual banter to such an extent that Van can speak about her as "punning in an Ophelian frenzy on the feminine glans" (394). Regardless of how Lucette came to be that way, Ada is probably right when she says "that child has the dirtiest mind imaginable" (289). Ada's opinion is borne out by Lucette's description of her preferred activities and topics:

> "I enjoy—oh, loads of things," she continued in a melancholy, musing tone of voice, as she poked with a fork at her blue trout which, to judge by its contorted shape and bulging eyes, had boiled alive, convulsed by awful agonies. "I love Flemish and Dutch oils, flowers, food, Flaubert, Shakespeare, shopping, sheeing, swimming, the kisses of beauties and beasts—but somehow all of it, this sauce and all the riches of Holland, form only a kind of *tonen'kiy-tonen'kiy* (thin little) layer, under which there is absolutely nothing, except, of course, your image, and that only adds depth and a trout's agonies to the emptiness." (464)

Lucette does not enjoy this banter, it is an effect of the agonized torment inflicted on her by her passion for Van. For all her participation in Van's and Ada's wordplay, she has "a dull life" (464); she watches, exchanges "nothings" with Ada, but is never—with the exception of an abortive triple tryst designed by Ada—allowed to come close to intercourse with Van. In this respect, she is a female version of "A Nursery Tale"'s Erwin: a reader who cannot sexually engage with the objects in the texts in front of her. She yearns to transcend language, to participate in sexual, as opposed to verbal, intercourse with Van:

> Long ago she had made up her mind that by forcing the man whom she absurdly but irrevocably loved to have intercourse with her, even once, she would, somehow, with the help of some prodigious act of nature, transform a brief tactile event into an eternal spiritual tie; but she also knew that if it did not happen on the first night of their voyage, their relationship would slip back into the exhausting, hopeless, hopelessly familiar pattern of banter and counterbanter, with the erotic edge taken for granted, but kept as raw as ever. (485)

Lucette's failure to produce this prodigious act of nature leads her to emulate Ophelia and jump into the sea, where "she did not see her whole life flash before her" and where, like "a dilettante Tobakoff" she swims in "a *circle* of brief pa*nic*" (494, emphasis added). (The original Tobakoff once fell into the deep and "swam around comfortably for hours, frightening away sharks with snatches of old songs and that sort of thing" (480), but Lucette is not so lucky.) Her death in the "complicated waters" (495), may be a return to origins, to the sexual yearning—*l'eau*/O—that has defined and ruined her "like a creature native and indued unto that element." It is also, however, an attempt to escape from the sexual frustration of *only* reading. The story she has been watching—and that we have been reading—has "teased her to death."

In empathizing with Lucette, in according this moment a moral pathos unrivaled elsewhere in the book, the reader who cares can seek to escape from the control of Ada's erotic poetics as well. Not surprisingly, Boyd isolates Lucette's drowning as the moment of the book's greatest moral relevance to the reader's extratextual existence. According to Boyd, it is from here that the book sends us spinning back through the text, appalled by the realization that we have been ignoring Lucette's pain and are somewhat complicit in her death.[13] Her fate, he argues, gives us a "healthy" and "stern lesson" that we can take out into real life (59, 183). The novel itself both supports and complicates this reading. A passage several hundred pages earlier seems particularly relevant:

> It would not be sufficient to say that in his love-making with Ada he discovered the pang, the *ogon'*, the agony of supreme "reality." Reality, better say, lost the quotes it wore like claws—in a world where independent and original minds must cling to things or pull things apart in order to ward off madness or death (which is the master madness). For one spasm or two, he was safe. The new naked reality needed no tentacle or anchor; it lasted a moment, but could be repeated as often as he and she were physically able to make love. (219–20)

For Van, sex is the locus of extraverbal reality. In this place of security he does not need to make sense of things. Outside of sex, we avoid death by frantically struggling either to make connections or to avoid making them.

---

13. Indeed, for Boyd, Lucette seems to represent the moral principal of reality itself: "Van can see that Lucette is not someone with whom he can just engage in sex without considering the rest of her life: she is simply too real for him. Yet he cannot see that others, too, whom he uses merely as whores, are equally real, have lives that extend beyond his need for them and that must be affected by their contact with him. [...] They may be degraded into accepting their being used as means, but nevertheless they too are real, and though Van recognizes the reality of Lucette's life, it is an appalling failure of his imagination that he can still treat all other women as if, almost, they had no life beyond their existence as a means to fulfilling his 'needs'" (167–68).

When the quotation marks are put back on, naked reality disappears, and we struggle in a sea of language to interpret. Indeed, the passage suggests that interpretation is what we must do to survive when we are not having sex. Moreover, in retrospect, the phrases "cling to things" and "the new naked reality needed no tentacle or anchor" seem ominous, directing us to the scene of Lucette's death, as dictated by Van to his typist: "owing to the tumultuous swell and her not being sure which way to peer through the spray and the darkness and her own tentaclinging hair—t, a, c, l—she could not make out the lights of the liner" (494). The connection of the two scenes suggests that Van's and Ada's extratextual reality does have a price—Lucette; their sexual intercourse sends out tentacles that lead to Lucette's suicide. Her death is reality's anchor: this is where the hard lessons of real life begin.

The spelling out of letters for Van's typist reinforces, as Boyd has argued, the linkage of Lucette to the theme of letters. It may even be that three of these letters (t, c, l) echo verbally or reflect visually both Lucette's name and the word (*klitor*) Lucette didn't realize she could make. For Rowe, the letters are crucial to finding Lucette's spirit in communication with Van after her death—he ingeniously points out that they are present in the erotic dream Van experiences in 1905 ("he sat on the *talc* of a tropical beach full of sun baskers, and one moment was rubbing the red, irritated shaft of a writhing boy") (520); and if he is correct, the dream marks a life after death for Lucette's sexual frenzy, even if it has shifted it from one sex to the other. Van awakes, and Ada enters his bedchamber, but before they can make love he has to visit the W.C., more letters that he here rechristens as "*the petit endroit*" (521), a phrase that recalls Lucette's nickname of Pet. Throughout this affair, Van and Ada "have the feeling of still being under the protection of those painted Priapi that the Romans once used...," but it seems more likely that they are under the protection of Lucette: "A boxwood-lined path, presided over by a nostalgic-looking sempervirent sequoia (which American visitors mistook for a 'Lebanese cedar'—if they remarked it at all) took them to the absurdly misnamed *rue du Mûrier,* where a princely paulownia ('mulberry tree!' snorted Ada), standing in state on its incongruous terrace above a public W.C., was shedding generously its heart-shaped dark green leaves, but retained enough foliage to cast arabesques of shadow onto the south side of its trunk" (522). Here the shedding of the leaves recalls Lucette's role as the eavesdropper and leavesdropper of an earlier scene (98). The tree misidentified as a mulberry should bring to mind the young Lucette's excited play in a bathroom with a cake of mulberry soap between her legs as she pretends to be Van in a state of sexual excitement (144); as Mason notes, even the tree's incorrect identification links it to Lucette, since it was by a cedar at Ardis that Ada and Lucette teased Van and kissed each other (41). Moreover, the mulberry's "standing in state" echoes one of the most frenzied moments of punning between Van and Lucette:

> Wincing and rearranging his legs, our young Vandemonian cursed under his breath the condition in which the image of the four embers of a vixen's cross had now solidly put him. One of the synonyms of "condition" is "state," and the adjective "human" may be construed as "manly" (since L'Humanité means "Mankind"!), and that's how, my dears, Lowden recently translated the title of the *malheureux* Pompier's cheap novel *La Condition Humaine,* wherein, incidentally, the term "Vandemonian" is hilariously glossed as *"Koulak tasmanien d'origine hollandaise."* Kick her out before it is too late. (377)

This passage, for all its organ talk (*con-dition*), bawdy diction, and disparagement of Lowell, Auden, and Malraux, makes the tree later "standing in state" sound particularly phallic.[14]

Boyd, who has made the most thoroughgoing case for the survival of Lucette's spirit after death, sees her continuing presence in the novel as a positive force. At a crucial moment after the death of Ada's husband, Ada and Van attempt to rekindle their earlier flame. It seems to be a failure, and Ada leaves, but the next morning she returns, and they are reunited for the rest of their lives. Before realizing that Ada has come back, Van has another dream: "that he was speaking in the lecturing hall of a transatlantic liner and that a bum resembling the hitch-hiker from Hilden was asking sneeringly how did the lecturer explain that in our dreams we know we shall awake, is not that analogous to the certainty of death, and if so, the future—" (561). This dream, too, has Lucette's telltale letters—transatlantic, lecturing, lecture, and so it is not surprising that Ada says she decided to turn around "'somewhere near Morzhey' ('morses' or 'walruses,' a Russian pun on 'Morges'—maybe a mermaid's message)" (562). Boyd sees this message as "an act of kindness" on the part of Lucette's spirit: "her mermaid's message is an action manifesting the generosity that characterized her in life, a free gift of kindness that becomes the basis for the happiness of Van and Ada's lives and so of *Ada* itself" (208).

---

14. Johnson has identified the various literary players (*Worlds in Regression,* 75). *Hollandaise* contains a Shakespearean vaginal or anal reference (Partridge, 121; Williams, 160); "state" is a euphemism for erection both in *Ada* ("an exhibition of his state with a humble appeal for a healing caress resulted in her drily remarking that distinguished gentlemen in public parks got quite lengthy prison terms for that sort of thing" (312) and in Sonnet 29 ("Haply I think on thee, and then my state / Like to the lark at break of day arises", see Pointer 136); "pompier," in addition to meaning "hack" may be a reference to fellatio (*faire le pompier*). When Auden, Lowell, and Malraux get together, it is difficult to say who is doing what to whom.

Boyd goes even further, arguing that "Lucette has inspired Van to write *Ada,*" because "in accordance with her deep kindness, she wishes others to share in the happiness of Van and Ada and to be warned of the need for the consideration whose absence contributed to her own suicide" (219). This is an ingenious idea, since it allows Boyd to value both the pleasures of the text and the text's ethical message, to provide a happy resolution to the aesthetic and moral dilemmas posed by the novel.[15] Boyd's sanguinity is problematic, however, for two reasons. First, Lucette may be posthumously watching over Van's and Ada's trysts, but she has not been cured of her Ophelian frenzy. As we have seen, many of the moments that recall Lucette evoke her libidinally. Even the place where Van and Ada have their happy encounter after receiving her mermaid's message—Mont Roux—equates Lucette with her genital fascination: the name reflects not only the distinctive color of Lucette's hair but also the lower "ember" of her vixen's cross: *Mon Trou.* (We are told that the mountain "lived up to its name and autumnal reputation, with a warm glow of curly chestnut trees; and on the opposite shore of Leman, Leman meaning Lover, loomed the crest of Sex Noir, Black Rock.")[16] Might Lucette's spiritual survival be a survival of "spirit" in the Shakespearean sense, of a perpetually aroused ghost that now truly has only words and letters to play with? Her continued verbal nymphomania would show that, like Luzhin, she has not escaped from the text after all; rather, she continues to observe the lovers as she did in her earlier life. For her and the reader there is no escape from the pleasure and the torture of disembodied language. Lucette does not succeed in getting "kicked out." As in Humbert's final verbal tour around Lolita's "torn and polluted" body, the language of the text indicates that nothing has (or "nothing" has not) changed. Indeed, the continued presence of Lucette's spirit indicates emphatically that yes, there is lust after death, a kind of disembodied existence where we will suffer the hell of being continually aroused. The notion of *Ada* as a dictionary of "pet diminutives"

---

15. Bobbie Mason, who also reads the novel as a moral lesson, does not see its conclusion as happy. Rather, she views the brevity of its final section as confirmation that "the Ada [Van] finally gets is a pale substitute for the delightful child sitting in the sunshine on the Ardis balcony. She is pale, bleached, and empty at the end, as is Van's goal of the pure light of paradise" (135). Mason, though, seeks to put a happy spin on the novel—and a happy ending to her study of it—by concluding with a rhetorical flourish unmotivated by the rest of her book: a celebration of "metamorphosis" that seeks to distinguish the solipsism of Van from "the imagination of the artist" (156).

16. In a posting on NABOKV-L, Boyd proposes that the actually existing Swiss town where Ada turns around may owe its appearance in *Ada* in part to a Russian intensifying expletive—*khui morzhovyi*—"walrus cock" ("Boyd on Walruses"). Boyd's suggestion should alert us—through the zoological and cryptological meanings of "morse" (see his *Nabokov's "Ada,"* 203)—to the quintessentially libidinal nature of code throughout the novel. He does not consider, however, the consequences of this insight for his assertion that the novel's happy ending implies the reconciliation of Lucette with her sibling-cousins.

would further suggest Lucette as its somewhat foul inspirer; Lucette received her own diminutive ("pet" from the French word for *fast*) on account of her "letting wee winds go free at table" (418), and these breezes serve as the lower-body equivalent of authorial, inspirational breath, a cousin to the hallucinatory "halitosis" of Kinbote in *Pale Fire* (98).

Earlier I resisted Stephen Blackwell's suggestion that Zina was a figure for the reader and a co-creator of Fyodor's novelistic text (*The Gift*). That argument would work much better for *Ada*. Occupying the position of the reader, watching, aroused by the language but textually disembodied, Lucette, if Boyd is right, inspires Van to write the novel itself. But if Lucette is capable of sending signs to the characters, and sexual ones at that, she should also be held at least partly accountable for the Ophelian erotic excitement of the entire book. Her creative presence would extend to *all* of the memoir, not just to the parts that relate to her posthumous spiritual existence.

The text hints that this is indeed the case. After Marina's death, Van "tortured himself with thoughts of insufficient filial affection—a long story of unconcern, amused scorn, physical repulsion, and habitual dismissal." He tries to make "wild amends, willing her spirit to give him an unequivocal, and indeed all-deciding, sign of continued being behind the veil of time, beyond the flesh of space." But no sign comes: "not a petal fell on his bench" (452). This is the moment when Van should realize that he is treating Lucette in many of the same ways he has treated his mother—his self-torture will be replayed after Lucette dies. However, this scene is also an echo of a previous moment, which even before Lucette's death ties this remorse (about Marina) to her and establishes Lucette as a source of signs from the earliest sections of the novel:

> After the first contact [in the Shattal tree], so light, so mute, between his soft lips and her softer skin had been established—high up in that dappled tree, with only that stray ardilla daintily leavesdropping—nothing seemed changed in one sense, all was lost in another. Such contacts evolve their own texture; a tactile sensation is a blind spot; we touch in silhouette. Henceforth, at certain moments of their otherwise indolent days, in certain recurrent circumstances of controlled madness, a secret sign was erected, a veil drawn between him and her—.(98)

The girl most immediately present in this passage is Ada, but Lucette's markings are all over—the signature squirrel (ardilla), close to the name (Ardelia) that Van mistakenly bestows on her (36), the leavesdropping, the letters in *tacti*le, the strange phrase: "we touch in *sil*h*ouette*" (this word, "silhouette," phonetically containing Lucette's name, will later be used to announce Lucette's presence in the bar [460]). The genital code is also working hard— "nothing seemed changed," Van's *cont*acts with Ada's genitals, and, above all, the "*controlled* madness" of the sex-crazed conscience which has so artfully weaved this text together.

The final pages of *Ada* artfully show how it is possible for Van and Ada to fade away into the pages of their book. This is a final acknowledgment of both their mortality within the novel and their two-dimensional immortality on the page: "One can even surmise that if our time-racked, flat-lying couple ever intended to die they would die, as it were, *into* the finished book, into Eden or Hades, into the prose of the book or the poetry of its blurb" (587). And they do, as the book segues into its own blurb in the last few paragraphs. It should be appreciated that Lucette also dies into the book—that accounts for the strange final words of the chapter relating her death, where Van desperately searches for her, "bawling the drowned girl's name in the black, foam-veined, complicated waters" (495). "Complicated" calls out itself for attention here, and I think Nabokov is using it as he did with its Russian equivalents (*skladyvat'* and *slozhnyi*) in *The Defense,* hinting at the etymology of "complicate" and the original meaning of "complicated": *folded together (Webster's New International,* 547; *OED* 3:616).[17] "One might dissolve completely that way," says Fyodor in *The Gift* (334). Lucette, the figured reader who has been kept away from the textual object of her desire, is now absorbed into the text and suffuses it entirely. Her fate, and the novel's poetics, are prefigured in the speech Van wants to make to the dying Phillip Rack, Lucette's music teacher and Ada's erstwhile lover. When Phillip is taken by the "second nothingness" of death, Van hopes that he may find not oblivion but an "Eternal Rack":

> We can imagine—I think we should imagine—tiny clusters of particles still retaining Rack's personality, gathering here and there in the here-and-there-after, clinging to each other, somehow, somewhere, a web of Rack's toothaches here, a bundle of Rack's nightmares there—rather like tiny groups of obscure refugees from some obliterated country huddling together for a little smelly warmth, for dingy charities or shared recollections of nameless tortures in Tartar camps. For an old man one special little torture must be to wait in a long long queue before a remote urinal. Well, Herr Rack, I submit that the surviving cells of aging Rackness will form such lines of torment, never, never reaching the coveted filth hole in the panic and pain of infinite night. (315)

This passage is the novel's metamessage (note the *clinging particles*): it explains just what those signs from Lucette mean in terms of the novel's formal and thematic composition. Lucette is a sign sender and code master,

---

17. See also the reference to "the complicated ecstasies accompanying the making of a young writer's first book" (*Ada,* 324).

but those mermaid's messages are also the sign of her textually eternal sexual martyrdom.[18] Co-creator of the text, Lucette is also the reader who cannot get into it and who cannot be kicked out. In this respect, *Ada* is the text Nabokov's perverse reader has been waiting for, for which he has been lovingly coached. Every nightmare is the fulfillment of a wish.

One of my principal points in this study has been to argue that Nabokov's texts work to establish perversity not as a characteristic of the author—*definitely* not of the author—and not exclusively as a trait of the characters, but as a property of the reader, who must adjust his interpretive focus and his notion of what it means to be a reader. Historically and psychoanalytically, perversion has been a negative term, but the task Nabokov sets his reader is to become (more) perverse, to linger uselessly in a state of interpretive uncertainty and pleasure, because it is only through occupying that anxious, stimulated position which comes with reading perversely that the reader can understand the rich metafictive core of Nabokov's poetics. *Ada* risks and perhaps succeeds in alienating readers because on virtually every page this novel implicitly states just what kind of reader Nabokov expects his good reader to be. The almost erect organ of Morris Bishop has given way to "the red, irritated shaft of a writhing boy."

In 1950 Walker Gibson coined the notion of a "mock reader," "the fictitious reader whose mask and costume the individual [reader] takes on in order to experience the language" (2). A bad book, Gibson wrote, is "a book in whose mock reader we discover a person we refuse to become, a mask we refuse to put on, a role we will not play." More than any other book by Nabokov, *Ada* equates complexity with complicity: to appreciate the book aesthetically—as opposed to morally—we are pushed by the author to define ourselves in a way that fundamentally touches upon our hermeneutic identity; do we want to be the type of person who appreciates this type of writing? *Ada* poses this problem of readerly identity so acutely that it risks losing the reader altogether. By making Lucette a kind of coauthor, the novel makes its reader jointly responsible not for horrific acts (child abuse or murder) but for excesses in style.

Put another way, it is probably unfair to Freud to treat him once and for all, as Nabokov does, as a reductive writer. There is Freud and there are

---

18. The description of Lucette's final moments, with her vision of "a series of receding Lucettes" and her insight into "the infinite fractions of solitude," recalls Rack's "tiny clusters of particles still retaining his personality." Rack's name may even be present phonetically in those "infinite fractions," as well as in the phrase that opens the sentence concluding with those fractions: "As she began losing *track* of herself" (494).

vulgar Freudians, and Freud was occasionally one of them. The same is true of Nabokov: in the revised *King, Queen, Knave* and in *Ada,* Nabokov was a vulgar Nabokovian, but it would be unfortunate if these moments of repetition and excess lead readers to conclude that Nabokov's work might not be addressed to the sort of readers they want to work to become.

In the second part of *Ada,* more than halfway through the novel, Nabokov introduces Eric van Veen, a cross between the Russian intelligentsia icon Nikolai Chernyshevsky, Hugh Hefner, and the Marquis de Sade.[19] Eric has the idea of establishing a chain of elite, utopian bordellos; after his untimely death, his father is able to bring his "organized dream" to fruition. The chapter describing the Villas is preceded by a description of Van falling asleep and is immediately followed by Van's lecture on dreams. As such, it provides a condensed, oneiric reworking of devices. The passage describing the Villas' buildings and grounds contains an astonishing number of the words put to use in *Ada's* dictionary of pet names. Indeed, the van Veen eclecticism in matters of architectural style hints that, although Shakespeare in sexual excess may still be preferable to Freud, at this level of textual saturation the differences between them virtually disappear:

> Eric's grandfather's range was wide—from dodo to dada, from Low Gothic to Hoch Modern. In his parodies of paradise he even permitted himself, just a few times, to express the rectilinear chaos of Cubism (with "abstract" cast in "concrete") by imitating—in the sense described so well in Vulner's paperback *History of English Architecture* given me by good Dr. Lagosse—such ultra-utilitarian boxes of brick as the *maisons closes* of El Freud in Lubetkin, Austria, or the great-necessity houses of Dudok in Friesland.
>
> But on the whole it was the idyllic and the romantic that he favored. English gentlemen of parts found many pleasures in Letchworth Lodge, an honest country house plastered up to its bulleyes, or Itchenor Chat

---

19. Boyd aptly links Eric van Veen to the founder of *Playboy* (*Ada* online). A nod at Chernyshevsky seems to be the reason for Nabokov's discussion of Eric's absurd obsession with quantities as well as his homosexual tendencies: "at least two of the maximum number of fifty inmates in the major floramors might be pretty boys, wearing frontlets and short smocks, not older than fourteen if fair, and not more than twelve if dark. However, in order to exclude a regular flow of 'inveterate pederasts,' boy love could be dabbled in by the jaded guest only between two sequences of three girls each" (348). In *The Gift,* Fyodor echoes Herzen's quip: "the novel ends not simply with a phalanstery but with 'a phalanstery in a brothel'" (277).

with its battered chimney breasts and hipped gables. None could help admiring David van Veen's knack of making his brand-new Regency mansion look like a renovated farmhouse or of producing a converted convent on a small offshore island with such miraculous effect that one could not distinguish the arabesque from the arbutus, ardor from art, the sore from the rose. We shall always remember Little Lemantry near Rantchester or the Pseudotherm in the lovely cul-de-sac south of the viaduct of fabulous Palermontovia. We appreciated greatly his blending local banality (that château girdled with chestnuts, that castello guarded by cypresses) with interior ornaments that pandered to all the orgies reflected in the ceiling mirrors of little Eric's erogenetics. Most effective, in a functional sense, was the protection the architect distilled, as it were, from the ambitus of his houses. Whether nestling in woodland dells or surrounded by a many-acred park, or overlooking terraced groves and gardens, access to Venus began by a private road and continued through a labyrinth of hedges and walls with inconspicuous doors to which only the guests and the guards had keys. Cunningly distributed spotlights followed the wandering of the masked and caped grandees through dark mazes of coppices; for one of the stipulations imagined by Eric was that "every establishment should open only at nightfall and close at sunrise." (350–51)

This passage is the destination toward which the more covert bawdy talk of Nabokov's earlier novels has been headed. (In other words, *Ada* plays the same role in Nabokov's oeuvre as *The Kreutzer Sonata* in Tolstoy's.) While self-parody is no surprise in Nabokov's fiction, I am struck by the reference to "little Eric's erogenetics." It is not that I see my name's appearance as an uncanny sign that yours truly has become a creature in a Nabokovian text from which he cannot escape. Nor am I disturbed by this confirmation that any narcissistic pleasure derived by a scholar performing Nabokov is always a pale reflection of the author's paronomastic joy. "My" name's use in *Ada* may be an echo of Aphrodite's temple of Eryx twice referenced in *Lolita*. It may also be a reflection of the sad tendency of too many psychologists having had parents enamored of that name. But it is more likely a reference to Eric Partridge's lexicography. In a world of language, the bawdy thesaurus finds its counterpart in the brothel, and we can also take this equivalence as a sign of what may happen when divinity is forced to lodge for just a bit too long in the perversion essential to Nabokov's art.

In the next, and last, chapter, we consider what happens when we finally take Nabokov's advice to Rowe and attempt to remove our belongings.

Epilogue

What If Nabokov Had Written "The Double":
Reading Dostoevsky after Nabokov

What did Nabokov teach Dostoevsky? When I took my first course in comparative literature—after several years of philological training in the citation, quotation, and parody analysis that is the bread and butter of Slavic Languages and Literatures—I became aware of a much underappreciated fact: It is a central purpose of comparative literature to enable us to speak of the influence of a living writer on a dead one. Or of one who died recently on writers dead years before his birth. We don't usually put it in such terms—a distinction is drawn between influence and comparison, but the latter word often serves to spring the scholar free of the historian's fetish of causation. A good comparative study, though, can often have the impact of an influence—or quotation—study run in reverse, with the later writer's work illuminating the poetics of the earlier one. In these pages I want to take this idea literally, engaging in a genre that might be called counterfactual literary analysis. Rather than asking directly what Dostoevsky learned from Nabokov, I'll pose a different, related query: How would we read Dostoevsky's work if we knew Nabokov had written it? Since nearly every worthwhile act of scholarly comparison involves assertions of unexpected similarity that then lead to productive insights into difference, it seems appropriate to take as the object of this exercise Dostoevsky's study of discomfiting and illuminating likeness, "The Double," which has the additional benefit of being the one work of his successor for which Nabokov admitted a fondness (*Lectures on Russian Literature,* 100).[1]

There is something appropriately—perhaps peculiarly—Nabokovian in the posing of this question. As we have seen, the task of Nabokov's reader entails the exercise of "preposterous oversight," the (re)reading of a text's beginning with the knowledge of what happens later on. As a concept, "preposterous oversight" should apply not only within a book but within literature as a whole. Just as a "true understanding" of *Pnin* requires the reader to read the early portions of the book with knowledge derived from the book's end, so later works of literature shine their lights of "backthought" back on their predecessors.

In his novels Nabokov often explored the preposterous nature of memory, where temporal posterity inevitably colors a narrator's characterization of an event.[2] In his introduction to *The Defense,* Nabokov remarked that a sequence in the central chapters "reminds one—or should remind one—of a certain type of chess problem [...] termed 'retrograde analysis,' the solver being required to prove from a back-cast study of the diagram position that Black's last move could not have been castling or must have been the capture of a white Pawn *en passant*" (10). And en passant he proposed such a model of literary history to his students at Cornell: "Had Dickens come before Austen, we should have said that the Price family is positively Dickensian and that the Price children tie up nicely with the child theme that runs through *Bleak House*" (*Lectures on Literature,* 56). Reading preposterously is a variation on "retrograde analysis" in literature.

Such an approach to the study of literature makes a great deal of sense. It points to the paradoxical nature of the very notion of literary history. In analyzing a literary text, we usually treat the entire work as present. By linking up distant moments in the text, we establish what Nabokov called "tacit tunnels" that reveal the work's meaning and poetics (*Stories,* 156). In his lecture on "The Art of Literature and Commonsense" Nabokov wrote: "Time and sequence cannot exist in the author's mind because no time element and no space element had ruled the initial vision. If the mind were constructed on optional lines and if a book could be read in the same way as a painting is taken in by the eye, that is without the bother of working from left to right

---

1. For a reassessment of Nabokov's attitude toward Dostoevsky, see Alexander Dolinin's "Nabokov, Dostoevskii i dostoevshchina," which argues that before coming to America Nabokov distinguished Dostoevsky from *dostoevshchina* [Dostoevsky-ism] and defended Dostoevsky's artistry from profanation by emigré and Soviet authors who sought to emphasize the religious, philosophical, social, or psychological aspects of his writing.

2. This is a particularly important motif in *Despair* and *Ada.*

and without the absurdity of beginnings and ends, this would be the ideal way of appreciating a novel, for thus the author saw it at the moment of its conception" (*Lectures on Literature,* 379–80). Yet we *can't* read this way, and an essential part of aesthetic appreciation is the reader's work to offset or reduce as much as possible the amnesia introduced by the temporality of reading. Rereading overcomes temporality, and as such it makes not only Dostoevsky but also his rereader immortal by removing them from the merciless linearity of time.[3]

Nabokov's insight into the atemporal power of rereading should empower literary scholars in their approach to the history of literature. Why should a literary scholar—when confronted by the notion of literary history—lay down the tools of her trade and so readily accept the time-bound approach of another? A disciplinary inferiority takes hold of us when in considering the rapport between two texts we accept the role of *historians* working in a literary ghetto. What would it mean to take the literature in literary history seriously? To a certain extent, the place of history in literary study is itself a fiction. We may try to segregate our reading of a work of fiction from our reading (and writing) about fiction's history, but the separation is not hermetic. Every understanding of a particular work of fiction is somewhat preposterous, colored by works written after it but which its readers have already read. Why not make aggressive, productive use of our inescapably contaminated sense of temporality? Can't we read and write history from our own, disciplinary position of strength?

Ironically, such questions are being asked with increasing frequency from the other side of the disciplinary divide. Recent years have witnessed an explosion of contributions to "virtual" or "counterfactual" history, essays that ask what would have happened had something earlier happened differently. Robert Cowley has edited two volumes titled *What If?* and Niall Ferguson has edited a third, a large collection entitled *Virtual History.* The introductions to such enterprises tend to be a bit defensive, yet historians justify counterfactuals in a number of ways—the boldest of which is that any assertion of causation—the meat and potatoes of history for centuries—is inherently and implicitly linked to counterfactual supposition. Had the

---

3. Nabokov's appreciation for reverse literary influence was shared by T. S. Eliot, who claimed that any genuinely new development in art affects the perception of earlier artistic monuments in the existing "ideal order" of art. Invoking the notion of the preposterous, though perhaps conscious of only its modern meaning, Eliot observed: "Whoever has approved this idea of order, of the form of European, of English literature will not find it preposterous that the past should be altered by the present as much as the present is directed by the past" (5). Eliot's remarks are cited approvingly by Borges in his short essay "Kafka and His Precursors," which in some respects sets the tone for this concluding chapter (199–201).

causal event or events not occurred, history would have turned out differently. As Johannes Bulhof has shown, implicit counterfactual thinking often underlies historians' efforts to stress the importance of a particular event or their evaluations of the capabilities and judgments of particular historical actors (145–68). Psychologists have found that counterfactual thinking is a frequent response to tragic or traumatic events; crime or accident victims seek to "undo" the past by imagining how things would have been different had they done something else (Turley, Sanna, and Reiter).

In his introduction to *Virtual History*, Ferguson is nervous about his enterprise becoming too imaginative, irrelevant, or silly. He defends counterfactual investigation as a necessary antidote to determinism. He seeks to keep counterfactual imagination within bounds by considering "as plausible or probable *only those alternatives which we can show on the basis of contemporary evidence that contemporaries actually considered*. [...] To understand how it actually was, we [...] need to understand *how it actually wasn't*—but how, to contemporaries, it might have been" (86–87). Finally, he resists the anticipated assertion that he is allowing history to be absorbed by literature; Ferguson asserts that literature represents precisely the determinism he is trying to resist. Approvingly, he quotes W. B. Gallie: "To follow a story...involves...appreciation of how what comes later depends upon what came earlier, in the sense that but for the latter, the former could not have, or could hardly have occurred in the way that it did occur" (66). In effect, Ferguson insists that historians resist determinism and calls for more fiction, less plot.

Ferguson's prescription for history sounds much like Gary Saul Morson's advocacy of "sideshadowing" (*Narrative and Freedom*). Both scholars' concern with the importance of contingency arises from an insistent conflation of literature and real life. Their opposition to structure and plotting stems from a privileging of ethics over aesthetics, and it results in what Bakhtin referred to as a "prosaic deviation"—*prozaicheskii uklon* (*Literaturno-kriticheskie stat'i*, 57).[4] In Nabokov's metafictive world, there is no contingency, and the very words "chance, by accident, incidentally" nearly always refer the reader to the author's all-powerful and all-conscious presence behind the text. Nabokov continually reminds us of his control, and there are a number of invariants that repeatedly mark his presence, not only butterflies and squirrels but

---

4. Michael Bernstein's study of "backshadowing" in accounts of the lives of European Jews before the Holocaust presents a similar concern with the way highly organized artistic structures can impoverish or do a disservice to the subjectivity of human beings and the richness of their everyday lives (*Foregone Conclusions*). Readers of literature will differ on whether and in what circumstances aesthetic experience should be tempered—or, Morson and Bernstein might suggest, enriched—by a sense of moral obligation to actually or once living human individuals.

natural phenomena, too, and, in particular, wind, which playfully alludes to an author's inspiration of life in his characters.

In a thoughtful study of metapoetic works in the Russian literary tradition, Michael Finke describes the dominant trait of metafiction as its preoccupation with "a semantic field dominated by the fiction/reality opposition, where poetics is revealed as an artificiality concealed beneath the surface of a discourse which, with deceptive innocence, purports to reflect some or other real world *out there*" (12–13). "For metafiction," Finke adds, "reference to poetics is a way of 'undoing' the referential function in literature" (13). It is as metafiction in this very Nabokovian sense that I want to read "The Double"—as an exploration of the madness induced from unwanted life as a literary character. One result of this anachronistic practice will be to diminish any lingering readerly sympathy for the work's hero by pointing out his obviously fictitious nature. Indeed, Nabokov is a master at using metafiction to "undo" fiction's pull on the reader's emotions. The conclusion of *Bend Sinister* is the most obvious example of this phenomenon. By showing his hand and undoing already narrated trauma, Nabokov uses metafiction the way many people use counterfactuals; indeed, we might want to refer to his poetics as counterfiction.

There is a particular benefit to engaging in this enterprise at this point in this book. What happens when we stop reading Nabokov? Nabokov claimed that "after reading Gogol' one's eyes may become gogolized and one is apt to see bits of his world in the most unexpected places" (*Nikolai Gogol,* 144). Nabokov probably has a similar effect. Rereading Nabokov is a bracing lesson in paying attention, taking risks and trying to find just the right way to twist the meaning of words to gain access to a work's "second story." When our eyes are Nabokovized and we read literature (or even nonliterature) not written by him, what sorts of things do we see?

It is relatively easy to know when you have finished reading a book. *Rereading* a book can last forever. If there is no such thing as reading, just rereading, then no author's work can ever be completed. But how long do we want to read Nabokov? Many scholars dedicate themselves to Nabokov permanently, occasionally permitting themselves a glance at Shakespeare or Pushkin. It can be difficult to turn one's attention to other authors, even if lesser books might make us into better people, if not better readers. Most readers of Nabokov, however, will soon turn to something else. (In fact, some turn to something else *while* they are reading Nabokov; yesterday I noticed the woman checking out books at Berkeley's Doe Library simultaneously reading *Invitation to a Beheading* and Shelby Steele's *White Guilt.*) I want to end this book by trying my own turn at Applied Nabokov Studies—not to see how reading Nabokov can help us live better lives, but to see how reading Nabokov might make us into better, or productively different, readers of *other* authors' stories and novels. I take Dostoevsky as an example, in part because Nabokov had such a fraught attitude toward his work. This experiment in preposterous reading allows us to revisit many of the features of Nabokov's poetics as we take leave of them. One of the challenges facing teachers and authors is how to write a good conclusion—or how to make a review session interesting.

What would be obvious to us in "The Double" if we knew it to be Nabokov's? We would, first of all, pay attention to the issue of unstated agency. Nabokov took the Symbolists' practice of using indefinite expressions ("someone," "somewhere" / *gde-to, kto-to*) to hint at the noumenal, "more real" world, but he applied them to figures of authorial control, so that indeterminacy is a hint at the higher, more real world from which the character is sent twinklings of the author's design. The excruciating loss of a character's control over his life is a central theme of "The Double." This motif is most emphatically highlighted by Golyadkin's body's assertion of independence in the form of Golyadkin's "double," but it is also in play in the many instances when Golyadkin loses control of his physical movements. Starting involuntarily is a hallmark of Dostoevskian motor response; in "The Double," however, the author is more explicit about the motivation for unanticipated corporeal movement. Let's look at the moment when Golyadkin resolves to depart homeward immediately from the house of Ol'sufii Ivanovich:

> Having thus settled the situation, Mr. Golyadkin stepped briskly forward, as if somebody had touched a spring inside him; [...] Mr. Golyadkin, forgetting for a moment everything that was going on, stepped like a bolt from the blue straight into the drawing room.
>
> As luck would have it [lit., as if on purpose], they were not dancing. (158)

> *Razreshiv takim obrazom svoe polozhenie, gospodin Goliadkin bystro podalsia vpered, slovno pruzhinu kakuiu kto tronul v nem; [...]gospodin Goliadkin pozabyl vse, chto vokrug nego delaetsia, i priamo, kak sneg na golovu, iavilsia v tantseval'nuiu zalu.*
>
> *Kak narochno v eto vremia ne tantsevali.* (132–33)[5]

---

5. All English translations are by Jessie Coulson (Fyodor Dostoevsky, *Notes from Underground / The Double*). Unless otherwise specified, all quotations from "Dvoinik" refer to Dostoevskii's *Polnoe sobranie sochinenii v tridtsati tomakh, vol. 1.*

In habitual, preposterously Freudian readings, the "somebody" here would be Golyadkin's unconscious; we would have to suspend the question of whether a character can have an unconscious in the first place. Knowing Nabokov, we can see the image of mechanical prompting as a reference to authorial control, and we can read the use of *slovno* ("as though," formed from the word *slovo,* meaning "word") as a wink at the verbal means by which the spring is pressed. The pause in the dancing is indeed intentional (*kak narochno*) and fits into a whole gamut of moments in which McFate is the author of Golyadkin's downfall: "Fate was carrying him on. Mr. Golyad-kin himself felt that it was fate that carried him on. . . . Mr. Golyadkin felt as if he was being undermined, as it were" (*Rok uvlekal ego. Gospodin Goliadkin sam eto chuvstvoval, chto rok-to ego uvlekal. . . .[G]ospodin Goliadkin chuvstvoval, chto ego kak budto by podmyvaet chto-to*) (160, *134*); "Mr. Golyadkin rushed away, following his nose, at the mercy of fate, to wherever chance would lead him") (*Brosilsia pogibshii i sovershenno spravedlivyi gospodin Goliadkin kuda glaza gliadiat, na voliu sud'by, kuda by ni vyneslo*) (230, *186–87*). "Fate, des-tiny," exclaims Golyadkin the younger, and the original Golyadkin echoes: "We must blame fate for the whole thing" (*Rok! Sud'ba! . . . Budem obviniat' sud'bu vo vsem etom*) (253, *203*). Glossing the "spring" passage in 1922, Viktor Vinogradov remarked that "the hero's actions are mechanized and he himself is transformed into a marionette, repeating a specific round of actions at the will of the author" (111). Nabokov injects such critical metaphors into the consciousness of the hero, transforming device into plot, so that the story becomes an investigation into the horror of living as a character in a world where divinity has been replaced by authorship.[6]

At times, Golyadkin seems willing to submit to the author's script: "I accept the benevolent authorities as my father, and blindly entrust my fate to them. [. . .] God's providence has created two people exactly alike, and our benevolent authorities, recognizing God's providence, have given shelter to those twins. That's good. . . You can see that's very good. . . and that I am far from a free-thinker" (*prinimaiu, deskat' blagodetel'noe nachal'stvo za ottsa i slepo vveriaiu sud'bu svoiu.* [. . .] *Promysl bozhii sozdal dvukh sovershenno podobnykh, a blagodetel'noe nachal'stvo, vidia promysl bozhii, priiutili dvukh bliznetsov-s. Eto khorosho . . . eto ochen' khorosho . . . i ia dalek vol'nodumstva*) (243–46, *196–98*).

---

6. In other words, "The Double" is a metafictive, earlier variation on the theme—later developed much more fully in "Notes from Underground"—of speaking, and living, as if one were in a book and as if one had no lines of one's own to utter. In moving from one work to the other, Dostoevsky took a metafictive insight and applied it to the ideological plight of the Russian intelligentsia.

At other times, though, he is a desperate freethinker, willing to question the justness of the world that his author has made:

> Our hero was now, if the comparison is allowable, in the position of a man on whom some joker has amused himself by focusing a burning-glass. "What is this, a dream?" he wondered. "Is it real, or just a continuation of yesterday? But why? what right has all this to happen? Who gave permission for the appointment of this employee, who authorized this?"

> *Geroi nash, esli vozmozhno sravnenie, byl teper' v polozhenii cheloveka, nad kotorym zabavlialsia prokaznik kakoi-nibud', dlia shutki navodia na nego ispod-tishka zazhigatl'noe steklo. "Chto zhe eto, son ili net,—dumal on,—nastoiash-chee ili prodolzhenie vcherashnego? Da kak zhe? Po kakomu zhe pravu vse eto delaetsia? Kto razreshil takogo chinovnika, kto dal pravo na eto?"* (177, 147)

The question at the end of this passage is answered at its start—note the typical Nabokovian device of narrative circularity—by the author's claim of responsibility in the conventional plural—the hero is *his*. In "The Double" the frequent repetitions of "our hero" deploy a trite literary convention to new, defamiliarized effect.

"Exactly who had a finger in this shameful business?" (181) *(Kto tut imenno v eto sramnoe delo ruku svoiu zameshal?)* (181, *150*). Occasionally Nabokov's narrator refers playfully to his own and, perhaps, to the reader's presence:

> If some casual and uninvolved passer-by had chanced to give an indifferent side-glance at Mr. Golyadkin's melancholy flight, even he would immediately have been stirred to the depths by all the dire horror of his disastrous plight, and would infallibly have said that Mr. Golyadkin looked as if he was trying to hide from himself, as if he wanted to run away from himself. Yes, it really was so!

> *Esli b teper' postoronnii, neinteresovannyi kakoi-nibud' nabliudatel' vzglianul by tak sebe, sboku, na tosklivuiu pobezhku gospodina Goliadkina, to i tot by razom proniknulsia vsem strashnym uzhasom ego bedstvii i nepremenno skazal by, chto gospodin Goliadkin gliadit teper' tak, kak budto sam ot sebia kuda-to spriatat'sia khochet, kak budto sam ot sebia ubezhat' kuda-nibud' khochet. Da! ono bylo deistvitel'no tak.* (166, *138–39*)

What is really so? That Golyadkin wants to hide from himself, or that he is watched by someone from the side? (By his creator? By his reader?) In the scene of the Double's appearance, from which this moment is taken, Golyadkin seems at the mercy of the elements, and especially the wind, which rushes at him from all sides, "as though purposely joining in league and concert with all his enemies" *(kak by narochno soobshchas' i soglasias' so vsemi vragami ego)* (166, *138*). His double seems to be created by the elements, and as Golyadkin rushes to and from him, it is "as though he was kept in motion by some outside force" (171) *(slovno dvigaemyi kakoiu-to postoronneiu siloiu"* (171, *142*). One almost expects supernatural force (*potustoronnei siloi*)—so frequently are the authorial and the supernatural enmeshed in Nabokov's worlds.

In Nabokov's novels, the author acts through a variety of sometimes ominous and sometimes comical loving agents.[7] Rutenshpitz is the most obvious candidate for this role in "The Double." The doctor emphasizes to Golyadkin that he must "in a certain sense" "change" or more literally "break [his] character" (*v nekotorom smysle perelomit' svoi kharakter*) (135, *115*); this ominous prescription for a hero who will soon split in two is immediately underscored: "Christian Ivanovich strongly emphasized the word 'change' and paused for a moment with a very significant air" (*Krest'ian Ivanovich sil'no udaril na slovo 'perelomit'' i ostanovilsia na minutu s ves'ma znachitel'nym vidom*) (135, *115*). Is Dr. Rutenshpitz the tip of the author's pen? When we first encounter him, he is writing prescriptions (*retsepty i predpisaniia*) for his patients, prescriptions the story seems to follow to the letter. Golyadkin seems to grasp the narrative power of the doctor's texts:

> Here he took up his pen, drew a sheet of paper towards himself, cut from it a piece such as doctors habitually use, and announced that he was ready to write what was required [lit., what followed] at once.
>
> —No, Christian Ivanovich, it's not required! [lit., it doesn't follow!] no, sir, that's not necessary at all! said Mr. Golyadkin, rising from his chair and grasping Christian Ivanovich's right hand; there's no need of anything of that sort here, Christian Ivanovich....
>
> But even while he was saying all this, Mr. Golyadkin was undergoing a strange transformation.

> *Tut on vzial pero, pridvinul bumagu, vykroil iz nee doktorskoi formy loskutik i ob"iavil, chto totchas propishet, chto sleduet.*
>
> *—Net-s, ne sleduet, Krest'ian Ivanovich! net-s, eto vovse ne sleduet!— progovoril Goliadkin, pristav s mesta i khvataia Krest'iana Ivanovicha za pravuiu ruku,—etogo, Krest'ian Ivanovich, zdes' vovse ne nadobno....*
>
> *A mezhdu tem, pokamest' govoril eto gospodin Goliadkin v nem proizoshla kakaia-to strannaia peremena* (138, *117–18*).

---

7. For a detailed consideration of various aspects of "agency" in Nabokov's work, see Tammi, 29–56.

We should read this passage as a character's rejection not just of necessity in general but of narrative necessity, of what must necessarily follow (*sleduet*).

When he collects Golyadkin on the story's final page, the doctor's announcement of Golyadkin's fate rings out like a "sentence" (*prigovor*), and Golyadkin despairs: "Alas! This was what he had known for a long time would happen!" (*Uvy! on eto davno uzhe predchuvstvoval!*) (287, 229). Golyadkin's repeated premonitions serve Nabokov as the story's rhythm: the hero's awareness of his approaching exit functions as evidence of the story's existence as a plotted, artistic work. The doctor drives Golyadkin off to his final, carceral home, denying the hero the power to determine his future course. (Unlike Pnin, Golyadkin does not drive off the final page in his own vehicle; rather, he follows a reverse course, beginning the story in his own hired livery but ending it in involuntary mobile confinement.)[8]

Many of Nabokov's novels tell of a hero's hopeless attempt to escape from the text that contains him. Golyadkin insists that he is not about to follow the prescriptions of "silly novels" (*glupye romany*) (276, 221), and in this respect he is a successor to Makar Devushkin, who takes umbrage at the portrait of "The Overcoat"'s Akakii Akakievich. What serves in *Poor Folk* as a humorous misunderstanding of the distinction between art and life becomes far more literal and painful in "The Double." Being shown out of His Excellency's residence near the novel's end, Golyadkin is helped into his coat by his evil twin: "'Overcoat, overcoat, overcoat, my friend's overcoat! My dearest friend's overcoat!' twittered the obnoxious creature, snatching the coat from the hands of one of the lackeys and flinging it in mean minded and nasty mockery straight over Mr. Golyadkin's head" (*"Shinel', shinel', shinel', shinel' druga moego! Shinel' moego luchshego druga!"—zashchebetal razvratnyi chelovek, vyryvaia iz ruk odnogo cheloveka shinel' i nabrasyvaia ee, dlia podloi i neblagopriatnoi nasmeshki, priamo na goluovu Gospodinu Goliadkinu*) (271–72, 218). This sort of flattening of a character into narrative two-dimensionality is typical of Nabokov's metafiction; Gogol's overcoat straitjackets Golyadkin into eternal textuality.[9]

---

8. We should not ignore the typical, Nabokovian auto-parodic reference to authorial agents that occurs when Golyadkin sits on a log in Olsufi Ivanovich's yard: "Oh my God! My God! What on earth am I talking about now?" (*Akh ty, gospodi bog moi! Gospodi bog moi! da o chem zhe eto ia teper; govoriu?*) (275, 220). God seems to answer: "'Will you be wanting to go soon, sir?' said a voice from above Mr. Golyadkin's head. Mr. Golyadkin started; but it was only his cabby who stood before him" (*Neshto skoro, sudar', izvolite ekhat'?—proiznes golos nad gospodinom Goliadkinym. Gospodin Goliadkin vzdrognul; no pered nim stoial ego izvozchik* (275, 220).

9. See Finke's reading of *The Idiot,* in which he views Myshkin's courtship of Aglaya Epanchin (*epancha* = cloak) as a counterpart to Akakii Akakievich's seeing his new overcoat as a wife (106).

Golyadkin is essentially being forced to repeat Akakii Akakievich. This duplication is a hallmark of the text. The plot itself is notoriously repetitive. Not only do words repeat but scenes as well; indeed, there are many scenes—such as Golyadkin's first encounter with his double, where repetition seems virtually ritualistic. Here Nabokov bares the patterning feature of all narrative and all interpretations of narrative: the double is a flagrant personification of the principle of literary form. We shall see, though, why "The Double" represents such a primitive—necessarily preliminary—stage in Nabokov's work. In later novels, the figure of the double is absorbed by and suffuses the fabric of the text. Poor Luzhin, successor to Golyadkin, can't cathect his repetition anxiety onto a single figure; he is stalked by the repetition of textuality itself.[10]

One more Nabokovian peculiarity seems worth recalling: the fascination with "strangeness" as a marker of aesthetic consummation. The word *strannyi* ("strange") makes frequent appearances in "The Double," where it is linked it to its etymological sister—*storona* ("side"). Golyadkin undergoes "a strange transformation" (*kakaia-to strannaia peremena*) (138, *118*) during his first, highly metafictive conversation with Christian Ivanovich, just as the doctor picks up the pen. The splitting off of Golyadkin's double is preceded by his experience of "the strange feeling, his terrible black depression" (*strannoe chuvstvo, strannaia temnaia toska*) (168, *140*) that he cannot shake off. Golyadkin has great lateral motion, and his involuntary leaps to the side when encountering his twin and his frequent protestations that he is *v storone* (not involved, lit., "on the side") might be seen as the text's ironic acknowledgment that the nature of Golyadkin's uncanny predicament is his painful subjugation to the uncanny power of art.

"The Double"'s repeated references to speech and language are striking and work on a metapoetic level to allow the reader's frustration with the verbal repetitions of the text to mirror Golyadkin's own sense of character-istic claustrophobia. It is worth mentioning here the extent to which Nabokov

---

10. Mikhail Bakhtin portrays the narrator as Golyadkin's double and compares him to Ivan Karamazov's devil because the narrator mocks Golyadkin by using Golyadkin's own language against him (*Problems of Dostoevsky's Poetics, 217–22*). This valuable insight can be seen as the discovery of a kind of persecution by texuality itself; Golyadkin is pursued and derided by his own discourse. Potentially, this understanding of the story might be put to the service of a psychological reading: Golyadkin cannot escape from himself. The narrator's lexical and stylistic register, however, is broader than Golyadkin's—would Golyadkin use the phrase *tosklivaia pobezhka* (melancholy flight)? The narrator has a broader vocabulary and a broader field of vision, he remains an authorial figure mocking his creation. In Bakhtin's view, this author-hero dynamic was important as a step toward full-fledged polyphony, rather than as a stage in the evolution of metafiction.

foregrounds the role of language in Golyadkin Junior's genesis and in Golyadkin Senior's persecution. This is, of course, an old trick of his, and the appearance of the Double at the end of chapter 5 strangely combines Gothic horror with the grounding of the hero's identity in discourse:

> His hair stood on end and he collapsed into a chair, insensible with horror. Mr. Golyadkin had recognized his nocturnal acquaintance. Mr. Golyadkin's nocturnal acquaintance was none other than himself. Mr. Golyadkin himself, another Mr. Golyadkin, but exactly the same as himself—in short [in a single word], in every respect what is called his double.

> *Volosy vstali na golove ego dybom, i on prisel bez chuvstv na meste ot uzhasa. Da i bylo ot chego, vprochem. Gospodin Goliadkin sovershenno uznal svoego nochnogo priiatelia. Nochnoi priiatel' ego byl ne kto inoi, kak on sam,—sam gospodin Goliadkin, drugoi gospodin Goliadkin, no sovershenno takoi zhe, kak i on sam,—odnim slovom, chto nazyvaetsia, dvoinik ego vo vsekh otnosheni-iakh.* (173, *143*)

The similarity of Golyadkin to his double is summed up "in a single word" and doubly verbalized by being presented as an item of lexical explanation ("what is called his double"). Throughout the story words play a leading role in the persecution of Golyadkin and in the inevitable finalization of any aesthetic personage: "Golyadkin was crushed—utterly crushed (lit., "killed, utterly killed"), in the full sense of the word" (*Goliadkin byl ubit—ubit vpolne, v polnom smysle slova*) (165, *138*). Here the full sense of "the word" refers to aesthetic utterance and not simply to the particular word "killed" (*ubit*). Golyadkin—like Cincinnatus and Luzhin—is killed by his insertion into the artistic text.

"The Double"'s frequent use of "*slovno*" [as though] further reinforces this link between aesthetic identity and linguistic pursuit. "As though" (*slovno*), of course, has been the pedal note of this entire, perversely allegorical chapter. The story of "The Double" serves as a kind of parable for what happens when a later author takes the place of a former; it may seem to my readers that Dostoevsky has been packed off with his hero, the intellectual content of his works eviscerated and replaced with those of Golyadkin Junior, who has assumed the authorship of all his works.

Reading Nabokov is a transforming experience; as I have tried to show, only a perverse reading is adequate to the complexity of his texts. Nabokov's most explicit instruction in this regard—"The other way, the other way.

I thank you" (*Poems and Problems,* 158)—finds its counterpart in Golyadkin's similar entreaty about his own writing, in a passage where *pis'mo* can refer not only to a specific epistle but to writing in general or "his" entire text:

> I implore you to read it in the opposite sense—exactly opposite, if you will be so kind, that is, deliberately turning all the words in the letter the other way round.
>
> *[U]moliaiu vas chitat' ego naoborot,—sovsem naoborot, to est narochno s nameremiem druzheskim, davaia obratnyi smysl vsem slovam pis'ma moego.* (253, *204*)

It can be difficult to recover once one has mastered such an injunction. Virtually everything seems to be metafiction. (I am convinced, for instance, that the awful unnamable doom long dreaded and finally understood by the hero of Henry James's "The Beast in the Jungle" is that he *is* a character in a story by Henry James.) But let us try to return to conventional, historically conscious modes of interpretation. What might we just have learned?

First, we may have discovered the ancestral text linking the early Nabokov and the early Bakhtin. *The Defense* and "Author and Hero" seem to be transpositions of the same concerns in different genres, and I suspect that they both owe much to a metafictive understanding of "The Double." In an article on *The Eye,* Julian Connolly has shown us just how closely Nabokov read "The Double" ("Madness and Doubling," 129–39), but Nabokov's borrowed insights were not merely into human psychology: they formed an important part of Nabokov's effort to remember "Dostoevsky the artist" (Dolinin, "Nabokov, Dostoevskii, i dostoevshchina," 42). An aggressive, anachronistic stance, I hope, has allowed us to see how the metafictive core of Nabokov's poetics is indebted to Dostoevsky. In addition, an understanding of the metafictive dimensions of "The Double" should allow us to reconsider the role of fiction in Bakhtin's work of the 1920s. Bakhtin's work has always struck me as belonging to a new genre of scholarly fiction, which is why its application is often so disappointing. But if Dostoevsky was already telling the story of author and hero, we can see Bakhtin's work by that name not as a fictionalization of the creative process but as a brilliant, philosophically inflected paraphrase of what was metafiction to begin with. Describing the relations between author and hero, Bakhtin was transposing a metafictive story into the story of all fiction, although initially Bakhtin, too, sought to cover his tracks by treating Dostoevsky as a perversion of the normal author-hero paradigm.[11] Finally, I hope I have made a case for "The Double" as a genuine breakthrough in the process of literary evolution. To the extent that the story is treated as a success, it is credited for recasting "Gogolian elements" in "a genuine exploration of encroaching madness" that reinforces "Gogol's acute perception of the grotesque effects on character of moral stagnation and social immobility" (Frank, 299–300). I suggest that the story be appreciated for taking the Gogolian fantastic into a new, metafictive dimension where the author rigorously and ruthlessly investigates what it means to be a character.

What other works by Dostoevsky may prove to have been written by Nabokov? The answer to this question may turn out to be increasingly complex, and Nabokov would not have liked the implicit association with Bacon. In all likelihood, as Dostoevsky's work degenerated, Nabokov wrote less of it, so that, for instance, there is only one scene in *The Brothers Karamazov* which he may have authored.[12] But one scene in *Crime and Punishment (Prestuplenie i nakazanie)* is clearly his, and it is on that note that I wish to end. Raskolnikov has just overheard a student and an officer discussing their hatred of the old pawnbroker and whether they would kill her. The "superstitious" Raskolnikov becomes "greatly agitated":

> Of course, it was all the most common and ordinary youthful talk and thinking, he had heard it many times before, only in different forms and on different subjects. But why precisely now did he have to hear precisely such talk and thinking, when . . . exactly the same thoughts had just been conceived in his own head? And why precisely now, as he was coming from the old woman's bearing the germ of his thought, should he chance upon a conversation about the same old woman? . . . This coincidence always seemed strange to him. This negligible tavern conversation had an extreme influence on him in the further development of the affair; as though there were indeed [lit., really] some predestination, some indication in it. . . . .

> *Raskol'nikov byl v chrezvychainom volnenii. Konechno, vse eto byli samye obyknovennye i samye chastye, ne raz uzhe slyshannye im, v drugikh tol'ko formakh i na drugie temy, molodye razgovory i mysli. No pochemu imenno teper' prishlos'*

---

11. See Bakhtin's comments in "Author and Hero in Aesthetic Activity," where he presents "almost all of Dostoevsky's heroes" as examples of faulty artistic consummation (*Art and Answerability,* 19–20). In this example of imperfect consummation lies the seed of what would become known as polyphony.

12. See Fyodor's appreciation of this passage in *The Gift,* 72–73.

emu vyslushat' imenno takoi razgovor i takie mysli, kogda v sobstvennoi golove ego tol'ko chto zarodilis' ...takie zhe tochno mysli? I pochemu imenno seichas, kak tol'ko on vynes zarodysh svoei mysli ot starukhi, kak raz i popadaet on na ragovor o starukhe? ...Strannym vsegda kazalos' emu eto sovpadenie. Etot nichtozhnyi, traktirnyi razgovor imel chrezvychainoe na nego vliianie pri dal'-neishem razvitii dela: kak budto deistvitel'no bylo tut kakoe-to predopredelenie, ukazanie. . . . .

(66, *Polnoe sobranie sochinenii, 6:55*)

The uncharacteristic ellipsis highlights the importance of the passage. The strange coincidence is a Nabokovian marker of authorial design, the stuff of which narrative is made. And in this moment, reflecting on the uncanniness of the moment, Raskolnikov almost has an insight: shimmering verbally before him, distorted—*predopredelenie, ukazanie*—as if it had come from Terra, lies the name of the indeed (*deistvitel'no*) existing novel whose narrative has controlled his destiny from the very moment of his birth on the page.

❧ Acknowledgments

This book would not have been written had Yuri Slezkine not kept reminding me that someone in my position really ought to be reading some good literature. Nor would it have gone very far if so many people did not care so very deeply about Nabokov's work. All scholars of Nabokov owe a tremendous debt to D. Barton Johnson, the founder of Nabokv-L, for doing so much to facilitate the study of VN; and I would like to acknowledge as well the contribution to this book of the many who have posted their thoughts on Nabokv-L during the past decade.

My colleagues at Berkeley, in particular Robert Alter, Anne Nesbet, Sam Otter, Irina Paperno, and Olga Matich, have provided a receptive but challenging audience for many of the ideas in these pages. The author of *The Cabinet of Earths* has supplied many of this book's better lines. With friendship and great respect I thank Robert P. Hughes for nearly three decades of insight, suggestions, and encouragement, beginning with the telephone call that first brought me to graduate school in Berkeley. Before that, Sergei Davydov introduced me to the excitement of reading Nabokov; each time I left his class, the world seemed a far richer place. Stephen Booth, one of the best good readers ever, spent a semester critiquing several of my early chapter drafts as part of the Initiative Program at the Townsend Center for the Humanities. I hope he valued that experience at least half as much as I. I am grateful to Dmitri Nabokov for the vitality he brought to his sojourn at Berkeley as a Regents Lecturer; his performance as his father in Terry Quinn's play and his work with our translation workshop remain deeply appreciated at this campus.

Students at Berkeley, some of whom are now colleagues, have been an inspirational audience. I have learned a great deal from them, in particular Polina Barskova, Anne Dwyer, Lina Ilic, Konstantin Klioutchkine, Jeremy Kuhn, Asya Ofshteyn, James Ramey, Lewis Rubman, Lucas Stratton, Sidsel Thorsen, Erica Valdovinos, and Boris Wolfson. A wider circle of readers and listeners have left their impact on this book as well. I have been fortunate to have the input of Eliot Borenstein, Stephen Blackwell, Evgeny Dobrenko, Caryl Emerson, Alexander Etkind, Gregory Freidin, Andrew Kahn, Joachim

Klein, Mark Leiderman, Dale Peterson, Galina Rylkova, and nearly all my anonymous reviewers. My conversations and electronic exchanges with Blackwell and Etkind have provided some of the most stimulating moments of work on this project.

I have profited greatly from the reactions of my listeners at Hampshire College, William and Mary, Pomona, Oberlin, the University of Illinois at Champagne-Urbana, Stanford, Harvard, Princeton, the University of Chicago, and the universities of Manchester, Sheffield, Konstanz, Tübingen, and the Free University of Berlin.

Earlier versions of parts of this book have appeared in *Comparative Literature* 58, no. 1, 2006; *Nabokov Studies* 5 and 8 (1998/99 and 2004); *Novoe literaturnoe obozrenie* 54 (2002); *Representations* 101 (2008); *The Russian Review* 64, no. 4 (2005); *Stanford Slavic Studies* 32 (2006), a special issue in honor of Robert P. Hughes and Olga Raevsky Hughes; and *Ulbandus* 10 (2007). Irene Masing-Delic, Irina Prokhorova, George E. Rowe, and Zoran Kuzmanovich were willing to bring out my work at early stages of this project, and I am deeply appreciative of their encouragement and readiness to take risks.

I thank the Artists Rights Society and the Art Institute of Chicago for permission to reproduce *Jeune Fille au Chat* by Balthus and Scholastic for permission to reprint the cover of the September 1935 issue of *The Instructor*. At Cornell University Press I have benefited from the enthusiastic support of John Ackerman, the thoughtful copyediting of Carolyn Pouncy, and the patience of Candace Akins. Frank Farzan of Metro Publishing helped secure the proper quality for visual images.

Lee Naiman provided the cover illustration; when she took that picture in 1956, did she already know she would be saving it for my future book? I am grateful to her and to Robert Naiman, my first readers, for many overly generous reviews, and to Cara and Tom Naiman for not minding that too much. I am pleased that Dr. Clark Sugg has displayed my first book so prominently, and I trust he will give this one as much publicity. Eleanor and Ada Naiman, I hope, will have another book written for them before they are old enough to want to read this one.

I cannot describe in any meaningful way how much I have enjoyed the seventeen and a half years spent with the dedicatee of this book. She constantly impresses me with her intelligence, grace, humor, and tolerance. (I may seem to take all that for granted, but I never do.) I will miss her terribly. So what if she prefers Dostoevsky? She is welcome back anytime.

✒ BIBLIOGRAPHY

Abbott, Edwin A. *Flatland.* Published with Burger, Dionys. *Sphereland.* New York: Harper Collins, 1983.

Ades, Dawn. *Surrealist Art: The Lindy and Edwin Bergman Collection at the Art Institute of Chicago.* London: Thames and Hudson, 1997.

Akhmatova, Anna. *Stikhotvoreniia i poemy.* Leningrad: Sovetskii pisatel', 1977.

Alexandrov, Vladimir E. "Nabokov and Bely." In *The Garland Companion to Vladimir Nabokov.* Ed. Vladimir E. Alexandrov. New York: Garland, 1995, 358–66.

——. "Nabokov and Tolstoy." In *Nabokov's World.* Volume 1: *The Shape of Nabokov's World.* Ed. Jane Grayson, Arnold McMillin, and Priscilla Meyer. Houndsmill, U.K.: Palgrave, 2002, 58–70.

——. *Nabokov's Otherworld.* Princeton, N.J.: Princeton University Press, 1991.

Alighieri, Dante. *The Purgatorio.* Trans. John Ciardi. New York: Mentor, 1961.

Allen, Paul. "Through the Veil." *The Guardian,* September 13, 2003.

Alter, Robert. "*Ada,* or the Perils of Paradise." In *Vladimir Nabokov, His Life, His Work, His World: A Tribute.* Ed. Peter Quennell. New York: William Morrow, 1980, 103–28.

——. *Partial Magic: The Novel as a Self-Conscious Genre.* Berkeley: University of California Press, 1975.

——. *The Pleasures of Reading in an Ideological Age.* New York: W. W. Norton, 1996.

Andreev, Leonid. "The Abyss." In *The Dedalus Book of Russian Decadence: Perversity, Despair and Collapse.* Ed. Kirsten Lodge. Trans. Margo Shohl Rosen with Grigory Dashevsky. Sawtry, Cambridgeshire: Dedalus, 2007, 221–35.

Anonymous. "Allegoriia." *Entsiklopedicheskii slovar'.* St. Petersburg: Brokgauz-Efron, 1890. Reprint Yaroslavl: Terra, 1990, 1:461.

Appel, Alfred, Jr. Introduction and notes to *The Annotated Lolita.* By Vladimir Nabokov. New York: Vintage, 1991. xvii–lxvii, 319–457.

——. *Nabokov's Dark Cinema.* New York: Oxford University Press, 1974.

Bader, Julia. *Crystal Land: Artifice in Nabokov's English Novels.* Berkeley: University of California Press, 1972.

Bakhtin, M. M. *Art and Answerability.* Trans. Vadim Liapunov. Austin: University of Texas Press, 1990.

——. *Literaturno-kriticheskie stat'i.* Moscow: Khudozhestvennaia literatura, 1986.

——. *Problems of Dostoevsky's Poetics.* Trans. Caryl Emerson. Minneapolis: University of Minnesota Press, 1984.

——. *Rabelais and His World.* Trans. Hélène Iswolsky. Bloomington: Indiana University Press, 1984.

Banchoff, Thomas F. "From Flatland to Hypergraphics: Interacting with Higher Dimensions." *Interdisciplinary Science Reviews* 15, no. 4 (1980): 364–72.

Barabtarlo, Gennady. *Phantom of Fact: A Guide to Nabokov's "Pnin."* Ann Arbor, Mich.: Ardis, 1989.

———. "Pushkin Embedded." *Vladimir Nabokov Research Newsletter* 8 (1982): 28–31.

———. "Those Who Favor Fire (On *The Enchanter*)." *Russian Literature Triquarterly* 24 (1991): 89–112.

Barra, Allen. "Reading *Lolita* in Alabama." Salon.com, 22 December 2005. http://dir.salon.com/story/books/review/2005/12/22/nabokov/index.html (accessed October 22, 2009).

Barskova, Polina. "Filial Feeling and Paternal Patterns: *Hamlet* in *The Gift.*" *Nabokov Studies* 9 (2005): 191–208.

Begnal, Michael H. "*Bend Sinister:* Joyce, Shakespeare, Nabokov." *Modern Language Studies* 15, no. 4 (1985): 22–27.

Bell, Michael. "*Lolita* and Pure Art." *Essays in Criticism* 24, no. 2 (1974): 169–84.

Bely, Andrei. "The Magic of Words." *Symbolism: An Anthology.* Trans. and ed. Thomas G. West. New York: Methuen, 1980, 120–43.

———. *Petersburg.* Trans. Robert A. Maguire and John E. Malmstad. Bloomington: Indiana University Press, 1978.

Belyi, Andrei. *Peterburg.* Moscow: Nauka, 1981.

Bernstein, Michael. *Foregone Conclusions: Against Apocalyptic History.* Berkeley: University of California Press, 1994.

Bershtein, Evgenii. "Tragediia pola: dve zametki o russkom veininigerianstve." *Novoe literaturnoe obozrenie* 65 (2004): 208–28.

Bertrang, Todd. "Experiences." http://toddbertrang.com/experiences/labiaexp.html (accessed February 16, 2004).

Bethea, David M. "Nabokov and Blok." In *The Garland Companion to Vladimir Nabokov.* Ed. Vladimir E. Alexandrov. New York: Garland, 1995, 374–82.

Biely, Andrey. *St. Petersburg.* Trans. John Cournos. New York: Grove Press, 1959.

Bitsilli, P. M. "Vozrozhdenie allegorii." *Sovremennye zapiski* 61 (1935): 191–204.

Blackwell, Stephen. "Edmund Wilson's Human Interest." Online posting, March 6, 2006, NABOKV-L. http://listserv.ucsb.edu/lsv-cgi-bin/wa?A2=ind0603&L=NABOKV-L&D=0&I=-3&P=1094 (accessed June 29, 2007).

———. *Zina's Paradox: The Figured Reader in Nabokov's "Gift."* New York: Peter Lang, 2000.

Blasons anatomiques du corps féminin, suivis de Contreblasons de la beauté des membres du corps humain. Paris: Gallimard, 1982.

Bodenstein, Jürgen. *"The Excitement of Verbal Adventure": A Study of Vladimir Nabokov's English Prose.* Inaugural Dissertation zur Erlangung der Doktorwürde der Neuphilologischen Fakultät der Ruprecht-Karl-Universität zu Heidelberg. 2 vols. Heidelberg, 1977.

Booth, Stephen. "Commentary." In *Shakespeare's Sonnets.* Ed. Stephen Booth. New Haven: Yale University Press, 1977, 135–538.

Borges, Jorge Luis. *Labyrinths.* Ed. Donald A. Yates and James E. Irby. New York: Modern Library, 1983.

Boyd, Brian. "Annotations to *Ada.* Part I. Chapter 6." *The Nabokovian* 36 (1996): 41–57. Boyd's annotations to *Ada* are continually updated and may be accessed at http://www.ada.auckland.ac.nz.

——. "Boyd on Walruses." Online posting, December 8, 2004, NABOKV-L. http://listserv.ucsb.edu/lsv-cgi-bin/wa?A2=ind0412&L=NABOKV-L&D=0&I=-3&P=7305 (accessed July 4, 2007).

——. "d'O you get the joke?" *The Nabokovian* 47 (2001): 9–14.

——. "Nabokov: A Centennial Toast." *Nabokov's World.* Volume 2: *Reading Nabokov.* Ed. Jane Grayson, Arnold McMillin, and Priscilla Meyer. Houndsmill, U.K.: Palgrave, 2002, 8–14.

——. *Nabokov's "Ada": The Place of Consciousness.* Christchurch: Cybereditions, 2001.

——. *Nabokov's "Pale Fire": The Magic of Artistic Discovery.* Princeton, N.J.: Princeton University Press, 1999.

——. Notes to *Novels and Memoirs, 1941–1951.* By Vladimir Nabokov. New York: The Library of America, 1996, 675–710.

——. "The Problem of Pattern: Nabokov's *Defense.*" *Modern Fiction Studies* 33, no. 4 (1987): 575–604.

——. "Reflections on Narcissus." *Nabokov Studies* 5 (1998/1999): 179–183.

——. "Scatology in *Ada.*" Online posting, January 14, 2004, NABOKV-L. http://listserv.ucsb.edu/lsv-cgi-bin/wa?A2=ind0401&L=NABOKV-L&P=R14990&I=-3 (accessed May 31, 2007).

——. *Vladimir Nabokov: The American Years.* Princeton, N.J.: Princeton University Press, 1991.

——. *Vladimir Nabokov: The Russian Years.* Princeton, N.J.: Princeton University Press, 1990.

Brittain, F. *Arthur Quiller-Couch: A Biographical Study of Q.* Cambridge: Cambridge University Press, 1948.

Brodsky, Anna. "Homosexuality and the Aesthetic of Nabokov's *Dar.*" *Nabokov Studies* 4 (1997): 95–116.

Bulhof, Johannes. "What If? Modality and History." *History and Theory* 38, no. 2 (1999): 145–68.

Butler, Diana. "Lolita Lepidoptera." *New World Writing* 16 (1960): 58–84.

Butler, Judith. *Bodies That Matter: On the Discursive Limits of "Sex."* New York: Routledge, 1993.

Cadwalader, Susan. "Letter to the Editor." *Nature Conservancy* (January–February 2000): 40.

Carroll, Lewis. *Alice in Wonderland and Through the Looking Glass.* Kingsport, Tenn.: Kingsport Press, 1946.

——. *Ania v strane chudes.* Trans. V. Sirin. Mineola, N.Y.: Dover, 1976.

——. *The Works of Lewis Carroll.* Feltham, U.K.: Hamlyn, 1965.

Cassiday, Julie. *The Enemy on Trial: Early Soviet Courts on Stage and Screen.* DeKalb: Northern Illinois University Press, 2000.

Centerwall, Brandon S. "Hiding in Plain Sight: Nabokov and Pedophilia." *Texas Studies in Literature and Language* 32, no. 3 (1990): 468–84.

Chernyshevskii, Nikolai. *Polnoe sobranie sochinenii.* 16 vols. Moscow: Khudozhestvennaia literatura, 1939–1953.

Chernyshevsky, Nikolai. *What Is to Be Done?* Trans. Michael R. Katz. Ithaca, N.Y.: Cornell University Press, 1989.

Clancy, Laurie. *The Novels of Vladimir Nabokov.* London: Macmillan, 1984.

Colman, E. A. M. *The Dramatic Use of Bawdy in Shakespeare.* London: Longman, 1974.

Connolly, Julian. "Madness and Doubling: From Dostoevsky's *The Double* to Nabokov's *The Eye.*" *Russian Literature Triquarterly* 24 (1991): 129–39.

———. *Nabokov's Early Fiction: Patterns of Self and Other.* Cambridge: Cambridge University Press, 1992.

Couturier, Maurice. *Nabokov, ou la cruauté du désir.* Paris: Champ Vallon, 2004.

———. *Nabokov, ou la tyrannie de l'auteur.* Paris: Éditions du Seuil, 1993.

Cowden Clarke, Charles and Mary. *The Shakespeare Key.* New York: Frederick Ungar, 1879.

Cowley, Robert, ed., *What If? The World's Foremost Military Historians Imagine What Might Have Been.* New York: Berkeley, 2000.

———. *What If? 2: Eminent Historians Imagine What Might Have Been.* New York: Putnam, 2001.

Coxeter, H. S. MacDonald. "Geometry, Non-Euclidean." *The Encyclopedia Brittanica. Macropaedia.* Chicago: Encyclopedia Brittanica, 1975 (15th ed.), 7:1112–20.

Creech, James. *Closet Writing / Gay Reading: The Case of Melville's "Pierre."* Chicago: University of Chicago Press, 1993.

Culler, Jonathan. *On Deconstruction: Theory and Criticism after Structuralism.* Ithaca, N.Y.: Cornell University Press, 1982.

Dabashi, Hamid. "Native Informers and the Making of the American Empire." *Al-Ahram Weekly,* June 1–7, 2006 (No. 797). Online edition http://weekly.ahram. org.eg/2006/797/special.htm (accessed October 22, 2009).

Dalzell, Tom, and Terry Victor. *The New Partridge Dictionary of Slang and Unconventional English.* 2 vols. London: Routledge, 2006.

Davydov, Sergei. "Nabokov and Pushkin." In *The Garland Companion to Vladimir Nabokov.* Ed. Vladimir E. Alexandrov. New York: Garland, 1995, 482–96.

———. *"Teksty-Matreshki" Vladimira Nabokova.* Slavistische Beiträge, Band 152. Munich: Otto Sagner, 1982.

De la Durantaye, Leland. "Lolita in *Lolita,* or the Garden, the Gate, and the Critics." *Nabokov Studies* 10 (2006): 175–97.

———. *Style Is Matter: The Moral Art of Vladimir Nabokov.* Ithaca, N.Y.: Cornell University Press, 2007.

Dmitrovskaia, M. A. "Fenomen vremeni: pervoaprel'skie igrovye strategii v proizvedeniiakh V. Nabokova-Sirina." *Nabokovskii sbornik, Iskusstvo kak priem.* Kaliningrad: Kalingradskii gosudarstvennyi universitet, 2001, 30–72.

Dolinin, Alexander. *Istinnaia zhizn' pisatelia Sirina. Raboty o Nabokove.* St. Petersburg: Akademicheskii proekt, 2004.

———. "Kommentarii." In *Lolita.* By Vladimir Nabokov. Moscow: Khudozhestvennaia literatura, 1991, 356–414.

———. "Lolita's Chestnut Lodge." Online posting. September 26, 1997, NABOKV-L. http://listserv.ucsb.edu/lsv-cgi-bin/wa?A2=ind9709&L=NABOKV-L&P= R2914&I=-3 (accessed June 30, 2007).

———. "Nabokov, Dostoevskii i dostoevshchina." *Literaturnoe obozrenie,* 1999, no. 2: 38–46.

———. "Nabokov's Time Doubling: From *The Gift* to *Lolita.*" *Nabokov Studies* 2 (1995): 3–40.

——. *"Primechaniia."* In *Sobranie sochinenii russkogo perioda* by Vladimir Nabokov. Sankt-Peterburg: Simpozium, 2000. 5 vols., 4: 600–768.

——. Untitled review of Aleksandr Etkind, *Tolkovanie puteshestvii. Novaia russkaia kniga,* 2002, no. 1: 82–88.

——. "VN and Translating Belyi." Online posting, February 28, 1999, NABOKV-L. http://listserv.ucsb.edu/lsv-cgi-bin/wa?A2=ind9902&L=NABOKV-L&D= 0&I=-3&P=8622 (accessed May 20, 2008).

Dostoevskii, F. M. *Polnoe sobranie sochinenii v tridtsati tomakh.* Leningrad: Nauka, 1972–1990. 30 vols.

Dostoevsky, Fyodor. *The Brothers Karamazov.* Trans. Constance Garnett and Ralph E. Matlaw. New York: W. W. Norton, 1976.

——. *Crime and Punishment.* Trans. Richard Pevear and Larissa Volokhonsky. New York: Vintage, 1993.

——. *Notes from Underground / The Double.* Trans. Jessie Coulson. Harmondsworth, U.K.: Penguin, 1972.

Drescher, A. N., and Jeff Edmunds. "Chestnut Lodge." Online posting, September 18, 1997, NABOKV-L. http://listserv.ucsb.edu/lsv-cgi-bin/wa?A2=ind 9709&L=nabokv-l&P=R1612 (accessed March 16, 2004).

Dwyer, Anne. "Krug, Paduk, Luzhin: Variations on Terror and Art in Vladimir Nabokov's *Bend Sinister."* Unpublished essay, 2001.

Eliot, T. S. *Selected Essays.* New York: Harcourt, Brace, 1950.

Ellis, Herbert A. *Shakespeare's Lusty Punning in "Love's Labour's Lost" with Contemporary Analogues.* The Hague: Mouton, 1973.

Emerson, Gloria. "The Other Iran." *The Nation,* 16 June 2003: 3.

Emery, Jacob. "Guides to Berlin." *Comparative Literature* 54, no. 4 (2002): 291–306.

Etkind, Alexander. *Tolkovanie puteshestvii. Rossiia i Amerika v travelogakh i intertekstakh.* Moscow: Novoe literaturnoe obozrenie, 2001.

Ferger, George. "Who's Who in the Sublimelight: 'Suave John Ray' and *Lolita's* 'Secret Points.'" *Nabokov Studies* 8 (2004): 137–98.

Ferguson, Niall, ed. *Virtual History: Alternatives and Counterfactuals.* New York: Basic Books, 1999.

Field, Andrew. *VN: The Life and Art of Vladimir Nabokov.* New York: Crown, 1986.

Finke, Michael C. *Metapoesis: The Russian Tradition from Pushkin to Chekhov.* Durham, N.C.: Duke University Press, 1995.

Fippinger, Andrew L. "Discussion Topic for NABOKV-L." Online posting, January 18, 2003, NABOKV-L. http://listserv.ucsb.edu/lsv-cgi-bin/wa?A2=ind 0301&L=nabokv-l&T=0&P=10387 (accessed May 22, 2007).

Flaubert, Gustave. *Madame Bovary.* Paris: Le Livre de Poche, 1972.

Frank, Joseph. *Dostoevsky: The Seeds of Revolt, 1821–1849.* Princeton, N.J.: Princeton University Press, 1976.

Freud, Sigmund, "Three Essays on the Theory of Sexuality." In *On Sexuality.* Harmondsworth, U.K.: Penguin, 1977.

Friedman, Jerry. "Thoughts on Canto One." Online posting, December 2, 2007, NABOKV-L. http://listserv.ucsb.edu/lsv-cgi-bin/wa?A2=ind0712&L=NAB OKV-L&P=R2676&I=-3 (accessed May 26, 2008).

Frye, Northrop. "Allegory." In *The Princeton Encyclopedia of Poetry and Poetics.* Ed. Alex Preminger. Princeton, N.J.: Princeton University Press, 1974, 12–15.

Gallop, Jane. *Around 1981: Academic Feminist Literary Theory.* New York: Routledge, 1992.

Gibson, Walker. "Authors, Speakers, Readers, and Mock Readers." In *Reader Response Criticism from Formalism to Post-Structuralism.* Ed. Jane P. Tompkins. Baltimore: Johns Hopkins University Press, 1980, 1–6.

Gilbert, Elliot L. "'Upward, Not Northward': *Flatland* and the Quest for the New." *English Literature in Transition* 34, no. 4 (1991): 391–404.

"Go Ask Alice." Columbia University's Health Question and Answer Internet Service. Online posting, April 6, 2001. http://www.goaskalice.columbia.edu/1879. html (accessed February 16, 2004).

Goldman, Eric. "'Knowing' Lolita: Sexual Deviance and Normality in Nabokov's *Lolita.*" *Nabokov Studies* 8 (2004): 87–104.

Grabes, Herbert. "Nabokov and Shakespeare: The English Works." In *The Garland Companion to Vladimir Nabokov.* Ed. Vladimir E. Alexandrov. New York: Garland, 1995, 496–512.

Grayson, Jane. *Nabokov Translated: A Comparison of Nabokov's Russian and English Prose.* Oxford: Oxford University Press, 1977.

Grebanier, Bernard. *The Heart of "Hamlet": the Play Shakespeare Wrote.* New York: Thomas Y. Crowell, 1960.

Green, Jonathan. *Cassell's Dictionary of Slang.* 2d ed. London: Weidenfeld and Nicolson, 1998.

Grose, Francis. *A Classical Dictionary of the Vulgar Tongue.* London: Scholartis, 1931.

Groys, Boris. *The Total Art of Stalinism: Avant-Garde, Aesthetic Dictatorship, and Beyond.* Trans. Charles Rougle. Princeton, N. J.: Princeton University Press, 1992.

Henderson, Linda Dalrymple. *The Fourth Dimension and Non-Euclidean Geometry in Modern Art.* Princeton, N. J.: Princeton University Press, 1983.

Henke, James T. *Courtesans and Cuckolds: A Glossary of Renaissance Dramatic Bawdy (Exclusive of Shakespeare).* New York: Garland, 1979.

Herbold, Sarah. "'(I have camouflaged everything, my love)': *Lolita* and the Woman Reader." *Nabokov Studies* 5 (1998/1999): 81–94.

——. "Reflections on Modernism: *Lolita* and Political Engagement or How the Left and the Right Both Have It Wrong." *Nabokov Studies* 3 (1996): 145–50.

Hewett, Heather. "'Bad' Books Hidden under the Veil of the Revolution: Iranian Women Resist Oppression by Reading Forbidden Novels." *The Christian Science Monitor,* March 27, 2003, 2.

Hinton, C. H. *Scientific Romances.* New York: Arno, 1976.

Hitchens, Christopher. "As American as Apple Pie." *Vanity Fair* (July 2006): 52–56.

Hyde, G. M. *Vladimir Nabokov: America's Russian Novelist.* London: Marion Boyars, 1977.

Ilic, Lina. "Cubism: Nabokov's Reaction to Andrei Bely." Unpublished paper, 1996.

Jakobson, Roman. "O khudozhestvennom realizme." In *Readings in Russian Poetics.* Ed. Ladislav Matejka. (Michigan Slavic Materials, 2). Ann Arbor: University of Michigan Press, 1962, 29–36.

Jann, Rosemary. "Abbott's *Flatland:* Scientific Imagination and 'Natural Christianity.'" *Victorian Studies* 28, no. 3 (1985): 473–90.

Johnson, D. Barton. "A Guide to Nabokov's 'A Guide to Berlin.'" *Slavic and East European Journal* 23, no. 3 (1979): 353–61.

——. "Belyi and Nabokov: A Comparative Overview." *Russian Literature* 9, no. 4 (1981): 379–402.

——. "Boyd Proposal for a List of Nabokov's Reading." Online posting, September 14, 2002, NABOKV-L. http://listserv.ucsb.edu/lsv-cgi-bin/wa?A2=ind0209&L= NABOKV-L&P=R42173&I=-3&m=5470 (accessed June 28, 2007).

——. "Drescher Query re Lolita's Chestnut Lodge." Online posting, September 22, 1997, NABOKV-L. http://listserv.ucsb.edu/lsv-cgi-bin/wa?A2=ind 9709&L=nabokv-l&P=R1689 (accessed March 16, 2004).

——. "NABOKV-L Subscription Info." Online posting, May 15, 1998, NABOKV-L. http://listserv.ucsb.edu/lsv-cgi-bin/wa?A2=ind9805&L=NABOKV-L&P= R1037&I=-3&m=2170 (accessed June 28, 2007).

——. *Worlds in Regression: Some Novels of Vladimir Nabokov.* Ann Arbor, Mich.: Ardis, 1985.

Johnson, Kurt. "'Laughter in the Dark' in the Latest *Nature Conservancy* Magazine." Online posting, December 15 1999, NABOKV-L. http://listserv.ucsb.edu/lsv-cgi-bin/wa?A2=ind9912&L=NABOKV-L&P=R2194&I=-3 (accessed October 22, 2009).

Johnson, Roy. "A Guide to Berlin." Online posting, November 3, 1994, NABOKV-L. http://listserv.ucsb.edu/lsv-cgi-bin/wa?A2=ind9411&L=nabokv-l&F=&S= &P=182 (accessed January 7, 2006).

——. "A Nursery Tale." Online posting, November 8, 1994, NABOKV-L. http://list serv.ucsb.edu/lsv-cgi-bin/wa?A2=ind9411&L=NABOKV-L&P=R171&I=-3 (accessed June 27, 2007).

Kartsev, Peter A. "Lolita's Chestnut Lodge." Online posting, September 26, 1997, NABOKV-L. http://listserv.ucsb.edu/lsv-cgi-bin/wa?A2=ind9709&L=nabokv-l&P=R2782 (accessed February 16, 2004).

Kauffman, Linda. *Special Delivery: Epistolary Modes in Modern Fiction.* Chicago: University of Chicago Press, 1992.

Kermode, Frank. "Nabokov's *Bend Sinister.*" In *Puzzles and Epiphanies: Essays and Reviews 1958–1961.* London: Routledge, 1962, 228–34.

Khrushcheva, Nina L. *Imagining Nabokov: Russia between Art and Politics.* New Haven: Yale University Press, 2007.

Koch, Stephen. Untitled review of *The Eye.* In *Nabokov: The Critical Heritage.* Ed. Norman Page. London: Routledge, 1982, 183–87.

Kökeritz, Helge. *Shakespeare's Pronunciation.* New Haven: Yale University Press, 1953.

Lambert, Jean-Clarence, ed. *Les blasons du corps feminine.* Saverne: Les libraires associés, 1963.

Lee, L. L. "*Bend Sinister:* Nabokov's Political Dream." In *Nabokov: The Man and His Work.* Ed. L. S. Dembo. Madison: University of Wisconsin Press, 1967, 95–105.

Lehman, Peter. "Revelation about Pornography." *Film Criticism* 20, no. 1–2 (1993): 3–16.

Levinton, G. A., and N. G. Okhotin. "Chto za delo im—khochu..." *Literaturnoe obozrenie,* 1991, no. 11: 28–35.

Lewis-Kraus, Gideon. "Pawn of the Neocons? The Debate over *Reading "Lolita" in Tehran.*" *Slate,* November 30, 2006. http://www.slate.com/id/2154700 (accessed May 21, 2008).

Liuksemburg, A. M., and G. F. Rakhimkulova. *Magistr igry Vivian Van Bok (Igra slov v proze Vladimira Nabokova v svete teorii kalambura)*. Rostov-on-Don: Rostov State University, 1996.

Lock, Charles. "Transparent Things and Opaque Words." In *Nabokov's World*. Ed. Jane Grayson, Arnold McMillin, and Priscilla Meyer. Houndsmill, U.K.: Palgrave, 2002. 2 vols., 1: 104–20.

Lokrantz, Jessie Thomas. *The Underside of the Weave: Some Stylistic Devices Used by Vladimir Nabokov*. Acta Universitatis Upsaliensis. Studia Angelistica Upsaliensia, 11. Uppsala: Uppsala University, 1973.

Malmstad, John. "Iz perepiski V. F. Khodasevicha (1925–1938)." *Minuvshee* 3 (1987): 262–91.

Marvell, Andrew. *The Complete Poems*. Ed. Elizabeth Story Donno. London: Penguin, 2005.

Mason, Bobbie Ann. *Nabokov's Garden: A Guide to Ada*. Ann Arbor: Ardis, 1974.

Matich, Olga. *Erotic Utopia: The Decadent Imagination in Russia's Fin de Siècle*. Madison: Wisconsin University Press, 2005.

McHale, Brian. "The Great (Textual) Communicator, or Blindness and Insight." *Nabokov Studies* 2 (1995): 277–89.

Meerson, Olga. "Vladimir Nabokov's Transformation of Dostoevskij in *The Defense: Zashchita Luzhina* or Zashchita Dostoevskogo?" *Zeitschrift fur Slavistik* 41, no. 1 (1996): 20–33.

Mel'nikov, N. G. *Klassik bez retushi: Literaturnyi mir o tvorchestve Vladimira Nabokova*. Moscow: Novoe literaturnoe obozrenie, 2000.

Miller, D. A. *The Novel and the Police*. Berkeley: University of California Press, 1989.

Morson, Gary Saul. *Narrative and Freedom: The Shadows of Time*. New Haven: Yale University Press, 1994.

Nabokov, Dmitri. "Edmund Wilson's Human Interest." Online posting, March 6, 2006, NABOKV-L. http://listserv.ucsb.edu/lsv-cgi-bin/wa?A2=ind0603&L= NABOKV-L&D=0&I=-3&P=1298 (accessed June 29, 2007).

——. "On a Book Entitled Lo's Diary." In *Lo's Diary*. By Pia Pera. New York: Foxrock, 1999, vii–x.

Nabokov, Vladimir. "A Nursery Tale." *Playboy* (January 1974): 99, 100, 116, 268–69.

——. *Ada, or Ardor: A Family Chronicle*. New York: Vintage, 1990.

——. *The Annotated Lolita*. Ed. Alfred Appel, Jr. New York: Vintage, 1991.

——. *Bend Sinister*. New York: Vintage, 1990.

——. *The Defense*. Trans. Michael Scammell in collaboration with the author. New York: Vintage, 1990.

——. *Despair*. New York: Vintage, 1989.

——. *The Enchanter*. Trans. Dmitri Nabokov. New York: Vintage, 1991.

——. *The Gift*. Trans. Michael Scammell in collaboration with the author. New York: Vintage, 1991.

——. *Invitation to a Beheading*. New York: Vintage, 1989. Trans. Dmitri Nabokov in collaboration with the author. New York: Vintage, 1989.

——. *King, Queen, Knave*. Trans. Michael Scammell in collaboration with the author. New York: Vintage, 1991.

——. *Laughter in the Dark*. New York: Vintage 1989.

——. *Lectures on Literature*. New York: Harvest, 1980.

——. *Lectures on Russian Literature.* New York: Harvest, 1981.

——. *Lolita: A Screenplay.* New York: Vintage, 1997.

——. *Lolita, Poems* (sound recording). LP. Spoken Arts, 1964.

——. *Look at the Harlequins!* New York: Vintage, 1990.

——. *Mary.* New York: Vintage, 1970.

——. *Nikolai Gogol.* New York: New Directions, 1961.

——. *Novels, 1969–74.* New York: The Library of America, 1996.

——. *The Original of Laura (Dying Is Fun).* New York: Knopf, 2009.

——. *Otchaianie.* Ann Arbor, Mich.: Ardis, 1978.

——. *Pale Fire.* New York: Vintage, 1989.

——. *Pnin.* New York: Vintage, 1989.

——. *Poems and Problems.* New York: McGraw Hill, 1970.

——. *The Real Life of Sebastian Knight.* New York: Vintage, 1992.

——. *Selected Letters 1940–1977.* Ed. Dmitri Nabokov and Matthew J. Bruccoli. San Diego: Harcourt Brace Jovanovich, 1989.

——. *Sobranie sochinenii russkogo perioda.* 5 vols. St. Petersburg: Simpozium, 1999.

——. *Speak, Memory: An Autobiography Revisited.* New York: Vintage, 1989.

——. *The Stories of Vladimir Nabokov,* New York: Vintage, 1995.

——. *Strong Opinions.* New York: Vintage, 1990.

——. *Transparent Things.* London: Penguin, 1993.

——. Untitled review of Frayne Williams, *Mr. Shakespeare of the Globe. The New Republic,* May 19, 1941: 702.

——. "Volshebnik." *Russian Literature Triquarterly.* no. 24 (1991): 9–41.

——. *Zashchita Luzhina.* Ann Arbor, Mich.: Ardis, 1979.

Nabokov, Vladimir, and Edmund Wilson. *Dear Bunny, Dear Volodya: The Nabokov-Wilson Letters, 1940–1971.* Ed. Simon Karlinsky. Berkeley: University of California Press, 2001.

"NABOKV-L." In *Zembla.* Ed. Jeff Edmunds. June 29, 2007. http://www.libraries. psu.edu/nabokov/forians.htm.

Naiman, Eric. "Drescher Query re: Lolita's Chestnut Lodge." Online posting, September 23, 1997, NABOKV-L. http://listserv.ucsb.edu/lsv-cgi-bin/wa?A2= ind9709&L=NABOKV-L&P=R2197&I=-3 (accessed October 22, 2009).

——. "Shklovsky's Dog and Mulvey's Pleasure: The Secret Life of Defamiliarization." *Comparative Literature,* 50, no. 4 (1998): 333–52.

——. "VN and Translating Bely." Online posting, February 28, 1999, NABOKV-L. http://listserv.ucsb.edu/lsv-cgi-bin/wa?A2=ind9902&L=NABOKV-L&D= 0&I=-3&P=8522 (accessed May 20, 2008).

Nafisi, Azar. *Reading "Lolita" in Tehran: A Memoir in Books.* New York: Random House, 2003.

——. "Reading *Lolita* in Tehran." *The Chronicle of Higher Education,* April 25, 2003, 7.

"Natural Selection." *Nature Conservancy.* 1999 (November/December), 42.

Naumann, Marina Turkevich. *Blue Evenings in Berlin: Nabokov's Short Stories of the 1920s.* New York: New York University Press, 1978.

Nesbet, Anne. "Tolstoy's Theater of War." Unpublished paper, 1991.

Nicol, Charles. "Pnin's History." *Novel* 4, no. 3 (1971): 197–208.

Oh, Kara. *How to Please a Man In and Out of Bed.* Santa Barbara, Calif.: Avambre Press, 2006.

Ohi, Kevin. "Narcissism and Queer Reading in *Pale Fire.*" *Nabokov Studies* 5 (1998/1999): 153–78.

Otten, Charlotte F. "Ophelia's 'Long Purples' or 'Dead Men's Fingers.'" *Shakespeare Quarterly* 30, no. 3 (1979): 397–402.

The Oxford English Dictionary. Prep. J. A. Simpson and E. S. C. Weiner. 2d ed. 20 vols. Oxford: Clarendon Press, 1989.

Page, Norman. *Nabokov: The Critical Heritage.* London: Routledge, 1982.

Painter, Robert, and Brian Parker. "Ophelia's Flowers Again." *Notes and Queries* 41 (1994): 42–44.

Paperno, Irina. *Chernyshevsky and the Age of Realism: A Study in the Semiotics of Behavior.* Stanford, Calif.: Stanford University Press, 1988.

———. "How Nabokov's *Gift* Is Made." "Literature, Culture and Society in the Modern Age: In Honor of Joseph Frank, Part 2." *Stanford Slavic Studies* 4, no. 2 (1992): 295–332.

Partridge, Eric. *Shakespeare's Bawdy.* 3d ed. London: Routledge, 1990.

Patnoe, Elizabeth. "Discourse, Ideology, and Hegemony: The Double Dramas in and around *Lolita.*" In *Discourse and Ideology in Nabokov's Prose.* Ed. David H. J. Larmour. London: Routledge, 2002, 111–36.

Penley, Constance. "Crackers and Whackers: The White Trashing of Porn." In *Porn Studies.* Ed. Linda Williams. Durham, N.C.: Duke University Press, 2004, 309–31.

Pera, Pia. *Lo's Diary.* Trans. Ann Goldstein. New York: Foxrock, 1999.

Pike, Robert E. "'The Blasons' in French Literature of the Sixteenth Century." *Romanic Review* 27 (1936): 233–42.

Podhoretz, Norman. "*Lolita,* My Mother-in-Law, the Marquis de Sade, and Larry Flynt." In *The Best of 1998: The Anchor Essay Annual.* Ed. Philip Lopate. New York: Anchor Books, 1998, 366–95.

Pointer, Frank Erik. *Bawdy and Soul: A Revaluation of Shakespeare's Sonnets.* Heidelberg, Universitätsverlag, 2003.

Proffer, Carl R. "A New Deck for Nabokov's Knaves." In *Nabokov: Criticism, Reminiscences, Translations, and Tributes.* Ed. Alfred Appel, Jr., and Charles Newman. New York: Clarion, 1970.

———. *Keys to "Lolita."* Bloomington: Indiana University Press, 1968.

Proskurin, Oleg. *Poeziia Pushkina, ili podvizhnyi palimpsest.* Moscow: Novoe literaturnoe obozrenie, 1999.

Pushkin, A. S. *Polnoe sobranie sochinenii.* 17 vols. Moscow: Akademiia nauk, 1937–1959.

Pushkin, Aleksandr. *Eugene Onegin: A Novel in Verse.* Trans. Vladimir Nabokov. 2 vols. (4 vols. in 2). Princeton, N.J.: Princeton University Press, 1990.

———. *Sobranie sochinenii.* 10 vols. Moscow: Khudozhestvennaia literatura, 1978.

Pyles, Thomas. "Innocuous Linguistic Indecorum: A Semantic Byway." *Modern Language Notes* 64 (1949): 1–8.

———. "Ophelia's Nothing." *Modern Language Notes* 64 (1949): 322–23.

Quiller-Couch, Sir Arthur. *Q Anthology: A Selection from the Prose and Verse of Sir Arthur Quiller-Couch.* Ed. F. Brittain. London: J. M. Dent, 1948.

———. *Shakespeare's Workmanship.* Cambridge: Cambridge University Press, 1951.

Radcliffe, Ann Ward. *The Mysteries of Udolpho.* Oxford: Oxford University Press, 1998.

Robert, Paul. *Le Petit Robert: Dictionnaire alphabétique et analogique de la langue française.* Paris: Le Robert, 1982.

Ronen, Omry. "Puti Shklovskogo v 'Putevoditele po Berlinu.'" *Zvezda,* 1999, no. 4: 164–72.

Ronsard, Pierre de. *Oeuvres complètes.* 2 vols. Paris: Bibliothèque de la Pléiade, 1950.

Rorty, Richard. *Contingency, Irony, and Solidarity.* Cambridge: Cambridge University Press, 1989.

Rowe, William Woodin. *Nabokov and Others: Patterns in Russian Literature.* Ann Arbor, Mich.: Ardis, 1979.

——. *Nabokov's Deceptive World.* New York: New York University Press, 1971.

——. *Nabokov's Spectral Dimension.* Ann Arbor, Mich.: Ardis, 1981.

——. "Twenty-Seven Footnotes to Nabokov's Innocence." *Encounter* 40, no. 3 (1973): 78–79.

Rozanov, V. V. *Liudi lunnogo sveta: Metafizika khristianstva.* St. Petersburg, 1911.

Rubinstein, Frankie. *A Dictionary of Shakespeare's Sexual Puns and Their Significance.* 2d ed. New York: St. Martin's Press, 1989.

Rylkova, Galina. "Okrylyonnyy Soglyadatay—The Winged Eavesdropper: Nabokov and Kuzmin." In *Discourse and Ideology in Nabokov's Prose.* Ed. David H. J. Larmour. London: Routledge Harwood, 2002, 43–58.

Sawday, Jonathan. *The Body Emblazoned: Dissection and the Human Body in Renaissance Culture.* London: Routledge, 1995.

Schiff, Marjorie A. "To Impress an Admissions Officer, Read Something Worth Writing About." *The Chronicle of Higher Education* 50, no. 12 (February 6, 2004): 15.

Schiff, Stacy. *Vera (Mrs. Vladimir Nabokov).* New York: Random House, 1999.

Schroeder, John W. "Spenser's Erotic Drama: The Orgoglio Episode." *English Literary History* 29, no. 2 (1962): 140–59.

Schuman, Samuel. "My First Time with *Lolita.*" Online posting, August 18, 2005, NABOKV-L. http://listserv.ucsb.edu/lsv-cgi-bin/wa?A2=ind0508&L=NABOKV-L&P=R26245&I=-3 (accessed May 22, 2007).

——. "Nabokov and Shakespeare: The Russian Works." In *The Garland Companion to Vladimir Nabokov.* Ed. Vladimir E. Alexandrov. New York: Garland, 1995, 512–17.

——. "Something Rotten in the State: *Hamlet* and *Bend Sinister.*" *Russian Literature Triquarterly* 24 (1991): 197–212.

Sedgwick, Eve Kosofsky. "Paranoid Reading and Reparative Reading; or, You're So Paranoid, You Probably Think This Introduction Is about You." In *Novel Gazing: Queer Readings in Fiction.* Ed. Eve Kosofsky Sedgwick. Durham, N.C.: Duke University Press, 1997, 1–37.

——. "Shame and Performativity." In *Henry James's New York Edition: The Construction of Authorship.* Ed. David McWhirter. Stanford, Calif.: Stanford University Press, 1995.

——. *Tendencies.* Durham, N.C.: Duke University Press, 1993.

Seifrid, Thomas. "Nabokov's Poetics of Vision, or What *Anna Karenina* is Doing in *Kamera obskura. Nabokov Studies* 3 (1996): 1–12.

Shakespeare, William. *Hamlet: The New Variorum Edidion.* Ed. Horace Howard Furness. 2 vols. Mineola, N.Y.: Dover, 2000.

———. *The Norton Shakespeare.* Ed. Stephen Greenblatt, Walter Cohen, Joan E. Howard, and Katherine Eisaman Maus. New York: W. W. Norton, 1997.

———. *Shakespeare's Sonnets.* Ed. Stephen Booth. New Haven: Yale University Press, 1977.

———. *Twelfth Night or What You Will.* Ed. Sir Arthur Quiller-Couch and John Dover Wilson. Cambridge: Cambridge University Press, 1930.

Shirland, Jonathan. "'A Singularity of Appearance Counts Doubly in a Democracy of Clothes': Whistler, Fancy Dress, and the Camping of Artists' Dress in the Late Nineteenth Century." *Visual Culture in Britain* 8, no. 1 (2007): 15–35.

Shklovsky, Viktor. "Art as Device." In *Russian Formalist Criticism.* Ed. Lee T. Lemon and Marion J. Reis. Lincoln: University of Nebraska Press, 1965, 3–24.

———. "Iskusstvo kak priem." *Sborniki po teorii poeticheskogo iazyka* 1919, no. 3: 101–14.

Shrayer, Maxim D. *The World of Nabokov's Stories.* Austin: University of Texas Press, 1999.

Shute, Jenefer P. "'So Nakedly Dressed': The Text of the Female Body in Nabokov's Novels." *Amerikastudien / American Studies* 30, no. 4 (1985): 538–43.

Skonechnaia, Olga. "Cherno-belyi kaleidoskop: Andrei Belyi v otrazheniiakh V. V. Nabokova." In *V. V. Nabokov: Pro et contra.* Ed. B. Averin, M. Malikova, and A. Dolinin. St. Petersburg: Izd. Russkogo khristianskogo gumanitarnogo instituta, 1997, 667–98.

———. "'People of the Moonlight': Silver Age Parodies in Nabokov's *The Eye* and *The Gift.*" *Nabokov Studies* 3 (1996): 33–52.

———. "Primechaniia." In *Sobranie sochinenii russkogo perioda.* By Vladimir Nabokov. 5 vols., 2:705–17.

Smith, Jonathan. *Fact and Feeling: Baconian Science and the Nineteenth-Century Literary Imagination.* Madison: University of Wisconsin Press, 1994.

Smith, Jonathan, Lawrence Berkove, and Gerald A. Baker. "A Grammar of Dissent: *Flatland,* Newman, and the Theology of Probability." *Victorian Studies* 9, no. 2 (1996): 129–50.

Solov'ev, Vladimir. *Sochineniia v dvukh tomakh.* 2 vols. Moscow: Mysl', 1988.

Sontag, Susan. *Against Interpretation.* New York: Delta, 1966.

Steele, Shelby. *White Guilt: How Blacks and Whites Together Destroyed the Promise of the Civil Rights Era.* New York: Harper Collins, 2006.

Stegner, Page. *Escape into Aesthetics: The Art of Vladimir Nabokov.* New York: Dial, 1966.

Stringer-Hye, Suellen. Review of *Reading "Lolita" in Tehran: A Memoir in Books,* by Azar Nafisi. *Nabokov Studies* 8 (2004): 209–11.

Syrovatko, L. V. "Paskhal'nyi i rozhdestvenskii rasskaz v tvorchestve V. Nabokova." In *Nabokovskii sbornik. Masterstvo pisatelia.* Ed. M. A. Dmitrovskaia. Kaliningrad: Kalingradskii gosudarstvennyi universitet, 2001, 126–44.

Tammi, Pekka. *Problems of Nabokov's Poetics: A Narratological Analysis.* Helsinki: Suomalainen Tiedeakatemia, 1985.

Tolstoy, Leo. *Anna Karenina.* Trans. Richard Pevear and Larissa Volokhonsky. New York: Penguin, 2000.

Toker, Leona. "Nabokov and Bergson on Duration and Reflexivity." In *Nabokov's World.* Volume 1: *The Shape of Nabokov's World.* Ed. Jane Grayson, Arnold McMillin, and Priscilla Meyer. Houndsmill, U.K.: Palgrave, 2002, 132–40.

——. *Nabokov: The Mystery of Literary Structures.* Ithaca, N.Y.: Cornell University Press, 1989.

Trilling, Lionel. "The Last Lover—Vladimir Nabokov's *Lolita.*" *Encounter* 11 (October 1958): 9–19.

Tsvetaeva, Marina. *Sochineniia v dvukh tomakh.* 2 vols. Moscow: Khudozhestvennaia literatura, 1984.

Turgenev, I. S. *Polnoe sobranie sochinenii i pisem v tridtsati tomakh. 30 vols.* Moscow: Nauka, 1981.

Turley, Kandi Jo, Lawrence J. Sanna, and Reneé L Reiter. "Counterfactual Thinking and Perceptions of Rape." *Basic and Applied Social Psychology* 17, no. 3 (1995): 285–303.

Twiggs, Jim. "Thoughts on Canto One" Online posting, November 29, 2007, NAB OKV-L. http://listserv.ucsb.edu/lsv-cgi-bin/wa?A2=ind0711&L=NABOKV-L&P=R12007&I=-3 (accessed October 14, 2009).

Updike, John. "Afterword." In *The Memoirs of Hecate County.* By Edmund Wilson. Boston: Nonpareil Books, 1980, 449–59.

Uspenskii, P. D. *Tertium Organum: Kliuch k zagadkam mira.* St. Petersburg: Andreev i synov'ia, 1992.

Vignerot-Duplessis-Richelieu, Armand Louis de. *Recueil de pièces choisies rassemblés par les soins du cosmopolite.* Leyden, 1865 [1735].

Vinogradov, V. V. *Poetika russkoi literatury.* Moscow: Nauka, 1976.

Weber, Nicholas Fox. *Balthus: A Biography.* New York: Knopf, 1999.

Webster's New International Dictionary, 2d ed. Ed. William Allan Neilson. Springfield, Mass.: G. and C. Merriam, 1952.

Wendel, Sylvia Weiser. "Chestnut Lodge." Online posting, September 25, 1997, NABOKV-L. http://listserv.ucsb.edu/lsv-cgi-bin/wa?A2=ind9709&L=nabokv-l&P=R2705 (accessed February 16, 2004).

West, Rebecca. *The Court and the Castle: Some Treatments of a Recurrent Theme.* New Haven: Yale University Press, 1957.

White, Duncan. "'(I have camouflaged everything, my love)': *Lolita*'s Pregnant Parentheses." *Nabokov Studies* 9 (2005): 47–64.

Willey, Basil. *The 'Q' Tradition.* Cambridge: Cambridge University Press, 1946.

Williams, Gordon. *A Glossary of Shakespeare's Sexual Language.* London: Athlone, 1997.

Wilson, Edmund. *The Forties.* Ed. Leon Edel. New York: Farrar, Straus, and Giroux, 1983.

——. *Memoirs of Hecate County.* Boston: Nonpareil, 1980.

Wilson, John Dover. *What Happens in "Hamlet."* New York: MacMillan, 1936.

Wood, Elizabeth A. *Performing Justice: Agitation Trials in Early Soviet Russia.* Ithaca, N.Y.: Cornell University Press, 2005.

Wood, Michael. *The Magician's Doubts: Nabokov and the Risks of Fiction.* Princeton, N.J.: Princeton University Press, 1994.

Yardley, Jonathan. "Defiant Words." *The Washington Post,* 10 April 2003, C 8.

YouTube. "Apostrophes: Vladimir Nabokov." Interview on Antenne Deux, 1975. http://www.youtube.com/watch?v=XheZIhnRKQI (accessed May 16, 2008).

❧ INDEX